Jeffery Plumb
March 1977.

A Guide
to Pastoral Care

A Guide to Pastoral Care

A Practical Primer of Pastoral Theology

R. E. O. White, B.D., M.A

May the God of peace
who brought again from the dead . . .
the great shepherd of the sheep
equip you.

Hebrews 13: 20,21 RSV

LONDON
PICKERING & INGLIS LTD
1976

PICKERING & INGLIS LTD
29 LUDGATE HILL, LONDON EC4M 7BP
26 BOTHWELL STREET, GLASGOW G2 6PA

ISBN 0 7208 0377 2
Cat. No. 01/0711

Printed in Great Britain by Robert MacLehose & Co. Ltd, Glasgow

CONTENTS

Typical Problems

A primer is for aspirants, not for experts. Like its companion volume, *A Guide to Preaching*, this manual is intended for those just entering upon pastoral responsibility, whether students for the full-time ministry or the large and increasing number who are called to lay leadership and part-time pastoral charge in evangelical fellowships.

Remembering, assembling, sifting and arranging the experience here harvested has only deepened the impression, gathered through thirty years, that of all ministries Christians are called to exercise within our confused, fear-ridden, rudderless, trivialised and imperilled society, that of pastoral care for individuals under spiritual stress is the most relevant, rewarding, and Christlike.

'The wise course is to profit from the mistakes of others' (Terence)

1 THE CURE OF SOULS

The Christian fellowship is a caring community: the obligation to build one another up in the faith is laid upon all Christians. Yet just as all are enjoined to be witnesses though few are specially commissioned to be preachers, so while all must care for one another some, whose Christian experience, spiritual gifts, and position in the Christian community so qualify them, are specially charged with Christian oversight and pastoral care. Not ministers alone but all who exercise leadership in churches, assemblies, youth groups and other Christian organisations know how delicate, how increasingly important amid contemporary problems and tensions, and how rewarding is 'the cure of souls'.

A mature Christian experience and the spiritual gift for this work are all important, and probably also some recognition of these by the Christian group, in electing a person to such leadership, is necessary to success. Beyond that it is tempting to rely for guidance on 'one's mother wit and where that fails the Holy Spirit'. But the work is too important and the cost to others of our failure is too high to depend on learning by mistakes. Some sharing of Christian insights and wider experience are essential if we are not to blunder in where experts fear to advise. Not least the Christian counsellor soon realises his need, in this work more than in any other, of even deeper and more thorough knowledge of the Scriptures and of Christian teaching. Face to face with souls in trouble, slick and superficial citation of ill-considered texts is soon revealed for the cruelty it really is. A man needs an adequate understanding of Christian doctrine, as well as a sympathetic understanding of ordinary people.

Pastoral Theology

That is why the accepted title for this discipline is 'pastoral theology'. The Christian cure of souls is simply *the application of Christian theology to pastoral situations*, bringing the gospel to bear upon individual needs and circumstances. Here the work of the Christian pastor is clearly distinguished from those of doctor, psychiatrist, social worker or mere busybody. He is a practitioner of the faith, clinically applying all he knows of God, of the saving grace

1

of Christ, of Christian teaching and experience, to specific moral and spiritual problems.

The pastor's *purpose* is larger and deeper than physical or mental health or social rehabilitation. He seeks besides these the reconciliation of individuals to God, to each other, and to life, which not only establishes the individual in peace and lays the foundation for abiding joy, but releases within the soul such faith, hope and love as enable it to meet all demands with equanimity and resource. His concept of the norm or ideal towards which he works is not the merely negative cure that consists in the absence of all tensions, insecurity, fears, anxieties and the like, but the creation of a positive, balanced, active and outgoing wholeness of personality, in which the image of Christ is reflected.

To this end the pastor's *methods* must be such as preserve at all times the individual's freedom of belief, decision and action. Any valid response to religious truth must be voluntary, understanding and heartfelt: coercion of any kind, pressure, command, or persuasion by anything less than the truth clearly spoken and freely understood, is out of the question for the Christian counsellor. Whatever place hypnotism and subliminal suggestion may have in other forms of healing, they are no part of Christian ministry. Nor is that accommodation of truth to what will suit the patient's condition to believe, which may achieve temporary pacification but no permanent—certainly no eternal—cure. It is as true of pastoral work as it is of preaching that the basic method of operation is 'the manifestation of the truth to every man's conscience in the sight of God'.

The pastor's *resources* are likewise very different from those available to other counsellors. If, on the one hand, he assumes the weak sinfulness of human nature and accepts man's creaturely limitations of wisdom, vision and strength as inescapable, on the other hand he believes implicitly on the possibility of redemption and recreation for every living soul. He sees moral failure as in one sense a sickness of the whole personality as Jesus saw it: and is confident that all such sickness can be cured by the Great Physician. He will frankly concede that most moral problems are due to the way that family, or society, or life itself has treated an individual without doubting that the individual may yet be changed by other moral forces brought to bear upon him. He will understand that many have been 'disturbed' to their hurt by the way the world has dealt with them, and the way they have reacted to such treatment—who can be 'disturbed' again to their healing by Christian truth and friendship, forgiveness and faith, releasing wholly new moral energies within the soul.

Above all he will work in the conviction that human personality is ever open to invasive forces of good as well as evil, and he will rely on the power of God released through faith and prayer to make a man whole. He will never merely urge a man 'to pull himself together'— a futile and frustrating prescription for the person who has already gone to pieces—but to surrender himself to Him who made men by his power and redeems men by his grace, and who loves every creature he has made.

Thus the Christian pastor relies upon more than his own goodwill and personal experience. He must know the gospel well and all the varieties of spiritual experience described in the New Testament, not just his own. He must learn how those have found Christ whose education, temperament, background and need were very different from his. He must learn what others have seen in Christ which his own Christian experience and cast of mind have not led him to discover for himself. He must have confidence in the effectiveness of truth sincerely spoken to win its own way and do its own work, and he must expect that often the resolution of a soul's problem, and the answer to his own prayers, will not come precisely as he anticipated but in some surprising dispensation of grace and providence, in which the hand of God is plainly to be seen.

Simply to list the spiritual forces that work in and through the pastor: the healing power of forgiveness; the creative and sustaining gratitude kindled in a penitent heart by the realisation that Christ loved him and gave himself for him; the energy of the Holy Spirit; the strong sympathy of the church fellowship; the kindling illumination of the gospel and the soul awakening beauty of Christ himself; the deep inspiration of finding oneself undeservedly loved and trusted; the undergirding acceptance into Christian society and Christian work; the upholding strength of tradition, habit and ritual; —simply to list these is to suggest at what deep levels the Christian pastor operates on the soul, and with what measureless resources he is commissioned to the work of Christ among men.

Too much piety?

Nevertheless this emphasis on a religious approach to personal caring brings its own dangers:

(i) The temptation to believe that the real work lies always in preaching, even to the extent of turning each counselling session into a preaching occasion. This may be because in his heart the gifted preacher has little patience with pastoral care. The public limelight of the pulpit, and the opportunity for satisfying self-expression in eloquent exposition of sacred things, are both fascinating and rewarding, while the private confidential ministry to individuals is often frustrated, sometimes exasperated, and usually unnoticed. The wider church and the world at large will usually judge a Christian leader's reputation by his public performances: his own people will far more often judge him by his private ministry.

The man who thinks he need not take great trouble over his preaching because his gift is for pastoral work will soon find he has no congregation to visit or to counsel, but the man who insists that preaching is the main thing, that his people can have either his head or his feet but not both, may soon find—or his people will—that his preaching is irrelevant, abstract, unrelated to real life situations, lacking warmth and human persuasiveness. It is easy for an evangelical preacher to imagine he can talk well to scores but yet to be tongue-tied when faced with a single listener. It is commonplace too to find pulpit generalities evaporate in vestry interviews. The Master loved to talk in private with individuals in need.

(ii) A second danger implicit in the religious emphasis in pastoral work is the temptation to suppose that the answer to every problem among unbelievers is conversion, or among Christians more prayer. This is sometimes true, sometimes foolish. True when what is meant is aligning life and its problems with God and his will, committing the self and its needs to Christ's control; foolish if we imagine that the individual's change of heart automatically removes every cause of friction, unfaithfulness, anxiety, ill health, poverty, unemployment, stupidity, addiction, and the rest of the ills and sins that beset human life. Pastoral help usually means showing *how* conversion or prayer would change the situation. Often the pastor after hearing some complicated story will not know how a better Christian attitude would resolve a problem, and he must not pretend to know. Instead he will go away to think through the problem in the light of Christian faith and ethics, and come back later with his Christian counsel.

Similarly, because our task is to apply the gospel to personal situations it is easy to fall into the prejudice that in any dispute, in any marital upset or quarrel, the Christian will be in the right and the non-Christian in the wrong. The Christian husband or wife will expect you to take that for granted. In fact, of course, some knowledge of your fellow Christians, of their occasionally censorious, infuriating, exasperating ways, will be enough to warn you that sometimes your sympathies should be with the unbeliever.

Firmly as the pastor will emphasise the religious basis, aim, and method of his ministry, he will be too much a realist to believe that instant religion is a cheap nostrum for all ills.

(iii) A further obvious danger is to allow the religious character of our caring to become a barrier and deterrent to those in need of help. To be, or to appear to be, professionally religious is a serious handicap: only the man who is naturally, constantly and without ceremony, an approachable and competent Christian friend is likely to be often consulted.

The *preacher* has time and warning about his engagements and can put on a second persona, becoming more careful of his thought, arranging his words, avoiding awkward issues and foreseeing difficult questions. Given some flair, self-assurance, and guile, the preacher can get away with much and people will still come to hear.

But the *pastor* cannot prepare in the same way for his detailed private ministry to individuals. His attention, sympathy, patience, and wisdom have to be immediately at command. The chief requirement is not cleverness but genuineness.

The pastor needs above all to be himself, a man of faith and experience, of such knowledge and wisdom as life has given him, with such insight and language as he possesses, and with a deep faith in the help of the Spirit. He will sit alongside a fellow Christian in trouble and out of his own heart's compassion will try to help. The professional role, a fixed time and office duly announced, professional dress, the pastoral filing cabinet and record cards well in evidence, a pseudo-psychiatric jargon colouring the usual things which a minister is popularly supposed to say on such occasions, all these are not only unnecessary but may imply claims to an authority we do not possess, and they always create gulfs which the person in need has to find the courage to cross.

Admittedly a deliberately cultivated informality of untidy appearance, careless speech, Christian-name relationships, and the rest, can be just as hypocritical—a non-professional image created for professional purposes—and it can become just as forbidding a barrier to a soul in need of comfort or guidance, who seeks serious and careful conversation with a responsible Christian, not chat from a brash cheerleader.

In practice people in distress will often approach the pastor in his garden, leaning on a fence, strolling in a park, standing at a street corner, or anywhere else, confident that he will be always the same sympathetic listener, predictable in reaction, cool in counsel. Frequently the only result of that ice-breaking appeal—perhaps emotionally impulsive, perhaps the sudden leading of the Spirit— will be to set the time and place for more convenient interview, but the first momentous step will have been taken that could transform a life, and it is made possible when a man of God is known to be a friend and pastor ready at all times and in all situations to listen and advise as God enables him.

(iv) At a deeper level, the emphasis upon divine resources for the work of pastoral care may sometimes obscure the demands made upon the counsellor himself. It is possible to profess great confidence that God will resolve a problem in answer to diligent prayer for no deeper reason than that such counsel avoids getting oneself involved. Such assurances may be no more than a pious brush-off, and the applicant turns away sorely aware that the pastor does not understand, or does not want to be troubled.

The truth here is that the kind of graciousness through which, especially in pastoral work, the grace and truth of Christ can flow to other souls, is very largely the result of acute and candid self-knowledge. A man needs to be able to stand off and watch himself counselling other people, fully aware of his own reactions, neither shirking them, repressing them by self-deceit, nor denying them. Because while dealing with others' problems, confessions, addictions, failures, a man is constantly reminded of his own most secret temptations, inadequacies and sins, a professional reaction would be to deny this even to oneself, hiding the truth in a 'superior' and censorious pose. The genuine reaction is to listen with inward honesty, acknowledge that you too have at times been stupidly angry, resentful, lustful, faithless, wayward, untruthful, and so to listen humbly, gently, with insight, aware of yourself—and aware of your Saviour.

Unless you have found an answer to your own inadequacies you will not be counselling others at all. Yet if you have forgotten your utter dependence upon divine grace, you ought not to be counselling anyone else. 'Genuineness' consists in being self-aware and pretending nothing: it does not require you to join your patients in their sorry confession and unhappiness: no good purpose will be served by suggesting that such failure is normal, or that the physician knows no better than the patient; but the pastor will know his own heart and seek with renewed penitence and prayer the words that will help others avoid his own mistakes.

Much that we have said can be expressed more bluntly in negative form:

The pastor must not play God in other people's lives, giving directions, solving problems, providing the approved answers to classified questions. Much counsel on counselling appears to assume that the counsellor can know God's will for another life. You cannot. You help others find God's will for themselves, but you cannot tell them what it is. The pastor can never say 'You must' or even 'You should': and he dare not say 'If you will not, I cannot waste time with you'. Always decisions must be theirs, freely made, before God.

The pastor does not offer simply his personal advice, for he stands always outside another's circumstances, observing from a very different background with a different experience and a different conscience. Any advice offered is therefore merely a spectator's comment, or else it descends to projecting oneself into other lives and telling what we would do if we were in their shoes. If we were, of course, we should be seeking counsel not giving it. Instead, the pastor listens, prompts, draws out the problem, the guilt, the fear, into the daylight of the patient's faith and conscience until the solution emerges in the telling, unspoken by the counsellor, perceived by the patient himself. Often the result is a grateful admission that it has helped to talk it over, and the patient goes away wondering why he consulted you when the solution was so plain. That is a highly successful interview.

The pastor is not, normally, conducting a confessional. Often he will discourage open confession: it may create a situation beyond his handling afterwards; it may make normal future relationships impossible because of what he knows; it may destroy the reticence, the modesty, which the healthy soul should diligently preserve. So the counsellor will prefer to kneel with the confessor and invite him to tell God there and then in silent prayer all that has happened, thinking it through in silence in God's presence. The pastor may then offer his own prayer, aloud, in general terms, bearing up the man's silent confession for him, and taking God's forgiveness for him and with him. Then he will let the man depart with his secret and his peace.

Finally, the Christian pastor is *never authorised to exploit other people's troubles and distress* for the sake of multiplying converts, gaining new church members, achieving a reputation for evangelical outreach, using his 'pastoral case-histories' to frame an appeal for money, or parading his evangelistic 'captures' to promote further campaigns. The publicity purposes to which other souls' tragedies are sometimes put are little short of disgraceful, however pious such purposes superficially appear to be. A man's only justification for intervening in others' lives is that he loves them, has been commissioned by God to help them, and believes that he possesses some insight, knows some truth, holds the key to some resources, which may solve their problems.

But when any man makes this appeal to high religious motives, resources and sanctions, he must accept unhesitatingly the austere discipline which such an appeal imposes. The 'successes' are not then his successes—though the failures may be; and the souls helped through him, their secrets and their new found help, are all in the highest degree sacred. He will feel for them a new interest and tenderness, but under no circumstances would he exploit his privileged position in their lives *for any purpose whatsoever*.

If we have dwelt on the dangers inherent in the high calling of the Christian pastor, it is only because its privileges, assumptions, and responsibilities are so great, and the possibilities of abuse so patent; but when the work is well done no task on earth is so rewarding or earns so ready and lasting gratitude from human hearts.

2 PASTORAL PRACTICE

An evangelical approach is doubtless essential to an effective pastoral ministry, but it is not sufficient. Competence requires also some instruction, some experience and careful thought. The area of instruction is admittedly limited: needs and backgrounds of people in distress are too varied, and the counsellors themselves are too different in outlook, temperament, and personality, for rule of thumb directions to be laid down. Since the goal in every instance is the fulfilment of God's will for an individual life, any attempt to systematise typical instructions for typical 'cases' would be irreverent.

Experience can be too dearly bought by the counsellor and by people in need. The only possible shortcut is to benefit by others' experience, sometimes by considering and rejecting their example; sometimes by learning from their mistakes; and sometimes by having one's own ideas and horizons greatly enlarged through sheer inspiration. The fruit of experience for the humble in mind is an ever increasing self-awareness.

Most of our thought about pastoral work will consist in sifting such experience and reflecting upon aspects of the gospel that seem relevant. We shall consider some specific pastoral tasks as illustrations of the pastor's range of work; and then some typical pastoral problems with possible lines of approach; our third theme will be deeper pastoral insights into the way that people, and especially Christian people, 'work'. We place these later as garnered from many particular experiences and easier to understand when some idea of the variety of problems has been gained. Those who feel that the insights should precede the applications may of course read our third section at this point.

Though detailed rules are impossible, in pastoral experience certain general principles do emerge which can increase efficiency and avoid a blundering or wasted effort.

(i) *The Principle of Clear Purpose*

It is well always to define your aim precisely and positively. Form a clear idea of what exactly you are trying to do at a marriage, at a funeral, beside a sick bed, or concerning an illegitimate child. You will be surprised how often as pastor you become involved in situations with only the vaguest notion why, what for, or to what end. You will not lack advisers: all around you people will tell you what they think you ought to do, but you must know for yourself your intention and your goal.

And it should be positively expressed, because too often the pastor finds himself merely trying to avoid something. He intervenes, or visits, or issues statements, to forestall criticism, to avoid any impression of indifference, to prevent some feared consequence of not doing so. Occasionally that may be a satisfactory reason, but is a poor pastoral ministry that merely pursues negatives. Spend your life looking for trouble to avoid and you will surely find it.

Too often the Christian leader and friend, looking back upon an attempt at ministry in some difficult circumstances, realises with disappointment and regret that he never paused to survey the whole problem, to isolate the real issues, to consider alternative courses of action, or to get clear in his own mind the best solution he could work towards. Eager to help, meaning well, praying and hoping for some good end to a sorry situation, he plunged in and 'got involved'. But to be involved in someone's problem may be no help at all unless some sense of direction, some policy and purpose inform one's words and acts. Simply to share bewilderment and frustration can be a true expression of sympathy and friendship, but it is not the cure of souls. For that, the one who seeks to help must contribute from his wider experience and objective viewpoint the understanding, foresight and guidance which the sorely troubled heart cannot attain. The counsellor therefore must know where he is going, and have as clear an idea as possible how to get there.

(ii) *The Principle of Deliberate Responsibility*

Always define your responsibility at least in your own mind. Pastoral responsibility can be very far reaching. While it is true that those who consult you must reach their own decisions in the end, yet in so far as those decisions are influenced by what you say or do not say, by how you persuade or warn or encourage, you will bear some responsibility for the consequences. Irresponsible counselling of others is a crime against all fellowship and trust, a betrayal of the pastoral calling.

And counselling can be irresponsible. As when a few Bible passages are thrust at some anguished parent or wife, careless of the price that will be paid in suffering, or loneliness, or tortured conscience, if your literal application of ancient texts is obeyed—or disobeyed. Or when a severe and ruthless warning of judgement 'puts the fear of God' into some timid and over-anxious soul, distorting for life all his thought of God and religion; or in extreme, but by no means rare, instances leading to madness or suicide. A girl may endure decades of unfulfilled maternal longing through the distorted attitudes to sex inculcated by some zealous but unbalanced Christian leader, whose teaching gained spurious authority from her hero-worship in adolescent years.

To offer counsel is to incur responsibility. There is no escape by declining to accept blame: the only escape is to decline gently but clearly to make any comment, or offer any guidance, because the problem is beyond you, or because you are not satisfied that the truth is known. Once a Christian pastor has held out his hand to help he cannot like Pilate wash his hands of the consequences. He can only seek in all things to act and speak carefully, prayerfully and with Christian responsibility.

Of course the degree of responsibility varies with the situation. Where you are asked to act, your action must always be on your own terms. A marriage you consent to conduct for example must be a Christian marriage as you understand it. This will be a matter of personal conscience; all your pastoral acts will be your own acts and must be irreproachably Christian. You do not judge those who act otherwise, nor forbid what others desire: but merely decline to take responsibility for actions that would be contrary to your own principles.

But where you intervene or are consulted in problems or disputes that lie largely outside your own effective action, your responsibility will usually be limited to seeking the best practicable solution. You will often help towards a compromise, having regard to the mixed group you seek to help, though if you had full control of the situation you would want a solution more fully Christian. Frequently you will feel that the outcome disappoints all Christian hopes and prayers; but where opportunity and freedom of action are denied, responsibility must be limited and shared.

Responsibility may, too, be many-sided. Few moral and spiritual problems are wholly individual. Not only in marital, parental or church disputes, but where a young lad or girl is in trouble, an invalid falling into despair, an addiction destroying a soul, there are always others involved, husband or wife, a family circle, employers, fellow Christians, and often young people who watch very closely and critically the leader's reactions. The pastor will remember, while seeking to help one, that he is responsible to others, and must so act and speak that no one is needlessly hurt.

He can receive no tales or gossip at face value; can accept no accusations without hearing the defence; can act upon no account of a dispute without hearing both sides. One who genuinely seeks help will understand this and consent to further inquiry; where consent is withheld you may be sure something important is being concealed.

Young people running from home, absconding husbands or wives, people fleeing from arrest or from punishment, even escaped convicts, may all appeal in desperation for Christian protection. Often the appeal is prefaced by a request that you will not betray to parents, partners, or the police. But the Christian pastor cannot condone injury done to the deserted and anxious family; nor assist a runaway marriage where it is obvious that great danger and lasting resentment may be the consequence; nor can he come between wrongdoing and the law by withholding evidence or sheltering wrongdoers.

The Christian leader consulted in such situations has to claim complete freedom of discretion, pledging himself to do only what he thinks right and wise. It is worth making the point that they would not consult him in such straits if they did not think he could be trusted, and that trust depends upon his absolute integrity and good faith, which helping to hide wrong would soon destroy.

Whenever any serious legal complication arises, it is well for the Christian counsellor to consult a sympathetic lawyer. In general the pastor can claim no legal privilege which would hinder the course of justice, injure others, or create immunity for himself. When you are caring for 'missing' young people or other runaways evading trouble whom you hope to send back to their homes, it may be well to inform the *senior* local police authority that you have 'someone' under your care whose name and situation you will report if enquiries are being made, but whom meanwhile you wish to keep incognito. Most police authorities are happy to co-operate if they are assured that they can get information in due course if that proves necessary.

(iii) *The Principle of Confidence*

The pastor and pastoral elder soon finds himself the repository of secrets. If his people discover that he cannot hold his tongue, he will soon cease to be their pastor in more than name. All Christian ministry can be destroyed by careless talk, veiled allusions, or what is even worse, deliberately covert hints of what one could tell if one chose. To any Christian privileged to enter in Christ's name into the secret places of another life, all confidences must be sacred for conscience's sake: they had better be also for his work's sake.

Some men who would never deliberately pass on private information betray it unconsciously in earnest conversations, and even in preaching, by what they fondly think are unrecognisable illustrations of faith, dedication, backsliding, or courage, drawn from situations and people they remember. Where your friends find that you are willing to discuss others' problems they at once perceive that you will talk about themselves also if occasion arises. However guarded, however intimate, the betrayal, the person receiving it will at once resolve 'I will never tell him anything'. Some men wonder that their people never consult them in trouble: they do not realise that their people long to do so—but have listened too carefully.

Yet keeping confidence is often *very* difficult. A situation may develop which concerns the Christian group and therefore comes under discussion by its leaders, of whom the pastor is one. His private knowledge may then become a real embarrassment. He may request to be allowed to handle the matter alone, without betraying anything he knows, or that he knows anything more than others; or he may judge it better simply to keep silent, contributing to the discussion only so far as common knowledge of the matter allows. Either way, keeping confidence and keeping faith at the same time often requires skill as well as integrity.

Some secrets are heavy to carry alone, and some can be dangerous. The pastor must know himself in this respect, his own vulnerability, and his own strength or weakness of purpose. Some secrets confer a sense of power that only mature and disciplined characters can hide; and some create a responsibility for delicate and solemn decisions for which a man may feel his own experience insufficient. The counsellor then needs his own counsellor and it is no breach of confidence when for your people's sake or for your own you take the gist of a problem, and even the weight of private information, to someone more wise and utterly to be trusted.

Among the dangerous confidences are those which involve a young Christian leader in delicate situations affecting the private lives of the other sex. The single counsellor will probably refuse to pursue such problems, introducing the soul in need to some wise and godly Christian woman. That the person seeking help does not wish to be so 'referred' may usually be taken as in itself a danger signal. The married counsellor may possibly feel on safer ground—but does his wife? Each man must know how far he can share such information and problems with his wife without placing her in a difficult position, making normal happy friendship with someone else impossible because of what she knows.

He may have to conclude that in a few matters his wife would find impartial judgement especially difficult, and decide to keep some things entirely to himself, but on other things he will know that his own family life will be safer, and his own judgement a great deal wiser, if he consults his wife whenever he can. Of course he will resolutely refuse to reveal or discuss with others what he will or will not share with her: that is entirely his own business.

There are again some confidences which a man must refuse to accept. A prior responsibility to parents makes it impossible for a Christian to bind himself to silence about some things a lad or girl may tell him. Responsibilities towards a husband may conflict with the wife's wish for secrecy. A pastor may come to know something which he at once realises the patient's doctor must be told; and some secrets involve third parties who will have no opportunity to defend themselves. It may be necessary in such cases to rebuke the teller. In every such situation a man must school himself to refuse to hear confidences his conscience will not let him keep.

And to refuse confidences which, from the outset, he knows he cannot act upon. So often people begin to share information on the understanding that the pastor will not do anything about it, or reveal what he knows by any attempt to put things right. Such confidences should at once be checked: they confer a responsibility you are forbidden to discharge. What usually happens in such cases is that someone who will not take right action himself, shirks his responsibility on to your shoulders—without accepting responsibility even for doing that. He can always say afterwards 'Well, I told the minister', forgetting to add that he bound you to do nothing. Foresee it, and decline it.

The wise counsellor will never force a confidence, or even encourage one. Discussion of spiritual problems is far better kept on the level of impersonal generalities—even when it is obvious that the issue closely affects the enquirer. Let the personal application remain unspoken. The secrets of every soul are sacred to that soul, and when the stress of the moment has passed an outburst of confidence about sad and shameful things may be bitterly regretted. If it was due in any degree to your pressure, it will be bitterly resented. In any case, confidences shared always change relationships. Neither can entirely forget what was said. Continuing Christian friendship may depend directly upon a man's being always willing to listen and to help, but never seeking to pry, or to weaken the natural reticence which shelters the heart from intrusion.

Confidences required in court are again a special problem. The Christian pastor or elder has no immunity from the processes of law. It may be possible to acquaint the court privately with what you know and accept the court's ruling on whether it must be made public, but the wise pastor will have sought the advice of a Christian lawyer before getting that far.

Confidences must, however, be held inviolate from the press whatever the temptations to seek public acclaim or sympathy for your work. To use private or professional knowledge to enhance personal reputation is despicable and dangerous. One who speaks to the press has no control whatever over what is printed, and no real remedy if harm results: recantations and apologies never catch up with original reports. An English archbishop was waylaid in New York with the question 'Will you be visiting any night clubs during your stay?' which he parried with 'Are there any night clubs in New York?' The headlines read 'Archbishop, before leaving the boat, asks: "Are there any night clubs in New York?" ' A young minister began a carefully balanced comment about gypsy encampments, 'Of course the local residents have a case when vagabonds leave filthy litter about the district; but these people have to live somewhere, and it is inhuman just to keep moving them on.' He was dismayed to see the report, 'Minister says local residents have a case; vagabonds leave filthy litter.' It is no use thinking you can word the report. The safe rules are: no utterance at all until you have the reporter's Press Card in your pocket; no personal *comment* at any time; remember your responsibility to all the people involved; it is no use regretting notoriety if you court publicity.

(iv) *The Principle of Shared Ministry*

Despite the need for confidence the pastor must not forget that pastoral care is the responsibility of the whole Christian fellowship. No small part of the function ascribed to apostles, prophets, pastors and teachers is 'the perfecting of the saints for the work of ministry'— creating a group fellowship in which, by the pooling of gifts and the sharing of resources, a total healing community is created.

One of the great advantages possessed by the Christian minister compared with other social workers, and one which some psychiatrists openly envy, is that the minister has a church around him to share his clinical practice of theology. The church is his casualty ward, his rehabilitation centre, his reserve of specialists. There a team of concerned people, with infinitely varied spiritual experience but sharing a like faith in the love of God for sinners and in the redemptive power of the gospel, waits to share in ministry to men.

They will need training and encouragement; they will need advice too on the dangers involved, on the need to keep secrets, on not interfering when some healing friendship has been set on foot, on how to make one needy soul at a time, or perhaps one family, a matter of prayer, study and active support. But the rewards are great—a church pastorally competent and caring, set within the community as an agency of redeeming grace and active love.

Often, this enlistment of others' help consists simply in introducing an enquirer to one trusted Christian within the fellowship who has faced the same problem—early bereavement, rebellious children, the agonies of childlessness, the problem of adoption, the dread of cancer, the fear of age without companionship. Confidence is preserved because permission is asked to do this, and the reasons explained. If the pastor undertakes to arrange the meeting and explain the need, very often a troubled heart will find great relief in talking to someone else who has trodden the same way. But having done this, step down! Do not pry or prod. If your choice was right you can leave it to them and to God.

Sometimes you will feel that the best solution lies in integrating the 'patient' into the church's common life and activity. It is wise not to be too explicit about your reasons. The heart in need should enter the fellowship like any other member. He must not become the church's current 'invalid' or 'problem'. But with care and prayerful preparation it is possible to organise a situation so that the repressed shall find self-expression, the lonely find regular enforced contact with others, the introspected be left no time for self-pity, the 'unwanted' find themselves looked for and useful. A church so equipped and outgoing in its ministry to inadequate and troubled lives may come to have more than its share of 'dependents': but it will be doing Christ's work, and the dependents will be left in no doubt that they in turn must become helpers whom others lean upon.

(v) *The Principle of Detachment*

It may seem strange to speak of 'detachment' as a requirement of pastoral efficiency. Yet experience reveals the danger that inadequate, distressed, frustrated or ashamed people can become unhealthily dependent upon their spiritual mentor, and the mentor himself come to enjoy and even look for that dependence, as somehow his due from truly grateful 'patients'.

Those whose problems you help to solve, whose marriages you share or later save, whose children you guide and whose parents you bury, will remember you with appreciation and perhaps affection, and that is well. But just as the preacher can sometimes revel in a following devoted to his particular gifts and talent; as the evangelist can sometimes be betrayed into building a personal coterie of converts for whom he is the centre of everything Christian; so can the pastor come to enjoy the special loyalty and uncritical praise of those whom at some time he has directly helped. He likes to feel he has been 'greatly used', and he may resent it very much if, having been helped, they then manifest a normal independence of mind and judgement.

Yet the goal of all his help ought to be just that independence of faith and decision. Sometimes people who 'have been through deep waters' enjoy being the minister's special problem; it can give them a self-importance and a sympathy which otherwise might not be theirs. When the result is a dependence so close and prolonged that the 'patient' can face no situation, take no decision, show no initiative, without first consulting the counsellor, then the counsellor has failed. Indeed a new problem has been created, that of psychological 'transference', threatening perhaps an even greater inadequacy-for-life than did the original situation.

At that stage detachment from the seemingly essential support and sympathy can be extremely dangerous. The patient may relapse into helplessness embittered by a feeling of rejection, of having been betrayed. Extra outside help may well be necessary. The danger must be forestalled by the very method and technique of counselling, as well as by the mingled sympathy and detachment of the counsellor. As we shall see he will at all times avoid making up other people's minds, directing their careers, acting as their conscience or their god. His aim is their self-sufficiency in Christ: and he succeeds in this when he makes himself dispensable.

Nor should an understanding pastor feel surprised if people whose inmost unhappy secrets he has shared, prefer not to meet him Sunday by Sunday and sit under his teaching ministry, wondering all the time how much he is remembering, and whether this or that remark is meant for them. Far better to worship elsewhere and leave distressful memories behind. For the pastor—he has done God's work in their lives and he must let them go.

On one further 'principle' of pastoral ministry earnest Christian workers may be divided. Some will argue that they have nothing at all to say, and no responsibility to discharge, to those who have not accepted the Christian faith and committed themselves to the

Christian way of life. With such, they say, they have no common ground from which to start, no agreed authority through which to appeal, no accepted goal or standard of living at which to aim. Such leaders will 'pastor' Christians, but can only evangelize unbelievers.

That position is defensible and consistent. Those who adopt it will realise that this, too, carries responsibility—the responsibility of declining to help. They will reply that this, though regrettable, is the consequence of refusing the gospel: it places out of reach all Christian solutions to life's problems.

Others, however, while fully recognising that without Christian faith few real-life problems are soluble at all, will yet feel under obligation to offer friendship, sympathy and assistance, even where the full gospel remedy is refused. They will argue that to counsel unbelievers on the Christian way of handling failure, sorrow, fear, affliction, shame, *is* evangelism, and they will appeal to Luke's picture of Jesus 'the man for others' whose heart was open to the lost, the least, the lowest, and the unloveliest. Here again a man must know himself, his own reactions and prejudices, his own convictions, intolerance and aversions.

This does not mean that a Christian must be naive, ready to be imposed upon by every rogue's plausible story. Sometimes he will refuse help because the plea is manifestly false: sometimes he will give help, openly expressing doubt, but preferring to be over-generous rather than over-suspicious. Aware of the dangers, his heart will remain open, though it be only with an effort, to all kinds of people, to liars, to the feckless, to the incorrigible and the hypocritical, and to fools. Not always to do what they ask, but to do them good.

And to all kinds of Christians too, Christians he does not like, Christians he cannot agree with, and some Christians he does not trust. Indeed he will be specially careful about these: a scrupulously fair and faithful pastor to members of the assembly and congregation whom he knows he dislikes. He must be aware of that dislike and over-compensate for it. He must act on principle, not prejudice or preference. He will then make some unexpected friends, and do some totally unforeseen good.

SPECIFIC TASKS

3 THE PASTOR AT WORSHIP

Among factors which shape spiritual experience, educate mind and conscience, heal the hurt soul, comfort and encourage the growing Christian, one of the most powerful is the regular worship-service shared with other Christians. Doubtless this subjective view of worship is partial, man-centred, and if considered alone would be a distortion of what worship is meant to be. Moreover not all who exercise pastoral oversight are called to conduct public services. Yet it is part of worship's meaning to behold the beauty of the Lord and enquire in His sanctuary, to receive the blessing of the Lord and strengthen one's hands in God; while many who never occupy a pulpit do preside at occasional meetings for devotion, Bible study, and prayer. Some understanding therefore of the *pastoral* value of worship-services is essential to a full pastoral ministry.

True worship can be a transforming, challenging and determinative experience. The Master's reiteration of the ancient command 'Thou shalt worship' is set, significantly, in the context of temptation, conflict with evil, and dedication to the work of God; while He set beside that command the promise 'Man shall not live by bread alone, but by every word of God'. The hour of worship is an hour on heaven's doorstep; in the service of praise, meditation and prayer the gospel is not only expressed but experienced. For men and women who spend every day in drab, noisy, contentious, or tempting surroundings, the worship-service is a draught of purer air, a glimpse of wider horizons, a reminder of dimensions, valuations, perspectives, not of this world.

For the hard-pressed, discouraged, or negligent, the regularity of worship is a valuable corrective of unworthy moods and flickering faith. To see above earth's sordidness the divine purity, above earth's lies and confusion the eternal truth, above earth's weakness divine resources of power, above earth's conflicts God's steadfast throne, above man's pitiful mortality the hope of everlasting life, is to prove that though worship is offered to God for His glory, its manward effect is the blessing and renewal that spell spiritual health.

'In worship we meet the power of God, and stand in its strengthening' says Nels Ferré. No pastor who realises the spiritual values of worship—the renewing power of that *appreciation* of God's

21

goodness which prompts praise; the *re-orientation* of thought and life which follows devout listening to God's word; the *prostration* of soul before the All-Highest which informs true prayer—will question that among all the opportunities open to him to influence and enrich his fellow-Christians, the conduct of worship is the greatest.

Not least among the rewarding functions of worship is the antidote it provides to ingrowing, enervating individualism. Penitence, faith, obedience, joy, are of the inner life and cannot be other than individual experiences; the heart knoweth its own secrets and its own Lord, its own regrets, confession, longing for holiness and for peace . Yet Christian discipleship is not, and Jesus did not mean it to be, a wholly individual concern. He banded men together, appointed a shared means of remembrance and witness, pledged His followers to a mutual loyalty in love like His own, spoke often of a kingdom and a family of God, and made His supreme law the limitless goodwill which binds a man to his neighbour and his foe.

Of this corporate dimension of Christianity, shared worship is the regular and appointed expression. In a worship-service, the littleness and limitation of individual experience are enlarged and stretched; personal quirks and eccentricities of mood and judgement are overwhelmed in the emotional and moral inspiration of a whole congregation caught up together in prayer, praise, and high thought. The lonely Christian finds companionship in God's presence; the timid, inadequate Christian gains confidence from shared faith; the self-absorbed and doubting soul can be lifted to a sense of ongoing Christian history, of generations of believers all rejoicing in the faithfulness of God, as hymn and prayer and ancient scripture usher him into the communion of saints.

Nothing of this happens, of course, without preparation and care. In planning every worship-service the experienced pastor has constantly in mind the circumstances and observed needs of his people. He will remember the direct bearing of their worship experience in educating and maturing the young Christian, enriching and stimulating the established believers, countering the spiritual effects of a week spent in a non-Christian environment, and binding isolated Christians into a strong, mutually-supporting fellowship.

Pastoral Worship-Patterns

The pattern of worship is largely fixed by each congregation's tradition and heritage. It is not lightly to be abandoned, nor changed without understanding; praise, prayer, scripture, sermon, are not so many 'items' to be juggled with in a desperate search for variety. From the strictly pastoral point of view, the aim will be to ensure that whatever any particular pattern is meant to achieve will be made easier for each worshipper by the care with which the service is prepared and conducted.

For many Christians, the basic pattern of worship is an offering made to God. Behind this thought lies the Old Testament liturgy of sacrifice, and New Testament teaching about presenting our bodies as living sacrifices to God, with the sacrifice of praise; the epistle to the Hebrews has much to support this conception of worship. In this pattern, the Lord's Supper usually has central place, and man's offering in worship is his response to Christ's self-offering on man's behalf. From the Prayer of Humble Access, through Confession and the acceptance of forgiveness, on to the hearing of God's word and the response in offered obedience, gathered up in the Act of Remembrance of Christ's sacrifice for us, all is centred upon God, and leads to a life surrendered to His purpose and glory. This being the intention, the pastor's plain task is to use such prayerful forethought in planning every part that each worshipper shall find it easy so to offer himself again to God in 'reasonable worship'.

Other Christians see worship as essentially communion with God, the determinative concept being that of encounter. Man approaches God in confession, praise and prayer, with offerings; God approaches man, speaking in scripture and sermon, conferring blessing in forgiveness, grace and benediction. In this pattern the Lord's Supper, too, will be 'communing' with the risen, ascended Saviour who died for our sins and was raised again for our justification. The Godward aspect of worship is here modified, at least by the expectation that God will 'respond' in truth and grace. Such a 'manward' reference will affect the pastor's preparation and conduct of the service, at least to the extent that the hymns will probably be more subjective and experiential, the sermon receive greater emphasis and more time, and perhaps opportunity will be afforded for silence and private prayer. Unless in the emotional tone of the service some sense of God's presence, in a heart-to-heart encounter, has been experienced, pastor and worshippers will feel disappointed.

In some Christian traditions, this concept of communion is taken further, and the pattern of worship becomes that of conversation, or dialogue. The basic thought is the more intellectual one of revelation and response: we expect God will speak to us, through scripture, sermon, hymns or in our inmost thought, making His truth plain and His will clear; we respond in prayer, thanksgiving, but above all in

B

inward faith, accepting God's new word. The Lord's Supper, when it is included in the service of worship, is yet another embodiment of the gospel truth—'God's acted Word'. Here the manward aspect of worship tends sometimes to predominate; the presiding pastor is spokesman both for God to men, as he reads and preaches, and for men to God as he prays, intercedes and gives thanks. The congregation 'sign their names' to what is said for them, by audible or silent 'Amen'.

Much facetious talk about the Reformed Order of Worship as a 'hymn sandwich' misses altogether the force and value of this conception of Christian worship as dialogue with God. Rightly understood, the 'direction' of the service is seen to alternate with a conversational rhythm:

The Bidding , or sentences	: Minister to people ('Let us . . .')
Opening Praise, and Prayer	: People to God, approaching
Old Testament Lesson	: God to people, promising
Hymn of response	: People to God, desiring more
New Testament Lesson	: God to people, declaring
Hymn (or Magnificat)	: People to God, thanks for gospel
Petition, intercession	: People to God
(Hymn)	: People to God, listening
Sermon expounding Word	: God to people, instructing
Hymn, Offering	: People to God, responding
Benediction	: Minister to people ('Go forth . . .')

Minor variations are of course frequently met, but such an Order should be appreciated before it is changed.

If he uses such a pattern for worship, the pastor would, of course, do all in his power to see that the 'dialogue' is genuine—that the worshippers truly listen to God, and truly respond, and that the choice of hymns, scripture and themes for sermon and prayer, help them to do so. Two other matters will also need his careful attention.

A conversation with God should surely 'get somewhere'. When this type of service is well planned, a certain progress is felt, the dialogue becomes a rewarding 'discussion'. In what God says there is 'progress' from the Old Testament reading of promise to the New Testament reading of fulfilment, to the truth of God directly spoken and applied to my own situation, in the sermon, and (in the full worship-service) to the word embodied by divine command in the Bread and Wine. In man's response there is progress from the approach with adoration to confession, petition, intercession for others, offering, and final thanksgiving. The pastor will know in his own experience that services which have moved and satisfied his heart have had this characteristic, something more than alternation and repetition—a sense of moving forward with God to higher understanding and more complete response.

Further, this type of worship-service tends to become over-intellectual. People vary considerably in what most touches and moves them in worship: to some the intellectual content is everything —even in the prayers and the hymns the meaning matters for them much more than the tune or the feeling expressed. For others, the fervour is everything, the ideas pass them by; to still others, all that matters is relevance to life, to duty and social problems, to character-building and the moral issues of the time. Most worshippers are susceptible to several lines of approach in different proportions and at different times; but services planned so as to express or satisfy only one or other part of total personality will be 'meaningless', or 'dead', or 'futile' for different individuals, according to which element is lacking. The pastor, as a student and man of words, will probably value most the intellectual elements of worship, and unless he takes care his preparation will always reflect his personal preference.

The worship-service which really meets a whole congregation's varied needs will therefore reveal a second rhythm: it will move between emotion in music and singing, heart and spirit in prayer and confession, intellect and imagination in reading and sermon, and will in offering and final resolve. Thus at different points and in varying order the whole man becomes involved, and those whose natures are more responsive to one form of appeal than to others, all find something to lift them nearer to God. It is here that pastoral care in the planning of worship becomes most evident. When service after service reflects only the pastor's type of personality, he is failing in ministry to some at least of his people, and must not be surprised if after a few years he is left with a congregation limited mainly to replicas of himself.

For some Christians, such talk about conscious 'patterns' of worship may seem artificial and contrived; for them, all that matters is 'a spiritual experience'—receiving 'a blessing'. Such will choose hymns only because they 'like' them; will seek out favourite passages of scripture, preachers who please and the form of service that is familiar. Here the manward aspect of worship is paramount; the service has become almost entirely an exercise in self-enrichment, Christian education or moral uplift. It is easy to criticise, even to caricature, this attitude but it has a place in the total spectrum of Christian worship, as the charismatic services at Corinth and the subjective silences of the Quakers may remind us.

But in this setting, the thoughtful pastor will strive to foster those elements in complete worship which look outward from the individual soul and its inner experiences to the long story of the church, the testimony and praise of past generations, the great acts of God in history, the series of scripture expositions which bring before the congregation passages and themes which might not have been chosen had not the planned studies directed attention to them. Spontaneity can never be wholly excluded from worship in which the divine Spirit is dealing with the souls of believing men. But spontaneity alone is not enough; it can result in superficiality as well as disorder. And sometimes we grow most mature, not by following our own spiritual 'instincts' and feelings, but by being confronted with the *objective* acts and words of God, and the *appointed* means of grace.

The pastor who observes and sympathises with his people will learn how rewarding, or disappointing, they find the pattern of worship to which they are accustomed, and will give much thought to ways of changing and enriching what no longer serves a spiritual purpose. But he will attempt reform only slowly, knowledgeably, and with full explanation. Above all, he will adhere to custom, or change it, for his people's sake and not his own: that is the discipline of pastoral care.

Pastoral Planning

What is true of the total pattern of worship is true also of the various elements within it. Each will be selected and introduced with similar pastoral intent, to edify and uplift, heal and bless those whose avenue to God the service is meant to be.

Direct instruction and inspiration are largely the task of *preaching*, and here a pastoral approach will affect deeply the selection of themes, the manner and level of treatment, and the balance of pulpit ministry over a period. The modern preacher, it is true, has to be more than pastor: he is evangelist, occasionally social prophet, spokesman for the church, public apologist for the faith; but it is with his pastoral role in the pulpit that we are here concerned. That will influence his choice of themes in three ways. Chiefly, he will constantly review his subjects, very critically, examining their relevance to the daily life, thought, faith, experience and circumstances of his hearers. Abstract discussions, theoretic Bible studies, doctrinal discourses, however attractive to himself, need to be pruned. They have their place in total ministry, and their fascination for certain minds, but the pastor in the preacher will want always to relate every passage, doctrine, historical illustration, parable or character-study to his people's daily discipleship. He remembers that they come to worship to be helped to live, and he will reserve his more academic disquisitions for other occasions.

The pastor's themes, too, will often arise from his people's experience, their illnesses, questionings, disappointments, hopes and activities. Frequently, his pastoral work will send him back to the scriptures for illustration and counsel, which then demands to be preached upon in more generalised form, not so explicitly related to individuals as to be recognised, but yet springing from what he has heard and observed among the congregation. From this follows a third effect of pastoral concern: the whole emphasis of a man's message in one fellowship may differ widely from his emphasis in another, precisely because he 'preaches to their condition'. As pastor, for example, of a congregation well schooled in the wonder and depth of evangelical experience but knowing little of the challenge to Christian morality and example in a permissive society, he will preach more often on Christian social duty and responsibility than on gospel theology. To a church well schooled in moral and social questions but lacking depth of faith and experience, he will do the opposite. A church of earnest, serious, scrupulous Christians may need a ministry of joy and relaxation; a church absorbed in so-called 'foreign missions' may need to be told often of the under-privileged about the church doors. This *is* pastoral preaching—preaching to correct what is wrong, supply what is missing, explore what is not sufficiently understood, until all come to mature manhood in Christ.

The pastoral approach will discipline in similar ways the preacher's treatment of each theme, his language, illustrations, intellectual level, application, being all directed wholly by his practical aim with those particular hearers. At regular intervals, the pastor will look back over his carefully preserved record, to consider how well he has remembered to minister to the old, the young, the well-educated or the ill-educated, the new converts or the mature members, the practical, go-ahead people or the introspective, 'spiritually-minded' people. He will examine whether he has, in the past six months, preached a full and balanced gospel. Often he may be shocked at his omission of whole areas of Christian teaching, themes of Christian duty, sections of the scriptures, as he turns again and again to his own favourite subjects and emphases. It is a salutary exercise honestly to assess what sort of Christians our people would be if all they knew of Christ was what we preached!

The *use of scripture* in Christian worship, deriving from synagogue custom of Christ's own day and earlier, determines not only the quality of our services but the attitude of the average Christian toward the Bible. Where the public reading of scripture is shortened to a minimum, the implied devaluation of the written Word communicates itself to our people, especially to the young. The passages to which the pastor continually turns will become for most of his hearers the familiar and important parts of the Bible, and those which he never reads or expounds, they will have every excuse to ignore. Indeed, it is probable that for many on the fringe of our Christian fellowships, listening to the scripture read at worship is all the Bible reading they ever do.

Moreover, the way the preacher handles the scriptures becomes the model which his constant hearers tend to copy. If he is fanciful, inconsistent, flippant, subjective, in his interpretation of the Word, his hearers will remain baffled, ignorant of the Bible's richness and relevance, vulnerable to every new twister of texts who assails their doorsteps. When they in turn offer their own fanciful, inconsistent, and subjective interpretations in defence of their own opinions, they will be hurt and resentful at their pastor's ready scorn. But when the pastor's choice of scripture is always purposeful and wide-ranging, his reading of the lesson impressive and illuminating, his comments disciplined by the strict rules of interpretation and loyalty to what the Bible writers meant their readers to understand—then he is informing, training and arming his people at the same time, as well as tempting them, Sunday by Sunday, to explore the Book for themselves. If in the worship-services the congregation occasionally reads the scripture with the pastor, they will the more rapidly come to love its music and hunger for its message, and often turn again to the same passage when alone, to read on—and on.

Similar considerations apply, with at least equal force, to *public prayer*. Here, more than anywhere, the pastor's heart is revealed, and the quality of the worship-service tested. If in the prayers the congregation is not drawn near in spirit to God, they are not likely to be aware of His presence in any other part of the service. Of course the most important question about pulpit prayer is, Will it be answered? But other questions also may be raised: What do the public prayers reveal, and teach, of the experience of prayer in the lives of Christians? What should public prayer include? How far are our public prayers public?

To hear some pastors lift to God a congregation's praise, adoration and gratitude in words fitting and heart-moving, is to learn once-for-all that *every* prayer, however private, however urgent and hurried, should contain such simple worshipping, that no Christian prayer should ever descend to a string of petitions, or to mere cosy chat with

God. Again, a pastor sensitive to his people's needs will soon learn always to include a public prayer for forgiveness, and a thanksgiving for free pardon given to the penitent soul. His people in their turn will quickly learn to seek daily forgiveness as they pray, while all who at worship are remembering (or should be remembering) how unworthy they are to come before God at all, are helped to set things right and renew their peace.

Even more perhaps do most people learn, from pulpit prayer, to pray for others—for friends, neighbours, the afflicted, the dying; for the world-wide work of Christ's church; for national and social problems and the welfare of the country; for those bereaved in public tragedies; for leaders and all in social and professional positions of responsibility; for the coming of God's kingdom. So Christians are prompted to relate all life around them, and all people, to God's infinite goodness and love. Private prayer can be intensely self-absorbed and narrow-hearted: the pastor's best antidote is not a lecture on how to pray, but a weekly exercise in intercession, informed and wide-ranging, for each other and for the world.

The pastor may sometimes suspect that for some of his fellow-worshippers, the prayer-time in church is the only period of the week deliberately set apart for praying. He will want to make the very most of it for their sake. So by example he will strive to show that without thanksgiving prayer is not worthy to be offered; without adoration it is not truly prayer to God; without confession it is not honest, and without petition it is not prayer at all; without intercession it is not Christian—and without sincere, believing prayer even public worship in the house of God is a profitless pretence.

The *music for worship*, too, must have, beside the best technical excellence obtainable, pastoral intent. For very many people the whole effect of a worship-service depends upon the hymns. Most of us are more influenced by emotion than by ideas: their combination in fine poetry wedded to good music leaves compulsive and enduring impression. Praise is also the part of the service where worshippers are most obviously united in thought, feeling and action, and often the only opportunity for active, vocal participation. It is not surprising that most popular theology is the theology not of the pulpit but of the best-loved hymns.

Once the pastor has realised the psychological importance of the worship-music he will take new care in whatever choice and handling of it fall to him. The secret here lies in discrimination. Some hymns are praise, adoration, thanksgiving, addressed to God, and should be so announced. Some are sung by the worshippers to each other—

'Courage, brother! do not stumble . . .'; 'Blessed assurance, Jesus is mine!' Such are strictly 'spiritual songs', and not hymns. So are those which the worshipper sings to himself—'Be still, my heart, be still . . .'; 'In heavenly love abiding, No change my heart shall fear . . .' They should be announced as songs, of assurance, of encouragement, of counsel, or whatever description is appropriate. A stirring affirmation of the Christian creed, such as 'At the Name of Jesus, Every knee shall bow . . .'; a moving expression of penitence like 'Just as I am, without one plea . . .'; a brave expression of trust through the darkness, 'God moves in a mysterious way', or a wistful longing for greater blessing, 'Pass me not, O gentle Saviour' or a declaration of personal testimony, 'I heard the voice of Jesus say . . .'—each should be noticed, distinguished, allotted an appropriate place in the service, not arranged haphazardly, and so *used* to liberate the heart of the worshipper. If the pastor will distinguish, and describe, sometimes announcing with a brief comment, and very occasionally telling the story of hymn or writer before inviting the congregation to sing it, the worshippers will not only sing more zealously but more profitably also.

The same care will prevent the pastor from unforgivable blunders —from announcing for congregational worship, for example, hymns that are meaningless ('. . . may heaven's tomorrow dawn on us of homes long expected possessed'); hymns that are cloying and sentimental ('My Jesus, I love Thee, I know Thou art mine'); those that are basically sexual ('I come to the garden alone . . . And He walks with me and He talks with me and He tells me I am His own . . .'); hymns that are untrue ('We are not divided, all one body we . . .') or those that are merely silly ('. . . saints . . . Some were eaten by strange wild beasts, and I want to be one too!').

The weekly choice of hymns should always be recorded, to avoid too frequent repetition, and direct attention to those which are too long ignored. (The simplest method is to enter the dates when a hymn has been used beside it, and then always choose the hymns from that book). It is so easy to select one hymn twenty times in a year, and a score of others not once in four years. Here, as always, the pastor has to keep constantly in mind the variety of taste, education, experience and temperament in his congregation. He will not regularly choose what they 'like', and certainly not always what he himself likes, but he will choose with them in mind. He will explore the whole hymnbook, and the treasury of the church's praise in all ages, that the people's contribution to each service shall be worthy, and worth while.

It should be repeated that Christian worship is centred upon God and offered to God. Its manward effect is only part of its total meaning and purpose. But it is that manward aspect that concerns especially the *pastor*, and he will serve his people well, and greatly reinforce his more individual ministry, when in the public services of worship he remembers that he is representative and servant of his people—not their idol.

4 SPIRITUAL LEADERSHIP

If the first corporate expression of pastoral care is the conducting of profitable worship-services, the second lies in providing spiritual leadership, which anyone carrying responsibility in Christian circles soon finds himself required to give. It is not individuals only who are sometimes bewildered, infirm of purpose, unsure of their goal, divided in mind: groups suffer the same disabilities. Pastoral care for the whole fellowship considered as a unit can be as important, and as demanding, as care for new converts, or for souls in trouble.

Of the constant need of such leadership there can be no doubt. If any local Christian assembly is not to be reduced to a religious rabble, if every new problem is not to prove divisive and disastrous, if the church at large is not to remain floundering and indecisive in a challenging and changing world, someone must provide the guidance, the steadiness, the vision that find God's way forward. The widespread hunger for revival is in some measure a longing for clear and kindling leadership in a day of wavering purposes, contradictory emphases, and conflicting trends.

Basically, no doubt, creative spiritual leadership is a gift of God, implied in some degree in every call to Christian service. Yet the gift needs to be understood, and improved. It is by no means the same kind of gift in every outstanding man of God: very different qualities create spiritual leadership in different people, and a man who would achieve leadership must be humbly aware of those he possesses, and of those he needs to cultivate.

In some men and women, the key to leadership is unquestionably abounding *energy*. In the New Testament, Peter is the obvious example. Of his foremost place in the apostolic church there can be no argument, but, in one thing only was he pre-eminent—his warm, eager, energetic nature. We recognise this in his impulsive speech, in his ready response to Christ, his heartfelt commitment—'Thou art the Christ . . . Lord to whom shall we go?'—in his violent language, and in his equally violent defence of Jesus in the garden. We admire it again in the courageous challenge he issued to the city that crucified his Lord. We know that in the end he will die for Christ.

This is the quality we call boldness, or zeal, when it works well, and impetuosity, fanaticism, when it works out badly. Essentially it is energy, dedication, drive, and there can be no leadership without it. The pastor, the youth 'leader', the elder or women's president, who is content to keep things quietly ticking over, to maintain the traditional pattern and programme, to conserve the past and postpone the future, betrays the trust of leadership. He or she is in a rut, and those who look for initiative find only inertia, discouragement of every new proposal, unwillingness to move—even forward.

Of course energy can be dangerous, as Peter's story shows. Where there is fire, fingers are liable to be burned; and energetic leadership may expose one to criticism, blunders, and opposition. Yet it is better to take risks than to take sedatives, when others look for inspiration. The servant of the living God, the vehicle of the free and forward-moving Spirit, can never afford to be lazy, lethargic or lifeless. He who would lead in God's work must bestir himself to keep up with God.

But energy alone is hardly enough. One leader emerged in the early church, most unexpectedly, of a type almost opposite to Peter. This was James. Slow to come to faith, he seems very quickly to have achieved responsibility. When Paul visits Jerusalem to see Peter, and stays fifteen days, James is the only other leader he meets, as though already James is sharing Peter's pre-eminence. A few years later, at the Council of Jerusalem, it is James who can call to order— 'Brethren, listen to me!' and James who can sum up unarguably— 'My judgement is . . .' By the end of his third missionary journey, Paul makes his report formally to James, as acknowledged leader of the church.

James' great quality was *judgement*. He is known later as a man of austerity, of prayer, and of a martyr's courage; but his nickname is 'James the Just'. In part, at least, that suggests impartiality, wisdom, judgement. One wonders if it really means 'James the Judicious'. If energy provides the drive, it is wise judgement that gives the direction, and makes leadership safe to follow.

Speed of thought, eloquence, wit, showmanship, all may kindle enthusiasm and win great popularity—which is often confused with leadership. It is steadfast and wise counsel, insight that time justifies, careful decisions that bear lasting fruit, which win trust and engender confidence. A quiet eye and penetrating mind, a deep reflection on the things of God and a far-seeing understanding of people, are not qualities that impress the passer-by. But of them is born the kind of leadership that long, testing years and many changes only enhance.

How does the pastor, the team-leader, the Bible-group teacher acquire that spiritual wisdom? James could listen, and weigh the

opinions of others, before he spoke: and there is much in that. The
habit of deliberate decision, too, is a mark of judgement. We cannot
always, like the medieval monks, insist on sleeping upon every
question, but the wise man is not ashamed to postpone his answer.
It is better to be slow, than to be superficial. Nor should any
Christian worker disdain to learn James' own secret: 'If any man lack
wisdom, let him ask of God, who giveth to all men liberally, and
without reproach.'

But the greatest test of leadership is something different again. It
is the *ability to get the best out of people*. As Paul so often insists, all
spiritual gifts are bestowed, not to enhance the possessor but to
enrich and edify others, 'for the perfecting of the saints'. So the real
mark of the leader is not skill in self-promotion, but deftness in
enabling others to grow, to be useful, and to work together.

Here the supreme New Testament example is Barnabas, whom the
apostles called—because it was true—'the son of encouragement'. He
got the best out of the unexpected developments at Antioch, when
the elders at Jerusalem sent him to investigate church life there.
He saw the grace of God and was glad. He got the best out of Paul,
when the Jerusalem church hesitated to admit the new convert to
membership, until Barnabas stood guarantor of his sincerity; and
again when he brought him from Tarsus to be pastor of the church at
Antioch, and stayed a year beside him, teaching him his trade. He
got the best out of young John Mark, when after his defection from
the first mission-journey, Paul refused to take him again. It was
Barnabas who gave Mark a second chance—even as he had given
Paul his first.

This is spiritual leadership of quite unique value to others, to the
church, and to the cause of Christ. It demands genuine appreciation
of others' qualities and gifts. It requires, too, a deep respect for
differences of opinion and outlook. Such a leader has to learn to take
care of others' consciences, and others' freedom, never descending to
coercion, bullying, or threats. And he must, like Barnabas, be always
ready to efface himself, that others may progress.

Of this quality there can be only one source: excellence of personal
character. 'Barnabas was a good man, full of the Holy Ghost, and of
faith.' Timid, reluctant workers, perhaps too conscious of their own
inadequacies, want of education, paucity of gifts, sometimes feel
themselves left behind by the forceful, overshadowed by the clever.
Yet they will respond gladly to the gracious, warm-hearted goodness
that invites, encourages, and supports, by its genuine interest,
confidence, and goodwill. Without this quality of integrity and grace,

other gifts, however valuable, will lack something of *spiritual* leadership; with it, even the poorly equipped pastor or elder may wield far greater influence over others than he will ever know.

For all that, the more intellectual gifts are to be prized also. Paul was different from Peter, from James, and from Barnabas, but he too had a host of friends and fellow-workers eager to follow where he pointed the way. His outstanding gift, among many, was for *clear thinking*, convincing exposition of the truth, powerful persuasion. He was well-informed, apt to teach, skilful and patient in helping others to see what he had seen.

This too is leadership. As Paul himself declared, 'If the trumpet give an uncertain sound, who shall prepare himself for battle?' The true leader keeps just ahead in thought, and action, and vision. He sees the issues, the work, the programme, the neighbourhood, the coming changes, the possibilities, before others do. And he is ever pressing toward some new mark, undiscouraged, untiring, and unsatisfied. He knows when to break new ground, forging ahead without waiting for unanimity. He knows when to take a firm line in dangerous situations, because he has thought ahead, and understands that some fears are better trodden down. On the other hand, he knows when to wait, and not drive; when to retire and not dominate.

This element in leading others must be largely one of intelligence, of thoughtfulness, of alertness and readiness of mind. It is not given to all: and we may be glad there are other kinds of leadership open to us. Nevertheless Paul would not have accepted intellectual explanations of his gift: he would insist 'It is not I, but the grace of God which was with me; not I, but Christ liveth in me.' And he would bid us pray for 'knowledge and all discernment' so that we 'may approve what is excellent' in all 'spiritual understanding'.

One manifestation of 'spiritual leadership' occasions considerable confusion in our time. In Christian as in secular circles, the strength of a man's influence is often judged by the size of his personal following—even if that has been achieved only by dividing some larger group. Some men become prominent by leading out from a wider fellowship malcontents whose only recommendation is their ability to change allegiance; and who, once the new leader's attention passes from them, will as readily desert him for someone else. It is tempting to prefer being absolute leader in some small unquestioning group, rather than first-among-equals in a true *koinonia*.

Yet such division must always imply failure in leadership—a failure to carry *all* with you. The task of the shepherd is to gather, not to scatter the sheep, to gather together in one all the children of God who are scattered abroad; to be the creator, the focus, and the guardian of a fellowship united in Christ.

Such leadership demands *the ability to unify a group*, despite all varieties of opinion and experience. It requires emphasis upon the positive, upon what is known to be true and proved to be Christlike. It requires the skill to hold the balance between opposite insights, and appreciate the many-sidedness of truth without losing conviction or blurring vital distinctions. It will value fellowship above controversy, the unity of the Spirit above pride of knowledge; it will never accept that the truth of God can be served by quarrelling.

In the New Testament, the great example of such leadership is the writer of the First Epistle of John. Nowhere is truth more clearly defined; nowhere are issues more uncompromisingly stated. Yet not once is any personal accusation levelled; never is an 'enemy' forced into a corner, or a position attributed to someone else from which he can only retreat with humiliation and shame. First John has very much to teach us of the art of defending God's truth without hurting God's people; of keeping faith without losing fellowship. And that is leadership indeed!

Something should be said, finally, about the place of *example* in spiritual leadership. To a young pastor striving to achieve leadership in the work of God was sent the counsel 'Show thyself an example to the believers, in speech and conduct, in love and faith and purity'. Paul's own leadership could be expressed in the same way: 'You know my manner of life . . . Be imitators of me, as I am of Christ.' Of all the qualities that comprise spiritual leadership this at least is indispensable: nothing can for long replace it—not brilliance, tact, talent, charm, boldness, training or daring. In Christian work the man who would lead the 'average Christian' must live above the average level.

Of course it is unfair for Christian people to require of their pastors and teachers a higher standard of Christian behaviour than they set for themselves. But leadership does require it. The front line is an exposed position, exposed to the criticism of those behind, as well as to the enemy. And the price of lasting Christian influence is just this—to be a little more conscientious than most people are, a little more scrupulous about doubtful things, a little more hard-working, and generous, and patient.

Such an example of devotion is not so much the price of leadership, it *is* leadership. In the end, among God's people, authority, responsibility, trust, have to be merited, earned, and won—not claimed, or assumed as a right of office. And so to have gained the confidence and loyalty of dedicated colleagues in some fine enterprise for God, is no small part of the reward for becoming 'leading men among the brethren'.

5 PASTORAL VISITATION

Whenever pastoral work is mentioned, the first thing that springs to many minds, sometimes the only thing, is—'visitation'. Most Christian groups can find someone to preach for them: they invite a pastor or elect elders, nevertheless, because they need also 'someone to do the visiting'. It is assumed that those who attend worship should be called upon in their homes, and that many other occasions will arise when the church's ministry will be exercised towards the sick, and those in spiritual need, through representative visitation. The pastor who does not undertake this task with meticulous regularity will be held to fail in his 'most obvious work'.

One unfortunate effect is to present pastoral visitation in the light of reluctant duty, a pointless traditional chore, time-consuming, never finished, yet yielding little result for the church's prosperity. With such a conception, or dislike, of the work, a diligent and energetic man may discipline himself to do it conscientiously, if only he will set himself a programme of thirty visits a week, and charge from house to house, notebook in one hand and watch in the other, determined to fulfil his schedule. His people may find the result humorous; they may also find it useless and exasperating. For he has no time to talk, no leisure to listen, no patience to wait until people have adjusted their mood and screwed up their courage to ask or confide the things they are longing to say.

The same constraining sense of duty prompts the man who visits other people's homes with all the determination and will-not-take-no insistence of a door-to-door salesman. He will sell religion as others sell vacuum cleaners, insurance, or cosmetics—a doorstep sermoniser who will complete his prepared statement of the gospel if necessary through the letter-box. The weakness of this whole approach is that the true motive shows through: the man has a duty to do, and does it. The patient are resigned to it, the tolerant are amused and slightly sympathetic, the irreligious resent it, and most people feel that they are again being exploited for someone else's good—for some new church, movement, or crusade. No one is blessed except the visitor, who feels virtuous.

Of course none of this is pastoral visitation. As everywhere in pastoral work, it is necessary to define your aim and keep it clearly before you. Any one of at least five deliberate aims may prompt a purposeful pastoral visit:

(i) The visiting pastor or elder *brings the church to the home*, bridges the gulf between Sunday and weekday, between church premises and the domestic scene, the 'special' atmosphere of the Christian group and the 'ordinary' life of the family together. The church leader meets the member in the setting of daily life, becomes acquainted with parents, brothers, sisters, children, environment, and enlarges considerably and at once both sympathy and understanding towards his fellow Christian. Sometimes the circumstances of the home throw wholly new light on the attitudes of the member; an invalid to be cared for, an afflicted sister or child, an unsuspected struggle against poverty, reveals the secret strain under which the member lives.

The home for its part sees the pastor or elder in a new 'human' light, as a natural, companionable friend, genuinely interested and easy to talk to. The 'best clothes and best behaviour' atmosphere of the place of worship is exchanged for the informal and intimate conversation of fireside or meal table, yet still the things of faith can be discussed and shared in a new warmth of fellowship. And the conversation about church affairs and events, about mutual friends, and plans, makes common Christian interests come alive as few group discussions at church ever do. The timid or puzzled can put their questions or offer their own comment or explanations, as they would rarely do outside their closest circle. In all such ways the church is 'brought home' to members in their families as a living fellowship of Christian hearts. Any pastoral visit which accomplishes so much is well worth making.

(ii) But the most important purpose of pastoral visitation, and perhaps the most delicate, is *to establish a relationship*. Its most significant achievement lies not in any measurable effect of two or three visits, but in what is thereby made possible, and easy, when some sudden emergency, sorrow, fear, or shame, shall arise. The pastor who is known at the fireside for a Christian and a friend will then move into a place already prepared, from which he can minister at need as no stranger could ever do.

The diligent pastor will soon accumulate his own memories of remarkable examples of visitation divinely guided and blessed. There will be times when an unplanned visit turns out to be the answer to someone's urgent prayer; when serious illness, bereavement, bad news, fierce temptation, threatened marriage breakdown, finds the pastor the key figure in a domestic crisis, able to say what needs to be said, and to take decisive action, with an understanding, authority and concern which are not questioned. But such things do not happen on first visits, or in a mechanical and perfunctory round of dutiful calls duly made. A foundation must be laid, a relationship created, wherein a potential for spiritual ministry exists in readiness for any opportunity that may arise. That is why one indispensable qualification for pastoral visitation is—patience.

But also ease, and simplicity. Here, as in all pastoral work, the pastor must be content to be his natural and genuine self. The man who is not only always the Christian, but always the minister, the church official, and always on duty, will not only fail to establish a fruitful relationship; each successive visit will make it more unlikely that he ever will. Such a man is—mentally—always in his pulpit. He feels he must 'improve the occasion', and especially that he must read and comment, perhaps rebuke, and always pray. *The gulf remains.* He may be respected, but he will rarely be welcome as the natural, happy friend whose companionship and conversation will enrich an evening. Instead, the less pious members of the family hastily retire to cold bedrooms, the children are banished to the boring kitchen, and everyone feels that the church has fallen upon the evening, determined to solemnise home-life.

In contrast is the man who calls, and calls again, finding excuses because he likes to call, without embarrassment or ceremony. Then, unexpectedly, finding the baby ill and the mother anxious, he will say with natural ease, 'Well, there's one obvious thing we can do— let's pray about him' and bending over the cot, in a brief prayer as simple as it is unexpected, he will bring God's own peace and strength to a distraught heart. When a lad is going to University; when the old people far away are unwell; when there is trouble at work—then the natural thing is to pray together: and the fact that it is *not* a formal and customary part of your visit makes it the more moving and significant.

The central purpose of pastoral visitation is pastoral relationship. Given that, there is no need at all to draw attention to one's religious status and purpose. 'God's grace', says J. R. Wood, 'interprets itself through the gracious man.'

(iii) Frequently, the predominant purpose of pastoral visiting is *to bring the church's worship to the home.* To those who through age, infirmity, affliction, illness, distance, or responsibility for others, are unable to share in worship-services, the pastor's visit is a link with what they miss, and so deeply long to share. In such circumstances the visit may be, and should be, more planned and formal. A deliberate manner, and expectancy, and an obvious preparation, will help recapture a little of the atmosphere of public worship. A previously selected portion of scripture, with a prepared comment or two, perhaps the reading of an appropriate hymn, and a prayer in which the work of the church, and the kingdom of God everywhere, is remembered as well as personal and family needs, will make fifteen minutes of solemn and refreshing worship, reminiscent of the missed means of grace.

Leave soon afterwards, that the memory of the service may remain: conversation should precede the worship, which becomes the climax of the visit. Occasionally it is helpful to recall, explicitly, the theme, scripture lessons, and message of one of the Sunday services. The sense of still being kept in touch is thereby strengthened, though (as with everything pastoral) to make this a habit would destroy its value. On a formal worship-visit of this kind, it is for the visitor to make the suggestion and create the occasion: often just setting out a Bible and hymnbook, with a moment or two of silence, is sufficient.

Illness or infirmity apart, the visitor will sometimes know that he is in a home where family worship is the custom, and he may ask permission to join their evening prayers before he leaves—without assuming that he must then conduct them. For him to remain, a silent sharer in the family's devotion, and then quietly leave, will be more deeply appreciated than he may realise. At other times he may be asked to take some part, and he will then know that he has been accepted as a very privileged friend into another Christian home.

In some Christian traditions it is customary for the Lord's Supper to be shared in their homes with members who are long housebound. Such a service can be a true means of grace and an immense comfort. Others feel that such a 'private' Supper contradicts the essentially corporate nature of the Memorial, which (they think) should always be a church occasion. Others again will point to the dangers of superstition surrounding the Bread and Wine, of indulging self-importance in certain 'leading members'; of frightening the sick with the suggestion that they are near enough to death for the 'last rites' to be administered.

At least it must be said that if the worship of the Lord's Table is taken to private homes, it is essential that—first—the representative and corporate nature of the service should be safeguarded: a group, however small, should be assembled, another elder, perhaps a lady member, a close Christian friend. There must be nothing private and clandestine about such worship. Secondly, it is essential that preparation be meticulous, the details not only of the order of service but of the carrying and setting out of the Bread and Wine, being dignified and reverent. The visitors should leave immediately afterwards. One accidental result of such careful arrangements would be to discourage too frequent or ill-considered requests. In any case, it is probably best that any such ministry of the Table in private homes should occur only when authorised, upon each individual request, by the leaders of the fellowship.

On all such worship-visits, the ideal will lie somewhere between the intensity and intimacy of private prayer and the more formal pattern and tone of public worship; the aim, to sense the near presence of God with individuals at fireside or in sickroom, while retaining the awareness of belonging to the world church of Christ. This is a very different experience to merely sitting together listening to a taped record of other people offering prayer, or listening to a sermon given to other people in other circumstances at another place. There will be occasions when records of special or historic services will be 'enjoyed' by those who could not be present, or by those who were present and wish to be reminded of the occasion. But spectating at a distance at other people's worshipping is not worship. The pastor's worship-visit must mean more than that.

(iv) What may be called *occasional pastoral visiting* is that prompted by needs or occasions that come to the pastor's notice, or are stored in his diary. Happy the man who can remember the wedding-date of the couple he married last year, and who drops in to congratulate on the anniversary day. And happy he who knows the first birthday of the baby, and calls to say so. An aged mother who comes to stay at the same time each year will be so glad to be remembered. The announcement of a son's or daughter's success at school, or first public concert, or engagement, or graduation, or the father's promotion or professional recognition—all are worthy occasions for the Christian friend to stop by with a word of greeting and good wishes.

The church's 'grape-vine' is an invaluable inspirer of such occasional visitation, and the alert pastor will store up many such 'excuses to call' as he listens to the conversation of church friends, and is kept informed by his wife. The local newspaper, too, can keep him in touch with what is happening to homes that he knows, and to some he does not. A bereavement, an accident, a domestic tragedy, anywhere in the neighbourhood, is an occasion when even the unknown pastor's word of sympathy and offer of help will forge a link that could hold some soul steady and sweeten a bitter day.

There will be opportunity on some such occasional visits to organise help in emergencies; to enrol fellow-members who have cars in a scheme of practical assistance to take the sick to hospital, to bring the infirm to church, to carry gifts to the housebound, to get the aged away to the country or the sea; to arrange for baby-minding during mother's sudden absence; to warn other members of the family, perhaps at a distance, of sudden needs; to take initiatives and carry responsibilities in a hundred different circumstances, in ways that will move hearts to deep gratitude when the emergency is past. Often there will be occasion to make use, for pastoral support in urgent need, of a charitable fund placed at the visitor's discretion, for which he gives account, in strictest confidence, to only one other member.

Among the occasions for pastoral visits there will be some that the pastor could not easily explain. An impulse, a strong pressure on one's spirit, a name that comes vividly to mind in prayer—these are enough, and the wise pastor never neglects them. The experienced man will have learned by repeated examples that God often directs the visiting in ways beyond our foresight to meet needs of which we never even knew.

(v) No pastoral visit calls for such delicacy and care as that which has *evangelistic purpose*. When such a visit is part of a campaign covering a district, the fact should be emphasised to avoid any impression of having singled out one 'godless' home. Early enquiry should be made concerning existing church-affiliation, lest the visit appear to be aimed merely at changing church loyalties. Sometimes as a result of such enquiry, long neglected links to former church fellowships may be restored.

Evangelistic visitation is occasionally the result of a campaign elsewhere, a profession of faith or a confession of need having prompted 'follow-up' in the home. Or an individual may have been moved to request a visit with a view to better understanding of the gospel. Perhaps the most obvious rule is to let the seeker set the pace, the visitor assuming no more, and no less, of understanding and faith than the individual is ready to profess. The eager visitor is so often anxious to bring the soul to the point—*his* point—too quickly, to press for premature decision, or church membership, when the first need is enlightenment, Christian friendship, and the infection of other Christians' joy.

It should not need to be said (though experience suggests it does) that evangelism in another's home calls for the utmost courtesy. You hold the audience captive, under obligation to be reasonably polite to you, since you are the guest: never presume upon that. There is never any Christian grace, or attractiveness, or spiritual power, in a bullying, self-righteous rudeness. The very lowest aim of every visit should be that at least you will be welcome when you call again; the highest aim would be that, after a quiet talk in which Christian truth has been graciously presented in heart-to-heart conversation, you will be greeted next time by one whose face and bearing testify to the transforming work of the Spirit in the silence and privacy of the individual heart.

Whatever the specific occasion for the visit, to be present in the home offers opportunity as need arises for pastoral counselling and encouragement. Though it may be, in some ways, more convenient to arrange for counselling interviews in one's own study or on church premises, where secrecy and security from interruptions are under the pastor's control, there are circumstances in which the right setting is a pastoral visit. Within the home, the dangers of professionalism and artificiality are less likely to distort the true relationship, and a close confidence is therefore more quickly established. The visiting pastor has always to be ready for the most casual call suddenly to develop into a most serious counselling session, as a soul in real trouble grasps the opportunity to unburden the heart.

Practical Considerations

Occasional, emergency, or impulsive pastoral calls must not overshadow the need for regular and systematic visitation, lest individual homes are overlooked altogether. Beside visiting immediately where there is need, a man should have some plan and schedule to deliver him from his own moods, from careless oversights, and from the natural tendency to visit oftenest the homes which welcome one most. Pastoral visitation should be as clearly a matter of conscience as the preparation of sermons.

A methodical plan will include an initial round of all the homes for which the visitor is responsible, by way of introduction, and to recognise those of greatest need. Thereafter, a regular monthly visit to those unable to attend worship, weekly perhaps to the sick or distressed, and maybe twice a year to others who are often met about the church, may suffice—provided such a schedule represents the minimum task, and never the maximum.

Organisation must not become bondage. An earnest invitation, news of sudden need, the guidance of the Spirit, a remembered special occasion, will adjust the planned route, and the frequency of calls, at any moment. And so, sometimes, will the visitor's own spiritual need. A well-loved minister of great experience, whose powerful preaching and gracious personality had enriched many, surprised a gathering of ministers with the candid counsel: 'When you are depressed, your faith is low, and you are fed up with the job, go visiting. Get out among your people. You may just possibly do them good: they certainly will do you good, and bring you to your senses!'

Visits should be regularly and accurately recorded, both by card-index and by a date beside addresses in the visiting pocket-book. If the cards only are used, there should be *regular* examination—at the same day and hour each week—for homes that have been missed. The cards should be for the visitor's eyes only, and contain, beside family details, ages, occupation, relationships and the like, something of the spiritual history of each member of the family, with dates of conversion or membership, kinds of Christian work done, and any private comment which will help subsequent visits to be made fruitful. To be able to produce details of visits paid is the best reply to criticism of neglect—where it is unjustified—and the best spur to regularity. Addresses will constantly be added, corrected, arranged in districts, for efficient organisation of time.

Frequently, as one ponders a visit just made, it will be clear that someone better qualified by age, or Christian experience, or the circumstances of life, might be more successful in such a home. The pastor should often delegate a particular ministry to another Christian, making the introduction, perhaps (unless confidence forbids) discussing the situation and the possible avenues of assistance with the one who is to concentrate on that home. A visiting-panel of fellow-members who share in this task, when well prepared and supported, can enormously multiply and enrich the contacts of the fellowship with its surrounding neighbourhood. The presence of ladies in such a group will remove one obvious danger in pastoral visitation, that of scandal or temptation. The pastor must never presume upon his reputation, nor assume that his office makes him immune from either suspicion or evil. Where the situation requires, he may be accompanied by his wife or a lady visitor, or arrange only to call when the family is present. Far better be wise, foreseeing trouble, than spend angry, hurtful weeks afterwards loudly protesting innocence.

A genuine concern for all kinds of people; careful, unbreakable secrecy about what you see and hear in other people's homes; willingness to speak with individuals face-to-face about the things it is sometimes easier to preach about; and unfailing courtesy especially towards non-Christians whose homes you are 'invading'—these are imperative conditions of a continuing and fruitful visitation ministry. Its sufficient reward, very often, is in the welcoming smile of the old and the young when next you call: and in the memories of times when seemingly idle visits bore fruit, perhaps long afterwards, in some exceptional experience of the transforming grace of God.

6 PERSONAL COUNSELLING

Personal counsel on the great and intimate issues of life is in these days so often lightly sought and freely given that it may be salutary to begin consideration of pastoral counselling with some ancient advice:

> Every counselor praises counsel,
>   but some give counsel in their own interest.
> Be wary of a counselor,
>   and learn first what is his interest—
>   for he will take thought for himself—
> lest he cast the lot against you
>   and tell you, 'Your way is good',
>   and then stand aloof and see what will happen to you.
> Do not consult with one who looks at you suspiciously;
>   hide your counsel from those who are jealous of you.
> Do not consult with a woman about her rival
>   or with a coward about war,
> with a merchant about barter
>   or with a buyer about selling,
> with a grudging man about gratitude
>   or with a merciless man about kindness,
> with an idler about any work
>   or with a man hired for a year about completing his work,
> with a lazy servant about a big task—
>   pay no attention to these in any matter of counsel.
> But stay constantly with a godly man
>   whom you know to be a keeper of the commandments,
> whose soul is in accord with your soul,
>   and who will sorrow with you if you fail.
> And establish the counsel of your own heart,
>   for no one is more faithful to you than it is.
> For a man's soul sometimes keeps him better informed
>   than seven watchmen sitting high on a watchtower.
> And besides all this pray to the Most High
>   that he may direct your way in truth.

So Jesus, son of Sirach, whose delicate blend of shrewdness, humour and piety will help a pastor keep a sense of proportion, an awareness of the pitfalls in advising others on how to run their lives, and a modest expectation of what may be achieved by pooling fallibility.

Nevertheless, such work is unavoidable, unless the pastor is to eschew all friendship, repulse all cries for help, and make his study a monastic cell. Without individual counselling he will scarcely be a pastor, certainly not a Christian pastor: for Jesus (it has been calculated) conducted no less than thirty-five recorded counselling interviews, so illustrating dramatically the meaning of ministry and the heart of the gospel.

How much of personal counselling a man may be called upon to give will depend partly upon his own personality: the excessively shy, cynical or dictatorial will attract few to seek his private ear. Few things in pastoral life so test the minister's character. The tense, anxious, 'highly strung' counsellor will not invite, or help, those similarly afflicted; a soul undermined with doubts will offer little to establish another's faith, until it has either resolved them or learned to carry them courageously. A pastor who loses his temper, who can be goaded, sarcastic, bitter, unforgiving, will rarely be consulted on problems of relationship—nor if there is any doubt whether he has solved his own elementary problems of truthfulness, self-discipline, unselfishness, loyalty, and trust in God. Though we point men beyond ourselves to Christ, yet we will never take them further than we ourselves have come.

In particular, personal counselling makes great demands upon sympathy, candour, and generosity. Appeals from people one does not like, to resolve situations that should have been forestalled, can severely test one's patience. To 'suffer fools gladly' comes very near to contempt. At least a man must discipline himself to listen fairly, until understanding, and eagerness to help, dawn within him: at best sympathy becomes identification, an emotional empathy, 'your ache in my heart'.

Candour is dangerous, yet without it counselling is superficial, and cowardly. To help an injured wife see the husband's point of view; an outraged man see the other side of a quarrel; a hurt, self-righteous soul see itself clearly—requires honesty of mind and speech. Yet unless the truth is spoken, in clarity as well as love, years of resentment, self-pity, and self-protective pride may never yield to more positive attitudes. And a true, practical generosity of time, thought, ingenuity and effort will be necessary, often to help those who have no claim upon you but that of Christian love, and who sometimes will show little appreciation. A narrow, calculating, time-scheduled ministry will not be troubled with much counselling.

A man's preaching, too, will determine how much counselling he will be asked for. Preaching that is friendly, person-to-person, relevant, will carry its own invitation, as hearers become aware that here is a man with whom one might discuss problems intelligently and with sympathy. Doctrinaire, dogmatic sermons will discourage such approaches. On the other hand, the more competent pastoral preaching is, the more will people find in the pulpit ministry the help they seek, and that is the more healthy, independent, reticent way to receive the counsel of God. Yet some will need further help to apply truth to their own situation, and the sermon will come alive again when broken into individual counsel.

What has been said of the need, in all pastoral work, of self-knowledge, maturity, sincerity; of the necessity, and dangers, of a religious approach; and of the importance of confidentiality and responsibility, applies with especial urgency to pastoral counselling. Some other general principles already mentioned will also have to be recalled as we discuss counselling methods.

Definition of Aim

The difficulty of defining one's purpose in counselling arises from the number and variety of people who seek help—and it is vital always to think of people, never of 'cases'. To categorise, systematise, diagnose by type-symptoms, mentally card-index or catalogue the multiplicity of human needs is to blunder at the outset. There are as many 'sorts' of people in trouble as there are kinds of people multiplied by kinds of trouble. To classify is to theorise, not to minister.

Some will seek interview 'just to talk things over'—an appeal for consultation, illumination, insight. Others will seek interview 'to see what you think'—an appeal to directive authority and presumed superior wisdom. A request to speak to the pastor 'so that he may understand' may be an appeal for sympathy and moral support. A request to speak 'in order that he shall know . . .' or 'so that I can explain' may reveal a wish to justify oneself. The request that is framed 'I must speak to you . . .' probably betrays a soul under stress, unable to cope, in fear of breaking down, or tempted to ruin home, career and happiness by some dreaded folly or sin. Anxiety, regret, sorrow, deep wounds inflicted by unfaithfulness or neglect, bewilderment at some turn in life's course, fear of some threatened crisis—an infinite number of situations may bring people emotionally disturbed, or morally distraught, or intellectually perplexed, to the counsellor's chair.

Depressive factors in religion itself—guilt, artificial spirituality, false self-denigration, unhealthy fear of God—may call for pastoral skill. A generalised anxiety-habit, or a generalised sense of inadequacy, reduces some lives to dumb struggle and a fear of all responsibility. Intellectual problems of belief are occasionally a thin smoke-screen for emotional or moral indiscipline. Marital problems are numberless. Over-emotional people break their hearts because feelings refuse to be dictated to; introverts tear themselves to pieces, extroverts complain that they cannot feel what others feel. There are people who habitually get into debt, and others who seem to find it impossible not to quarrel with those they most need for friends. Loneliness accentuates all other weaknesses, and creates problems of its own, including the fear of being alone, and jealous resentment against all who have company.

Even such a sample of problems demonstrates the danger of typecasting souls in distress. Keeping the general pastoral aim in view, the counsellor will realise that perfect Christians are rare, and that approximate ends, often heroically sustained amidst unfortunate circumstances, heritage, deprivation or inadequacy, are the working patterns toward which he directs his endeavours:

the reduction of over-all anxiety to tolerable intensity;

the attainment of a somewhat more objective attitude towards a problem-situation or relationship;

the removal of intellectual stumbling-blocks to obedience, without hoping to answer all the questions raised;

a better understanding of God and a firmer trust in His unswerving faithfulness and love, though disappointment and regret remain;

a maturity of faith which no longer shrinks at every setback, adverse providence, or unanswered prayer, yet still expects miracles— sometimes;

a self-confidence sufficiently restored to enable formerly 'useless' people to undertake responsibility and co-operate with others;

enough reassurance of God's love and unfailing support to make life again bearable for inadequate, defeated souls;

the replacement of crippling, poisoning guilt with the healing wonder of confession, forgiveness, cleansing, through God's grace in Christ;

the liberation of little, inhibited souls into the freedom and power of a Spirit-filled Christian experience;

the illumination of baffling frustrations as, after all, but the ache of unused capacities, requiring the redirection of life's energies towards more satisfying goals;

the inculcation, sometimes, of the simplest habits of private prayer, meditation, trust, and gratitude, in hearts straining desperately to fulfil Christianity's obligations without experiencing its renewing springs and radiant faith.

How can one define such varied purposes? It might be easier to state the aim of counselling from the counsellor's point of view: to serve the pilgrim footsteps of one's fellows; 'to warn every man, and teach

every man, in all wisdom, that we may present every man mature in
Christ'; 'to be made all things to all men that we might by all means
save some'. But that could mislead, if it makes us forget that the
focus of all Christian counselling is not the counsellor but the soul
in need.

Discussion of Method

A considerable methodology of counselling exists, with a most
unattractive jargon, but the practical issues may be distilled in
simple terms: what degree of pressure may rightly be brought to bear
upon an individual needing help, and what means may be employed
to achieve the end in view?

When one consults a lawyer, a doctor, a banker, one expects to be
told what to do; understanding *why* is not essential, and not usually
expected. One seeks qualified advice, and accepts it as given with
competence and authority. When however one consults a good
teacher, this attitude is modified considerably. In some subjects,
doubtless, (like languages and mathematics) authoritative direction
of study will be appropriate but as education advances towards
creative levels, as in art, history, philosophy, science, good teaching
must increasingly centre not upon the authority of the teacher but
upon the capacity and originality of the taught. Emphasis falls less
and less upon what the teacher has to impart, more and more upon
what the student needs to learn to achieve his individual best. In the
realm of faith, conscience, personal relationships, moral behaviour
and religious experience, this dependence upon the learner's initiative
and response becomes paramount. He must discern the way, struggle
with the difficulties, and discover faith, for himself.

Some would insist that this reduces pastoral counselling to
impotence. They would argue that the Christian counsellor's task is
to declare the Word of God in each situation, to expound the
principles of Christian theology and ethics with the authority of the
trained pastoral mind, and to use whatever pressures of warning or
persuasion may be necessary to evoke obedience to what is right—
while fully acknowledging that decision whether to obey, or to
disobey, and take the consequences, rests with the individual
concerned.

Others hold that this is bullying, if not blackmail, and must in
most cases be ineffective. It could only work where the authority of
the counsellor is conceded; and even there it cannot produce strong
and self-dependent attitudes but only a submissive, pliable character

with second-hand convictions. The pastor, we said, must not play
God: the moral initiative of Christian men and women must be
preserved, and when immediate problems have been resolved, a fully
independent discipleship should be resumed. Plainly, the amount of
directive authority expressed in counselling will vary with the
individual and the situation confronted. To say, 'Do not try to prove
to. a counselee that he is right or wrong' (Hamilton) suggests
abandoning in all cases not only the temptation to judge but all
endeavour to convert or to warn. If the counselling is to be Christian,
it cannot be purely subjective, or impromptu; certain convictions
and codes will direct it. If it is to be profitable, it must be in some way
manipulated, or organised, towards an acceptable end. Nevertheless,
when all is said and explained, spiritual health can only be restored
by voluntary response to the offer of God in Christ.

Moreover, this is but one aspect of the counsellor's task. The other
need is to get inside the situation with the person counselled, to see
and feel it from his standpoint, to sympathise with his reaction
toward it and assess it from within his frame of reference, his level of
culture, his opportunities, age, capacity and experience, and not from
within our own. Only in this way can we carry him with us in any
resolution attempted. Yet in framing that resolution it is the
counsellor who represents and works toward the optimum result, and
to that extent 'directs' the process of counselling to the end he thinks
nearest to God's will for men. How far the pastor's counsel, how far
the patient's self-discovery, contribute to the result will vary with
every particular problem.

Avenues of Help

The same issue may be approached by considering the avenues of
therapy open to the Christian counsellor. These are sometimes said to
be 'broadly speaking, two: the intellectual and the emotional'. But
that is unnecessarily restrictive: the pastor must often look for wider
sources of assistance.

(i) 'Intellectual' help would include such persuasion and stimulus
as may be brought to bear through better instruction in the faith and
in the ways of God, through explanation of the causes and cure of
various spiritual maladjustments, through reasoning a patient into a
better frame of mind, or by analysing a situation objectively and
seeing it in truer perspective. The appeal here is to reason and
insight; and the assumption, that to understand is to cure. In many
cases this is true: to bring to light the hidden causes of trouble, to

discover the subconscious sources of conscious distress, 'to see life steadily and see it whole', has therapeutic power; and even where the trouble is not cured it becomes less frightening. In all such help, the directive expertise of the counsellor as teacher is foremost, even though his understanding must be shared by the enquirer, not imposed upon him.

(ii) But many personal problems will not yield to the intellectual approach. People vary greatly in what operates to change them, and to many who seek counsel in emotional difficulties, all the talk and wisdom in the world will mean nothing. They are emotionally disturbed, and must be emotionally healed. This may be achieved by unleashing long-pent-up feelings, repressed by a reserved or proud nature, clamped down by a sense of shame at passions so strong and elementary, at fires of jealousy, envy, vengefulness, fear, remorse or anger, that the subject is frightened to admit. To 'come out with it all' in the confidence of the pastor's study, to 'break down' and unburden the heart to a sympathetic, trusted, and unjudging fellow Christian may work its own healing. Therein the counsellor's role will be mainly passive, receptive, a silent response of understanding.

But painful emotional stress may be countered in other ways. Sometimes, emotional energy may be redirected: faith and trust, courage and devotion, gratitude and hope, concern for another's distress, may divert strong feeling into useful and admirable channels. But such balancing-emotions (strictly, substitute-emotions) will not usually be kindled by argument, but by recollected scenes and friendships, familiar scripture passages of comfort and promise, moving prayers and hymns, remembered joys of earlier Christian experience, traditions of home and the loved circle. Much modern religion is emotionally starved, and human nature takes its revenge: the answer lies in religious faith emotionally nourished.

Or in action. Harmful emotion may find useful release in being harnessed to planned and sustained activity. Long festering memories of disobedience, of injury done, of neglected opportunity, or resented bereavement, may be turned to good account in actions that can redeem lost years, comfort other hearts, or spend itself—and its regrets—in helping others injured by similar wrongdoing. Here the role of the counsellor will inevitably be more active, and his manner more pressing.

(iii) Activity is an avenue of therapy the pastor will need very often to explore. Many 'spiritual' problems are not solved by prayer or faith or exhortation, but by action. The essence of counselling then lies in bringing the patient to resolute decision, usually fixing a time, place, and pattern of remedial action to be deliberately followed. A wrong done must be undone, by apology and perhaps by restitution; a quarrel must be reconciled by genuine approach of friendship, however costly; within a broken marriage, one further attempt must be made at reconciliation before irrevocable decisions are taken; a change of employment to avoid temptation, a change of neighbourhood to break dangerous associations, or to move from loneliness to friendship, may need to be undertaken. The whole pattern of leisure activities may need to be revised, self-absorbed people introduced to outgoing and demanding tasks, and self-pitying people brought face to face with the desperate circumstances in which others live, before our counselling is through.

So very often those who come to talk must be challenged to *do* something about their problems. Pastoral ministry can involve the counsellor in scores of unforeseen tasks, searching advertisements, writing letters, providing introductions, interviewing employers, organising others' life-patterns. Counselling rarely means just a kindly sympathy and a word of prayer!

(iv) 'Integrity therapy' is the curious term sometimes given to a view of personal problems which traces them almost exclusively to a loss of self-confidence and self-respect, a chronic sense of inadequacy for life. The causes may be varied—moral failure, self-betrayal, guilt, rejection by others. Inability to live with oneself, to organise life around any positive self-valuation and attainable goal, leads to inward conflict and despair; personality disintegrates and the individual is left vulnerable to every passing temptation, impulse, or exploitation.

Here the Christian counsellor possesses a means of healing available to no one else, in a gospel that proclaims the forgiveness of sin without condoning it, through atonement made and right upheld by love. The application of that saving truth to the burdened, self-loathing conscience needs more patience, skill and realism than some evangelist-counsellors might admit, but the healing, liberating, re-integrating power of an assured pardon and a welcoming, supporting love, working through rekindled gratitude and hope, is immense. To lead a sin-sickened soul through mere remorse, and emotional absorption in the sordid details of its story, to a true assessment and a truly moral revulsion, on to an honest, unexcusing but unexaggerated confession, acceptance of forgiveness, and whatever practical restitution may be possible, is to lay the foundation for a new beginning which may turn the evil past to good account and reverse the very strength of despair into moral endeavour and courage. That is redemption.

Some understanding of moral psychology and the causes of 'weakness' of will; some understanding of how personality 'works'; instruction on how to avoid, and to counter, temptation; how to build moral resistance to evil by constant habits of devotion, and by so planning one's day, and one's friendships, as to ensure that every incentive is present to be true to one's new, best self—this too will be required of the pastor who would rescue and support the morally endangered. Redemptive counselling is never achieved by pious, or theological, conversations.

(v) One form of ministry frequently required in individual counselling is the firm and clear exposition of the just proportions of religious truth. So much disappointment and distress is due to failure to keep the balance of the gospel. There seems to be no Christian idea which may not at some time be ridden to death, so emphasised as to obscure all other aspects of faith. So often the pastor will ask himself what element of the total gospel is being forgotten, or has never been understood, to produce an attitude so extreme, a character so unbalanced, a conscience so curiously inconsistent. Sometimes he will emphasise again the justice and holiness of God, to those whose conception of His mercy has obscured the fact that He still is God, and is not to be mocked. Perhaps more often he will need to teach hard, censorious Christians, and some whose hardness turns inward in despair, that God is tender, patient, and kind. To those who are despairing of ever reforming society by witness and good works he will recall that the Christian hope is not in human effort but in the divine inbreaking in God's good time; to those for whom the Advent hope has become excuse for irresponsible and unproductive prophecy-mongering, he will warn that the only 'vigilance' the New Testament commends is that of the shining lamp, the faithful servant and the well-invested talent. To the careless he will speak of judgement; to the burdened, of forgiveness. To the energetic doer of all good works, impatient of devotion, he will speak of the inner sources from which alone true endeavour can be fed; to the mystic entranced with the joy of inward experiences he will speak solemnly of the sick, the naked, the hungry and the prisoner in whom Christ is to be served. The cure of souls demands a skilled physician familiar with the whole spiritual pharmacopoeia, and not confined to a few simples and remedies distilled from his own limited experience.

(vi) In many situations, the honest and humble counsellor will find himself out of his depth. Medical, legal, or financial complications

c

will require expert advice; public authorities, or voluntary associations like Alcoholics Anonymous and Marriage Guidance Clinics, will provide services he cannot rival. It is the pastor's business to know of them, with their office addresses, hours of business and telephone numbers: he becomes the intermediary between souls perplexed, perhaps badly frightened, and those who have skill, resources and power to render aid.

Sometimes the experts will be within the Christian fellowship, and the counsellor *will seek permission* to introduce the patient to the doctor, lawyer, or social worker who can help. To do so without permission would be to break confidence; nor will the pastor make the introduction casually—merely 'sending' the patient on—but by personal contact. If permission is refused, the pastor should not enquire why, but suggest others: reticence and confidence must be respected, and there could be a family connection the pastor does not suspect. And the pastor will maintain his own special ministry meanwhile: the soul who turned to a *pastor* seeking help does not want to be handed over as a 'special case' to someone entirely different. The enlistment into pastoral ministry of mature and experienced members of the fellowship has already been emphasised: others, who have come the same way and learned God's graciousness first-hand, can often do better what the counsellor could only attempt to describe at second-hand. While continuing his own concern, the pastor will, in such cases, abstain from 'overseeing' or interfering, once the new supporting friendship is under way.

(vii) The most difficult of all decisions facing the personal counsellor is when to 'refer' a distressed soul for psychiatric treatment. Psychiatric and spiritual disorders are obviously near-allied, but the counsellor *must* understand the difference of field, function, and resources between psychiatric and pastoral care. The pastor deals with (otherwise) normal people whose distress arises from insufficient, or insufficiently understood, religious faith and experience; his remedy is a better expression of true religion in thought, behaviour and the pattern of life. The psychiatrist deals with abnormal people whose mental life reveals disease or disorders of various kinds, but whose symptoms, coloured by religious background, upbringing or habit, may take 'religious' forms. The remedy then must be not more and better religious faith and behaviour, but expert psychiatric attention.

It would be *extreme, irresponsible and culpable folly* for the pastor to meddle in psychiatric illness on the basis of some child-psychology, or religious psychology, studied during training. The difficulty is to recognise such illness with sufficient certainty to justify suggesting psychiatric help. When the patient is a danger to himself, or to others, is totally incoherent, or has lost touch with the real world altogether, the question decides itself. But early stages of mental ill-health are not easy to recognise, and the consequences of even mentioning psychiatry can be so serious that the pastor may well hesitate—and should do so. To refer a problem to the mental authorities merely because a patient is troublesome, or because no other solution offers itself, is indefensible—and would soon put an end to the pastor's usefulness.

The pastor will realise the shock which any suggestion of 'insanity' will bring to a distressed soul, probably already terrified of the possibility, and to the family. He must realise, too, the long hard road ahead for any man suspected of mental ill-balance: the attitude of neighbours, friends, employers, though irrational and indefensible, has to be reckoned with. The pastor must also realise that in the end little may be done, and that a psychiatrist unsympathetic to religion may rob the man of such comfort and support as he already has.

Nevertheless, the pastor may remain convinced that all he can do is to suggest psychiatry. *He will be well advised to do this, wherever possible, through the patient's present medical adviser*. He will suggest a consultation with the doctor, meanwhile himself reporting to the doctor privately what made him so advise. If he is able personally to introduce the patient to a Christian psychiatrist, he may do so directly. In either case, he will again maintain his pastoral ministry to the end, not abandoning the patient to others; and he will do much to prepare the patient and the family for what lies before them.

He will seek to persuade of the need for psychiatric healing; he may urge that only the psychiatrist can decide whether mental treatment is necessary, just as only a doctor can decide if medical treatment is necessary. Referral is but seeking expert diagnosis. He will strive to represent disorders of the mind as no less curable, no more permanent, no more frightening, than disorders of the lungs or circulation—percentages of cures are rising all the time. He will insist that mental illness is not inherited, necessarily, and set his face sternly against any implication that it is something to be ashamed of, and hidden away. He may need also to reassure the patient that to consult a psychiatrist shows no more 'lack of faith' than to consult a physician or a lawyer; and he may have to counter much religious prejudice, or fear, created by forms of psychiatry that seem inimical to faith and morality. Introduction to a truly Christian psychiatrist and the solemn promise to continue his own ministry throughout the treatment, will do more than anything else to allay such fears.

The need for caution in such situations is obvious, and some risk is always present: but the individual's need, too, may be desperate, and the pastor cannot shirk responsibility. In the end he can only act as seems right at the time, and leave the issue, and the patient, in God's hands.

The Counselling Interview

Appropriate treatment of a personal problem can only emerge during conversations in which the circumstances are analysed and the trouble shared. Pre-arranged interviews give opportunity to plan a relaxed and comfortable setting, free of interruptions and assured of secrecy. Yet both these desirable conditions need thought: counselling interviews can become tense, emotional, tearful; the well-timed interruption of a wife or housekeeper with refreshments can contribute greatly towards keeping the emotional temperature down, one's feet on the ground, and propriety secure. Some who profess to seek Christian counsel are cranks, some sneaks, some over-sexed and flirtatious, some even blackmailing. No one is invulnerable, or beyond suspicion, and the plea for secrecy must not be allowed to create compromising situations. It is an excellent rule never to interview a member of the other sex without another person within call: let it be understood that you never do, and do not break the rule for someone you happen to trust—the implication about others will be plain!

It is necessary not only to have time, but to be seen to have time. Some psychiatrists allow a hundred hours to reach the problem: even pastors discover that compassion and efficiency demand leisure to cultivate confidence. Haste inhibits the slow self-revelation that is essential before many people can bring themselves to say what they really mean, or come to the point, or even find what the point is! A hurried ten minutes before a meeting, when the counsellor's thoughts are elsewhere, his comprehension probably very sketchy, his comments ill-advised, can only do harm.

While it is pedantic and artificial to speak of the 'technique' of pastoral interviewing, in so far as the interview is conversation with a purpose it is possible to identify progressive stages and comment upon possible frustrations.

(i) Once the interviewee is set at ease and the purpose of the visit unhurriedly enquired, the first task is, of course, just to listen—for some pastors, the hardest part of the whole process. Listening may be an art, it is certainly a discipline. An obvious temptation is to give polite attention while part of the mind is speculating upon what is coming, another part is theorising, and even diagnosing, before the trouble has been described, let alone been analysed. Another temptation is to interrupt with probing questions, turning conversation into cross-examination, and quickly throwing the visitor on the defensive.

Quite unforgivable is the arrogance which attempts to tell another what his problem is. Few things antagonise so speedily, or so irretrievably as the dogmatic lecture, before the trouble is half told— 'Oh yes, I know your problem: what you need is a bit of humility . . . or more faith . . . or if you came to prayer meeting oftener this would not happen.' Unless, indeed, it is the conceited, overbearing, pseudo-scientific dictum: 'Aye, I recognise a manic-depressive obsession when I see one!' or, 'Obviously, brother, an oedipus complex masquerading as a passion for geriatrics!' A counsellor who can so react to a soul in distress needs himself to be psycho-analysed.

'Be prepared', says a Christian psychiatrist, 'to stay with what is, with whatever the sufferer says, wherever it leads. Go with the sufferer to *his* place of torment, do not struggle to drag him to where you are.' Let him talk the matter out, and let your listening balance sympathy with kindly cynicism until truth emerges. A gentle question will occasionally be right, to clarify a fact, a date, or a muddle in your own mind, sometimes to retrieve the thread where the story-telling has wandered, or to interrupt the flow of mesmeric words in which the client is getting lost—or running away. In moments of tension, or shame, the matter-of-fact, unemotional remark or question can effectively ventilate the atmosphere. But all the while you do not stop *listening*, with your eyes as well as your ears, as clenching hands or stirring in the chair reveal what allusions are most painful, what details are not to be probed. One listens to the overtones of words hesitated over; to the silences that reveal calculation, the pauses that betray tension, the speed of telling what the speaker hopes will not be noticed, to the points repeatedly approached and shied away from. The pastor who knows how to listen is too busy to interrupt. If any single phrase could define the initial stage of counselling it would be 'to listen, to elicit, and to lead'.

(ii) The second step is to seek agreement upon what precisely is the problem. What is first presented may well be not the heart of the matter but a smoke-screen put up to allow the timid, or devious, enquirer to manoeuvre into position. Sometimes the client has thought long, prepared many 'openings', anxious to explain exactly what the trouble is in fewest possible words, or in the best possible light, and the interview begins with a careful rehearsal of the position as the interviewee wants the counsellor to see it. Or the presented problem is a disguise, deliberately or unconsciously adopted, while the interviewee tries out the pastor's reactions, estimates how deeply he will be shocked by sad revelations, how censorious he is likely to be, or how gullible. Some people, of course, love to shock parsons, by language, attitude or confession: it is a form of exhibitionism, occasionally a defence-mechanism.

On the other hand, some barely articulate souls never can reveal their inmost thoughts without prolonged travail and hesitation. The sort of people who in trouble seek at last the help of a pastor are often acutely embarrassed, dreading loss of face and status, clinging desperately to the good opinion of church and Christian friends as their last resource against disaster. Some will be hypersensitive to their pastor's least frown or barely conscious indrawing of breath, and immediately freeze into silence or evasion. On the other hand, a girl whose whole world has fallen in, and whose future seems full of loneliness, fear, shame and panic, will suddenly feel very differently as the honoured leader coolly says, 'Well, it's a pity of course, but it has happened before, and the point is what shall we do about it'— and the world comes right side up again.

Only patience, sympathy, and skill gained with experience, can distinguish the well-expressed, true problem from the substitute-problem which gains time and leaves open the possibility of not revealing the real trouble in the end. If the latter is suspected, the counsellor can only wait, sympathetically but with an air of expecting something more, though not asking for it. The client must be allowed, without pressure, to change his mind about telling his secrets, even at the last moment.

(iii) The third step is the analysis and interpretation of the position revealed. Since no condition arises without previous pre-disposing causes, the history of a situation is usually illuminating—though it is not necessary in every case to begin at the cradle, nor is it always required to probe past mistakes or sins, especially where these have been already well-handled, and have no obvious relation to present problems.

Interpretation will be required where attitudes, motives or actions, of the client or of others, are being misrepresented, or are assumed to be virtuous or evil without evidence. It is vital however that neither analysis nor interpretation be imposed upon the enquirer: he must be led to see the situation, the facts, the real motives of people and the problem in right perspective, and to see himself in the midst of it, with his own eyes. Often this insight arises of itself, as a heart that has long brooded in private over its difficulty or regret, tries to present it clearly, and 'respectably' to a mature and sympathetic Christian friend. Attempting to describe it objectively, he comes to see it objectively for himself—and the cure is plain.

At other times, some suggestion or enquiry concerning how others involved might regard an incident, an attempt to imagine how Jesus might comment on such a situation, will bring self-understanding. However it is done, the counsellor is not the arbiter who pronounces upon the right analysis, interpretation or diagnosis. He is the midwife who brings to birth the incipient stirrings of conscience or spiritual unease which first brought the individual to seek Christian help; he is the expert who enables others to discern the thoughts and intents of their own hearts.

(iv) The fourth stage of most interviews—or series of interviews—will be agreement upon underlying causes, the ultimate source of the trouble, and upon what is to be done about it. Clearly to see a problem and identify its cause is frequently all the help a Christian needs: the solution will lie in familiar gospel truth and duty. Where more far-reaching adjustments or reparations are required, it may be necessary to consider together what actions are wise and arrange for practical steps and support. Some delay may be advised, so that the new insights can be fully weighed before decisions are reached; at other times promptness may be important to crystallise the new attitude—it may be well to indicate possible courses of action and obtain a definite promise that one or other will be followed. How much added persuasion, or moral support, may be needed will depend upon the personality of the person interviewed. Where difficult steps—of apology, reparation, confession, resignation—have to be taken, it is often good to fix dates, times, methods, for the action and arrange for report on the results, so guarding against evasion and prevarication. If large decisions about home or employment are involved, or referral to other sources of help, then time for investigation will be needed, and plans to meet again at some definite time and place will be made. Whatever moral support may be offered, planned and promised, the *free choice, full responsibility,* and *ultimate detachment* of the person being helped must not be obscured. A brief final prayer for grace to do well what has to be done, will close the interview.

In all Christian counselling, what matters in the end is not what either has told the other, not what the counsellor has authoritatively imparted or the client has discovered for himself: but what has emerged between them of the truth of Christ concerning that situation, and the way forward which follows from that. Often the result of such work may seem woefully inconclusive, experimental. Definitive action is rarely possible, nor is it the counsellor's to take. He may arm himself for disappointment by recalling how Apollos resisted the counsel of the apostle Paul (1 Corinthians 16: 12). To balance that, he may recall also how Paul stoutly resisted the counsel of many and against all advice pressed forward toward Jerusalem (Acts 21: 1–15). While for his own heart, lest he be exalted above measure by the number who seek his help in living their Christian lives, the pastoral counsellor may well bear often in mind the penetrating and gentle wisdom of the son of Sirach, with whom this introduction to a large subject began:

> A man may be shrewd, and the teacher of many,
>   and yet be unprofitable to himself.

7   THE CHRISTIAN MARRIAGE

Simply to say 'Christian marriage' almost defines the pastor's aim in this area of ministry: yet who shall say, without some thought, what is a Christian marriage, how that ideal may be attained amid the pressures of today, or what the pastor can contribute to it?

The third question is the easiest. In all the kinds of marriages which a pastor is called to share, those of members, adherents, strangers, old people, divorced people, people under duress of pregnancy, immature people, happy and unhappy people, he has three clear functions. He must minister to the parties concerned, filling a decisive hour of their lives with the most Christian meaning they can take and he has it in him to give. Of no use to say, 'the service means nothing to them'—that is his work. And ministry effectively offered at such a time ensures for the pastor a foothold in a new home and a place in grateful hearts.

The pastor must, too, perform a social task: he conducts society's approved rites at one of society's special occasions. This can be meaningless ritual, in which all religious significance is lost beneath ostentation, flippancy, stupidity—even drunkenness—or it can hallow and make responsible a contract between two members of society, a contract at once intensely personal and of far-reaching social significance and effect. Thirdly, the pastor is called also to bear a clear Christian witness, not indeed seeking to manipulate the occasion for evangelistic purposes, but so to declare and to assume the Christian standard, origin and purposes of marriage as to make very plain where Christians stand in the contemporary debate. Except at weddings, the public rarely hears any positive Christian teaching on the values of faithfulness and family life: to some outsiders, 'Christian marriage' must appear to be what Christians are left with by their opposition to divorce!

What is Marriage?

In western society, marriage may be described as a total friendship between man and woman in which natural sexual privileges are voluntarily and exclusively exchanged. Normally, the procreation of children, and the provision for them of affection, security and training, rank high among the purposes of such a relationship: but neither childlessness nor advanced age destroys a marriage. No right to *unnatural* sexual practices is conferred by marriage; nor do sexual privileges alone constitute marriage—it is the context of faithful and affectionate friendship which distinguishes marriage from a wholly sexual relationship, whether occasional or permanent. On the other hand it is the exclusive exchange of sexual rights that distinguishes marriage from all other friendships.

The unavoidable social consequences of such a relationship surround marriage with conditions, expressed mainly in law. These are designed for the good ordering of society, for the protection of women, for the security of the mother who in the years of child-bearing and child-care is dependent upon protection and support, for the safeguarding of children, for the avoidance of fraud, and the just management of property and inheritance. So the essentially private relationship comes to be enshrined formally in a legal contract of mutual and exclusive loyalty. The marriage contract must be entered into freely and in public, after due public notice given of that intention, with full understanding of its terms, by those free and qualified (by age and sanity) to do so, in the presence of witnesses, including a duly appointed officer of society, in a form duly approved; and the contract is then recorded in permanent and safe form to which legal appeal can at any time be made.

The record is of the contractual intention to fulfil such terms and obligations of marriage; the contract is said to be consummated at the first exchange of sexual privilege. Where consummation fails to follow contract, the marriage is said to be null, and the contract may be cancelled ('annulled'). Where it can be shown that the purposes of marriage were never intended to be fulfilled, or that either party was not free to enter such a contract (being already married, or too closely related), or that either was acting under duress, or without understanding, or that some deceit or false identity frustrated the true intention of either partner, the marriage may be declared invalid. This may follow too if any legal requirement as to place, time, persons, age, or form, was not properly observed.

It is impossible here to summarise legal requirements of marriage which vary in different countries, different states, different parts of the same country. Usually, it is an indictable offence to conduct the marriage ceremony without proper warrant from the marriage registration authorities, and neither ignorance, accident, falsehood of others, or mere play-acting, is acceptable as defence. Usually, too, there are strict regulations governing the time, place and duration of the publication of the notice of intention to marry; governing also the time, place, form, officer, and registration of marriages, the age of the partners, and sometimes the words to be spoken. Often, clear opportunity must be given for objections to the marriage to be lodged beforehand, or to be made at the ceremony—that is why previous information, and access to the place of marriage, must be available to the public. In some areas, a pastor may himself be appointed the official representative of the legal authority for marriages, to conduct and register marriages on his own authority; where however a local officer of the registration authority has to be present, it is essential to consult him before the date and time of the wedding can be fixed. It is for the pastor to familiarise himself with the legal requirements for marriage in his pastoral district: the registration authorities are normally very ready to instruct, to advise, and to provide specimens of marriage forms and other documents.

It cannot be too strongly emphasised that the legal requirements must be *strictly* adhered to, with utmost care and absolute sincerity. At even the slightest suggestion of untruth, the pastor must consult the registration authorities. A great deal may depend upon the integrity of the wedding service—a child's legitimacy, a girl's honour and security, some questions of property, insurance, and even legal liability (as giving evidence). Unless the pastor is entirely satisfied, he must refuse to proceed.

But social and legal requirements do not make marriage Christian. Around the private and public contract is woven the Christian meaning, the depth and wealth of a Christian dedication to each other and to God in Christ that makes a human relationship into a divine joy. Traditionally, the purposes of a Christian marriage have been defined as the procreation and nurture of children, mutual help and comfort, and a remedy against sin. Its origin is in the will of God, who created man male and female. It takes precedence over all previous natural ties—'for this reason shall a man leave his father and mother and cleave unto his wife'. It is guarded expressly by ancient sanctions attached to adultery, and by the words of Jesus insisting 'whom God has joined together, let no man put asunder'. Christian marriage is entered only in the will of God—a recognition that it is as some Christians would say, a 'sacrament', as all would agree 'a holy estate'. The mutual legal contract is therefore founded in religious vows taken in the presence of God, and usually (though not necessarily) in the context of worship. Such religious implications of marriage are not confined to Christianity: they have been acknowledged in all generations and cultures, and are rooted in the sacredness attached to sex, birth and parenthood among all civilised peoples.

Such a Christian marriage is, in ideal and intention, monogamous, permanent, and strictly indissoluble. Monogamy was the later form of

Judaist marriage inherited by Christianity and greatly strengthened by the Christian doctrine of unity and spiritual equality in Christ of man and woman, as 'heirs together of the grace of life', and by the supremacy of their faith and religious dedication over personal desire (Ephesians 5: 22–33, 1 Peter 3: 1–7). Permanence, likewise, is implied in the religious nature of the vow, and in the mutual respect of equal partners, neither of whom may in Christian love simply be discarded when no longer desired; it is implied even more in the depth of that total friendship, rooted in common experience of the grace of God and shared through years of spiritual development together, which issues in a rich and mature fellowship between two who have in every moral, psychological and spiritual sense 'become one'.

To say that Christian marriage is indissoluble is to add that it is in the strictest sense *irreversible*. In this the marriage contract resembles no other human contract; it so deeply affects the individual in body, mind, spirit, emotion, that it cannot be unmade without deep hurt to one or both. There *is* no return to virginity, to the situation that obtained before such vows and privileges were enacted, nor to the position where no third life was involved. The memory of love, the existence of a child, the unforgiving years, all ensure that no legal or social agreement to *cancel* what happened can ever in fact *erase* it. This is the truth, the reality of human relationship, which the Christian ideal of faithfulness unto death enshrines.

In our mixed society, some difficult questions of conscience face the pastor who holds to anything approximating this 'theology' of Christian marriage. (i) He may insist that as a Christian pastor he can conduct marriage only on Christian principles—that is, such marriage as seeks God's blessing by vowing before God lifelong sexual loyalty and affection. (ii) He may then refuse to share in non-Christian marriages—trial marriages, or any marriages where the full Christian vows are declined; though he need not, of course, refuse to follow a civil marriage ceremony with a Christian service in which the religious meaning is added to the civil contract. (iii) He may, however, consent to conduct Christian marriage for non-Christians, provided they accept the Christian standard of marriage, honestly desire God's blessing, and fully intend to observe lifelong sexual loyalty. A Christian girl may wish to marry a non-Christian boy who accepts *her* standards as to marriage; the non-Christian child of a Christian home, though not yet confessing faith in Christ, may sincerely want his or her marriage to be like that of the revered parents. The pastor who consents will probably feel that he must explore with the Christian partner all that is likely to be involved in such a 'mixed' marriage, so that nothing shall be done in ignorance, without consideration of the consequences. (iv) The pastor may, however, be convinced that only Christians can take Christian vows or maintain a Christian standard within marriage: and so refuse to marry any but fully committed Christians to each other—declining all non-Christian or 'mixed' marriages. This is a painful situation, especially where the child of devoted church-members wishes to marry outside the fellowship, and the parents look wistfully to their pastor to set the young people on the best possible road. The pastor may then feel that he must submit the decision to his colleagues in the fellowship; or perhaps allow another pastor to conduct the wedding, so relieving his own conscience. He cannot justly condemn such a marriage altogether (that would be libellous); he can decline to take any active part in it. (v) Fearful of these implications, the pastor may consider that Christian marriage is for Christians, and offer to perform something less than full Christian marriage for non-Christians.

The dilemma seems complete: is it ever right for a Christian pastor to refuse ministry to anyone who asks for it? But is it possible for a Christian pastor to offer any kind of 'ministry' which from the outset contradicts the principles which made him both Christian and pastor? Each must decide for himself, striving to be true to his own conscience, and fair alike to his church and to other Christian, and non-Christian, people.

A further pastoral obligation that seems to be imposed by such a theology of marriage as here outlined is the rule: 'no marriage without preparative counselling'. The possibility can sometimes arise that strangers armed with legal warrants set out to 'find a parson' and proceed with marriage. The pastor who regards marriage in Christian light can hardly consent to sudden and 'anonymous' performance of the sacred vows. Spiritual preparation for so great a step seems essential, and preparation takes time, requires interviews. Where the parties are unwilling for such delay, the pastor may conclude that he is being used for others' purposes, not appealed to as a servant of Christ.

Much of the blame for the meaninglessness of marriage in modern culture, and for the breakdown of many marriages that started out full of hope and idealism, lies with the church, which too often has 'dispensed' marriage irresponsibly to all comers, without enquiry, instruction or preparation. Often the first intimation the pastor receives that he is going to be involved is a shy question, 'Will you marry us?'—to which the only intelligent answer is 'No, that is something you have to learn to do yourselves. But I will gladly help you begin—when can we talk it over together?'

The Preparatory Interview

Ideally, the interview preparatory to marriage should do many things. It should explain the meaning of marriage, helping the couple understand the contract they propose to make and the life into which it will introduce them. It should explain the wedding service, and settle the details of form, music, and the rest, in good time. It should also anticipate frankly some of the special questions that marriage will raise, but which as yet have not been considered quietly by the blissful pair. The sensible and sympathetic approach of a third party can bring into daylight matters needing thought, before they become problems which can hurt. Not least, the understanding pastor can help the two get to know each other, in his presence, in areas of their thinking and attitudes which are never explored in their more private and romantic moments together, or which possibly they have carefully avoided. It may be, too, that something will fall to be said about sexual relationships, pitfalls, and joys.

Plainly, all this will require time, and more than one session. Happy the pastor who has established the rule that he never marries any couple in less than one month from their first request! Happy, too, the man who is on such good terms with his young people that he is among the first to know when betrothal takes place, so that he can congratulate the pair and quietly add: 'Your engagement brings your pastor new duties. I want to talk to you both about this exciting prospect long before we get involved in details. Come and have an engagement supper at the manse, and let's hear all about it.' Unfortunately, for many marriages he will have simply to insist on a preliminary interview or refuse to be involved.

Some advise three interviews, one with each partner and then one having both together. Most will feel that is dangerous, especially if the result of serious counselling is the cancellation of the marriage. Only special circumstances could justify a procedure so open to misconstruction, and so stultifying to one of the chief purposes of the preparation—helping the pair to know each other better. At least two joint interviews seem necessary, of which, whenever possible, the first should be on preparation for *marriage* and the second on preparation for the *wedding*; it may take some gentle firmness, though, to prevent the second purpose monopolising all conversation.

The preparation-for-marriage interview will be occupied with the essential character of marriage, its social implications, legal conditions, religious significance and richness. The pastor's emphasis will be upon the positive and joyous possibilities of Christian marriage— it is because we value it so highly that we want to guard it strictly; it is too precious to throw away by carelessness or irresponsibility. That is why the Christian vow is for life, as Jesus said, because only such a vow recognises its sacredness.

It may be necessary to follow mention of legal implications with detailed guidance on the steps to be taken in giving required notice, obtaining documents and fulfilling regulations. The pastor should have available accurate and clear information, with addresses, telephone numbers, office hours; and he will warn of the need to engage well in advance the officials, helpers and premises needed for the wedding service.

Reference to the social implications of marriage will suggest the inevitable place which parents have, both in the wedding and in subsequent years. A question or two can elicit any sore feelings or fears, and the pastor can do much to help the young people see that 'interference' is often love blunderingly expressing concern, that neither mother nor father can cut their grown-up children out of their hearts at will, nor help *feeling* jealous that an external love has supplanted them in their child's immediate attention. Admittedly, parents should not show this feeling, but they do. Wisdom and happiness lie not in resentment or collision but in understanding and handling the in-law situation, and in showing that the new love has not destroyed the old. It is easy to pass on the suggestion that, sexual matters apart, the essence of married love is utter and unbreakable *loyalty*. The answer to all who ask questions, who pry into the new home, who offer advice or warning—including the pastor!—is simply to *refuse to discuss each other with anyone else*. That is love. 'Say what you will to each other: never say anything, good or bad, to others about each other. Keep the whole world at bay! Let your refusal be polite if possible; if that does not work, then refuse bluntly—and change the subject.'

When husband is papering a room, or wife is making up a dress, a great deal of 'marrying' goes on, as the pieces are pushed and pulled into alignment, and the pattern emerges. Just so, a happy marriage has to be made, by constant adjustment either to other, as new facets of mind and character are revealed in daily developing relationships. There are thousands of topics they have never talked about, scores of things they do not know about each other, innumerable situations they have never observed each other in, or shared together. Marriage therefore is made as you go; some of its foundations, paramount in youth, will not last until the end, other binding factors taking their place. So marriage changes in content and emphasis, as love certainly changes with the growing years—though not necessarily becoming less, or less satisfying.

Two things especially are necessary to a mature marriage relationship—forgiveness, and independence. Forgiveness, because neither is perfect, nor consistently tender, loving, understanding, good-humoured, unselfish, and there will be plenty of opportunity for mutual forgivingness. The habit of evening prayer together, however brief and simple, is a marvellous safeguard against letting quarrels last on and resentments fester.

The pastor may surprise his hearers by urging independence, but any mature relationship involves co-operation between individuals who are persons, each in his own right. When two share a common life, one of two things must happen: either a balanced, good-humoured, loving tug-of-war between strong-minded adults, each possessing mind, heart, conscience independently; or one is submerged in the stronger character of the other. Submergence-marriages can work well, where the wholly dependent character finds content-ment and security in conforming, and the stronger is not overbearing or selfish. But increasingly in these days, the balance of two educated, independent, equally competent partners, differing but loyal, is the pattern of a Christian marriage. It demands some wisdom, and much mutual consideration so to grow together without destroying the variety and freedom which can make shared life so changeful and so rich.

Of course there are times when a single decision has to be reached but no agreement has emerged. The common-sense arrangement would seem to be that whoever will bear major responsibility if the decision proves to have been unwise, should have his or her own way—sometimes one, sometimes the other, according to which will have to find the money, nurse the children, clear up the mess, or face the music if things go wrong. But whoever decides a disputed issue, so far as the children, or the parents, or the world will ever know, it was a *joint* decision. That, again, is loyalty.

It becomes easy, with practice, to introduce into the conversation the couple's intentions and hopes as to work, money, children, and then to share experiences of the dangers and rewards of different experiments one has observed among church families. Some have found that when both partners continue working for a predetermined time, the initial financial burdens are eased before children arrive; but others have found that living on two incomes becomes a habit, and children are postponed too long, to their everlasting regret in later years. In other, tragic cases, children have arrived 'out of turn' and have been resented, unwanted, blamed for lack of comforts or loss of career opportunities. It is a danger to be faced with candour.

Some homes are happy to share all money arrangements in detail; in others, the wife is in charge of all income, expenditure and savings; in yet others, the husband takes full responsibility, shielding the wife

from worry. It is useful to enquire if they know their parents,
arrangement—and leave them to talk it out later. It is well, too, to
introduce the subject of children, and test the degree of understanding already reached on the prospect of a family. Sometimes
shyness, sometimes fear of disagreement, sometimes an assumption
that such matters solve themselves, keep a couple from revealing
their private hopes and fears, so storing up obvious, and serious,
disappointments or tensions for the future.

In all such conversation, it is plain, the two already in love are
getting to know each other in new ways, coming to understand more
fully how each looks at life, how their minds work, what their
experience has made of them. Much of the value of such counselling
preparatory to marriage lies, not in what either says to the pastor,
but in what they reveal in each other's presence, and even more in
what they say to each other, in confidence, as they leave.

A delicate decision for the pastor concerns the extent to which he is
prepared to counsel on intimate sexual matters, and especially on
ethical and religious aspects of contraception. Each must decide for
himself with a full sense of the responsibility incurred both by
offering counsel and by refusing to do so. Abundant literature exists
(much will reach the minister unsolicited) detailing methods and aids
to family planning, and he may think it right, on request, to have the
best of it to hand to couples at the right time. Or he may think it
wiser to refer all questions of a physical nature to medical advisers
and discuss only ethical aspects of contraception. It is probably
better to let the suggestion for such topics arise from the couple;
a general offer of help on any subject at any time will leave the way
open for future approach. If he wishes to be more positive, the pastor
may mention that in these days numerous engaged couples undergo
medical examination before marriage, and that could be sufficient to
introduce the subject. But it is well for the eager counsellor to keep
in mind that ordinary people have arranged these matters, on the
whole very well, for many generations, without the intrusive counsel
of third parties! Normal, healthy young people truly in love can
usually make their own discoveries in their own time and to their
own greater delight, without grandfatherly guidance. For the pastor
to be obviously willing, and able, to help if needed is quite enough:
in the vast majority of cases Nature and love between them manage
very well.

Before the interview ends, it is useful to pre-empt a definite date
before the wedding for a second talk about the service itself, lest this
need be crowded out as domestic preparations get under way. On

rare occasions, however, the result of the first interview may be disconcerting. One or other partner, seeing marriage clearly for the first time, or seeing the partner in a new light, finds that topics long avoided have been aired, doubts long repressed have surfaced, and sometimes basic ethical and religious attitudes have been revealed which show how far apart the couple stand. The pastor will feel responsible, and deeply concerned, if the result is a postponed marriage or a broken engagement. Yet it is obviously better to suffer this before irrevocable decisions are taken, than to regret ever afterwards that such dangers were not brought to light. The risk has to be taken. It is part of the responsibility implicit in all spiritual counselling: if a man wishes to avoid it, he had better not engage in pastoral ministry.

But only very rarely will the outcome of such interviews be unhappy. Usually, the pastor has made a friendship for life. The couple have seen their whole joy in each other, and all their hopes, set in a wider, firmer, deeper context of human life as a whole, and of God's will for His creatures. Their love will have become still more wonderful, the prospect still more exciting. When in a brief and intimate prayer the pastor commends these two, their love and their future, to the Father after whom all families in heaven and earth are named, he may well find their tears of joy his abundant reward.

The Wedding Interview

Nearer the wedding date, the second interview arranges details of the service with such care that no blunder or omission shall spoil a sacred and joyous occasion. The more familiar the couple are beforehand with all the elements of the service, the more relaxed and ready to participate they will be. It is not remembering what to do and say, but understanding what is going on and why, which gets rid of nervousness. It is not necessary to memorise anything, since the pastor will recall each step at the appropriate time.

The bride usually comes to this interview too preoccupied with organisational details to attend to more fundamental things. It is well to get these details out of the way first, by producing a check-list of things to be planned, and going through it openly, making written notes:

(i) What hymns, and other music, are desired? Will anyone contribute music during the signing of the record (preferably *not* during the service)? Who will arrange accompanists, and see that required music is available?

(ii) How many bridesmaids (that seats may be arranged where needed)? Any child-attendants (needing primary-chairs)?

(iii) What photography is planned?—not between opening prayer and benediction, even if allowed in church at all.

(iv) Who arranges for flowers, and what is to be done with them afterwards? If the ceremony is conducted at the Lord's Table, ask that flowers be not placed centrally—better, an open Bible.

(v) Who will sign the record as witnesses?—(over twenty-one, and from both families if possible; avoid discussion at the last moment).

(vi) Indicate all fees expected, and to whom payable: the pastor may wish to return his fee to members and friends, but he should collect from all alike.

(vii) Warn that you will ask the bride to dispose of flowers and gloves to bridesmaids at beginning of the service—to facilitate placing the ring later, and before nervousness makes removal more difficult.

(viii) If you intend to invite the bridal party to sit during scripture and prayer, give warning, that the bride may instruct groom and maids whether she will sit or not (it will depend upon details of her dress).

(ix) If you so intend, warn bride and groom that at the close of your prayer you will invite them to repeat aloud with you, for the first time as husband and wife, the Lord's Prayer.

(x) Will the ancient custom be observed of the bride's father giving her to the groom? If so, who will perform it? (The modern significance lies in the public assent so given by the bride's family to the marriage.)

(xi) Explain your usual arrangements for greeting the bride at the church, warning the organist, stewarding, conducting the party to the register-signing, and then returning to the Table for dismissal. (Rehearsal may be arranged if required.)

(xii) Invite the couple to ask any questions of detail and organisation that occur to them.

These matters out of the way, the pastor may proceed to explain the pattern of the service. Most church traditions have their own treasured forms of marriage; some incorporate phrases required by law, others include forms of vows that have been used for five hundred years. The pastor will follow, edit or adapt the pattern as he thinks best. But the basic order is the natural and logical one of four 'marriage steps':

1 Are you free to marry each other?
2 Do you want to marry each other?
3 Then do it (= 'I take thee . . . With this ring I thee wed . . .')
4 Now the pastor declares it done.

(Some legal authorities require responses to be more than simple affirmative answers, prescribing necessary forms of words to be repeated by each party.

If the 'giving away' by the bride's father or a representative is included, it follows the second step.)

Take the couple once or twice through these four essential steps, as expressed in the form of service to be used. Explain that the religious context is arranged around them: an opening prayer for God's presence and blessing, a hymn, and a brief statement of the Christian view of marriage; then the four marriage steps; then scripture lesson, greetings from the pastor and church, where appropriate, possibly a brief address, further prayer, ending with the Lord's Prayer offered by pastor and couple; a closing hymn and benediction. The order is best reviewed and explained twice, and possible preferences for scripture passages to be used, and for special prayers for absent or sick members of the family noted. It is important that this review of the service be presented not as 'instructions' or warning but as pleasurable anticipation, and a relaxing of tension. The pastor should assure the couple that he will be in complete control of the service, and they should leave all in his hands, simply doing and saying what he directs, worrying about *nothing*. Prayer together for God's blessing on the service, the families, and the day, will fitly close the interview.

Conducting the Wedding

Common sense, coolness, and command are the only requisites from the pastor for a happy wedding service in which the participants are put at ease and the real purpose in hand, to seek God's seal upon a lifelong contract, is not obscured by trivialities. Experience suggests simple, but useful, guidelines:

Be in good time to meet bridegroom and attendant friend before the service to make *sure* the necessary papers, the ring, and any required officials are present; that the seating and flowers are arranged as you wish.

See that your note of names, hymns, scripture passages is in place in your service-book. (If the slip of paper is larger than the page, with the full names at the top, you will be able to refresh your memory with the merest glance.)

See that you, alone, receive the signal that the bridal party has arrived, and that you alone, invite the congregation to stand to receive her, remembering to tell them to sit when you wish them to do so (probably at the close of the first hymn). The immediate impression of a pastor who knows exactly what he is doing and what he wants done, is wonderfully relaxing to others, if not to you!

Remember to ask the bride to dispose of flowers and gloves; take your time to arrange the party as you want them; quietly welcome them to church—if you know the bride well, a compliment will warm her heart.

After opening prayer and hymn, the brief preamble setting out the Christian view of marriage should lead naturally into the four marriage steps in the words and responses arranged. Allow time for the meaning of the words to be grasped, and for clear answers to be given. If spoken declarations are required, break down the statements into short and natural phrases. If either stumbles, go over that phrase again, with a laugh; if you let it pass, they will worry afterwards whether the marriage is valid! Let all be easy, leisured, good-humoured, relaxed: it is their happiest hour, and the pastor should help them enjoy it—not endure it.

In some forms of service a solemn enquiry is made whether anyone present objects to the marriage. Pause long enough to give opportunity for reply; though objection is very rarely made at that point, be ready for it. If any is made, take bride, bridegroom, registration officer, and the two fathers, with the objector, *and no one else at all*, into another room, first asking the bridal party, and the congregation, to sit in quietness while enquiry is made. Keep firm control: if necessary remind the congregation where they are.

In the retiral room, first *yourself* warn the objector of the seriousness of the position; he is liable for stern penalties if he is behaving frivolously, slanderously, or maliciously; the right place for objections to be lodged is where the notice of intention was published, and the reason for delaying until the public moment in church should be enquired. If the replies are serious and sincere, the ground of objection should then be enquired. The only legal grounds are, that one partner is under age, or being under age lacks a required parental consent, or is under duress, or is not free to marry, not sane, not comprehending what is being done, or that the two are too closely related, or that some legal formality has been omitted. Confer with the registration official if one is present; but if any proof of the allegation is offered, or if too much doubt has been raised to resolve there and then, the wedding *must* be postponed. The objector's name, address and signature should be obtained. It is best for the pastor to announce any postponement to the congregation, without explanation, asking them to disperse quietly and await further announcement from the families. The bride's mother, and the bridegroom's, should be escorted to the retiral room, and arrangements made for transport home.

If no reasonable objection is alleged, or no proof offered, no serious doubt raised, the wedding may proceed. Escort the party back to their places in church, and when all is ready, make the brief statement that 'the objection raised is nothing to hinder the wedding we are all waiting to share ... Now, where was I ... ?'

The marriage steps concluded, the bridal party may wish to be seated to hear scripture and greetings, and to join in prayer. The choice of scripture should be apt without being romantic or sentimental. Ruth's great vow of loyalty (Ruth 1: 16,17) sounds yet more wonderful in the setting of a marriage service. Moffatt's version of 1 Corinthians 13: 4–8a is appropriate, beside John 2: 1–11, Ephesians 4: 32–5: 2, and 5: 21–33, Proverbs 3: 3–6, Matthew 19:4–6.

The wedding prayer should remember gratefully the homes from which the two come, their nurture from childhood, and the hopes, and the new loneliness, of the parents; should offer thanksgiving for the gift of love, companionship, and joy, and for the guidance that has united two lives and two hearts under divine blessing; any references to the future home and hope of children should be reticent and careful, and prayer might be offered that the home shall become a centre of Christian friendship, witness, and hospitality. Requests for prayer for absent friends should have been noted beforehand; the plea that under God's blessing the excitement and joy of present love may mature and deepen with the passing years, will help to recall the permanence of what has now been done. A petition that the service may renew gratitude and love in all who have witnessed it, will make the prayer relevant to the whole company, and the quiet sharing of the couple in the Lord's Prayer will bring the service back again to their own hearts. After a second hymn, and benediction, conduct the bridal party to where the signing of the record is to be done—first announcing any musical items which may make the waiting pleasant. Signing completed, conduct the couple only back to the Lord's Table, asking the congregation to rise, and dismiss husband and wife with handshake and a final blessing.

Three Recurrent Problems

Special problems in marriage-ministry which recur fairly frequently in these days are three:

(1) *The Pregnant Bride*. No responsibility in pastoral ministry is quite so delicate, or so rewarding, as the opportunity to retrieve a situation which could mean only shame and regret, but which—through pastoral help—can yet renew lasting trust and find happiness. When the privileges properly reserved for marriage have been anticipated, and yet one or both partners still choose to seek a pastor's help, whether reluctantly, defiantly, or under family pressure, there is good ground for positive ministry. The pastor, of course, is not authorised to cross-examine, to judge, or to condemn; nor is he to be used merely to give respectability to a regrettable situation; neither may he wash his hands of anyone who asks his ministry. The pastor's rule is—'What would Jesus do?' and there is

no doubt that He would seek only to redeem the situation for two unhappy hearts, and *to make their future*.

Two inflexible rules guide the pastor's reaction. (1) He will insist upon a private interview, without promises, with the two who are asking to be married, and with them only, before he commits himself to any action. An angry, self-righteous mother, or even a bullying father, may be easier to handle than a tearful, ashamed mother—but exclude them all. You are not to marry the mothers, or the families. (2) He will resolve, privately, that in no circumstances will he marry two people who do not, quite freely, in spite of the pregnancy, tell him each alone and in confidence that they would still want to marry each other, and stay loyal, even if circumstances and the family were not pressing. But *he will not tell them of that resolve*, or he may never learn the strict truth of the situation.

Arrange for them to attend together: that silent admission of parentage is significant. But see each first alone, the girl first. Having established a sympathetic interest, and removed embarrassment by enquiries about expected dates and arrangements, gently probe the background relationship. How long has she known the boy? Where, how, did they meet—what does she really know about him, and think about him? Is she looking forward to life with him, or was there someone else on the horizon? Are the parents pressing for marriage? What, in strict confidence, does she really want? And so at last to the only vital question, if she were not in this situation now, would she, speaking quite honestly, want to marry him? It is difficult, but necessary, to receive the answer in silence, and go on with other questions to conceal its importance.

For you must next lead the boy, also alone, through the same process, question by question. It will do no harm to express admiration for his willingness to stand by what he has done; nor to obtain his admission (if there is the least doubt of his attitude) that he is the father. Try to get him talking freely about the girl, watching his language and reactions. For him, too, the crucial question is whether he would marry this girl if the circumstances left him a free, unpressured choice.

If either admits that but for the coming baby he or she would not marry the other, your duty is clear: you must refuse. To marry them in face of expressed reluctance, only because of the present situation, would be to add mistake to mistake, creating a still worse situation eventually. If either is doubtful, unable to think or decide objectively because the coming of the child (or resentment about it) overshadows everything else, then the next step is to postpone decision until—

say—six months after the child is born. Let the question, to marry or not to marry, wait until the pressure is over, and the decision can be free. Haste will probably mean a mistaken decision, leaving ever after the suspicion that, but for the child, the marriage would never have taken place. 'I only married you because I had to' is no basis for joy.

But if each is clear that, pregnancy or no, they would have married, though perhaps not yet (and most of those in such circumstances who seek a pastor's help will say so, their intimacy having arisen from a genuine love) then again your duty is clear. But present your decision carefully.

Having the pair together now, tell them plainly that you consent to marry them because of what each has told you, privately, without pressure, of their real love. Tell her, in front of him, that he has pledged to you that he would have married her, wanted to, still wants to, irrespective of what has happened. Tell him, in front of her, that she has said the same, that she wants him, irrespective of baby, or family, or what has happened. Then let each promise you, in each other's presence, first that they will never forget that *this was why they married*, because they love each other; and secondly, that never until they die will either ever 'throw it up' to the other that 'they had to marry'. That done, let there be no further word, anywhere, by anyone, privately or publicly, about the circumstances. They are a couple entering Christian marriage because they love each other—the rest is between themselves, and God.

(2) *The Divorced Person.* The remarriage of divorced persons is ruled out altogether by some church traditions, and by some pastors' conscientious understanding of the scriptures. Other churches leave the issue to the discretion of pastors in individual cases, and some pastors then feel that a request for help may spring from a genuine wish for Christian guidance and support, and may present an opportunity to remake two lives in Christian ways. For those who so incline towards helping the divorced person, two inflexible rules may again offer firm guidelines:

(1) Always see, handle, and read the documents of divorce. It may be difficult to request this, of persons known to you, but it is safest: people so easily hoodwink Christians! And it is a wise defence against criticism by others who think they know things you do not; the reply is sufficient, 'I have seen the Court's decree'—though you would never divulge what it said. If you make the rule invariable, there is no embarrassment in saying so, in particular cases. Silently note who

obtained the divorce, its ground, and its date. If the party now seeking remarriage was the one in whose favour the divorce was granted, you will probably feel freer to proceed—though legal rulings cannot always be taken as proof of innocence or blame. If the party was the one against whom the divorce was granted, you will need to satisfy your own conscience (a) that there has been a genuine change of heart and conduct; (b) that the other party to the proposed marriage knows the truth: this needs care—ask him or her if he or she knows what the paper says, and if not, ask *the person divorced* to show it; it is not yours to show, but you cannot condone deception; (c) that both parties now fully and deliberately intend a Christian, lifelong marriage. If there are financial obligations left from the first marriage, these too should be understood by the new partner, and fully assented to. Unless you are so satisfied, it is probably best to have no share in the new marriage—while making no judgement on what *they* do.

(2) Your second inflexible rule you keep to yourself until you make your decision: never marry the divorced person to the one who helped to destroy the former marriage, lest you become party to the whole sorry story. Before explaining this, you talk round the matter fairly lightly, perhaps while drinking coffee. What is his work? and hers? How did they meet? Where do they hope to live? How long have they known each other? Usually they will try to impress you with the length and depth of their mutual friendship—but you have that date in mind, and the time it takes to obtain a decree. It should soon be apparent if in fact you are being asked to make the last, respectable gesture in a story of betrayal. If however this is not the case, if the present proposed marriage is a new and sincere attempt to start again, on Christian foundations, you may feel able to go ahead. That once decided, no further reference should be made to the past, though as with all couples, the full Christian vows and their implications should be clearly explained, and accepted.

(3) '*Mixed*' *Marriages*. Beside the 'mixed' marriages already considered, between believer and unbeliever, there are marriages of mixed faiths, and of different Christian traditions, better termed 'inter-church' marriages. The pastoral task here is to help young people realise that what appear now, in the light of their new and exciting love, small scruples of conscience, will in fact grow in importance, and not disappear, with the maturing of their relationship and the deepening of their character. They must be helped to see that sooner or later decisions will have to be taken concerning the

religious training of any children they may have, and then any concession by one to the other, or by both, may become very painful.

Plainly, the seriousness of the issues involved will depend upon the depth of the commitment of each to his or her form of faith, and the width of the difference between them. Where the religious allegiance is purely formal, the proposed marriage is probably not so much 'inter-church' as 'non-church'; and where the difference of denomination is small, it may be that the marriage will lead to closer and richer church fellowship. But it should be pointed out, however gently, that to ask God's blessing on a marriage that deliberately involves abandonment of religious principles once held sacred, is scarcely consistent.

The most difficult case, of course, is that of a Roman Catholic–Protestant marriage. Where formerly the Roman Catholic church did not permit such marriages to its members unless both partners promised that any children should be baptised and trained in the Roman Catholic faith, since 1970 the Roman Catholic partner is required to promise to do all in his or her power to have all the children baptised and brought up in the Roman church; and the non-Roman partner must be informed of that promise and obligation. Permission must be obtained for the marriage of a Roman Catholic in a non-Roman church, or the marriage may not be recognised. Some Catholics, however, will still feel barred from communion with the Roman church, and the unease is more likely to grow than to diminish. Further difficulties arise, in some areas, over the general education of the children in later years; either the choice of school must be confined to one partner only—which is a surrender of responsibility by the other partner; or the matter is allowed to go entirely by default.

In numerous instances, a fresh difficulty is introduced where the two families, whom the marriage should bring into fellowship and unite in affection for children and grandchildren, are of so different persuasions as never to meet without conflict. That must bring added complication into the adjustments to 'in-laws' which all happy marriages require. Finally, the discussion and practice of religion at home and with the children, which should be a delight, binding a Christian family in common faith, worship, and loyalty, becomes impossible where convictions and practices are wide apart. Then religion becomes a subject wholly to be avoided, even at home, while any suggestion that family attend worship together and support the children in so doing, is ruled out from the beginning.

Some of these obstacles will be less serious for older partners to a new marriage; others will be more serious just because character and habit are more fixed. On the whole, the practical religious difficulties and deprivations involved in marriages across deep religious gulfs, together with the added complications introduced into a relationship that already demands care, unselfishness, and great willingness to adjust, scarcely recommend such marriages as likely to yield fullest satisfaction. It is not for pastors to assess the probable success of a marriage before deciding whether to share it. But most will probably feel bound to explore all sides of the question, shirking none of the difficulties involved, in a very frank consultation. Whether any pastor carries his 'discouragement' of such marriages to the point of declining to conduct the service, is a matter for his own conscience alone.

The whole subject of marriage-ministry obviously demands considerable thought and care. The counselling of those already married, and facing unexpected problems, adds yet another range of opportunity and responsibility. But the pastor has here a unique privilege. He stands very close to people at the highest emotional moment of their lives; he may become part of their most precious memories, one who helped to make the dearest things in life still dearer and more sacred. It is among the most rewarding spheres of ministry. To be the ever welcome visitor at a new and happy home you helped to found, to have the couple bring their babe to show to you and to your wife with reverent and happy pride, is to feel that all the time and trouble was worth while. And it is to know that the gospel is bearing still its loveliest fruit—a Christian home that is a shrine of Christ.

8 THE CHRISTIAN FUNERAL

As in conducting a wedding, so in conducting a funeral the Christian pastor simultaneously performs a social service, with legal overtones, offers a ministry, and bears a Christian witness in one of the crucial experiences of life.

It is right that by reverent and respectful disposal of the dead society should safeguard the dignity of the individual and express its underlying beliefs about human life and destiny. The ceremonies and conventions observed at funerals, where they have any meaning at all, usually serve this purpose: they should not be despised, but made to carry maximum significance. What the expected social rites are, must be carefully investigated by any pastor moving into a new locality; few communities observe quite the same customs.

Legal requirements likewise vary considerably, though the rule for most States is that the disposal of a human body must be notified beforehand to properly constituted authority, and proceeds only with formal permission. This is usually given by some form of Certificate of Death, registering the fact and cause of death, whether from natural causes as certified by a qualified medical authority, or from other causes which have been investigated or are to be investigated by the proper legal authority, which itself issues the certificate permitting disposal of the body. The reasons for these safeguards are obvious: it is imperative that the pastor take no part in disposal proceedings without proper authority.

In some areas, the Death and Disposal Certificate is delivered by the family to the pastor, who can then act upon it, and yield it up eventually to the funeral managers ('Undertakers' or morticians) or to the burial or cremation officials. More usually, the Certificate is obtained by the funeral managers, who take full responsibility for the disposal of the body, engaging a pastor for the religious service only. After the disposal, either the pastor, or the funeral manager, or both, sign the record of the event. It is impossible to describe in detail the widely varying arrangements for permission, responsibility and record: an experienced minister or funeral manager will usually be happy to explain to a newcomer what the local regulations are.

Nearer to the pastor's central concerns is the ministry of comfort, practical assistance, and often of instruction, involving visits to the bereaved home, before and after the funeral, and the conduct of the service. The service itself is somewhat unusual in being almost entirely man-orientated, ministry rather than worship: and it is of course intended for the living—the family, the mourners, the community. No judgement, speculation or prayers affecting the dead would be fitting: thanksgiving for them, regret at losing them, tribute to their known work and character, are alone in order.

The sources of comfort at such a time are manifold, and the aim is to set the immediate bereavement in the perspective of human experience as a whole. (i) The sovereignty of God, who gave life and who alone takes it away, combined with the certainty that God loves all His creatures, 'hating nothing that he hath made', provides the background to life and death. It is for this reason that the great biblical passages on the majesty of God, as well as those on His love, find place in funeral services. (ii) The assurance of divine sympathy and compassion, that God sees our tears and carries our sorrows, is willing constantly to be gracious and to strengthen hearts that lean on Him, is a nearer source of comfort. God seems so far away in the hour of loss and loneliness: we have to declare that then He is closest of all. (iii) The Christian hope of immortality and reunion, based on the unbreakable fellowship of God with those who love Him and confirmed for us by the resurrection of Christ, is for faith the strongest comfort of all; while for those who do not yet possess faith, the Christian hope may at this time become more meaningful and relevant than ever before. (iv) An immediate need, very often, is for assurance about the changed situation occasioned by the bereavement, for trust that God will surely guide and overrule in all the consequences and adjustments now to be faced. Here again, in the confusion and loneliness of bereavement, some find for the first time how religious faith can bring serenity, confidence and strong courage.

The third aim of the pastor in this area is to bear a public witness to Christian faith and hope. It is only at funeral services that the public hears what Christians think about death and the hereafter, and the pastor will affirm here (as he does privately at the deathbed) a Christian 'theology of death'. The story of Christ's resurrection, read in the context of human bereavement, gains enormously in relevance and power. The validity of the Christian hope for *this* life's perspectives, and the challenge as well as comfort of the Christian understanding of the future life, are all notes that need to be sounded in these bewildered days.

Yet it is both discourteous and unwise to use another's sorrow to proselytise among a captive audience. In these circumstances, it is best to take for granted the full Christian gospel, in conversation in the home, and in the public service; it should be confidently assumed, not argued about, and its basis in the scriptures silently exposed by the choice of verses for reading and for quotation in prayer. The quietly triumphant manner in which a Christian funeral is conducted, and the courageous bearing of Christians in sorrow, are far more effective exponents of the evangel than gospel sermons at the graveside or in the crematorium.

Types of Funerals

The different kinds of funeral with which the pastor may become involved may illustrate some of the issues he will need to consider.

(i) The funeral of a fellow Christian gives fullest opportunity to assume the Christian understanding of life and death; the service will be sad, but not miserable, marked by a sense of completion, of victory, of life fulfilled in the grace of Christ, and abounding hope. Assurance of the church's sympathy and continuing prayer for those bereaved, and perhaps a brief eulogy of the life now gathered to be with Christ, will be appreciated: but the cynicism evoked by most graveside eulogies should temper enthusiasm with strict truth, simple sincerity, and forthright brevity.

(ii) The funeral of a church-adherent, or a friend of church-members, is no occasion for speculating on his true position or his probable destiny; while optimistic assumptions on the matter will sound hypocritical and hollow. Discretion, truth, and (not least) kindness are demanded. Only God knows *any* heart's true story: the great Christian affirmations should be made with no suggestion whether they were, or were not, fulfilled in the life now ended.

(iii) The funeral of a total stranger will pose greater problems of sincerity. Whenever possible, the mourners should not *be* strangers by the time the service is held. The home should have been visited, the ice broken, a word of prayer offered in the home on the day prior to the funeral, so that at the service the pastor's voice, manner and friendliness are already familiar. Sometimes a town's rota of ministers available to serve at short notice a particular graveyard or crematorium prevents even this brief acquaintance. Even so, the Christian rite of burial may be followed, the Christian's faith declared, in general terms, implying nothing of their fulfilment in particular cases.

(iv) The funeral of a child needs especial care, in selection of scripture passages, in avoiding emotive (or sentimental) expressions which could wrench parents' hearts and undermine their self-control, and in evading every attempt to theorise about explanations and causes. A very old man once greatly comforted a young mother with the suggestion that perhaps—like old men—God liked having little ones around Him. Jesus certainly declared that 'of such is the kingdom of heaven'. It is probably best to admit the mystery, affirm God's love, assume that the child is ever within the circle of divine compassion—and pray for the bereaved.

(v) The funeral of a public figure can cause the young pastor some anxieties—what other recognition or ceremonial, social, military, professional and the like, should be included, and what references to the deceased should be made? A simple rule can save embarrassment and blundering: let representative figures make whatever eulogies or other speeches are appropriate, and the appointed officers of military or ritualistic 'orders' conduct whatever ceremonies they think right (provided of course that nothing is said or done to conflict with a *Christian* funeral)—but let these additions to Christian obsequies *follow* the service, and not intrude within it or replace it. It is a simple matter to invite someone to speak, or act, following the closing prayer, and perhaps then close with a sentence of thanks. If the pastor is quietly but firmly clear that that is what he expects to happen, his lead will usually be followed. In this way, responsibility for what is said and done is clearly and publicly assigned, and the Christian ministry and witness are not obscured.

(vi) The funeral of a suicide, or of a victim of violence, can be a testing occasion. It is wisest to ignore, so far as possible, the circumstances of death. Concentrate upon the bereaved, for whom alone the service is being held: avoid all references or hints that could add to their hurt. Formality, here, is kindness. Let the Christian truth shine through the service, and the private ministry, but not in too direct and personal a manner; commit all issues of judgement to God who alone knows all truth. The headline-writers may be disappointed, but the mourners may be comforted, and will be grateful. In no circumstances will a pastor who understands the inherent dignity of his task, discuss with the press anything he has said or heard in his ministry to grieving hearts.

The Service

Most church traditions have their own forms of service for the burial of the dead, which each pastor would naturally edit and adapt as circumstances, and his own preferences, indicate. In some districts it is still expected that the dead shall lie at home, and be carried thence with due ceremony to either grave or crematorium, pausing on the way for a service either at the family's church or at a church provided at the disposal point. Increasingly, however, the dead lie at the premises of the funeral managers, and the service is held there prior to disposal. In planning his ministry, the pastor must first ascertain where the 'main service' is expected, usually depending upon where the greatest number of friends can be present.

Where the main service is to be at home, a previous visit will have made the pastor familiar with the members of the family and with domestic conditions. It is a relief to everyone if he takes charge as soon as he arrives, assuming (courteously, of course) that everyone will do exactly as he wishes. He will usher the mourners into the appointed room, and (if at all possible) get *everyone* seated. He will have announced himself, if necessary, to the funeral managers, and discovered if the mourning party is complete, delaying as long as possible for late-comers. It is convenient to ask, aloud, that one of the younger members of the group will attend the door if anyone should arrive during the service. The pastor should station himself where he has sufficient light, and not too much heat, and within reach of the door, so that when the service is over he can indicate the fact to the managers, and when they are ready escort the party—chief mourners first—from the home. There will follow, at the graveside or crematorium, a brief service of 'Committal', at which sometimes only representative friends are present.

Where the main service is to be at church, whether home-church, cemetery-church, or funeral parlour (funeral managers' chapel) followed by burial or cremation elsewhere, the ceremony at the house will be much briefer. Invite a few moments of silent remembrance, to pay tribute to all that the departed meant to home and family and immediate friends, then close with a short prayer of thanksgiving and petition for strength and a quiet mind, to listen to God's word with faith and do what has to be done with courage and dignity. Then leave the home together.

At the church or funeral chapel it is well to alight first from the cortege to welcome the mourners at the door and lead them to their places. The service should close with prayer for comfort and peace (not the Benediction) and the quiet announcement that 'Our service will be concluded at the graveside (or crematorium)'. The Committal service will then follow at the appropriate place.

Where the main service is to be at the graveside or the crematorium, the same initial courtesies in the home and on assembling for the service are in place, but this time the Committal service is incorporated in the main service, and the proceedings end with either the Benediction or some other 'final' prayer.

In deciding which pattern is desired, the public prominence of the deceased, the identification of the family with the church, the available accommodation, and time, and the costs involved, must all be weighed, and it is best to let the family instruct the funeral managers when the several possible arrangements have been laid before them. The pastor may, however, find that too little time is being allowed for reverent ministry: funeral managers are in business, and their day's programme may be overfilled. For his own sake and the family's, the pastor will sometimes insist upon proper consideration and attention, while careful not to increase costs.

The funeral service may begin with brief prayer for grace to hear the gospel in such circumstances with simple trust, and to receive the comfort and hope of the scriptures in the strength of the Spirit. A hymn may follow, if arranged beforehand, though it is difficult to find funeral hymns that are not brashly realistic or mawkish and emotional; one chosen for its long associations, by the chief mourners, will be best appreciated. Scripture readings should be reasonably familiar without being hackneyed, and should be chosen with the particular funeral and family in mind: one of the stories of Jesus' resurrection should always be included.

Most service books include John 6: 35,37–40; Isaiah 40: 6–8 (where the final words are the whole point); Psalm 90, and Psalm 23; Psalm 34: 18,19,22; Psalm 68: 5; and 46: 1; John 11: 25,26; 2 Corinthians 4: 16, 5: 1–10; Matthew 19: 14; Deuteronomy 33: 27; John 10: 27–29; Romans 14: 8,9; 1 Peter 1: 3–9; Psalm 103: 8–18; John 14: 1–6 and 27; Romans 8: 18,28,35–39; from 1 Corinthians 15: 20–57; 1 Thessalonians 4: 13–18; Revelation 7: 9–10 and 13–17; Revelation 14: 13; (Wisdom of Solomon 3: 1–3; and 4: 13–17). Deliberately, this list is not arranged, nor is it exhaustive; it must be emphasised that for an alert pastor, prayerfully preparing such a service, each family and situation will suggest one or two of these and other appropriate passages. Freshness and relevance are everything. (If the familiar service book does not contain a desired passage, it is easy to cut from a Testament and paste the verses in.)

It is most helpful to arrange the readings in some simple and easily remembered pattern: 'Comfort . . . Hope . . . Victory'; 'God our comfort here; God our eternal reward' are examples. A very few verses under each key-word or key-phrase will enable the hearers to follow and retain the message for reflection afterwards. As this is the main witness and teaching in the service, it demands care.

D

88   A GUIDE TO PASTORAL CARE

A brief expression of sympathy, where appropriate, and perhaps a
public tribute, if spoken by the pastor or on behalf of the church,
may follow the scripture, and at the graveside or in the crematorium
the Committal would then follow, in some such words as—

> Since it has pleased Almighty God our heavenly Father to call from
> this life the soul of our *brother*, we therefore commit *his* body to the
> ground (in cremation: 'to the elements'), in sure and certain hope of
> the resurrection to life immortal through our Lord, Jesus Christ, who
> himself died, and is risen again, and is even at the right hand of God.
> Let us all pray . . .

Prayer at this point may give thanks for the gospel, for the hope of
immortality, and for the memory of all good in the life now closed;
and may ask for comfort, for guidance in the new situation, for the
fellowship of God day by day in the new loneliness that stretches
ahead. It may be well to pray, in gentle words, that the sorrow shall
by God's help leave no bitterness, but that grace may be given
bravely to accept the event and say with Jesus 'Thy will be done'.
Those who served the deceased in illness should be remembered
gratefully, and any absent members of the family; while a petition
may be offered for all who share darkness and sorrow at that time.
A prayer that all present may be reminded of the solemnity and
responsibility of life, and the necessity of faith and hope, may help
the company to return from the funeral to common things with a new
sense of God. Plan beforehand whether to conclude with the Lord's
Prayer offered together: it may be the only part of the service in
which those present audibly share, and those who grieve may be
greatly helped by actually speaking words so familiar and revered.

A second hymn, if desired, may be followed either by the
Benediction or with Hebrews 13: 20,21 and the announcement (if
necessary) that the service will conclude elsewhere.

The Committal moment is the most harrowing for truly bereaved
hearts. If the main service has been held at home or at church, the
Committal at graveside or crematorium will be very brief: a few
verses of scripture, the Committal pronouncement, a short prayer
and Benediction. The prayer may especially request that at
subsequent visits to the hallowed spot it may ever be remembered
that the loved one is not here, but with Christ in glory. In some areas,
the coffin is lowered into the grave before the graveside service
begins; in others, it is the custom to lower the coffin while the words
are being spoken. After the Benediction, and a few moments' pause,
it is helpful to lead the chief mourners away, lest grief overcome
them as the need for self-control relaxes.

In the cremation service, the coffin usually lies in view until the Committal moment is reached, when it is withdrawn or lowered, mechanically or by the attendants, either on some pre-arranged signal or as the Committal words are spoken. Often the congregation does not know whether to bow as in prayer, to crane their heads, or to peep through their fingers, to see the coffin disappear, or simply to look embarrassed. It is therefore more dignified, and more respectful, to give firm instructions: let all stand to face the coffin, while the pastor too faces it or possibly steps forward to touch it, as he commits the body to the elements. Then let the congregation immediately sit for prayer. Clear, firm directions will help greatly to control emotional tensions.

A few simple details require forethought and decision if all is to go smoothly. One traditional form of Committal, for example, includes the phrases 'earth to earth, dust to dust, ashes to ashes' (whatever that may mean) accompanied by handfuls of soil thrown into the grave. Some find the ritual impressive, others find it meaningless and melodramatic: the pastor should know whether he will include the words or not, and warn the funeral managers.

When the Committal service is separate from the main service, good planning will reserve some portions of scripture, and some themes of prayer, for use then, lest the second part of the proceedings dribble into empty repetition. Beside a grave, the closing verses of Romans 8, used as prayer, are wonderfully appropriate.

Quiet, but clear and firm speaking is far more effective than emotional histrionics or a synthetic piteousness, especially as the time-honoured scripture phrases yield their own depth of meaning and power in solemn circumstances. The pastor sets the emotional tone, which should be real sympathy but never artificial sadness. *Remember the value of formality* in getting through emotional scenes with dignity. The pastor soon learns that the deepest, most genuine feelings are often those most carefully controlled and even concealed. In any case, his ministry is to help people through such experiences, not to make them more difficult. On the other hand, where a cynical indifference is manifest, some expression of Christian feeling may be called for, to make others realise for the first time the depth of conviction that the service enshrines.

Peripheral Considerations

Numerous questions can arise, and even emergencies, in which the bereaved family will look to the pastor for a wise and clear lead, though he may never have met such circumstances before. He can only think quickly, and keep the ultimate good of the people themselves clearly in mind. Any lingering memories of disturbance, or ill-behaviour, of clumsiness or accident, will be exceedingly painful for the immediate family, and to protect them the pastor will on occasion be very firm indeed (with any signs of drunkenness, for example). He will remember that in such circumstances he who manifestly expects to be obeyed, will be; and a firm lead will always be followed. He will keep control, and proceed with dignity and quietness, whatever happens.

But he will also foresee trouble. There is often one mourner who either cannot control emotional outbursts, or who enjoys the public attention which dramatic fainting and hysteria will ensure. Usually the same person stands as near the open grave as possible, in imminent danger of collapsing into it; in all probability he or she will take good care not to, but the possibility will seriously disturb everyone else, and the service. The experienced pastor will have noted such an individual earlier, and as the mourners assemble will quietly direct people where he wants them, two stalwart men within reach of the person who might need upholding, and all standing well back, in a larger circle than is really necessary, to avert all danger. If anyone resists, the pastor will simply wait until all is as he wishes; and if anyone does faint, he should publicly ask the funeral manager to help that person from the scene (or from the church) and quietly carry on.

It is possible to find oneself directed to the wrong grave, or that the coffin is too big for the grave, or that some mourners have been delayed, or that a storm of rain or hail makes it inadvisable to stand around the grave. Again, the pastor retains leadership: quietly explaining the difficulty, he says what will be done—always better than making suggestions. The party will proceed to the right grave, together, by the route indicated; or will retire to the church porch to await whatever needs to be done; or will sit quietly conversing (silence would soon be unbearable) until the absent friends arrive; when all is well, he will proceed without comment. In very bad weather, after conferring with the chief mourners, the pastor may announce that only five or six of the younger men will proceed to the grave while the rest remain in church until they return. Whenever the weather is inclement, the conflict of reverence and common sense should be resolved by the pastor's inviting the men to retain their hats if they wish to do so. It is not unknown for a grave to be half-filled with water: the pastor will do a real service (at some risk to his own reputation for dictatorial methods!) if he insists that the mourners stand far back from the grave—without explanation—and then disperses them firmly. That is better than to allow the family to carry away with them, and brood long over, the picture of the coffin floating in mud.

After-care of a bereaved home can extend the funeral ministry into pastoral and evangelistic opportunity. For the pastor to return to the home after the funeral may give real support to a bewildered, or poor, or divided family, though to stay long may be trying to himself and to them. But he will always return after a day or two, to enquire, and perhaps to pray, when home and hearts are quiet again. Any temptation to capitalise sorrow by pressurised evangelism is more likely to evoke resentment and cynicism than to win hearts, but sincere friendship, an invitation to keep in touch, and especially to make contact if any help is needed, will be appreciated. Any response to the service, and any enquiry concerning Christian faith and friendship, would, of course, create a new situation, which the pastor will know how to use.

The receiving of fees for funeral ministry is always a delicate matter. For the public service accomplished, the local Disposal authority sometimes pays a public fee; funeral managers who engage the minister usually include his services in their charges and pay him. It is wisest for the pastor to accept whatever is arranged without differentiation. He may sometimes feel it right to return the fee privately to church families (who should not have to pay for such ministry by their own pastor), and to poor and stricken homes. In some cases it may be more considerate to send a note saying that the fee has been donated to some charity in which the deceased was especially interested, and in his or her name and memory.

A question requiring careful forethought, but often posed with immediate urgency, is—Cremation or burial? Some, convinced that cremation is not scriptural, have no hesitation; others notice that rock-entombment is not burial, and hold that considerations of health, the use of available ground, and the ultimate neglect of burying-places, argue cremation to be the better method of disposal. Theological considerations hardly apply: neither reverence for what God created, nor the hope of resurrection, seems to require the slow process of dissolution rather than the quicker process of combustion: the end result is the same. The question is one of feeling, more than of logic or doctrine.

But when the pastor is asked his advice, more often than not no one is in the mental state for a lecture on social hygiene, logic or theology, and it is not his opinion which matters. The sensible solution is for families to know each other's mind before the need for decision arises: the wish of the deceased is then paramount. But unless this is clear, the pastor will foresee the after-thoughts and regrets that will surely arise if by argument or family pressure the *feeling* of the next of kin is overridden. His counsel may therefore be, 'We all have our opinions, but let the next of kin say what should be done, and let us not discuss it. Perhaps in calmer days you may like to think it over and decide for yourselves—but not now.'

In the hour of death and bereavement all the truly fundamental issues of human life and destiny come to the surface, not to be evaded, obscured, or denied. This is the one crisis of experience in which the truth or falsehood of religion stares one in the face—death makes believers or pagans of us all. In consequence, it is the one crisis of experience in which only the pastor has any ministry at all to offer men—even the preacher is out of place. The pastor, befriending the sorrowing, instructing the bewildered, supporting the stricken, affirming the gospel, becomes for a time the very embodiment of faith, hope and love to hearts at their most susceptible moment and in their most receptive mood. Robert Menzies quotes the counsel of Professor G. D. Henderson of Glasgow, 'Never refuse to take a funeral, for you will never get a better chance to preach the gospel.'

The faithful man will not take advantage of that immeasurable privilege for selfish or sectarian ends; but he will, sometimes more than he realises, make God and the eternal world at last real to hearts that never before have faced the final facts. Often he will feel utterly helpless in face of unrelieved human sorrow, yet now and again he will discover that his careful ministry in the very shadow of death has opened for someone the gates of everlasting life.

9 PASTORAL EVANGELISM

If the church has learned anything about evangelism in recent years it is that all evangelism is ultimately pastoral. This is not a wilful confusion of convenient distinctions, nor does it mean that no place exists for the gifted, dedicated, full-time evangelist, free of permanent commitment to any local Christian fellowship and able to offer leadership and expertise for occasional campaigns. There is obvious need, opportunity, scripture warrant, and blessing, for such specialised outreach ministry. But who today would conduct such a campaign, or a single evangelistic service, without efficient *counselling* arrangements? Though barriers are removed, indifference dissolved, the soul stirred and kindled to earnest enquiry, by passionate gospel preaching, it is in the pastoral interview that the individual application and the personal resolve are registered.

Moreover, the church's failure to captivate, assimilate, educate or incorporate the converts won at great public campaigns revealed the necessity of pastoral care as not so much the 'follow up' as the 'follow through' of evangelism. The failure was not entirely the church's fault: no local Christian fellowship could sustain the level of publicity, numbers and excitement, the band-wagon atmosphere, of the Tent or Arena, and where these were equated with spiritual life and power, disappointment was inevitable. But many churches learned, for their part, how unready they were to understand, or to sympathise with, converts wholly unfamiliar with church ways, or to adjust their language, their programmes or their moral attitudes to make newcomers feel at home.

One result of this new self-knowledge has been an altogether greater emphasis within the church upon preparation for evangelism. Weekly programmes and activities that for years have had no further end than to maintain their own existence, have been looked at critically; the concept of the church as a close and enriching friendship for good causes in a vaguely religious atmosphere, with an underlying assumption that worship is good for society and often helpful to individuals under stress, has given way to a more positive and activist concept—that of 'mission'.

In more extreme reaction, exaggerations like 'the church is mission', 'evangelise or perish', have urged that evangelism is all the church exists for, the only method of her preservation. Sometimes evangelism is seriously proposed as the only hope of (a) saving our young people from dreaded behaviour-patterns, and so preserving our homes and families intact; (b) saving our society from the secularising, corrupting tendencies of the age; (c) saving our churches from extinction; (d) delivering our own consciences from guilt in face of the clear scriptural obligation to evangelise—all utterly selfish reasons. The rarest of all motives for evangelism, even yet, is genuine concern that other people should share the joy of Christian living. Nevertheless, the new concern, the new urgency about soul-winning, is of God, and welcome.

The Evangelistic Pastor

There is some truth, of course, in all such arguments in favour of evangelistic effort. But from the pastor's viewpoint, the essential truth is that a living church is evangelistic, by its inherent attractiveness, vitality, relevance, and joy; and a pastoral ministry is evangelistic, all the time. For pastoral ministry is, by definition, 'bringing the gospel to bear upon individual needs and circumstances': and where the need and circumstance is plainly that of an unconvinced mind, an uncommitted life, struggling with problems which Christ could help to solve, the application of the gospel will necessarily be evangelistic.

This approach is all-important. The pastor does not strive at every opportunity to register conversions, but he is, in doing the work of a pastor, doing also the work of an evangelist, in detail, with individuals.

Thus, while he does not in sickroom or hospital ward, at wedding or funeral services, at every Young People's Meeting or pastoral visit, embarrass, bore or antagonise his captive audience by 'going for them with the gospel', yet because he sees every need and situation in a Christian light, and sustains a Christian witness to the meaning of life, sickness, marriage, age and death, he is presenting the gospel all the time, in friendship, counsel, invitation and prayer. An alert and beloved pastor, with an alert and welcoming church behind him, will over the years win souls for Christ, consistently and permanently, as few other evangelistic agencies can do.

All of the pastor's specific tasks, and most of the problems brought to him, give him entry to hearts and homes at especially open and responsive moments; and he will often be aware that his counsel, like his conduct of wedding and funeral services, his prayer in a sickroom, presupposes a commitment to Christ which his clients have not yet made. It is more effective to let this fact appear, and make its own challenge, than to insist upon a decision to follow Christ as the only solution, or as the condition of offering any further help. For the pastor is often painfully aware that such a decision, *of itself*, will solve little unless it leads to a totally new, Christian approach towards the problem, the need, or other people involved.

Nevertheless, the pastor cannot evade the responsibility to make his day-to-day pastoral duties evangelistic in intention, expectation and reward. To say, 'But I am essentially a teacher, a pastor, not an evangelist' is to hide timidity under sophistry. One cannot be a gospel-teacher, a gospel-pastor, without being ready to seize the evangelistic initiative in every opportunity presented, for example in *pastoral preaching*. This is not the place to discuss evangelistic sermons in detail:* but the pastor needs to question false generalities about the type of people who attend Christian worship. It is true that worship-services no longer attract the proportion of unbelievers that once they did; the social convention of attendance at church that once provided great pulpiteers with constant evangelistic opportunity no longer binds the great majority. Yet in every congregation there are people at all stages of belief and unbelief. Some who are considerably involved in church activities understand little of the personal experience of salvation. In most church families, attending worship together, there are some members as yet unsaved.

Every normal congregation will have, too, all the time, within its sphere of influence, some young people growing up who need to be confronted with the living Christ. Some still attend church occasions for friendship, music, stimulus, tradition or conscience—who yet are not Christians. Whenever such are expected to be present, a sermon with evangelistic purpose and emphasis will be relevant, and all the more persuasive because it comes from a man known, respected and trusted, rather than from some stranger, however eloquent.

The evangelistic initiative will also inform the pastor's share in the church's *education programme*. He will take care to make his presence familiar to younger children in the church's classes, and to keep the true purpose of Christian education before the minds and on the hearts of the teaching staff. But most of all the evangelistic pastor will see that he has under his own care, for half the year or so, a group of those who have reached the age of decision. The 'Senior Class' in any Sunday school should be his charge, even if he then hands the scholars on to someone else for Bible class and Discussion Groups.

* See the author's *Guide to Preaching*, chapter 12.

This pastoral class of constantly changing individuals should be the permanent 'church membership class' where, without any previous assumptions about eventual decision, the whole of the school's teaching is summarised and brought to the point of individual experience, practical discipleship, and membership of Christ's church. All scholars should in turn pass through this course, in personal contact with the pastor. No pressure should be exercised: those who withhold response must still feel themselves as welcome within the Christian circle as before. But from such a pastoral ministry among the older scholars will come in time many converts, not swept into the kingdom but led by patient and detailed teaching. And from among these will emerge in later years some of the most faithful and mature members and workers the church will ever know.

The evangelistic initiative will affect similarly the pastor's leadership in all *Youth activities* fostered within the Christian fellowship. A church's ministry to youth includes three main purposes: (1) to educate and train young Christians towards increasing usefulness and responsibility within Christian circles and in social endeavour; (2) to use these young Christians to attract and hold young people not yet Christian, providing for them useful, enjoyable and profitable group activities of many kinds in a Christian atmosphere among Christian friends, as counter-attraction to temptation and refuge from the pressures of a menacing environment; (3) to exercise every gentle, positive and winsome persuasion to move young people from group (2) to group (1).

Much evangelism in such a setting will be unspoken, emanating from well-chosen leaders, from Christian example, friendship and gaiety, and from a carefully devised programme which *assumes* the spiritual needs of young people as naturally as their need of food, fun, friendship and romance. The pastor's influence will probably lie as much in selecting the leaders and framing the programme as in direct activity, though he will take care to be known, and available, as occasion offers.

Other *church organisations*—young wives' clubs, 'women's meetings', men's societies, music and reading circles and the like, tend to be satisfied with a loose connection with church life. Where the attendance is chiefly of Christian members, the pastor will probably feel no obligation to make such groups explicitly religious, or recruiting grounds. Yet for some people, such smaller circles can become the only connection with the church: some women who would never attend Sunday worship will often be faithful members of a women's gospel meeting where the informality of programme and dress makes fewer demands. The alert pastor will assess the need and opportunity of each group, and see that he is known, available, and on good terms with its leaders and members.

When opportunity offers, he will remember that he is asked to contribute to the programme or to give his counsel as *pastor*—often a silent appeal for truly spiritual leadership and support—and he will respond with forthright, though courteous, Christian witness and conviction. As in every area of church life, an evangelistic intention will *underlie* his contacts, occasional talks, conversations, with such fringe-groups. He will neither repel by over-eagerness, solemnity, persistence or rudeness, nor discourage by aloofness, flippancy, uncertainty of mood, or unreadiness to listen. Without evangelising all the time, he will *be* an evangelist, expressing and embodying the gospel so naturally, so consistently and so gladly, that to be in his presence in spiritual need is to open one's heart and find blessing.

The Evangelistic Church

But pastoral evangelism is necessarily a corporate enterprise, and the pastor's second and equally important task is to create and foster an evangelistic church. An evangelistic church is one favourable in atmosphere and attitude towards evangelistic effort, and willing to be trained in evangelistic methods.

As to attitude: not all churches are favourably disposed toward evangelism—strangely, not even all 'evangelical' churches. The more a Christian fellowship insists upon clear convictions, deep personal experience of the grace of God, and high standards of behaviour, the greater is the temptation to be exclusive and inward-looking, to shun the world, to be cautious in welcoming new members, reluctant to adjust its programme to suit outsiders who come in, rigorous in its discipline and censorious of all who do not at once conform to traditional patterns. Always glad to welcome new people *of the right type*, such churches remain unfavourably disposed towards those who do not yet conform, who have all the finesse of Christian life and fellowship still to learn, whose language, manner, and moral attitudes are immature, 'uncouth', ignorant—because they have only just learned to love their Lord, and little else.

Other churches are unfavourably disposed towards evangelism for other reasons: theological, social, or superficial. The pastor's evangelistic task will be the same in all, to create and then to nourish an attitude and atmosphere in which the work of evangelism will be undertaken and the fruits of evangelism warmly and sympathetically accepted. This means teaching the church to seek, to welcome, and to educate the outsider.

(i) *To seek* means much more than advertising, enticing or inviting outsiders to come *where we are*, in church, hall, tent, home, coffee-bar: it means our going *where they are*. That could involve Christians in visiting some strange places, not only 'into the mountains' where sheep stray, and 'the streets and lanes of the city', but into the highways and under the hedges of our society. It could involve mixing with strange types, the poor, the maimed, the halt, the blind, outcasts and sinners, and risking from fellow Christians the rebuke flung at Jesus—'Too friendly with the wrong sort of people!' The evangelist is always open to accusations of guilt-by-association.

To remark that through the greater part of their lives most people are to be found either at home, at school, at work, at leisure, on holiday, or in care, is to name at once six places where the church must seek them out. Efficient, regular and kindly *house-visitation* is essential if a church is to minister to the community in which it is set, and it opens doors to many kinds of service for the old, the sick, the children, and the handicapped. Invitations to special services, and an *interesting* church Newsletter distributed regularly through a district will build up through the years a rapport between church and community which will yield incalculable results.

The evangelistic pastor will see that the presence and interest of himself and his church are known in the local *schools and colleges*. He will attend school occasions, link church and school by all means open to him, offering facilities for school-worship, making himself available whenever opportunity arises to visit Christian groups within the school, and to help with specific problems of discipline or stress among the pupils. Genuine, unselfish, and of course un-sectarian, offers of help are rarely discouraged by school or college Principals.

Many factories, offices and other *places of employment* have Christian groups which meet for occasional fellowship, and a local pastor is often welcome as guest and supporter. From this there frequently arises opportunity for chaplaincy and counselling ministry to the whole organisation, and sometimes for totally unexpected links with individuals and families far outside the church's fellowship.

To seek people *at leisure* and *on holiday* may involve infiltrating local sports clubs and societies with individuals or groups seeking their own entertainment where people can be met, and there loyally contributing as Christians to the common interest and welfare. A church music group, sports group, debating society, willing to mix with other groups in all innocent enjoyment and competition may reveal the quality of Christian living to people who never otherwise have personal contact with Christianity. Summer evening epilogues, or children's services or story-time, on the beaches and in public parks, the adjustment of service times to suit holiday-makers, and providing a social centre where visitors from various places can meet for coffee and conversation—many such arrangements can extend the church's ministry with deep-level evangelistic intent once the will to meet and mix with those we seek has been created.

People *in care* of hospital, nursing home, geriatric clinic, mental home and prison are as much an obligation upon Christian concern as targets for Christian evangelism. If genuine love is shown, the religious spring of that love will soon be revealed. A church should take steps to be well known to every healing and caring institution in its neighbourhood, continually sending its pastor, its choir, its individual entertainers, its young people to relieve hard-pressed nursing staffs, its gifts of fruit and flowers, its carefully chosen visitors, and sometimes its car drivers to get patients home. Always the test of such ministry is the genuineness of its professed concern, and that will be revealed by consistency, kindness, courtesy, far more than by aggressive propaganda. 'To be among men as one who serves' is to be like Christ: the evangelistic impact will take care of itself.

Thus, to seek and to save them that are lost requires far greater enterprise than mere 'outreach'—staying safely within church walls and putting out tentative and timid feelers to passers-by. It means going forth bearing precious seed, in the rough weather of the outside world, in the faith that eventually we, or others who enter into our labours, will doubtless come again rejoicing, bringing their sheaves with them.

(ii) Truly *to welcome* the outsider into Christian fellowship may involve similar disturbance of our own comfort and preferences. The 'welcome' can sometimes be very tardy, cool, suspicious, as was the reception that Saul of Tarsus received when he stood on the threshold of the church in Jerusalem. Every evangelistic church needs the heart and spirit of Barnabas, who saw the grace of God in strange places and strange people, and was glad. Some new converts look so different—so 'unchurchly'—possessing no Sunday clothes and wanting none, speaking with new accents, having never learned the language of Zion. On occasion, their manners, habits, behaviour, ignorance and criticism are hard to bear. We much prefer converts from right backgrounds, fully fledged Christians of matured faith, already familiar with gospel truths and Christian ways, their manners and attitudes refined by grace.

But the pastor knows that those won to Christ from pagan homes and vicious ways have very much to learn—and unlearn. He has every right to expect his fellow Christians to make them welcome and treat them kindly, with great gentleness towards their faults, while they grow up into Christ. Admittedly, there are problems, and risks. The pastor will sometimes be deeply disturbed, and even angry, when he sees Christian parents withdrawing their own young people from contact with the 'incoming world'. He must try to understand, to explain, to be patient; he must himself be deeply concerned for any moral or spiritual danger he may be introducing to sheltered and immature children of the church. Frank and firm consultation with the youth of the church and with their parents is necessary. The young people themselves will sometimes solve this problem by their own outgoing generosity of heart, while their elders still argue about it; though here again the pastor may think it wise to forbid anyone with less than two years' Christian experience to engage in certain areas of Christian work. With older Christians he will be equally firm: they must, in Christ's name, welcome all whom Christ has welcomed, and is saving.

On his own part, the pastor must resist the temptation to focus all attention on his new 'trophies', to sacrifice everything to keeping them happy, to over-expose them to publicity and spoil them for the rest of their lives for any humble, self-effacing Christian service. Incoming outsiders must be welcomed, but they need not be, and should not be, continually feted.

(iii) All the same, *to educate* the incoming outsider will mean that the activities and interests of maturer Christians, designed to advance the instruction, fellowship and experience of believers of long standing, will have to yield something to fringe activities, with lighter and more varied programmes, helpful to people who 'belong to the Christian community rather than to the community of Christians'. Inevitably, this will seem to some to be an intrusion of 'unspiritual', 'unevangelical' ways into the cosiness of a close-knit fellowship—yet its motive is evangelistic.

Similarly, the education programme has to be adjusted to accommodate beginners in the faith. Themes and Bible studies on very elementary topics affecting Christian belief, behaviour, and church loyalty must be given attention; old truths must be translated into new, unfamiliar language understood by those to whom church-talk is an alien tongue. New translations of the scriptures will appear, some with garish titles and covers; the 'reverent' organ has to give place a little to the 'irreverent' guitar; ancient hymns become mixed with modern folk-praise; the church becomes noisy, lively, untidy. The pious silence of rows of quiet people attending devoutly to a religious address is replaced sometimes by the give and take of open discussion, with occasionally outrageous views, as new converts explore their astonishing new faith.

Always, the crucial question is, will the established Christians understand? Will they support the effort, will they remain to enrich, deepen and train the newcomers—or will they withdraw to some more comfortable and sheltered refuge in a closed circle of 'spiritual people' safely insulated from the complications of evangelism?

Plainly, to create and foster an evangelistic church requires far-ranging vision, considerable tact, clear understanding alike of the fears of the flock and of the impatience of the lost sheep; immense patience, courage, and firm leadership. In some situations, nothing less is needed than a total rethinking, *together*, of the nature and function of the church—and even of the nature and function of the Faith. For Christianity was a mission before it became an institution, a campaign before it became a church. The institution, the fellowship, the church justifies its existence only as it serves the mission Christ came to pursue. We may never forget that He indignantly 'cleansed' a Temple which had come to ignore the crying needs of the city about its courts; which was concentrating its endeavours upon preserving its own privileges. Having driven out its officials, He gathered into its courts, instead, the blind and the lame for healing, the children to sing, the ignorant for instruction. For the house of God is not merely a refuge for the sensitive: it is a bridgehead into society, a base from which Christians advance into irreligious areas of life.

To stimulate a fellowship into such revision of cherished ideas involves much that is uncongenial; a readiness for change to appeal to a changing world; a fellowship made not only enjoyable but adhesive, inclusive, absorbent—so that no soul, however dimly interested, can get within a mile of it without being hauled in. It will become a group no longer hard to get into, but hard to keep out of. Some of the traditional, more advanced, ministries and disciplines must be maintained: for unless the inner heart of the church is soundly nourished, there will be no point at all in bringing newcomers in. Yet outreach must be as eager as upreach. It is nice to talk of the church as a spiritual home: the evangelistic pastor has to teach his people to talk of it *also* as a railway station where the troop trains come and go to frontiers where the real conflict lies.

For the real purpose of being in the church of Christ is—to get out of it.

As to training: once a truly evangelistic outlook has been engendered, the demand for training arises of itself, and the pastor will find great joy in devising schemes of preparation for evangelistic experiments. He will need to acquaint himself, through booklets and magazines, with as much as possible of what other men and churches have tried and discovered—always remembering that what succeeds in one place, with one team of workers, may fail dismally elsewhere. And he will need to be persuaded himself, and to persuade others, that while something can be done to prepare mind and heart for the adventure, the work of evangelism is mainly learned in evangelising.

(i) A first, elementary point of instruction is the duty and opportunity of simple daily witnessing. 'You are an epistle of Christ . . . read and known of all men' . . . 'Men took knowledge of them that they had been with Jesus.' The duty is clear: the enormous range of opportunity may occasion surprise. Talk of evangelism usually raises questions about striking publicity, effective organisation, team-assembly, sufficient funds, outstanding speakers—how to make contacts, and generate a lasting impression. In sober fact, this is no problem.

Any Christian assembly, in village or town, has all the contacts with the community that it needs, far more than it can handle. Forty members, each living next door to four neighbours, travelling to work, or shopping, beside two more, working beside two colleagues, speaking to an additional five during each day, writing, telephoning or visiting one more, and buying milk, bread or newspapers from one more, *has six hundred contacts with the community every day*; two hundred and nineteen thousand every year! That, without the least effort, or expenditure. A church of four hundred members has six thousand contacts daily, two million one hundred and ninety thousand in a year. Just by being there! If every member is a witnessing Christian, a truly tremendous evangelistic impact is being made all the time. To be a Christian, talk like a Christian, care in a Christian way for others, express Christian views and attitudes on the topics of the day, be available with Christian understanding, friendship and counsel to all who seek help—this is daily witnessing. It needs little instruction, just consistency.

(ii) A second area of instruction might well occupy weeknight study-services over a winter's preparation. This would aim to isolate and expound the essentials of Christian belief and Christian ethics, the simple heart of the Christian gospel, defined in contrast with the ideas non-Christians profess—agnosticism, humanism, amoralism, materialism, communism. Useful, too, would be a course on the cults that deviate from Christianity, and where appropriate, something about immigrant religions. The intention would be to enable believers to give a reason for the hope that is within them, to keep to the essential Christian point, to avoid mere argument and rivalry, and to bear a straightforward and relevant testimony to the Christian gospel and its meaning for today.

(iii) A third area of instruction might deal with the deepest personal motivation, the spirit in which Christians approach others with evangelistic intention. What *right* have we to evangelise? Old people suspect all propaganda, the young resent being exploited, and both reject all instruction, correction, 'being done good to', by busybodies with a mission to fulfil, a duty to discharge, or who find some spiritual satisfaction in lecturing their neighbours on religion.

None of us would presume to offer advice, unasked, about another's marriage, or money, how many children he should have, or how he disciplines his wife: but we earnestly, insistently, press upon other people spiritual counsel, testimony, beliefs and warnings, concerning the most personal issues of all, without thinking it unusual! That is arrogance. It cannot be said too often that the indispensable self-preparation for evangelism is, that none shall go upon any mission, campaign, visitation, or outreach of any kind, until he can genuinely and undisguisedly do so *for the sake of the evangelised, and for that alone.* Until he can do that, he will not get a hearing, nor deserve one.

The essential truth here is that before I can engage upon evangelism, I must justify the wish to speak to others about spiritual things; I must earn for myself the right to speak to others about spiritual things; I must myself create the most favourable opportunity to speak to others about spiritual things; and I must first establish the relationship in which what I say will have weight, and truth, and meaning.

All of which implies that the evangelistic approach must be entirely sincere, and *well-prepared* by real friendship, true concern, practical help, genuine neighbourliness. One pastor who trained a whole church in evangelistic enterprise to a level of competence which all might envy, used to say 'the best tract for a sick neighbour is a rice pudding every day—and not a word about religion until she asks you why!' The outsider will counter argument with argument, assertion with contradiction, testimony with scepticism: but against a radiant and practical Christian friendship he has no answer. When he sees the gospel in the Christian, and learns that behind the Christian is a church whose corporate life embodies all that the gospel teaches, he is already half persuaded, not only to listen but to believe. But until we have so won an entrance for the word we bring, by the love we show, we shall talk in vain.

(iv) Such consistent care for individuals and families, preparing the way of the Lord, will be mainly an individual and long-term task. But a fourth area of evangelistic instruction might concern methods of joint activity. The simplest starting-point, and one of the most fruitful, is shared systematic district visitation, either to publicise special events or—better—to provide the foundation for the church's ministry to the area around it. Couples would be selected of varied age, sex and background, and advice given on approach, timing, the information to be gathered; while to prevent wasted effort, fixed streets would be allotted to each couple for—say—a year's work. The primary purpose of the first visit would be to convey the church's greeting and interest to every home, and to leave some permanent information-literature to recall the visit afterwards. The secondary purpose would be to record names, existing church-affiliations, and any details useful to children's or youth groups or other circles in the church.

Thereon, the visitors must be guided by circumstances and reactions. In each home will be a new situation, often with real need; as opportunity offers and the Spirit guides, testimony may be given, practical assistance volunteered, or prayer offered, but only as seems right at the time, *never* as 'evangelistic routine'. The visitors will be ready also with detailed information about all the activities and societies to which the visited are invited. As soon as possible after each visit, the information should be registered, back at church, by those able to collate and file efficiently. Where there is revealed some serious need for pastoral, or medical, or social-department care, the required action will be set on foot. A separate list of homes that showed interest and promised response, or were not linked to any other church, will provide the basis for second and third visits— plainly a much shorter, more concentrated task. Information about lapsed members of other churches may be passed to their ministers.

Out of such an enterprise will arise endless opportunities for personal invitations, children's rallies, practical ministries, individual friendships, while a church thus made familiar and shown to be friendly will often be called upon by local families for help in trouble, in sorrow, or in wedding festivities. But all needs the most careful and prolonged preparation, and efficient organisation; promises made must be kept, homes contacted must not afterwards be neglected. Mere impulsiveness and short-lived interest are here not merely useless but dangerous: better not to start such an effort than to do it badly, or abandon it unfinished. And better to make two friendships that are maintained than twenty that are swiftly forgotten.

Yet from the workers' point of view, one of the most useful results will be the discovery of *corporateness* in evangelism. Some who would never venture alone discover unexpected joy in sharing such work. Old and young, who have hardly spoken to each other before, find new appreciation as they admit their nervousness, help each other, and then discuss together afterwards their impressions and experiences. Quickly, different types of worker learn when to take the lead, when to be silent, adapting to the circumstances found in any home. Not least, some who imagine themselves wholly competent to evangelise in any situation, learn that in some cases they are helpless and the quiet 'ineffective' soul who hardly has a word to say reveals some unsuspected gift for getting alongside strangers and finding the right approach. Others again who 'cannot bring themselves' to talk to strangers about Christ, or whose physical handicaps prevent street-tramping, will throw themselves energetically into keeping files, addressing invitations, referring needs to those who can help, providing refreshments for returning visitors. Many pastors have found that whatever the results of such corporate effort may have been for the visited, the reflex effect in deepening church fellowship has made everything worth while.

(v) Instruction in the purpose of all evangelism, the response to be aimed at, may seem superfluous, but it could be very important. Some eager personal evangelists count their work done if they have stated, in their own words, what they consider to be the essence of the gospel—whether or not it has been clearly understood, persuasively presented, or shown to be relevant to the hearer's need. Of course there can be no evangelism without the eventual exposition of what it means to believe on the Lord Jesus Christ and be saved. But that truth has to be communicated, not merely presented, and that means wrestling with the hearer's language, understanding, objections, and lack of experience. The personal evangelist is not responsible for his hearer's unbelief: but he is for his hearer's incomprehension.

Yet evangelism is not indoctrination. We cannot pretend to provide ready-made religious convictions, or answers for every problem posed. As Peter learned at Caesarea Philippi and Paul at Damascus, the truth about Christ is revealed at last to every heart by the Father; the work of illumination and conviction is the work of the Holy Spirit, who takes of the things of Christ and reveals them unto men. We can lead others to the place of personal revelation, can provide the background information, tell the divine story, explain and illustrate its bearing upon modern life, and add (if we think it wise) our own testimony. But in the end we seek to lead men towards their own moment of insight. What we are after is not conformity to an inherited pattern of ideas, but rediscovery of the inherent truth. All new converts must see the inexhaustible Christ with fresh eyes, and explore the gospel with new wonder, and then themselves go out to tell their new experience in new terms, new songs, new ways, often impatient of traditional customs and second-hand convictions. Therein lies the perpetual freshness of Christian experience.

Yet even in helping would-be evangelists to see clearly what they are aiming at, the pastor will warn against over-intellectualising the gospel. Doctrine, discovery, belief, illumination, insight—all are well over the heads of many whom we would win for Christ. Very often, therefore, the evangelist will aim, not first at clear understanding, but at enlistment, the involvement of the hearer in the Christian circle and fellowship, the Christian cause, the Christian pilgrimage and obedience. Some will find their understanding—so far as they ever will—through sharing the life and activity in which that understanding is enshrined. They will experience God's grace before they grasp its meaning, and come to share peace and joy before they know what makes it theirs. Who will question that experience is a valid way to find the truth?

It is often remarked that Jesus approached the woman of Samaria not with an offer but with a request—'Give me to drink'. Robert Menzies adds to that illustration of the 'involvement method' an incident from the life of Moses. 'Moses entreated Hobab to go with them on their wilderness journey: "Come with us, and we will do thee good." And Hobab stoutly refused to go. Then Moses tried another line, "Come with us, and be eyes to us in the desert." And Hobab immediately capitulated, and went.' That reaction will often be met with: some resent being offered help of which they as yet feel no need, but will gladly bring their skill, energies, interest and labour, if asked, to serve and support the church and those to whom she ministers. It is a beginning. It can become an unspoken but deeply felt expression of belief; to become involved in the fellowship and work of the gospel may, for some people, be the most articulate confession of faith of which they are capable. It can lead, by God's grace, to a full and happy Christian life.

Instruction is of course only a part of training. The rest is experiment, practice, accumulated experience. The pastor will be at hand to support, encourage, and advise, and he will frequently call together the evangelistic team to discuss problems, share and sift experiences, work out together the answers to unforeseen questions, and unite in thanksgiving and prayer. A church so led by a pastor who is himself inspired at all levels of ministry with evangelistic zeal, taught by his vision and example to expect results, and including within its fellowship a team so trained and equipped, should enjoy continual reinforcement of its membership and reinvigorating of its life, while the Lord adds to the church daily such as are being saved.

TYPICAL PROBLEMS

10 PARENT AND CHILD

Domestic life in the western world has been under varied pressure in recent years, and the Christian pastor often becomes involved in ministry to the family as a Christian unit. His role, as wise and independent counsellor, is mainly to illuminate, interpret and mediate, helping the members of the family to understand each other and find richness, rather than division, through their differences. Especially is this his work in the special difficulties that arise between the generations.

Family trouble is as diverse as most sorts of trouble, and rarely understood by outsiders; while advice about it is frequently resented by all sides. A great deal depends on whether it is parent, child, or third party (teacher, grandparent, youth leader, neighbour, or mere busybody) who suggests that the pastor might help resolve a problem. In every case he is likely to begin on the defensive, and must take extreme care to hear all sides of a story, and think carefully around the total situation, before he ventures any comment.

Though we have all been members of families, we do not always see our family life with objective impartiality. It is well therefore to see the basic family-situation in general, and the particular ways in which modern changes affect it; to distinguish which strains are natural and inevitable, which arise from personal failings. Then to see *why* those strains, and those failings, arise is to move towards better relationships and family harmony. Moreover it is obvious, though often forgotten, that the same home and family looks very different seen from eyes a generation apart.

(1) *The Parental Situation*

(i) *The basic situation*, from the parents' point of view, is that the child 'belongs' to them, is 'their' child, the fruit of their love. This assumption is emotionally strengthened, first by the infant's helplessness: the 'belonging' is not for the parents all privilege, for it involves care, and the sacrifice of time, freedom and resources, all gladly given in accepted obligation towards the new life they have created. The assumption is strengthened, secondly, by the child's own affectionate response, clinging to parental strength and love—

a powerful and long-lasting psychological bond. It is strengthened, thirdly, in time as home, plans, savings, future, and even the day-to-day programme of family life, focus largely upon the presence and needs of the child. Much that the parents for months, perhaps years, have 'lived towards', and now deliberately live for, centres in 'their very own' family.

Here lies at once the foundation of the problem inherent in every family situation. The assumption is false, as time will relentlessly reveal. The child belongs to no one: it is its own, an end in itself, an independent existence, a new life. In Christian thought especially, the child must never become the means to others' happiness, a tool of others' self-fulfilment, a 'thing' possessed.

(ii) *The changing situation* which so often imposes strain upon family relationships is precisely the surfacing of this inherent falsehood. The child very early begins to assert its own individuality and freedom, to make its own demands, express its own preferences, exercise self-will. The process continues through childhood, puberty, adolescence, with growing emphasis and rapidity, parents retreating reluctantly, never altogether consenting to relinquish the ownership which is emotionally so precious *to them*.

Parents realise, intellectually, that the young animal must leave the den; they are slower to accept that growing away from home is a necessary element in the maturing of their own offspring. It takes time to bring parental emotions into line with insight, and to persuade that if the young are let go, they will usually return of their own accord; whereas if they are bound firmly to home by pare ntal prohibitions, they will eventually break away in resentment, andnot return. Very generally, it may be said that boys find their main interests outside home between ten and fourteen years and return to father, or to a substitute father-hero, around eighteen; girls turn from home around fifteen to seventeen and return to mother at the approach of marriage or the coming of their first baby. Some such pattern, complicated by innumerable accidental factors, is wholly *natural*: the alternative is prolonged immaturity. When parents misread the growing-up process as rebelliousness, ingratitude, selfishness, want of love, they merely show their own immaturity.

(iii) *The widening gap* between parent and child is likewise inevitable, inherent in the family situation. No two generations ever lived in the same world, or the same home. Each inherits a new environment, lives with different people, is one stage further down the line of history. The natural gaps, of age and status, of dependence and *priority* (who gave life to whom) are all widened by the different cultures in which the forty-year-old and the fourteen-year-old live, even in the same house. They are widened further by every advance in education, creating for the child a world of thought, knowledge, opinion and interest very different from that of its parents. The better the education the parents provide, the further the children may be driven from them, especially where parents themselves are inarticulate, or educationally underprivileged: but that is *not* the child's fault. The responsibility for bridging every gap of education lies of course on the better educated, but this may be made unnecessarily difficult by the conceit or impatience of the young, or the pride of parents who resent the 'rudeness' which seeks to instruct them.

Better education brings better opportunities, and greater economic freedom. While parents still provide home and basic needs, growing children, with few demands, may command greater income than the parents possessed at their age. The burdened middle-aged can become very envious of the adolescent's resources, freedom and enjoyment, which seems sheer irresponsibility. The young cannot understand, nor the old explain, the underlying fears born of memories of insecurity: while real selfishness, thoughtlessness, and extravagance sometimes turns a natural difference of viewpoint into serious estrangement.

(iv) So-called *parental responsibilities* can emphasise yet further the distance between the generations. In the eyes of parents, experience is the only source of wisdom; on all questions of behaviour, personal relationships and responsibility, books, discussions, 'modern ideas', and the like are useless, and suspect. In part, the appeal to longer experience is a substitute for missed education, but it has some basis in fact: parents have seen how certain courses of action, certain types of behaviour, tend to work out. They cannot deny their own experience, or the urge to share it in the form of guidance with those who lack it. And experience seems to confer authority: 'living longer implies knowing more implies the right to rule the young.' The young, of course, see that the equation is false; but they rarely see behind it the desire to shield from evil, to avoid repetition of the parents' own unhappy mistakes—or the older person's fear of novelty and untried ways.

The desire to shield may become oppressive as over-protectiveness. It is as natural to want to shield the young from immorality as from falling downstairs, all the more so if the parents have guilty memories, or are themselves enduring an unhappy marriage. Absence of all protectiveness would leave the young vulnerable, exploitable‘

insecure. Logic may urge that 'the only consequence of saving people from the consequences of their folly is to fill the world with fools', but love answers, 'nevertheless, the young are ours, and we must save them, in spite of themselves'. It takes true insight, and self-control, to see eventually that to shield too long is to create the very weakness and immaturity that is feared. The only way to teach responsibility is to let the young carry it by making larger and larger decisions for themselves. George Lawton voices a familiar plea of the adolescent, 'Don't keep us young too long'. The one valid hallmark of parental success is to prepare the young to live well when parents are no longer there; it is a parent's duty, like a teacher's, to make himself superfluous.

Nevertheless, as parents know but the young rarely realise, the practical responsibilities of the family do fall ultimately upon parents, whatever independence the young pretend. The pregnant daughter cannot be abandoned; the peace and happiness of the parental home are destroyed after long years of building it together. The lad who falls foul of the law involves his parents, if not in paying the fine, still in facing the neighbours—and each other, in carrying the shame and disappointment, the anguish of heart and fear for the future, which no youthful scorn can comprehend. The sheer rowdiness and crowdedness of a 'home' no longer their own, as the young dispossess the parents of the home they planned and saved for, only to leave it in the end shabby and soiled, is part of the price parents pay for the freedom they afford the growing family. Yet it is a price the young cannot appreciate. And when foolishness, wildness, viciousness, result in accident, failure, unemployment, loss of health, or of capacity or sanity, it is the parental budget that must somehow meet the economic consequences.

To retort that parents need not, and ought not, to feel such responsibilities, because the young do not wish it but rather resent it, is to argue that the negligent, irresponsible parent is the best. And it merely shifts the obligation on to society at large—that is, on to other people's parents. The situation is not one to be shrugged off, nor changed by indignant repudiation: the attempt only widens the gap.

(v) All such sources of possible strain within the family-pattern, though inescapable are not—given patience and goodwill—insoluble. There are other sources of trouble that are not inherent, but can embitter relationships. Some arise from *the decay and souring of parental attitudes in themselves defensible*. The authority claimed for age sometimes deteriorates into bullying that goes beyond anything experience could justify, into an unreasoning, unyielding discipline that concedes no measure of self-decision or personal judgement to the child. Such parental tyranny becomes disastrous when reinforced by 'religious' claims and sanctions not self-evidently true to the child, and not supported by parental example and attractiveness. The 'authority of experience' is then but a hypocritical term for the blind collision of wills.

What originally was love, and a delight in being depended upon, can develop into possessiveness, possibly fed by a morbid anxiety, a too dramatic imagination picturing all the dreadful things that will go wrong once young people are out of their parents' sight. Or it may be merely selfish, a determination not to leave behind a stage the parents enjoyed, when the little one was helpless. Sometimes a mother dare not face the possibility of losing her dominant place with the children, lest she become no longer necessary to anyone. And often the parents cannot see the growing lad or girl, but only the baby that was: they cling to the pride that used to be, and miss the deeper pride they could enjoy in the developing personality and maturing character.

The parents' economic responsibility can change from wise provision to a threat wielded in anger, a sanction held over every command and prohibition—'So long as I pay for your food and clothes, you will do what you are told!' Strangely, after months of such distorted admission of obligation, parents can still feel deeply hurt when the young adopt the obvious course, setting up an independent room somewhere and 'living free'.

The natural gap in thought, opinion, and education can deepen into parental refusal to listen, understand, learn or communicate at all. It is a startling feature of modern homes that parents and children may rarely converse together, maintaining only such bare communication as living on the same premises makes necessary. All adolescent talk is treated with caustic contempt, gibes at what 'they' teach in school these days, sullen silence, or—'Shut up or get out, the telly's on!'

(vi) Yet other complicating and embittering factors can arise from *attitudes basically and originally wrong*. Jealousy can alienate parents from children: the mother jealous of the natural closeness of father and daughter, the father similarly jealous of mother and son. Father may become jealous of the place the children hold in the home and in the mother's affection. So sorry, and painful, a situation needs to be pointed out only with extreme care. Parents can be jealous, too, of youth's freedom, money, and opportunity; of the child's straying affection, when other figures begin to supplant the family; and of the authority which others outside the home begin to exercise—teacher, youth leader, minister, becoming the temporary hero of ardent, and tactless, hearts.

A parental sense of failure can mar confidence. The father's career-aspirations may not have succeeded as he hoped; the standard of the home may disappoint the mother as she realises that much of life is passing with her dreams unfulfilled. The marriage itself may be a secret, nagging disillusionment. Often a sense of imprisonment, of being bound by moral and family obligations, with little happiness, can fret the middle-aged. The coming of the children, with their incessant demands, their prior claims, their inhibiting of the parents' freedom, is felt as part of the total cause, and parents sometimes visit their personal disappointments on the children, often unconsciously. When the social ambition of the young people grows, and they are unwilling to bring their 'socially superior' friends home, the parents' failure is brought cruelly to the surface, and hearts, and relationships, grow sore indeed.

Moral shortcomings of the parents can of course place family harmony well-nigh out of reach. Opposite to the social ambitions of young people may be set the snobbery of parental insistence that their children shall outdo the neighbours' children in education, sport, beauty, income, education, level of friendships, and everything else; shall more than satisfy the neighbours' standards as to behaviour, deportment, dress and speech. Timid children merely endure the misery of endless comparison; stronger children, seeing the triviality and folly of the whole situation, over-react by deliberately outraging neighbourhood standards, courting scandal and rejection. That is their only means of protest, and usually parents can see this when it is firmly pointed out to them.

More serious moral failures of parents are another matter. The narrow, sex-starved, affection-starved, listless, mismanaging or spiteful mother, the drunken, selfish, vicious, bullying father, will see clearly all the actual faults of the young people and imagine faults not there. Nor is there much hope of telling them the truth, without risking the breakdown of family life altogether.

The wise and careful pastor, genuinely concerned and having a privileged intimacy with scores of families, can often help parents see themselves, understand why they are failing to get beside their children, and how they can 'become adults fit for a child to live with'. When the young people have shared their confidences with the pastor, his position can be very delicate, and his method of approach must be discreet, even devious. Yet few parents will resent a genuine interest in their own children's welfare, and many are grateful for help. The natural immediate response to any suggestion of failure on their part is self-defensive, or self-righteous; yet truth spoken kindly will bring about its own silent changes, and a better spirit eventually prevail.

(2) *The Child's Situation*

From the viewpoint of the younger members of the family, all is changed: 'the child sees the under side of every leaf'.

(i) *The basic situation* for the child is that of felt helplessness, expressed in fear, insecurity, the need of adults, and of constant attention. Hence arises the child's anxiety to conform, often remarked by teachers, the will to please adults by giving the expected answer, by appearing to behave in the required way, not simply to avoid trouble but because of constant dependence upon adult goodwill. Yet this dependent conformity clashes from the start with the natural and necessary self-assertiveness of the child, the need to command attention by tantrums, noise and if necessary ill-behaviour. Individuality consists in self-expression, which in the child's struggle with the unpredictable world of adults so often appears as stubborn self-will.

Thus the child lives at the mercy of the need to be loved, supported, admired and shielded, and the equal need to be independent, different, aggressive, rebellious. The small child will run away from parental control in great glee—and burst into tears if the parent turns his back. The growing girl will run out into the waves alone with courageous abandon, and in sudden panic howl like a baby again. The growing lad will edge along a tree branch, testing its strength, defying commands to come down—and suddenly squeal if abandoned to his wilfulness. Strong and well, he is a growing man of the world: hurt, or ill, and he retreats to his cradle! And sometimes the basic contradictory situation is further complicated by rivals—brothers, cousins, schoolmates—against whose claims he must assert his own need, and defeat before whom will make him sullen, feeling unwanted, rejected, and afraid.

(ii) *The changing situation* is mainly one of advancing strength, independence and skills, constantly pitted against others, intellectually, in sport, in music, dancing, dress, or—equally naturally—in gang activities and schoolboy fights. Personality grows only in confrontation of mind with mind, of emotion, imagination, will against those of others, and the girl no less than the boy widens experience, knowledge and self-confidence by continual competition and comparison. It is natural too that some of this self-identification by confrontation should occur at home: to pit oneself against those who 'belong' is both daring and yet safe—they will continue to belong. While to pit oneself against adults is triumph indeed, and also safe: they will remain one's parents, even if things go wrong!

At the same time the child's situation is extended as he ventures, or is taken, outside the home, to explore other homes strangely different from his own, to meet other adults, other children; and later to meet other codes of behaviour, other forms of discipline or indiscipline, other standards of pocket-money, holidays, clothes and freedom. This can evoke a new appreciation of privileges formerly assumed to be universal: oftener, it kindles criticism of things familiar, together with some confusion as the new, adventurous ways challenge past experience. For the first time the child begins to look critically at its own parents, and to wonder if others are kinder, more understanding, less strict, more generous. Self-assertion, wonder, bewilderment, criticism, are symptoms of developing childhood.

(iii) *The changing self* is the crux of this troublesome process towards maturity. Puberty is full of problems to be solved, yet it is wrong to treat adolescence as wholly difficult: it is also one of the most exciting and enjoyable experiences life offers. The ancient Greek picture, beloved of youth's mentors, of the charioteer struggling at the same time to urge forward and yet control his plunging steeds, does have within it the essential truth. Adolescence is a crisis of energy versus discipline; the emergence, from a hitherto largely passive and receptive personality, of self-generated drives, and the need to harness them constructively in the total pattern of living.

The new sexual drive is the most obvious and the most powerful of these disruptive forces. It is no less than the thrust of life itself towards yet another generation. It arrives earlier for the girl than for the boy, proceeds faster, and tends to dominate life more completely. Physical changes can be frightening, in the lad as in the girl, the more so as a totally new shyness can prevent the young from seeking explanation or help. The emotional changes are chaotic—a wholly new delight in strength and manliness, beauty and grace, wonder and gentleness, stirs the young heart; day-dreaming, vision, romance, music, poetry are evidence of a new dimension of inward experience that makes childhood seem silly. But at the same time the new awareness of sex is all too often associated with feelings of guilt and furtiveness; the contradiction is seen in strange alternations of mood, extremes of exhilaration and depression, such as only the young can measure.

In part, the sexual problem is natural: what to do with the sex interest and desire before marriage can channel its drive and joy into acceptable patterns. In part the problem is artificial, the confusing, contradictory, and hypocritical attitude of a society which alternately prohibits and exploits sexual talk, images, curiosity, satisfaction and enticements. In part, again, the problem is parental fear: on almost every other matter—health, education, money, dress—parents have enough to say; on this, aware of the dangers inherent in sex, themselves confused by society's changing standards, embarrassed, and on this subject inarticulate, they merely forbid, scold, and threaten, when the young lad or girl longs simply to understand, and be helped. Information sought secretly, and physical relief sought furtively, can engender intense self-loathing; the youngster feels morally helpless and in consequence ashamed, frightened by such proof of weakness and personal inadequacy.

The pastor and his colleagues have here an absolutely vital role, even if it be largely unconscious. Occasionally explicit teaching or counsel may be called for; much more influential will be the frank and healthy acceptance of sex and its manifold delights as part of divine creation, a joyous enrichment of human experience, something that a complete Christian life takes in its stride as a gift from God. The pastor will never avoid the subject, and never obtrude it: but by his sermon illustrations, his conversation, his obvious interest in the pairing-off of his young friends, and his own happy relationships, he will be constantly helping the young who silently observe and listen to see how sex fits in to a total Christian character. When approached, he will be ready with the explanations, illumination and perspectives that rob the whole subject of its furtiveness and fears, and enable the youngster to understand what is happening in himself; if ever a girl sought such help, common sense would require that reply would be made only in a group, and preferably a mixed one.

The new relationship-drive is so complicated by sex as to appear the same problem, though it expresses in fact a separate and even deeper need. Hitherto, the relationships which have formed so much of the child's experience have been *there*, provided for him. In adolescence, even these familiar relationships look different: the sexual relationship of one's own parents is a surprise, and brothers and sisters take on a new emotional significance. And beyond home, a whole circle of new relationships with very different kinds of people opens with dis-

E

concerting rapidity. The emerging personality longs to be accepted and admired. First, tentative, approaches to the opposite sex can be tormenting; the desire to be approved is crossed by the dread of being rebuffed, of proving inadequate: groups of boys looking askance at groups of girls, afraid to approach yet unwilling to ignore, illustrate the inward ambivalence. Some will impatiently over-compensate in bold, self-assertive, gauché aggression, unaware that such pretence at maturity is in fact failure to cope with immaturity. The longing to be accepted explains also the extreme sensitiveness of the young to any facial blemishes, malformation, defect of the senses, or physical awkwardness; the clumsy youth, all feet and hands, is pathetically grateful when someone points out that for the body to grow faster than skill in controlling it is perfectly natural, and temporary!

In time the young learn how to obtain, or to do without, approval at home, but face a new need to be accepted by teachers, employers, fellow students and others of the same age-group; a new set of required responses has to be learned, and since these new relation-ships are voluntary, and dispensable, the task of winning and holding acceptance is harder. For the gifted lad or girl, admiration comes readily, and the young scholar, musician, entertainer or sportsman is soon on the way to stardom, eager to conform and to outdo all rivals. Others, reacting against felt incapacity, become antagonistic to groups that reject them, and seek an inverted attention by refusing to conform, or adopting minority-patterns of behaviour that ensure notoriety. Others again, caught in the contradiction between what is required for approval at home and what is needed for approval outside the home, may develop a dual personality, their language, manner, conversation and appearance sharply changing once they are beyond home's observation.

Despairing of any happy relationships, the young may turn inward in self-isolating alienation, either competent and satisfying as with the great creative minds, or incompetent and self-pitying as with the morbidly introspective 'lone wolves' who pretend to despise the pack. It is no wonder that when some adolescent relationship is formed, with teachers, heroes, idols, it tends to be intense, all-or-nothing, and obsessive. The need for acceptance is often torturing, and the loss of it despair. The value of an alert Christian youth group is in this respect immeasurable. As the enquirer or young convert comes within range, the whole process of seeking acceptance and approval is lifted to a new plane—for the new friends are representative, and idealised. The standards must be high, the welcome sincere and sustained: short-lived notice and *bonhomie*, never carried forward into friendship, will merely repel and drive the newcomer in upon himself. Some pastoral training of the young Christians in the creation and function of group-relationships would well repay the pastor's efforts.

Complicating still further this turbulent time is *the new identity drive*. The child who by conflict and conformity has found his place, rights and duties within the family, finds as he moves beyond that close-knit circle that the process of finding his self-understanding must be repeated. He must discover anew his significance and status in a larger world, and find where he belongs in a society that has never before heard of him and cares little for him. 'Who am I?' becomes an insistent question only to be answered by 'Showing 'em' —asserting individuality, doing one's own thing, exploiting the new economic and personal freedom so as to claim notice, status, and a place in the world. Like the child, the adolescent needs to prove himself: that the method chosen is frequently non-conformist only underlines the strength of the need to do something startling to assert himself. It does not at all follow that the youngster is vicious or anti-social: he may be only 'a scared soul in search of a self' (J. I. Hamilton). Until he achieves an independent identity he cannot possess convictions or character. Second-hand opinions, however religious, and second-hand principles, however moral, are never genuine; nor is the weak, impressionable adolescent who lives by them ever safe.

Failing to find such self-identity may also drive a young person into a sheltering group of similar 'misfits', to find a substitute-identity through absolute conformity in talk, dress, appearance, behaviour, enthusiasms, clichés and emotions. The 'commune', 'movement', 'people' concept, with its crowd-originating mores, is for many the substitute for individual maturity and self-reliance, a confession of insufficiency in the difficult art of being oneself. Even a Christian youth group will have its positive, contributing members, gifted and thrustful, and its negative, dependent members, content to be led, happy to be in the company of more forceful, stimulating people whom they can trust. Here again the group may need to be taught to exercise this pastoral care, in containing, nourishing and protecting its temporarily weaker members.

Too little note is commonly taken of the fourth change in the growing self: *the new drive towards altruism*. The young child may have learned, laboriously, to share good things, be kind to pets and to poor or handicapped strangers, but it is an acquired virtue.

Adolescence very often brings an outburst of concern, social criticism, wide-ranging charity, and reforming zeal. Great unselfishness, generosity and compassion may reinforce the energy with which various causes are taken up, and the cynical assumption that it will be short-lived and superficial is by no means justified. The pastor or church which does not recognise and provide outlet for this phase of adolescent enthusiasm deserves to fail with youth; but the provision must be serious—temporary and needless tasks about the church just to keep them busy are insulting. Gospel and church have a true claim upon youth's time and gifts, but many young people feel more concern for practical ministries of social and compassionate nature, and the church should be ready, not to exploit but to advise and harness this wider altruism also. Nor should spare-time social activity alone be in view: a career of socially useful dedication in one of the innumerable caring agencies of modern society seeking workers of proved character and integrity, should be held before youth as a truly Christian vocation. If the pastor takes trouble to arm himself with information concerning training and career prospects, and is willing when necessary to intercede for the young with parents whose ambitions take little account of youth's idealism, he will earn the gratitude of many who find deep satisfaction in a life-work they might have missed.

With so much happening within the self and outside, it is hardly surprising that the adolescent is often confused, inconsistent, bewildered, moody, impulsive and unsure. The watchful, friendly pastor will find enduring reward as he introduces one after another to the living Christ, as One to identify with, love, lean upon and serve, and sees them discover that self-understanding, self-discipline, self-fulfilment and self-dedication which are the ingredients of maturity and the springs of happiness.

(iv) *The changing home* results in part from the mere passage of time: the small child among adults becomes the young adult among older adults; conversation and planning become co-operative; a pooling of varied interests, friendships and opinions enriches family life. Home itself begins to belong to the young—parts of it as their separate 'dens', all of it theirs to help organise. Additional pocket-money, occasional employment, scholastic grants, and later regular wages, remove the economic dependence which was a main argument for obedience. Things hitherto prohibited by cost now become possible without parental permission; when the young pay the insurance, and the fines, they can drive as fast as they wish! If home seems too repressive, one can always leave: though the young usually wish for only limited independence, enough to remove restrictions but not to forfeit the ultimate refuge and resources of home if the going gets rough.

With widening experience and relationships, something nearer friendship can spring up between daughter and mother, son and father. But also criticism. Unsuspected faults are discovered in parents and in home arrangements; to see father as weak and henpecked, mother as extravagant and foolish, the standards of honesty, purity, piety, demanded of the children betrayed by parents who 'appropriate' an employer's goods, read the sex magazines, drink heavily, excuse themselves from church loyalties, is a severe blow to any child. It is true that youthful criticism is merciless, demanding from adults a consistency which they themselves rarely show. But it often proceeds too alongside a struggle to be affectionate and loyal. It begins, usually, with a sense of being sadly let down, and only becomes hostile when parents resent, and refuse to discuss, what the young people say.

Inevitably criticism becomes challenge of what the elders believe, and pronounce to be right. Developing freedom naturally seeks to overthrow limits set by tradition, and differing adult standards in other homes justify the attempt. It is equally natural for the quickening mind to ask fundamental questions which the older generation has forgotten they ever asked, and to test what foundation or truth the accepted philosophy of life possesses. To resent such challenges as 'rebellious', 'ungrateful', or 'insolent disrespect', is stupidly to misread the situation, and the motive. It is true that youth sometimes hides its real need behind over-zealous contentiousness, and a delight in debate and quickness with words; youth tends, also, to ask its questions by means of very belligerent-sounding statements. Yet, these immaturities apart, to challenge is wholly natural and justified, and the only intelligent, indeed the only adult response, to a challenge is—to answer it.

The young have every right to know why adults believe and behave as they do, if adult standards are to be imposed upon them. And adults must be ready to explain, to share their experience and their thought, to face questions honestly and offer sincere replies. In the great majority of families with which pastors have to do, the young do not look for clever or infallible answers, but only the patience to listen and to answer as best parents can, with truthfulness. Affection makes up for a great lack of expertise! Often young people are grateful (though they would not say so!) for a firm and reasoned guideline, a clear limit of permission; to closest friends they will sometimes admit that parental firmness saves them from having to decide, when the pressures to do wrong are fierce. It is a safe, and yet face-saving refuge to pretend, 'I am quite willing to be wicked, but with my sort of parents it is not worth while.' Others of course are quite willing to accept responsibility for deciding, so long as parents are there to blame when the decision proves wrong—that is being young!

Christian parents are as prone as others to silence challenges with charges of stupidity or irreverence, and to demand more loudly an 'implicit' obedience, to cover their want of argument. Prone, too, to practise the emotional blackmail of tears and distress at so-called unappreciated love. Especially are second-generation Christians liable to this insensitiveness to enquiring youth—Christians who themselves live by a code they do not truly understand, and a creed they simply never thought about. For them, it is enough to remember godly parents whose faith and gracious living was sufficient justification for accepting the symbols of piety without question, but also without the deep experience of God that gave the symbols meaning. The third generation, in its turn, has no such memories to hallow the Christian tradition, only a shallow and second-hand, pedestrian religiousness in parents who cannot explain or defend what they never personally understood. The besetting weakness of a merely inherited, borrowed religion is precisely that it has nothing to hand on, nothing with which to kindle fire in other hearts. The pastor will often recall the stories of Jacob—and Ahaz.

The cosy philosophy of childhood, 'Mother, father, knows best', will not endure into adolescence. Without explanation and persuasion, commands, prohibitions, threats must provoke collision painful to both sides. Parents will think the young glory in defiance, though in fact they long to be at once responsible and approved: no normal lad or girl wants to be thought a 'problem'. One feature of such conflicts that can infuriate the young, is the triviality of the issues that parents choose to collide upon, hair styles, length of ribbon, tastes in music, chewing gum. Many stages that youth would rapidly grow through are given ridiculous importance by becoming battle-grounds where the young feel impelled to show their strength. Meanwhile, having lost all contact, reasonableness and friendship over pointless oppositions, parents feel hurt and outraged at their inability to discuss with their children the serious issues of sex, drink, faith, or dangerous friendships. 'Choose well your battlefield' is sound advice from all old campaigners.

In modern conditions, with widespread university education,

mobility of labour, urbanisation, the splitting of families, the readiness of business to exploit the affluence of youth, and the prevailing laxity of discipline, adulthood is thrust early upon young people. Going out to work, to university, or to city lodgings, can be as cataclysmic at seventeen as going to school without Mummy was at five. It demands real courage to grow up—and friendship, understanding, example, counsel, warning sometimes, and often reassurance and the faith to begin again. That is the pastor's opportunity.

The Pastor's Role

To understand, interpret, mediate, and help people understand each other, while contributing all he can by preaching, marriage guidance, and counsel towards creating Christian homes: these are obvious pastoral tasks. The pastor will insist, too, that if Christianity does not work at home, it is hypocritical to make large claims for it as the solution to the problems of society and the world. He will also find himself driven to defend youth, to protest vigorously against all the impatience that would declare the young to be useless, boring, a menace, irreverent, a danger to the premises—and all the rest. Such attitudes are to be proscribed within the church. Some young people may be troublesome, all need salvation; but wicked or winsome, youth is part of the church's stewardship for Christ, a golden investment in the future, each young mind and heart a pearl of great price worth the church's selling all else to purchase for Christ. Of that, the pastor must never let the church express a doubt.

In his own relationship with the young, the pastor's best rule will be to treat each individual as two or three years older than he is. Treat an adolescent as a child, and he will react childishly, petulant, wilful, sulky. Treat him as an adult, needing to discuss and decide for himself, and he will surprise you (and himself) with his sudden maturity. The pastor's faith assumes from the outset the value, freedom, responsibility, and divine purpose, enshrined in every individual; the church is a fellowship in which that assumption inspires a unique care for every one within reach. Herein any young life may find acceptance, identity, ideals, a cause, and a Master whom to know is to love, and to love is to serve in perfect and passionate freedom.

The pastor, and the youth leader, must be aware that something of youth's enthusiasm will overflow upon themselves. Young people whose homes and parents are unsatisfying will seek eagerly for substitutes, and leading figures within the fellowship will be idealised and made objects of a somewhat jealous loyalty, while it will sometimes be difficult to get the young off the church premises and on their way 'home'. Such clinging to that which represents their new-found faith is not unhealthy, if handled aright, and it can be a great help towards steadfast character. But there are obvious dangers. Those liable to this intense attachment must be very carefully chosen: sexual and other serious implications are plainly possible. Moreover no one is immune from the subtle flattery involved in becoming a young soul's 'spiritual hero'; but to indulge it is childish.

Responsibility towards parents requires that the young be pointed back towards home as the first place to show Christian loyalty and obedience; (if the pastor finds himself unwilling to do this, he would do well to examine very carefully his own motives). Simple common sense and self-knowledge should warn against allowing young people to suppose that one is infallible, perfect, blameless, or unusually wise, and the young's deprecating flatteries must be firmly rejected. They must grow up in the real world, and learn that *all* adults are good and bad, strong and weak, inconsistent, fallible and discourageable. The stern, black-and-white, non-compromising attitude of the young must give place to balanced and realistic judgements. To play upon their perfectionist idealism in order to minister to one's own pride, even by implication in one's criticism of others ('less spiritual, less consecrated pastors . . . That sort of church knows no better . . .') is unforgivable: it merely prepares for further disillusionment as they discover the feet of clay.

In any case, the young Christians must learn to get along without idols. The word of Jesus to the 'rich young ruler', whatever it meant originally, must be our word to young people in search of perfection: 'there is but one good, that is God'. To centre adolescent faith on the supreme father-figure of God revealed in Christ is to build securely in a disappointing world and an imperfect church.

So very urgent is youth's need of help, whether confessed or not, that the frank, approachable and understanding pastor who treats young people as his equals, will never lack clients, confidants, or converts. If among young people he finds his deepest anxieties and disappointments, yet it is also among young people he will find his most rewarding successes, his most lasting fruitfulness, and his most precious trophies of grace.

11 YOUNG PEOPLE IN DIFFICULTIES

Every pastor knows that the possibilities involved in ministry among young people are incalculable. Whole lives may be shaped in half-an-hour's talk; life-long friendships may be formed—the young feel their problems keenly, and rarely forget even the most halting attempts truly to sympathise and assist. The pastor himself finds stimulus in rethinking with younger minds the Christian answer to new questions. When the cosy reverence afforded to his every word by older Christians becomes a little stuffy and unhealthy, the fresh wind of youth's frankness, originality, and lack of false respect can bring a renewing draught to his soul.

It will often become evident that the years that separate the pastor, or the youth leader, from adolescents are both a barrier and a great advantage. He will remember that the barrier seems higher from youth's side than from his own, and that it is not to be broken through by any special techniques of approach. Nor by presuming upon authority or respect due to additional years—in youth's eyes a handicap and not an asset; nor certainly by pretending to be younger, and adopting attitudes, behaving, speaking, in imitation of adolescents. That brings only ridicule. Genuine friendship, true understanding, born of sympathy and the wish to help, count for far more; and the only training is patient listening, watching, analysing, and *respecting* youth. Given these, the difference of age becomes no longer an obstacle, and its advantage appears. As George Eliot said: 'The middle-aged, who have lived through their strongest emotions, but are yet in the time when memory is still half passionate, should be a sort of natural priesthood, whom life has disciplined and consecrated to be the refuge and the rescue of early stumblers and victims of despair.'

Not all young people get into trouble that they cannot perfectly well handle for themselves: wise is the pastor who knows when not to help, but to let the lad, the girl, face the music, resolve the mess, and grow in character in so doing. For him then to be approachable, accessible, and helpful if needed, may be all youth requires. But as with a doctor, so with a pastor, the closest relationships often spring out of emergencies faced together. In addition to 'parent-trouble', three situations may be taken as typical.

(1) *The Young Agnostic*

The need that each new convert be led to fresh personal discovery, and not merely indoctrinated with inherited attitudes, implies a renewed Christian dialogue with each new generation. As we have seen, it is healthy, right, and promising for the maturing young to challenge, question and investigate: wherever the spiritual dialogue is not initiated by parents, pastors or teachers, it will be introduced by the young for themselves. Where it is resisted, ridiculed, ignored, the young will turn to flat denial and rejection—if only to command attention.

The less articulate may show their rejection in rebellion, temper, scorn, outrageously challenging behaviour; the more articulate on their part may be rationalising sexual or home problems, inadequacy, lack of identity, and the rest—the heat of the argument will usually betray a more than intellectual interest in its outcome. The inarticulate protest, and the intellectualist smoke-screen, are alike cries for help, equally requiring sympathetic understanding.

Articulateness can sometimes be mistaken, by the young student himself and by his listeners, for maturity; and quick intelligence can occasionally make the lad or girl feel less socially secure and less emotionally stable than the more stolid, silent, type. Airing advanced ideas is not adulthood, and facility with words, theories and contemporary opinions, often changed overnight, may conceal a retarded wisdom, compared with that of other young people, whose experience of work and the ways of the world is wider than the classroom. The point which the pastor must remember here is that however self-possessed the young disputant may sound, he is facing the same problems of growing up that afflict other young people— that the religious challenge is probably disturbing him in areas already over-sensitive.

The whole problem of finding self-identity in the broadening experience of society is sharpened by the demand for religious decision and commitment, and by religion's stress upon personal responsibility. The problem of group-relationships is sharpened by the social nature of religion and the need to 'join-up'—a requirement that can be of immense help to some, but frightening to others. The stress of religion upon personal guilt and forgiveness, often expressed in contexts which touch upon sexual sensitiveness, complicates that problem also, and not always helpfully. Religious hero-worship sometimes only rebukes a felt personal inadequacy; as the claim to spiritual authority challenges sorely the growing sense of freedom and self-affirmation.

In an intellectual climate of change, of challenge towards all inherited ideas, modern young people must be expected to rationalise many of their natural 'growing pains' into intellectual posers that make Christian beliefs 'preposterous and incredible'. That the young agnostic fledgling, trying his intellectual wings, trots out as brilliant discoveries some of the most trivial and hackneyed 'arguments' borrowed from a few fashionable publicists, professional or political agnostics, or war-embittered poets, may give the pastor opportunity for clever and caustic replies: but it is vital to remember that the arguments are not trivial nor hackneyed to the speaker, nor are they the real point. Special care is needed where professed intellectual difficulties are merely the temporary form of seething revolt against uncomprehending authoritarianism imposed by repressively religious parents, to whom all free enquiry is 'blasphemy' and all genuine seeking for ethical explanation seems like 'wilful trampling upon all morality and decency'. A better understanding of the parents' experience and fears will be much more useful than theoretic debate about theistic philosophy.

Professed agnosticism can of course sometimes be a defence against conscience or fear aroused by actual wrong done. Sinners can run away from spiritual conviction into intellectual contradictoriness at any age. On the other hand, the intellectual problems may be perfectly genuine. An infallible, inspired book written two thousand years ago, before the revelations of modern science dawned upon the world, does take some believing. A college chaplain reports a widespread feeling among adolescents that religion is a subjective, intuitive and private emotional experience; that God may well be different for different 'observers', and that morality is a matter of personal taste and conviction, like aesthetics. That position is not Christian, but it merits reply, not scorn.

In general, the pastor's aim with the young agnostic is to keep the dialogue going. He must have confidence in the power of truth to win its own victories, provided no false pressures of dogma provoke rejection, and provided both sides of the dialogue are conducted with respect and honesty. Dialogue implies that in turn each side *listens*— and some pastors find it impossible to listen to young people. 'Father,' said one seventeen-year-old to a Protestant minister, 'you are the first man older than me who has ever listened to me in all my life'—and justified the assertion. It is sometimes suggested that in dialogue with young people, the Christian leader should never do more than one third of the talking.

Respect should not be difficult for the pastor aware of youth's frequent concern for justice and compassion. Honesty should be native to the Christian: but sometimes the middle-aged forget the questions that once deeply troubled their own minds, and become inured to the awful contradiction between the suffering of the world and the love of God, which youth feels with passionate intensity. *That* problem it would be unchristian to brush aside. Young minds are often troubled, too, at the lack of fully rational, conclusive proofs of the existence of God, at many of the stories and ideas in the Bible, at some of the episodes in church history. The honest apologist will not pretend to prove the unprovable, or to defend the indefensible, to press acceptance for tradition's sake, or represent everything in Christendom as worthy of Christ. On the other hand the pastor will require equal honesty from the young, as they assert sweeping generalisations and draw far-reaching conclusions from selective evidence, and as they seek to rest upon mere doubts and denials. If the Christian explanation of life be untrue, the Christian standards of value illusory—that in itself is no sufficient philosophy of life: some better explanation and standard must be discovered, and subjected to the same rigorous logical analysis and historical tests. The young agnostic may fairly be asked what he *does* believe, and *why*, and how it helps him to explain, and to endure, suffering, war, injustice, evil, and mortality.

Fear of insecurity can lead young minds to retreat into fanatical dogmatism, satisfied with mystical, emotional, subjective 'experiences', refusing all uncertainty, all unwelcome facts, suspecting all careful explanations as special pleading, and all honest suspension of judgement as hypocrisy. Often, a closed mind on religious questions exists alongside high intellectual ability in other spheres—the mind split into compartments, no 'worldly' science or logic being allowed to disturb the fundamental religious tradition, tenaciously but irrationally clung to as 'beyond discussion'. The pastor will recognise that the underlying insecurity is a more serious problem here than the intellectual formulation of it. Allied to it is the aggressive, all-or-nothing response of youth to moral issues, rejecting all compromise, defining all questions in black and white, insisting upon total loyalty to every principle, in all circumstances, by all Christians, at whatever cost. The practical best in given tortuous circumstances seems to the ardent young simple betrayal, and the cruelty of their inflexible demands upon other Christians, in tragic circumstances or with deprived backgrounds, is quite unconscious. The pastor's patience will be sorely tried as he strives to lead to more mature and understanding attitudes; but he must do so, for intellectual and moral dogmatism is perilously vulnerable, as experience of the real world assaults such romanticism.

Unfortunately, the pastor (and the evangelist) may succumb to the temptation to exploit youth's dogmatism and call it conversion; to play up to youth's uncompromising idealism, and call it consecration. The pastor can become equally dogmatic, hiding his own misgivings by still more emphatic assertion, because he knows that some of his young people will respond, and will rally to defend him. Such a man will greatly enjoy his 'success with young people', but he will carry heavy responsibility for middle-age breakdowns when the harsh truths and uncertainties of wider experience find Christians unequipped for honest faith and courageous endurance.

Dialogue with young challengers will probably prove most profitable if (i) the pastor encourages the careful expression and thorough analysis of the young person's own opinions and questions. Within a group, or alone, this frequently leads further than positive assertions of Christian truth. Half-examined objections and theories, when pursued and fully understood, so often leave the real questions unresolved: when this is clear, the Christian answer may then be suggested, tentatively, as at least one possible solution. (ii) The discussion will get furthest if the pastor insists upon keeping it to vital issues concerning Christ, Christian ideals, the Christian interpretation of life, refusing to discuss Jonah, Cain's wife, or the plagues of Egypt, as not entirely central to Christian discipleship, nor really the concern of people who have not yet faced up to Jesus.

(iii) In the same way, the wise pastor will keep the discussion firmly on the ground, by acknowledging that intellectual theorising is a pleasant pastime, but not the real issue: the state of society, the real church and its varied ministry, history, the facts of human progress, character, suffering, mortality, the truth of his own experience and testimony—these are the material for debate, not fine-spun webs of words on which unwary intellectual gadflies get caught and their integrity devoured. (iv) The determination to avoid dogmatism, to keep the dialogue open, to avoid pressing for premature agreement in order to leave room for slow change of mind, does not at all mean that the pastor is not quietly, humbly confident of the things he does know. That he limits his certainty to a few central truths, admitting there is much he does not know, will make his confidence all the more persuasive. But all the while, his own assurance that Christ is unique, unrivalled, and unchallengeable; that two thousand years of Christian testimony are not going to be overthrown by a facile and superficial fashion like agnosticism; and that truth is invincible and shall prevail, will reinforce his patience, and—if he does his work sincerely and well—leave his young hearers envious. And envy is so often the first step towards faith.

(2) *The Young Offender*

Young people watch as well as listen. The real influence of pastor or youth leader will often be determined by his action—or inaction— when young church members, adherents, or the children of church families get into trouble with the law, or with school authorities. The pastor who withdraws all interest because some young person has been caught stealing, drunk, breaking into premises, or borrowing a car, need not expect *his other young people* to take much notice henceforth of his expositions of redemptive love. They will silently assess his real attitudes, and draw their own conclusions.

Yet the pastor has to bear in mind his threefold role. He is a citizen, bound to uphold the law and the rules of society, to aid the police, to give evidence when required, even to report offences or share guilt as an accessory to law-breaking. If Christians do not defend order in society, who will? If on supposed conscientious grounds the Christian leader declines to support law, he cannot complain when others, for their own reasons, follow his example. The pastor is also friend, shield, spokesman, for the offender, 'staying with' him when all others desert him. This must not imply pretence, manufacturing excuses, laying blame elsewhere, whitewashing offences, or in any way weakening the individual's responsibility. The Christian attitude to the wrong done must be clear: but Christian goodwill to the wrongdoer must not be in doubt either. The pastor neither condones the offence nor condemns the offender: his attitude is wholly positive and redemptive. But the pastor is yet again the spokesman of a Christian community, upholding within the church the higher-than-average standards of Christian behaviour, without casting out those who fall short, or making their position in the fellowship intolerable. He must not weaken the conscience of the group, provide excuse for others to relax standards, treat offences lightly, or misrepresent the facts—as by insisting on 'the good character' of someone just convicted of public wrong. For the sake of younger members especially, he must be frank, clear, and generous. He will do best, in almost every case, to take the members of the fellowship deliberately into his confidence, sharing his sorrow and regret with them, and explicitly *assuming* their co-operation and their prayers in seeking to restore the situation.

To 'restore the situation' is the essence of the pastor's purpose. The first need will be for his presence, in the home, in court, with the family, attending any enquiry if allowed to do so, and being at home with them afterwards. In all this he may be officially silent, when he has no useful evidence or testimony to contribute: but his presence will give countenance and moral support, will sometimes prevent angry recriminations, and help to assure everyone that this trouble is not the end of the world. Sometimes, the pastor's standing by the young offender will shame the parents into doing likewise. Meanwhile, observing, listening, gently leading conversations, he will be forming his own interpretation as to the real causes, the personal or family inadequacies, the weaknesses of character or training, the hidden resentments, that explain the whole event, and the possible steps towards better relationships and better behaviour.

But when the public proceedings are over, the pastor will make opportunity, perhaps without revealing his purpose, for counselling interviews with those closely affected. Where family relationship is already close, and the regret of offender and parent is shared, he may interview both together, simply to offer reassurance, friendship, a sense of proportion, and prayer. More often in such cases, group counselling may be hazardous; a family quarrel may get out of hand and preclude further assistance. Usually the offender, and the parents, both need help to understand themselves and each other, and this necessitates separate interviews.

(i) *Interviewing the Offender* should come first—it will seem much fairer to the young mind to be heard first! As the delinquent finds himself confronted by the pastor, he will probably be wary, sullen, suspicious, perhaps defiant, though either attitude can equally well be a disguise for deep regret, anger with himself, or shame. The pastor's cool acceptance that such things happen is always helpful. A relaxed atmosphere, a genuine friendliness, in which the fact of the offence is at once brought into the open, may have unexpected results. The pastor's 'Well, you seem to be in a spot: care to tell me how you got yourself there? Not quite your style, I would have thought—what happened exactly?' may well be the very first time that *anyone* has asked for his own view of the matter in that spirit.

When others are blamed for unkindness, or harsh judgements are resented, such comment as 'Well, I can see why they felt like that,

but they need not have said so . . . Yes, I guess that would make you
sore!' will encourage confidence without committing the pastor to
agreement. As always, the pastor will listen and watch for what is
only hinted at, or concealed, or spoken too emphatically, or needlessly
repeated, trying to assess attitudes, fears, tensions of which the
offender himself is only dimly aware.

Three intentions will guide the interview: (a) to probe underlying
causes of such behaviour, to discover what need, inadequacy,
frustration, the wrongdoing was expected to resolve. Was it shortage
of money, insufficient status in the group, anger at some injustice,
the need for attention, boredom, over-compensation for some
conscious lack? If such can be brought to light, the better responses
that are possible to such problems usually emerge of themselves. The
lad or girl may find in such new self-understanding a sense of relief
so great that character is redirected there and then.

(b) But the offender will need also to be helped to accept the
consequences of wrongdoing without whining, self-pity or bitterness.
He must be led to see for himself that parents, school, society,
church, could not do otherwise than disapprove: admitting so much
can take most of the sting from punishment—'Well, their frowns
wont break your heart—unless you let them! It's up to you to show
them, patiently, that you disapprove of it now, also.' The pastor can
help greatly by undertaking to intercede with parents, employers,
the group, lending the weight of his own status and authority to
support the retracing of steps. More delicate may be the undertaking
to help a girl-friend, or a boy-friend, to see things more fairly and
react more gently. The pastor may privately think that a break in
such a friendship may be wiser for the girl or boy, but he may ask for
that to be postponed a little, for the offender's sake.

(c) The pastor will have suggestions to make about more positive
reactions to the whole experience. He will not crudely draw moral
lessons, but he will leave in the young mind suggestions how a surer
faith, a clearer decision for Christian discipleship, a better circle of
friends, fuller and more rewarding interests, would help avoid
repeating mistakes. He will try, too, to win from the experience a
better understanding of home, parents, the family circumstances and
attitudes. Very occasionally he may even advise leaving a wholly
unsatisfactory home and starting afresh. The main need is to
encourage a definite and positive practical reaction to the experience
—no mere verbal formula of regret and emotional revulsion, but a
reorganising of time and relationships, a clear recognition of better
levels of experience to be explored.

(ii) *Interviewing the Parents* may well be more difficult. Parents of young people in trouble seek a pastor's help for very varied reasons—in need of comfort, to justify themselves, to seek support in taking revenge on the offender, to pull strings in order to minimise punishment or costs, to lend countenance to get them out of neighbourhood disgrace, or even to blame the pastor and the church for not preventing the trouble in the first place.

When the prime need is for comfort and support, the pastor obviously will seek, so far as truth allows, to show that the trouble is not so serious as it feels, that the lad or girl is not so wrong as this episode might suggest, that the attitude of others whose judgement matters at all is more of sympathy, and perhaps confusion, than of condemnation. He will assure them of his continued friendship for the offender, and share with them his own reflections on the underlying causes and attitudes. Often he can explain the event, the working of the young mind, in ways the parents have been too upset to understand, and without breaking confidence he can describe the hom as the son or daughter sees it—'I have often found that where the home . . .'. From his more objective viewpoint he will urge the parents neither to exaggerate the significance of what has happened, nor to miss its revelation of some need to revise attitudes and patterns of life.

When the parents' real anxiety is to justify themselves, blame others, or evade the consequences of their own neglect or harshness, the pastor will need all his skill and tolerance. He must remember that even bad parents can be frightened, upset, inwardly ashamed: yet unless they realise their share in producing the trouble, improvement is unlikely. As all the blame is heaped upon the young head—'He has always been ungrateful, selfish, thoughtless, bad tempered . . .' it is tempting (and occasionally may be necessary) to stem the abuse by hinting that character is never purely accidental and enquiring what made him so, and who he takes after. As blame is heaped on school, employers, neighbour's children, bad friends, the pastor may long to point out that of course *they* will look on the episode the other way round! It is usually best simply to listen, letting the parents talk themselves out, sometimes to talk themselves into self-revelation. To defend, challenge or argue may relieve the pastor's feelings but could make further progress impossible.

In trying to present their hurt, anger, bitterness, in some respectable form, parents may begin to see themselves in the pastor's eyes. A question or two—'Who is this friend—has he been in trouble?'—'Did the school report suggest any warnings of bad behaviour?' will sometimes cool the atmosphere and get complaints into perspective. Or the pastor may proceed, 'Well, things like this do not happen out of the blue, if he is happy and things going well. Why do *you* think he broke out in this way? Has there been any change recently in circumstances or plans, or in his manner? Has he been disappointed in any way?' If the parents are altogether sure of themselves and of their own innocence, the pastor may get somewhere by asking, 'Then what precisely do you want of me, if all is well and as it should be?' Sometimes, when all is talked out, it is possible silently to dismiss every point made with 'Well this seems a purely exceptional business, a mere mistake, impulsive and out of character. If all you say is true, he will not do it again. The sooner it is forgotten the better'—which may produce unexpected penitence.

The pastor will listen and watch alertly for any talking at each other, for conflicts between the parents or within them, or between them and the child. Difference of viewpoint, and varying anxiety, between father and mother is natural, but basic disagreements should be brought into the open, and their effect upon the child discussed. Assume always that the parents intend to stand by their lad or girl— if they refuse, it may be best to say firmly that in that case you cannot help them. Enable them to feel the inner distress the delinquent is experiencing, and the still greater need, now, for their trust and acceptance, though the young person's manner may not suggest it. Where definite complaint against the parents has come to light, it is well to expose real situations, for parents often create their own problems quite unconsciously. If a lad is merely forbidden to bring a girl home, without explanation, the parents are *inviting* secretiveness and deceit; to let him do as he asks will at the least enable him to see her against his own home background, and assure him of his parents' genuine interest in his welfare. If he cannot have friends in, of course he will be 'out every night some-where or other, never at home'. If all his friends, interests, hobbies are continually criticised, of course he will 'never tell them what he is doing'.

It is not often that any 'follow up' ministry can help in problems of domestic relationship. It is better to express continuing interest, and willingness to help as needed, but to make clear that parents will best know how to understand and support their own children—and children have to learn to understand and appreciate their own parents. The longer that either parents or young people look to a third party for help, the longer the difficulties will last. The sooner his counsel is superfluous, the more successful the pastor has been.

(3) *The Pregnant Girl*

The 'unattached' girl who becomes pregnant presents a different pastoral problem from that of the intended bride in the same position. Some pastors recoil with strong distaste from the deserted or promiscuous girl who is 'in trouble' through 'immorality'. The first need therefore is that the pastor analyse his own reaction to this all too frequent situation, in the light of the gospel, before individual cases, perhaps involving people he knows, can arise to cloud his judgement. What has been said of the pastor's duty to the Christian fellowship and to other young people applies here also; he must maintain the highest standards of Christian behaviour and excuse or condone no wrongdoing. Here also, if the situation is known in the Christian group, he would do well to make opportunity, without making specific reference to the case, to illustrate the Christian attitude to such problems, letting the young people perceive for themselves the relevance of the insights he shares with them to the current instance.

In reaching those insights, and in explaining them, the pastor will remember the very great significance of such a girl's turning to the church of Christ for help and friendship. In itself, that constitutes a claim upon care, responsibility and compassion. He will hardly forget the attitude of Jesus to the woman of the city and the woman taken in adultery, and the prohibition Jesus laid down against all judgement of our fellows. Condemnation is unchristian: Christ Himself came not to condemn but to save; condemnation is too late, once the evil has been committed, and it will preclude all attempt at redemptive good. Such considerations leave little doubt that the Christian reaction must be positive, practical, evangelical, condoning nothing but condemning no one.

What the pastor can do may depend very much on what it is the girl seeks from him. His cool acceptance of the situation as neither hopeless nor the end of all happiness and joy, and his evident readiness to befriend without judgement or inquisition, may well in itself bring new hope and courage to a distressed, despairing heart. But sometimes the girl hopes for advice and support in fixing responsibility and obtaining financial assistance. *This calls for the utmost caution*. One obvious danger is that usually only the girl's word is available for evidence of paternity; and however well the pastor thinks he knows the girl, however sure he is that her story is true, he cannot *know* this fact with legal certainty. He should always refuse to act in this direction, unless strong independent testimony (for example the father's admission) is forthcoming—and then he would do well simply to introduce the girl to a reliable legal adviser.

But he must warn the girl that nothing may be gained from such a course, even if the verdict were in her favour. She cannot hope to find happiness in a legally enforced marriage, even if such were possible. It is extremely difficult to compel payment of maintenance from an unwilling or protesting father; while in the course of legal proceedings not only will the whole story be made public to her own great embarrassment, but damaging countercharges may be made against her character, to which no adequate defence before public opinion is ever possible. Where such publicity is invited, and where supporting payments are received, the effect of the whole event on any possible future marriage to someone else must be remembered. On the whole, therefore, the pastor will probably counsel that (except where there is a voluntary agreement to maintain the child, duly undertaken in legal form) an unfortunate situation will only be made worse by litigation. The girl will be well advised to accept the unfairness that leaves her to face alone the consequences of joint misdoing, to preserve her personal dignity, and to give her attention instead to planning with intelligence and courage what she has to do.

The alternatives are abortion, acceptance, or adoption. The pastor will need to have read and considered carefully the ethical issues involved in abortion, which are by no means simple. Merely to name the different possible situations—abortion after rape, abortion where life or sanity is endangered, abortion where the mother is plainly too young to nurture a child, abortion for selfish, economic, family, or career reasons, abortion to conceal misconduct—is to indicate how complex are the judgements required. Sometimes the child is scarcely considered at all, except as the nuisance to be got rid of; at other times it is the child's own most probable destiny that prompts the wish for abortion. The pastor should have reached some working conclusions for his own counselling, and should know what the law requires, or forbids, before offering advice. He will insist that he can speak only as a Christian from the viewpoint of conscience, avoiding all comment on the serious medical issues that only the girl's doctor will understand. Whatever his own position on the question, the pastor will warn the girl that a price has to be paid for abortion, in emotional and spiritual reaction afterwards. Facing the fear and distress of bearing the child, she may feel that abortion is the easy solution; she must remember that afterwards she will feel very differently about what she has done, and must be prepared to live with her decision for the years ahead.

Where age and circumstances permit, the pastor will probably feel that the most Christian reaction to a difficult situation is for the coming child to be accepted, not as a punishment or 'consequence' of ill-doing, but as an individual in its own right, with its own claim to love, welfare and happiness—and much love and happiness to confer. To face responsibility without running away, to respond with deliberate intention to bring good out of evil, is to redeem the situation by using it well. There will be need to weigh carefully the practical problems that must arise: the available financial resources or assistance; where mother and child may live; how to work and yet care for the child; the parents' attitude and co-operation; whether the girl's sense of doing what is right will sustain her through the years in face of all the questions that will have to be answered from time to time. In this solution also, the long view must be kept in mind. The growing child will limit freedom, hamper employment opportunities, possibly affect future prospects of marriage. On the other hand the child will bring its own affection, joy and deep satisfaction. Nor will the pastor hesitate to promise that though God does not always make the right path easy, He always makes it possible, walks it with us, and sees us through.

Adoption may ensure better care and opportunity for the child, where the mother is very young, her resources are limited, or her family refuses co-operation. It may therefore be the most responsible provision the mother can make, accepting the loss to herself for the sake of the child; or it may be an easy evasion of all responsibility— passing it to those willing to accept it. Even when he regrets the motive, however, the pastor may conclude that adoption offers better hope that the child will be cared for. The pastor will have available the necessary information about legal formalities and reputable adoption agencies who may be consulted; but he will warn that— apart from temporary fostering-arrangements while the mother regains her strength—adoption must be all or nothing. The distraught young girl so often imagines that she can ensure the child's welfare by handing it to adoptive parents, while retaining for herself some claim, some opportunity for contact, and some future option to change her mind. It is essential to insist that this cannot be. For the child's sake, and for the adoptive parents' sake, there can be no compromise. Adoption means relinquishing the child, and that can mean heartache in after years, if the mother regrets, but cannot undo, her decision.

In every case an experienced pastor will advise that no decision on adoption be taken until at least three months after the baby's birth.

Wise foresight is extremely difficult under the pressure of the last months of pregnancy. At that time, for most girls, the *birth* is all they can think of: within an hour of the event, the *baby* is everything. Once the 'emergency' is past, and the baby is held, tended, and worshipped, all looks very different. A mother's response to her own child is something natural, instinctive, essential to womanhood, old as the race, powerful beyond any young girl's understanding—until it happens. When the time comes, the young mother may find she cannot possibly part with the child which the young mother-to-be was certain she could never possibly keep or care for. Trying to make her foresee this, the pastor will probably suggest that tentative contacts be made with an adoption society, but that final decision be deferred until calmer months ahead.

Whatever the solution chosen, the pastor will promise continued support, friendship and counsel for a girl whose spiritual need will not disappear when the practical problems are resolved. But such after-care is not a task for him or for his wife alone, but for some kindly, motherly Christian soul within the fellowship, whose own children and grandchildren are too far away to be enjoyed, and who will take mother and babe into her heart, for Christ's sake and the church's. The pastor will seek permission to explain, introduce, inaugurate the friendship, and retire into the background, until mother and child can be welcomed into the church's fellowship and care exactly as any other family might be.

Frequently during his ministry among young people the pastor will have occasion to remember the moving words of Mark concerning Jesus and the young ruler of the synagogue: 'Jesus, looking upon him, loved him.' His own heart will kindle with a like affection and joy over many who respond to his counsel with wholehearted eagerness. Even where the outcome is not all that he would desire, he will feel inexpressibly grateful for opportunity to show that love of Christ to troubled youth, and at least to give them the chance to know the young Prince of glory, the incomparable Lord and Leader of the young in all generations.

12 MARITAL SITUATIONS

It is well for the pastor not to over-estimate his powers in marriage repair. So long as marriage was regarded as a quasi-religious relationship, many strained unions were held together by religious feeling, and where external help was sought at all, it was natural to turn to the Christian pastor. The secularisation of marriage has removed both this bond and this relief. However willing he may be to help, it is difficult to see what the pastor can offer, other than his unusually wide experience of human relationships, to mend a deliberately non-Christian marriage. Most who turn to him will consider their mutual vows 'sacred', and he will often find himself doing, belatedly, what should have been done in pre-marital counselling—or repeating what was then suggested.

Probably the first and most important principle to grasp in this area of need is that there are no typical marriage problems. All individuals are different, all relationships vary, there are infinite permutations in the many elements that contribute to marital unhappiness. The cardinal error is to identify a 'case' as a 'typical example' of something or other, and lose sight of the persons involved, with their unique background, their individual character, and their very personal disappointment. Nevertheless it is necessary to identify some of the more frequent contributory factors in disturbed marital situations, whether personal failings or merely 'organisational' problems, always remembering that every instance is different, and every situation, however familiar to the pastor, is new and tragic to the people concerned.

Ingredients of Unhappiness

Among the more common personal difficulties are:

(i) *The invasion of revised moral standards*. There is little doubt that some marriages suffer from comparison with the sexual freedoms practised by many contemporaries. In the first excitement of engagement and wedding, the exclusive, lifelong nature of Christian marriage may well have been taken for granted; alternative liaisons were simply not in mind, or ever intended to be. After seven years or so, when the responsibilities of marriage have overtaken the excitements, those Christian standards may not seem nearly so obvious—except to the committed Christian. Envy of the freedom of other men and women may prompt attempts to revise the basis of marriage to allow one or both parties to seek fresh excitements elsewhere. The protest that this was not the quality of marriage originally promised may be dismissed as 'mere possessive jealousy', and talk of sacred vows as out of date and superstitious. The aggrieved partner may retaliate in kind, or be compelled to see a dream dissolve, and accept the mutability of human character.

It may not change much to help the betrayed partner to see how tenuous was the moral basis of the marriage from the start, in half-understood, half-intended moral loyalties, though it may remove some of the bitterness and self-reproach. The pastor can often advise on the protection of the deserted partner, and any children, from the practical difficulties that arise: there is no Christian reason why one who forswears a solemn and voluntary oath should escape all consequences and responsibilities. If opportunity offers, the pastor will strive to present an objective view of what has been done, in the hope that the erring partner may repent. He may also advise separation (as Paul did in somewhat similar situations at Corinth), though he will probably urge that the hurt mind shall not be permanently closed against all possibility of reconciliation. But if renewal of the marriage should ever prove possible, the pastor will strive to see that a better foundation is laid in a full agreement as to what true marriage entails, and what promises are being made. Even when no repair of the situation seems possible, the enormous value of just listening, supporting, comforting the deserted husband or wife must not be under-estimated. To be able to unburden a very sore heart, without meeting criticism or condemnation, and without fear of breaking confidence, to someone trusted and respected, has immeasurable therapeutic value, and by itself can mean the difference between moral and spiritual breakdown, and the regaining of dignity, confidence and courage.

(ii) *Disappointment in each other*, or of one partner in the other, is often due either to the superficial way in which the marriage began, or to unfulfilled 'role expectations'. Unquestionably the sexual-romantic basis of many modern marriages, with its foolish talk of 'falling' in love, of compulsive fate or fortune—marriages founded upon nothing more permanent than boyish charm and girlish ways, or upon more crudely sexual characteristics in a fantasy-world of over-emotional heroes and heroines—merely stores up inevitable disappointment as the practical realities of life together make new demands upon character. Minds filled with make-believe invite disillusion. How can two people make and preserve a home without some domestic capability, some understanding and skill in child-care, some financial responsibility, and ability to organise, to keep in employment, to protect wife and home from foreseeable risks, to show sympathy in sickness and bereavement? Yet none of this is guaranteed by vital statistics, the colour of eyes and hair, or the ability to dance, or dress well. The expectation that each would find the other a *competent* marriage partner may have had no grounds at all, and accusations of failure may be patently unfair.

There may be no agreement, either, as to what that expectation should be. If the girl came from a happy home, she will probably expect, perhaps unconsciously, that her husband will automatically be and do all that her father was and did; if her home was unhappy, she may as lightly assume that her husband will be the opposite to her father in every way. The husband himself may have only the vaguest idea of what is expected of him, or how he fails. So he will measure all her ways with his 'wonderful' mother, or against his most unsatisfactory mother or sister! It may be that with deliberate wisdom they agree to forego this family-definition of roles, and fall instead into comparing their partner's ways with those of other fellows' wives, other girls' husbands. Such comparisons will affect hundreds of details: how he sits about the house, whether he is handy with tools or helpless, how she cares for her clothes, how he eats his food or speaks to the children, how she appears at breakfast, or leaves personal things lying about, how he 'bosses' or she 'nags'.

The outcome must depend on how well each knew the other, and accepted the basic pattern of each other's character, from the start; how determined each is to enjoy the endless rediscovery of growing together in understanding, how willing each is to stretch love's endless compromise. Well managed pre-marital counselling should have given opportunity, and spur, to better knowledge of each other's attitudes and opinions on many things. The pastor will often find himself insisting that each must let the other be himself, herself; that neither was free to accept only what they found especially attractive in each other, but must marry the whole person; that each alike must contribute to mutual understanding and freedom by the fullest and kindest discussion of whatever irritates or disappoints. Often it is enough for either complaining partner to be made to see how unfair, and unreasonable, are the comparisons being half-consciously made; how trivial are the irritations beside their mutual joys; how invaluable a sense of humour and a gift of tenderness may be—if the will to play one's part as well as possible first be present.

(iii) *Inability to communicate* is often related to disappointment in each other, arising from similar causes. A couple may scarcely have known each other, may have had very little to enjoy together, from the start. Where courtship days were filled with shared excursions, holidays, parties, games, mutual friends and romantic interludes, there might be no opportunity, and no great need, for sharing of mind with mind. Serious topics may well have been avoided, lest a precious evening together be spoiled by argument; the surrender of personal interests in music, sport, hobbies, when opportunities of meeting were rare, raised no difficulties. But spending day after day together creates a new situation. The need of common themes to talk about, of common interests to share, of freedom for each to pursue some personal hobby without resentment from the other, becomes apparent; a great gulf of communication can yawn 'when the kissing has to stop'.

Differences of ability and education can still create serious difficulties. The well-trained or academically-inclined husband may assert frequently that he did not choose his bride for her brains: but he has to live with her lack of them, and should recognise the resulting situation, his own reactions to it, and his wife's feeling about it, with great frankness. The very talented, or highly intellectual wife will probably have recognised with amused tolerance the slowness and stolidity of her devoted swain—but she has to accept the situation in daily detail with great sensitivity. Either can draw away from the other into a superior aloofness or a timid retreat, communicating only in essential and trivial things, while living in painful loneliness. He may spend considerable effort and money, to her great annoyance, striving to do something he *thought* she wanted done; she may go on providing or arranging what she fondly imagines he dotes upon, but which he once praised only to please her! At times, talk is deliberately trivialised lest openness should reveal gulfs that frighten. Worst of all is the silence that falls between two hearts longing to communicate again, whether the silence be resentful, disdainful, or just helpless. For silence in such circumstances always isolates, alienates, and wounds.

This is one situation where merely to talk over the problem with a sympathetic but shrewd and objective third party may be sufficient to solve it. To see what is happening clearly enough to describe it will sometimes reveal how ludicrous it is, how unfair, how childish. The pastor may help trace causes backwards to insufficient communication in courtship days; he may venture to point out that we all have to live with our choices, and not blame others for them; but he will emphasise more the enrichment that arises from differences, when differences are truly accepted and appreciated, rather than regretted and resented.

(iv) *Undisclosed Intentions* are rooted likewise in ignorance of each other, and the reluctance to discuss differences openly. The wife may not have fully disclosed, before marriage, her intention to continue working and to postpone a family; or that one or two children, well spaced, were all she wanted. The husband may not have revealed that he expected to retain all his earlier friendships, male and female, or to continue his bachelor's level of pocket-money, and freedom in spending it; or that he thought it good for husbands and wives to take holidays apart. Human nature's propensity for postponing the disagreeable is a fruitful source of trouble; so is the starry-eyed optimism that assumes that time and love will clarify everything. More serious is the assumption that what is not very important to us will not be important to the other person intimately involved. It is easy for a pastor to point out that many such matters really ought to have been discussed and decided earlier—though many such questions are almost unforeseeable. To help the couple towards unemotional, objective discussion of the real issues involved in each point of disagreement; to make an unyielding partner see that refusal to discuss is an admission of weakness; and where discussion is insufficient to contrive some fifty-fifty plan of mutual surrender, is probably all that a counsellor can do in a situation that common sense should have avoided.

(v) *The direct clash of wills*, or of 'temperament', usually called 'incompatibility', is a perpetual risk in all mature human relation-ships. Handling that risk, so as to win from the diversity of two equally independent, developing characters a lively partnership, in which a fundamental unity of purpose is held in manifold tension, is *the* art of marriage. Pre-marital counselling should have made clear the place of independence within most marriages, while allowing that 'submergence' of one partner to the stronger, protective character of the other, given always consideration and unselfishness, can also provide the basis for real happiness. The nature of love is essentially loyalty within difference of function: and the simple technique of division of spheres of decision according to responsibility, while sustaining united attitudes before all observers, may need to be talked through again in the light of experience. It often heals much unnecessary hurt simply to explain that Christian marriage does *not* mean fifty years together without a single difference of opinion or collision of purposes. One should expect that not in a marriage but a morgue.

(vi) *Sexual adjustments failing* after the first few years may cause intense disappointment and lead to sore misinterpretation of each other as 'no longer in love' or 'emotionally frigid'. The cause may be purely physical, when the pastor would unhesitatingly refer the couple to a medical authority, either the family doctor, or one whom he knows will be especially helpful, or a marriage guidance clinic. The cause can also be simple misunderstanding. There are two main types of marriage, equally valid and successful: one begins in sexual attraction and achieves affection and companionship; the other begins with companionship, shared interest, work, good causes, and achieves sexual adjustment as an adjunct to the total relationship. Occasionally one partner thinks mainly of the first approach, the other of the second approach to the same marriage—with obvious room for difficulty. But at least as often, the causes may be psychological, even religious.

It is still possible for a man not to realise that a woman has sexual needs scarcely less powerful than his own, and so never to have conducted their relationship with that two-sided understanding. His wife therefore may never have found in this side of marriage any joy or satisfaction, but only 'duty'. It is possible too, even yet, for some women not to realise that the sexual drive in man is not 'a selfish habit' but a need as natural as the appetite for food, and that married love is the appointed, healthy and joyous satisfaction of that *need*.

At other times the root problem is the repugnance felt by one partner towards anything to do with sex, as 'unspiritual', 'sensual', having no real place in a holy Christian life except as a regrettable necessity if children are desired, and to be left behind when the family is complete. Much Christian teaching is certainly to blame for this inhibition of sexual pleasure, and the pastor may have real difficulty in leading gently towards a healthier, more human, more Christian attitude. For God did not only make man, male and female, for bisexual procreation: He made the process pleasurable to the point of mutual ecstasy. Jesus repeatedly uses the *joy* of marriage as illustration of higher joys: the New Testament insists that the marriage bed is undefiled. Man and woman are creatures of the senses as well as of the spirit: from that fact stems all art and music, all enjoyment of nature and of food, and through the richness of liturgy, much of the *pleasure* of worship. What determines the Christian quality of the sensual life is its discipline by reason, tenderness, respect, consideration, responsibility, abstinence when necessary (but not 'so as to defraud one another'), and exclusive loyalty to one partner only. An artificial spirituality, which pretends that sexual relationship is to be endured by Christians but never enjoyed, denies the deep joy of mutual self-giving which God Himself made the heart of married love.

Religious scruples about the avoidance of unwanted pregnancy are frequently at the root of failure in this side of marriage. The pastor will know that no Christian church has ever condemned birth-control, but only sought to distinguish 'natural' from 'artificial' methods of achieving that end. Advice as to method is not, of course, within the pastor's competence, and might well be resented. He may wish to draw attention to an *ethical* distinction between methods which harm in any way the natural functions, so risking health, and those which do not: but his main contribution to the discussion would probably be the liberating truth that sexual enjoyment has never been regarded by Christians as merely utilitarian—for the procreation of children—but as by its own right part of that comfort which one ought to have of the other in married happiness. That once realised, the wisdom and innocence of taking some steps to avoid too large a family seem to follow, though precisely *what* steps, it is better to leave to a doctor to advise.

The distinction between personal and organisational problems in marriage is debatable, and difficult to maintain: but it is useful sometimes in cooling an emotional situation to be able to say 'this is just lack of planning, not lack of love'. (vii) Thus the opposite problem to that of unwanted pregnancies, *the heartache of childlessness*, is plainly more one of organising together to face a mutual disappointment, than of what either thinks of the other or is willing to give the other. It is still possible, though fortunately more rare than used to be the case, to be confronted with a husband's conviction that his wife has been 'cursed' or 'punished' by God with barrenness. With this barbarous and superstitious notion the pastor must deal with what patience he can find. The impossibility of reconciling such a thought of God with our Lord's teaching, should be plain. The explanation of childlessness lies, of course, in physical or possibly psychological conditions, and the pastor's first counsel will be to consult the doctor and take whatever medical steps he advises. Where the husband rejects this recommendation, or refuses such medical advice, the pastor should point out fairly forthrightly that such a refusal suggests the husband really suspects the 'curse' is upon himself, and fears to test the matter. That suggestion should at least protect the wife from further slanders. If fear of childbirth, or fear of bearing a malformed child, or the husband's jealousy of the place that a child will take in his wife's affections, be the root cause, careful analysis by the pastor of real attitudes should bring to light the sub-conscious motivations and fears, and suggest healthier responses.

Where all treatment fails, the pastor should be ready to persuade that there are more ways of 'having' children and caring for them than just bearing your own. So many needy children in the world make it tragic, and wrong, that a Christian home and loving Christian hearts should be 'wasted' through the accident of childlessness. To foster others' children, even temporarily, and even more to adopt another's child as one's own, is to react positively to misfortune, and very largely to resolve the parental disappointment while doing a Christlike service in another life. The pastor will be firm that the 'dangers' of adoption are grossly exaggerated: heredity does count for something in character formation, but environment, training, and example count for much more, and these the couple can supply with their love. The uncertainty about how young people will develop is not really greater with 'chosen' children than with one's own; and to have given some hitherto unwanted child the opportunity of a good, healthy, happy life, and years of care and companionship, is to have served Christ in one of His little ones—even if all that the parents hoped for did not happen. To this extent, childlessness is not just a misfortune of health: it becomes a matter of choice—whether to accept it, or to circumvent it by adoption.

(viii) *Diverse family loyalties*, with complaints of interference, and undue concern for the 'outside' opinions of mother, father, sisters, can develop into longstanding grievance. Though it will appear to be, and may indeed become, a personal quarrel over personal relation-ships, fundamentally the difficulty arises from failure to plan together how the two families—his and hers—are to be approached; how far each shall be consulted, or informed, of matters concerning the new home; and the solemn undertaking that neither will discuss the other with their families or with anyone else. Where families are balanced in numbers, it should be easy to compromise: either both are told, or neither. And once the trouble is expressed in words, it ought to be easy to extract the promise from both partners that neither will accept advice or suggestions from the families except in some such form as 'I will tell him (or her) what you suggest, and we will think it over'. Loyalty, the pastor cannot say too often, is the essence of love.

Once hostilities and jealousies have been allowed to develop, it is difficult to begin again. The pastor may remind the couple of what he said (or would have said) on this subject in pre-marital counselling. He may also help each partner to look again at the other's fears, and loyalties, and at his or her own jealousies. He may persuade them that it is not what other people say to either of them which causes trouble, but the spirit in which it is reported. A firm promise that *nothing* that others say or do will be allowed to come between them, except as a comment or suggestion to be weighed together, will take most of the heat out of the situation. Here again, just to see themselves and their own behaviour in the eyes of a kindly observer may do all that is needed to create a better understanding.

(ix) *Monetary disagreements*, also, stem from failure to organise shared life intelligently, but they can lead to suspicions of meanness, extravagance, selfishness, even to such quarrelling and anxiety over debt as to destroy all confidence and tenderness. There is no general pattern of domestic arrangement, and a well-prepared couple ought to have compared notes previously about how their parents managed their finances, and how they themselves intended to do so. Fully shared responsibility means shared knowledge in detail about the family income and expenditure, and agreement on priorities. In other homes, the woman takes all responsibility, receiving all income and returning what is agreed as pocket-money to the rest of the family; in yet others, the husband shoulders ultimate responsibility for the larger 'overhead' expenses, making a regular allowance for house-keeping, so relieving the wife of larger anxieties and dividing functions. Whatever is planned should in fairness be adhered to and only changed by agreement—though where the wit to plan at all is present, there ought not to be serious unhappiness.

One cause of tension is the loss of that freedom of spending which modern society has conferred upon many young people; house buying and family responsibilities demand so much from the common resources. The temptation is to blame each other for what being married *costs*. A great deal of mistrust is removed at a stroke by a simple agreement that wife and husband shall take equal spending money, for similar personal expenses, luxuries, gifts, to be used quite separately from household expenditure. But some individuals are simply feckless and incompetent about money; years of unemployment, casual labour, inadequate training grants, or bachelor affluence, all discourage habits of thrift and well-planned spending. The pastor may help a couple decide, quite frankly, which of them is most likely to make a success of budgetary matters, and plan some sensible compromise.

Where this is insufficient, the pastor may arrange for some well-chosen woman of the fellowship quietly to teach a young wife better household planning, or for a friendly man to take the lad aside and tell him how *they* manage things at home: the helpers should obviously be on the same income-level. The acknowledgement together before the pastor that it is 'misunderstanding about money' which is the cause of unhappiness, the realisation that it is not something to quarrel about but to organise intelligently, and the admission by both that living together is much more costly than either had expected, will often do all that is needed.

(x) *Disagreements over the children* include especially questions of discipline, of extent of freedom and spending-money, questions of education, choice of school, and of career. Because the children are personally precious, and the issues so important, it is hard for either parent to relinquish all decision to the other, and a battle of wills may easily develop in which the real aims are obscured. When, possibly among other causes of strife, a tug of war over the children is evident, it is well to resolve it promptly, and it need not be difficult. Usually there is immediate agreement that the welfare of the child is the common aim; the parents are united in what they are after for the child, disagreeing only about method. They may be brought to agree also that responsibility for the children belongs equally to both, that neither can be expected to surrender on such a matter and 'contract out'. If there is hesitation here, it is worth asking if either partner really wants the *whole* responsibility henceforth.

Given then that agreement, or some workable compromise, is essential, why the difficulty about method? *Why* does he think his policy best, and *why* is she equally sure that she is right? The answer will almost certainly lie in each following, or reacting against, his or her childhood experience, or possibly the experiences retailed in family stories. A checking of the details, a cool assessment of the soundness of the parallels being drawn, will reduce hostility to plain difference of opinion. If the solution has not already emerged, goodwill having been restored they can be left to work at the problem together.

(xi) *Inevitable changes due to age* can bring serious trouble to a marriage, mainly through failure to plan with foresight. If in the foundation of the marriage, sexual attraction has from the first been subordinate to shared interests, companionship, a common faith and purpose, advancing years will make less difference than if the physical relationship was primary. As the years pass, physical union must come to mean less and mental and spiritual union to mean

more, if only because of the waning of desire, the completion of the
family, the pressures of work, and impaired health. Where mental or
spiritual interests are limited, the simple domestic advantage of
remaining together in a comfortable tolerance of each other's foibles
may replace the earlier raptures quite adequately as a basis for a
relationship that has come to take 'love' and loyalty entirely for
granted.

The chief danger arises when the physical and psychological
changes in the two partners do not keep pace. Parents, or custom,
once decreed an ages gap of five to ten years between bridegroom and
younger bride, to ensure that middle-aged diminution of ardour
would roughly coincide! Where eager young people make their own
decisions, and where the emphasis falls mainly upon sex, this kind of
foresight is harder to inculcate. But a pastor's patient explanation
that the inevitable changes which time brings involve no loss of love
or loyalty, but only a change in their expression; and the simple
common sense which plans for age as once it planned for youth, and
which discovers or arranges for wider interests, occupations and
activities to share, should remove disappointments, suspicion or
resentment, and banish fancied estrangements.

(xii) A special instance of the changes due to age is the *wife-
mother-wife* development, sometimes called 'the empty nest syn-
drome'. As the children arrive, they tend to monopolise the mother's
time, energy and emotion; she changes, for most of her thought,
activity and interest, from the young bride-wife to the fully-
preoccupied mother, at first with the full co-operation of her
bridegroom-husband, but later increasingly to his chagrin as he finds
himself taking second place in attention, resources, and apparently
in affection. When, at between forty and fifty, the mother finds the
children growing away from her, either leaving home or asserting
independence while remaining under the parental roof, she may well
face a real crisis, as she turns back to a husband who has become
largely a stranger, older, unromantic, repressed, absorbed now in his
work, sport, playing or drinking, and in his own friendships outside
the home. He too has grown away from her.

Often, the mother-turned-wife-again will severely blame both
children and husband for the situation resulting from her own
actions. In her desperate need to feel needed, she will think much of
her 'sacrifices' in 'giving the best years of her life to the family'
(meaning the children), and she may resent bitterly their 'unfairness'
towards herself. Often menopausal complications, depression, and the
shock of suddenly approaching age, add considerably to the wife's un-

F

happiness. Meanwhile the husband, feeling himself unfairly blamed for a situation he never desired, and probably protested often enough against, resents his wife's continual moodiness and complaint.

Pastoral counsel will usually concentrate upon helping the partners see how the situation came to be, so removing the tendencies to blame and resentment. He will persuade that neither intended, or wanted, things to turn out so; they have drifted into a position they dislike through want of foresight, but it can now be adjusted, given goodwill, by understanding, appreciation of what each has done, and planning together for the new circumstances without the family. The husband may have to change somewhat his interests and habits to readmit his wife into his pattern of living; the wife may well be led to consider new ventures in employment, education, or voluntary work in church, hospital, or social causes. Both must be helped to believe that growing old together can be as interesting, as enriching, and in some ways even more satisfying and contented, than being young together, and must set themselves to make it so.

Little has here been said about prayer and family worship, and the way in which true loyalty to Christ would resolve most family problems. The fact is that where a couple maintains shared devotional life, no problem is likely to become so complicated, or so embittered by ill-will, that an outsider's help is needed, except for purely practical advice. Whenever he has been consulted, before his counselling is through a pastor would naturally commend the home to God in prayer—perhaps with the very brief reminder that as the marriage began in God's presence, so it will only continue at its best under His blessing.

Counselling Tactics

A friendly, approachable pastor will usually find that people in marital trouble seek of themselves for his help and guidance when the need is urgent; then his way is clear. At other times, he may observe for himself a growing unhappiness, and may intervene with direct enquiry, provided he does so graciously, for the sake of a Christian friend for whom he feels concerned. Where one Christian within a home reports trouble 'in confidence' without consent of other members of the family, his approach—if made at all—will call for much ingenuity and care. He will probably only take action if personal enquiry and visitation confirms the report. He will likewise refuse to do anything in response to neighbourly gossip, however disguised as 'spiritual concern'.

Absence of either partner from worship may provide both a symptom of trouble and a ground upon which to base enquiry. A son or daughter whose evident unhappiness, absence, or behaviour is causing the pastor concern, may well provide the necessary line of approach: exploring *with* the parents the possible source of the trouble—school, friends, employment, neighbours, church, or home? —may well reveal that all is not well between the parents, and give the needed opportunity. If the young people have reported trouble at home, their confidence must be scrupulously kept, and action taken only upon the pastor's personal observation, so alerted.

However the matter comes under notice, eventually some kind of interview will result. In one sense, every marriage-counselling interview will be a joint one: though only one partner actually attends, the absent partner's viewpoint, motives and complaints must be kept in mind, explored and examined until they are understood. Mere accusations of total unreasonableness, selfishness, stupidity, will be discounted; the impartial analysis of a consultant who is sympathetic but not gullible will do much to set self-pitying exaggerations into truer perspective.

Whether the first interview should include both partners requires careful thought. The counsellor can better assess the situation as they talk in each other's presence—Who talks most? which is the stronger personality? who blames whom? What subjects does either deliberately avoid or quickly dismiss? A joint interview also avoids charges of talebearing. But it could also be painful, and an open quarrel in the pastor's presence might be final. Moreover, the needed steps towards reform can, with some people, be more difficult when either partner knows this was what the pastor prescribed, than when one partner attempts silently to mend his or her ways. The pastor's personal relationship with each, the strength of resentments involved, and the urgency of the crisis reached, will affect the decision. If after a single-partner interview a joint-interview seems desirable, *the pastor himself* should invite the absent one, explaining how the invitation arises, and taking full responsibility for advising it, while making very clear that he has not prejudged the situation, but wishes only to know the full facts before offering any assistance. The permission of the partner who consulted him would, of course, be essential.

The necessary probing beneath the surface of the situation calls for gentleness, patience to listen without comment or surprise, and reticence—not asking for more information than is necessary to clarify confusion or overcome any tendency to self-justification. Where more than this is needed, because something is being deliberately or unconsciously concealed, 'surgical questioning' may be necessary. If the person interviewed hesitates at more intimate references, the pastor's forthright use of words ('You find yourself resenting intimacy?'—'She is no longer sexually responsive?') will help to establish a clinical atmosphere.

Two possible starting points suggest themselves, once the story is told. 'Let us fill in the background: how long have you known each other? Where, when, did you meet? What happened? Where were you married? How did things go on from there?' Such questions purposely recall the emotions, affections and hopes of earlier days, which can of itself induce a wistful, more penitent mood; it also gives opportunity for the pastor to watch carefully for regrets, sore points, and subjects at which memory winces.

Or the probing may start with: 'Well, you were much in love once: tell me about that—where did it begin to go wrong?' This is more abrupt, and may provoke more abrupt and forthright replies. 'She was very lovely—at least I thought so—and very lively in those days, and very gay, until the baby came. That changed her. She had a bad time, and I was very worried about her. But I had worries about money too, and how we were going to provide for the baby. She got the idea I did not really want the baby—perhaps because I did not help with it. But I just did not know how to cope with babies' (often so, if he was an only child, or the youngest at home). 'So she blamed me, and swore she would not have another . . .'

Or: 'Everything was all right, we were quite happy, until mother came to live with us . . .'; 'till I had to change my job, and we were poorer and missed our holidays . . .'; 'she was never the same since she was so ill—it frightened her, I think, and she will not let me touch her now, though I am willing to take precautions . . .' Or: 'He was a fine fellow when we married, gentle always, and he used to help till the second baby came. He did not want that to happen, and blamed me. But I was very lonely as a child, and I think there should always be at least two . . .' (lack of previous communication on a deeply-felt principle); 'he did well, and gave me all I asked, until he lost his job, then he became very mean . . .' (lack of communication on his part of the shock and fear unemployment brought). Or: 'He was fine until he started going mad about cars . . . gambling . . . spending a lot of time and money outside the house . . .' (what was the reason for this seeking new interests?) 'He did not like my sister coming to live with us, but I insisted . . .' (dominating, without counting the cost!) 'Oh, I was ill for a time, and unless he could have all he wanted he did not seem to care. And then there was a girl—Oh, I forgave him, it was nothing really . . .' (then why 'forgave'?) '. . . but I never felt the same again when we were alone together' (that means she did *not* forgive).

Occasionally the story may reveal very deep maladjustments. 'We were very wild in those days, and careless—hardly knew each other— and when I found the baby was on the way, well, we had to marry. But he (or she) has always resented it—felt trapped, and angry inside. Never took to baby at all. We have never really been close, just living together at a distance, regretting it ever happened . . .' This demands severe testing. Is he (or she) *sure* the other resents, or just imagining it: after all he or she did consent to marry and has cared enough to 'stay with it'. Could it possibly be *vice versa*—the other partner always thinking that the speaker feels trapped and resentful. Probably a joint interview of complete frankness, in hope of facing present facts as adults seeking happiness, will be necessary, but it could completely transform the home, if only for the child's sake.

While the probing continues, the pastor hears the story behind the situation, the facts behind the facts that are being told. The 'until' is the sign that he is possibly nearer to the real issue than the presented problem ever was. Out of the real facts, the background story, the needed insight usually appears. When an impasse is reached, however, or the root-problem appears to be mainly organisational, a change of approach may be profitable, to play down emotion and recall a different mood, as well as to bring some further illumination. The pastor will listen for unconscious comparisons—for the comforts, freedom, car, holidays, once enjoyed and now regarded as 'sacrificed' for marriage; or for personal relationships at home, idealised in childhood memories and used to disparage present relationships. The sources of much disappointment may emerge in such unconscious self-revelation.

Where the immediate problem is, for example, disagreement over money, the pastor may interject among these memories, 'Tell me, as you remember your home, how did your parents handle this money arrangement?' An answer like 'Oh, it never arose; mother was queen of our home, and never had to ask for a thing; she managed every- thing beautifully . . .' may reveal a girl who looked for a weak husband like Dad and got a man instead! Or: 'Oh my Dad would never have stood for it, as I do: he carried all responsibility and sheltered mother from all anxiety . . .' may reveal a man looking for a mouse-like, submissive wife, such as he thinks his mother was; or (on the wife's lips) may reveal a woman idealising her father but inheriting too much of his strong character to repeat the pattern for herself!

Such answers always need checking. The question 'Was your mother, then, a nonentity at home?' may bring a strong denial—and the realisation that neither can *any* wife be expected to be. 'Did your father, then, dodge all responsibility?' may bring a new light on a home situation not really understood. To ask for instances, or to place the asserted knowledge in an unfavourable light, often leads to the admission that they do not know what the parental arrangements were, but always thought . . . From this may come understanding that neither can expect the present partner to reproduce a barely-understood role, or live a generation behind. In any case, neither of them in fact chose that kind of person—and they would not have liked him or her for their partner, anyway.

The purpose of the probing of such attitudes and assertions must always be kept uppermost in the conversation: curiosity, or cross-examination are sure to be resented. The pastor expresses repeatedly his desire to understand how those being interviewed see a particular point. The aim throughout is clarification, bringing to the surface of the discussion, and of their own minds, half-revealed, half-understood feelings, resentments, fears, motives, comparisons, and regrets.

The crucial element in Christian marriage-counselling is the application of specifically Christian concepts to the situation finally revealed. Here it is well to keep to basic and forthright statement of Christian ways of handling such difficulties. Thus, it is always Christian to return to one's starting point. In the case of marital difficulties, to return to the original attraction, and love, and promises made; to the relationship out of which the children were born—refusing to deny, forget, or become cynical about happier days. These were God's gifts, and nothing is to be gained by denying, nor is it Christian to deny, the joy that life once brought.

It is always Christian, too, to return to first principles. Even for experienced couples it is never too late to recall what marriage is, the essence of love as loyalty, the necessity for a more enduring basis than the things that the years must take away. In fact, it is never too late for the pastor to repeat his elementary instruction upon marriage. Experience will prove, and not contradict, its basic wisdom.

The Christian concept of reconciliation, with true forgiveness, is always binding upon believers and relevant to every stressful human relationship. It is not alone the duty of forgiveness that needs emphasis, however, but the hope of real reconciliation, the earnest prayer for change of character and relationship, the expectation that divine grace can transform situations and persons. The gospel of new birth holds out continual possibilities of altered attitudes, and so requires of the Christian the readiness to let people change, and to try again. It is important that the pastor shall not let this Christian duty be imposed upon by insincere professions of amendment, made to avoid consequences, or to blackmail a wronged partner into acquiescence. Some dependable evidence of changed attitudes, some clear alteration in the pattern of behaviour, should be insisted upon before Christian forgiveness can be required in response. But where such is forthcoming, and time has shown it to be sincere, forgiveness may be the right way forward. Implacable refusal would expose a still more tragic deficiency, and evangelism rather than marriage-counselling would be the next step.

Even the most elementary Christian principles may sometimes need to be recalled and applied to the home situation. The duty of being just, fair, and truthful, never so self-pitying as to misrepresent the other's motives, never so angry as to exaggerate the other's faults, may need to be pointed out. If the pastor's impartiality is resented, that may itself be used to expose the speaker's unfairness. Nor may the aggrieved Christian ignore the deep unhappiness of a partner tied to an unsatisfactory marriage. Both the pain, and the wrong, are being shared; the Christian should not be allowed to forget the duty of loving concern even for one who has caused the disappointment. Vindictiveness, or indifference, must be unchristian. So is the determination not to value another person for what he or she actually is, but only as he or she conforms to our own standards, and submits to our own pattern of life.

To run away from a situation because it is less than perfect may be too easy, too weak and cowardly, to commend itself to Christian hearts. The teaching of 1 Corinthians 7, about remaining in a painful position with divine grace to make it tolerable—'therein abide with God'—may be the truly Christian reaction, the one which will most clearly testify to the patience and the strength which Christ gives. The pastor will never impose such duties on other consciences: he will be too deeply aware of the cost in daily discipline and pain to speak lightly of what another soul *ought* to do. But with utmost sympathy he will suggest, remind, ask leading questions about the possibility of showing such heroic determination to *use* a testing situation for good and for God's glory. And he will certainly assure the willing heart of God's presence and help in every time of testing.

To close such an interview with a brief, three-sentence prayer may be well: but not to encourage the superficial hope that the 'solution' to difficult personal problems lies in praying. It does not. Readjustments of behaviour, and of attitude, revised judgements about people, a rethinking of one's own position and response (the literal meaning of *repentance*), and new decisions about the pattern of life, are at least equally important. It is necessary also to allow for the pain of swallowing natural pride; to be prepared to accept a *silent* apology, and not extort humiliation; to give time for changed attitudes to show themselves. Time and opportunity must be given also for prayer to be answered. For the pastor may certainly assure those truly willing to repair a strained Christian marriage that God is on their side.

13   MINISTRY TO THE SICK

Opportunities for pastoral visitation, for bringing the church's worship to the individual, and for pastoral counselling, frequently arise in the context of illness or the more leisured, more reflective mood of convalescence. Their aims will be unchanged, but the delicacies and practicalities of the sickroom must, of course, be borne in mind. Nursing, washing, feeding, injections, sleep and like ministries, including some not to be explained to the visitor, have to be allowed for without comment, together with the short and limited concentration that can make well-meaning conversation a trial and not a blessing.

Sickness, however, creates an added need for ministry: it is another experience to be faced in Christian faith and fortitude. The pastor may find his skill and insight taxed to the full: he needs to be very clear about what he is doing, and more than usually perceptive and gentle in doing it. His purpose is not simply to comfort and bring cheer, or to express the interest and goodwill of the Christian fellowship. He should expect the querulous and never-settled question, 'Why should this happen to me, pastor?' and be prepared with something more than the spiritual platitudes and bromides usually expected of him in face of suffering. But with growing experience he will realise that his most illuminating reflections on pain in human life are not enough; the experience has not only to be understood, but faced, accepted, endured and used in positive Christian ways. He will find that both explanation and courage are in fact discovered by the patient himself as he seeks the will of God for the weeks of illness. Such a definition of pastoral aims plainly calls for both a theology of suffering, and a strategy of conquest, if the ministry is to match the need.

Theology of Suffering

Doubtless the problem of suffering is but part of the larger problem of evil, and of an imperfect, unfinished, wayward universe. The trained pastor will have met that problem before, but the sickroom is not the place for refined philosophical discussion. A thoughtful convalescent may be interested in the pastor's thoughts on the meaning of suffering; most patients' questions will be more immediately personal and practical—how to be a Christian when one is ill and in pain.

Man's heightened capacity for suffering is surely the strangest feature distinguishing him from the rest of creation. In the scale of life, wider and deeper vulnerability to pain is the price paid for increasing complexity and richness of experience. Man's more highly developed nervous system, the basis of his intellectual and creative powers, leaves him more sensitive to want, injury, and agony. His priceless gift of imagination, the essence of all art, vision and humour, is also the source of all his fears, including his dread of death. Man alone, apparently, is subject to the sustained sadness of long-remembered sorrow: it is the price we pay for the treasure-house of memory. Man alone, again, seems troubled by the limitation of his powers, the weakness, brevity, frustration, dependence, of his existence—because man alone among the creatures has the power to reflect on his own situation in the universe. Only man is susceptible of moral suffering, the burden of shame, the cost of duty, the struggle for character, the agony of remorse, the bitterness of failure. And all the range of man's infinitely enriching social nature—his sympathy, friendship, affection, loyalty, and love—brings with it the inevitable liability to greatly extended suffering through sharing others' burdens, bitterness, and grief.

It is odd that the full stature of humanity should be measurable in this way, yet the choice seems clear: we could only be freed from suffering by being less than human. The problem is by no means peculiar to Christianity; we do not solve it by denying the Christian conception of God—the suffering then remains to be borne, and explained—*without* God. All religions and philosophies have to wrestle with this element in the human condition. The Stoic sought to discipline himself not to feel pain, treating it with proud dignity and often with insensitive contempt. The Mohammedan, translating stoicism into religious terms, accepts all that happens as the will of Allah, irresistible, unavoidable, incurable, tending to sink into fatalism. The Buddhist would exalt himself into a world beyond pain *and joy*, finding deliverance from suffering in a void existence emptied of all desire, good or bad. Christian Science imitates that intellectualist reaction to suffering, by attempting to deny its reality: pain is a psychological illusion, a figment of a falsely conditioned imagination—a flat denial of the obvious which is scarcely scientific, and in its implications for the suffering of Christ, certainly unchristian.

The modern hedonist, assuming that life is designed for pleasure, turns his mind resolutely away from all unhappiness, often callous towards others' pain, filled with self-pity towards his own, and bitter at life's meaninglessness and injustice when experience destroys his illusions. The Jewish reaction was more complex and more candid. Suffering is there, in life and in God's world. Traditionally, from Eden and the Law to Job's friends and the Pharisees, suffering was 'explained' directly by sin and by corporate involvement in wrong-doing. The thorns of experience are all of man's planting; a man is born blind because of his sin or his parents'; the collapse of a tower in Siloam is God's judgement on those who died. The assumption that God's favour spells prosperity and ease must carry this implication, that suffering and want prove divine disfavour. But another attitude insisted that the innocent suffered no less than the guilty. Job, some psalmists, and the author of Isaiah's songs were sure that sin was no sufficient explanation—that even the Servant of the Lord would suffer, though He had done no violence, neither was deceit found in His mouth. With insight born of faith and integrity, such thinkers came within sight of the final truth about suffering, its possible redemptive power and vicarious fruitfulness.

Here Christian reflection begins. Christian realism too accepts that thorns disfigure God's world; so far from denying suffering, it sets pain at the heart of human duty by demanding love's compassionate service of the hungry, the naked, the sick, the lonely, the lost and unloved. In contrast to all other teachings, Christianity sets suffering and mortality at the heart of its gospel, in the story of the cross. Jesus roundly denied any direct connection between individual suffering and sin. Occasionally sin may lie somewhere behind the suffering: Jesus *forgave* the paralytic before dealing with the con-sequences (in his case) of wrongdoing—and the pastor will remember this sometimes. But he will never condone the cruel, unchristian assumption that the believer suffers only because he lacks faith or withholds obedience. Where the pastor thinks it might be so, or where the patient raises this question, he will urge repentance, and offer assurance of God's forgiveness: but the occasions for this will be very rare indeed. Even brief pastoral experience will soon demonstrate that often the best suffer most.

The Christian faith accepts the fact that the world is spoiled by human folly, misuse of freedom, and grievous fault: it offers little new about the ultimate explanation. Instead, it demonstrates how the thorns man's sin has planted, and which man's hate will some-times weave into a wreath to torture earth's best, may yet be so accepted and so worn as to make a crown of heroism, and of glory. This is the Christian theology of suffering. Christ took our pain and loneliness, ingratitude and agony, betrayal and mortality, and from them He fashioned the redemption of the world. Why me? It happened to Him—every kind of pain, distress, injustice, cruelty and shame! Yet His character shone through: neither recrimination, threats, bitterness, self-pity, defiance, nor whimpering for mercy, spoils the final portrait. He died greatly, with gentleness and care for one beside Him, forgiveness and love for those beneath.

The agony of Jesus makes certain things clear: (i) suffering need not corrupt or destroy, though it can do both. Indeed, suffering can refine and ennoble—without hardship there could be no heroism, without pain no patience, without adversity no endurance, without conflict no courage, without darkness no faith. Offered as comfort to the tortured, this may be superficial and sentimental; but when suffering challenges the moral character of the world, it is a valid comment. (ii) Suffering need not contradict the love of God—for Christian hearts, the crucial question. Weakness, pain, fear and distress make radiant, quiet trust appear impossible; God *feels* far away, or is displeased, or hides Himself. That Jesus knew and shared that inner darkness, yet still could call God Father, and into loving hands commit His spirit, is answer enough. Thousands testify to the courage, calmness and undergirding strength that the suffering Christ's assurance of divine love has brought them in the midst of pain and doubt. The questions remain, but their sharp urgency is gone; we do not understand, but we know that nothing shall defeat us, that neither tribulation, distress, peril, things present or things to come shall separate us from the love of God in Jesus Christ our Lord.

(iii) Suffering confronted with faith and fidelity can yield positive good. The experience need not be so much wasted time and strength, but may fulfil God's gracious purposes. Christ's suffering achieved the redemption of the world: in some sense, at an infinite distance, we know the fellowship of His sufferings, and ours, too, are not for nothing. Hearts that love God, and accept His purpose for their purpose, find that God makes all things work together for good—the supreme good for which we are 'destined and called and justified'— that we should be conformed to the image of His Son. It is no accident that that courageous affirmation of faith should be set between 'the sufferings of this present time', futility, bondage, groaning in travail, and 'tribulation, distress, persecution, famine, nakedness, peril and sword'. It is the darker side of Christian experience that fills Paul's mind as he writes, and he knew at first hand the suffering he describes. But if that darker side of experience finds its place in the loving purpose of God to make us Christlike, then Paul believes that we can in all adversity be more than conquerors through Him that loved us.

For the visiting pastor, that conquest of suffering is the immediate priority, but he will be wise to have thought through some such 'theology' of pain, and of its place in Christian life, if his ministry in the sick-room is to be more than a bewildered and impulsive sympathy, a helpless concern that means well but fails to enlighten or to strengthen faith.

Conquest of Suffering

Suffering is overcome either by healing, or by endurance: each is a victory. Spiritual healing is a subject on which it seems difficult to be temperate, neither fanatical nor faithless. The assumption that no Christian should ever be ill; that every sickness or affliction would be divinely removed if 'enough' faith or prayer were exercised, is certainly unscriptural. Epaphroditus 'was ill, near to death . . . he nearly died for the work of Christ'; Trophimus was 'left at Miletus, sick'; Timothy was advised to try wine for his frequent infirmity; Paul preached in Galatia 'because of a bodily ailment', having with him (almost certainly) Luke 'the beloved physician'. But neither Luke nor repeated prayer could remove Paul's 'thorn in the flesh': the infirmity remained. No enthusiastic proclamation of 'a full and fourfold gospel' offering health to all who believe can evade this sobering evidence that the apostolic circle had its ailments, its frustrations, and its invalids.

For all that, there can be no doubt, either, that health is one of God's gifts to His people, and one of the promises offered in the gospel—when health is God's will. Hezekiah's prayer and Psalm 103 are ancient testimonies that God is the 'Lord that healeth', while the first evidence of the presence of the kingdom of God among men in the person of Jesus was that the lame walked, lepers were cleansed, the dumb spoke, the blind saw, the sick were made well. With the gospels in our hands we cannot doubt either the will or the power of Christ to heal.

To remind sufferers that all healing is God's handiwork, and to direct their thought and faith, hopefully, towards divine resources for body and mind, is essential to sick-ministry. James' picture of the sick believer *calling* for the elders, who hear his confession, who administer the common alleviating treatments (anointing with oil was the universal medicament in the east, not a superstitious charm) and who pray for him with confident faith, is the classic picture of pastoral sick-visitation—and of divine healing.

No experienced pastor will question the place which courage and hopefulness, a quiet mind, a reconciled spirit resting in the goodness of God, may have in the process of healing. One single instance where these are absent, where self-pity, fear, resentment, despair, rule the patient's mood, will teach him the truth unforgettably. As skilled hands and informed care can nurse the body back to health, so can skilled ministry nurse the mind and spirit, releasing within the personality healing forces that assist recovery and confirm the cure. No pastor should permit himself to doubt that, where his message is believed and his ministry accepted, his work has real place in the task of healing, alongside the more technical ministries of physician, surgeon and psychiatrist.

But sometimes he will feel impelled to go further. He will need to exercise extreme care in recognising such occasions, in weighing circumstances, and especially in foreseeing what *harm* as well as what good may result from more definite action. He will be responsible for whatever disappointment or relapse occurs, however sincere his motives, if by any word or action he encourages a hope that proves to be false, or supports the patient in rejecting common-sense precautions, refusing human aids, because of some 'spiritual conviction' that imperils both cure and life itself.

Yet with all due responsibility and caution, a Christian pastor may still feel convinced that the deepest danger lies within the attitude of the patient, in a despair of life, a lack of will to live, a fatalist acceptance of death as inevitable, sometimes miscalled 'resignation'. The pastor will not, if he is wise, oppose or contradict more qualified opinion in fields beyond his own expertness: but he may resolve nevertheless that more might be attempted to rally faith, determination, and courage. In such cases he may, in assured faith and with definite prayer, perhaps with a few friends who can keep their counsel gathered with him about the sick-bed, *lay hold on life* in God's name for the sick soul. He will bring to bear all the pressure of Christian affirmation, shared faith, the conviction of God's love and purpose—acknowledging always that God's will is final, yet confident that God does *not* mean the life He loves to be maimed henceforth, or thrown away. More often than he expects, such exercise of faith in God's healing power will bring results too wonderful, and too humbling, to be rudely publicised, or even reported without bated breath.

Nevertheless, healing is not always God's will. Trophimus may wait at Miletus, and Paul pray in vain. Then endurance, without resentment, is the victory required. This is, indeed, precisely the meaning of 'overcoming' in Paul's great affirmation of confidence. 'In all these things,' he says, closing the list of varied forms of distress, 'in all these things we are more than conquerors . . . For I am persuaded that . . . nothing shall separate us from the love of God.' That *is* victory: to pass through pain and darkness, disappointment and sorrow, *not* unscathed, *not* pretending that nothing hurts us, not even unshaken in heart, but when all is past, still to have our hand in the hand of God. Still, in spite of all, to remain within the love of God in Christ, 'not to be separated', that is more than conquering. As John says, 'This is the victory, even our faith.' To lead sick and fearful believers to share that spiritual triumph is ministry indeed.

To help counsel the afflicted toward that victory of endurance we have the self-unveiling of the apostle. Faced with his own 'thorn', a messenger of Satan to harass him, Paul says he *prayed*, not once or twice, that it be removed. Something of Paul's anguish of soul is in his confession: the hindrance to his work, the trial of his patience, the frustration of faith itself, yet the prayer—though heard—is not granted. To pray is right: to attempt to dictate to God is wrong, and foolish; but to lift the whole experience to God expecting to be heard, is the Christian's natural first reaction to any trouble. The second is, to cast about to *find a meaning* in the experience. There will be a meaning, and God may make it clear, or He may not. Paul knew the meaning of his own distress; his suffering was a counterpoise to high spiritual privilege 'lest he be exalted above measure'. For others, the purpose may be very different, but the heart that seeks will probably find what God is doing, and such understanding is half-way to conquest.

The third step is to expect, and to *receive the grace* that is sufficient for every hardship, adversity or grief. More was given than Paul has asked—not healing, but grace to endure without bitterness, to suffer without being spoiled. So to live in the sense of God's favour, by the strength that is made perfect in our weakness, can make any day tolerable, any pain bearable—if only God is near. Paul's fourth step was surrender, the *active acceptance* of the total situation, even 'glorying in infirmity, that the power of God may rest upon me'. Even prayer for deliverance may then cease, and the heart find perfect rest in letting God have His way. This is not bowing to the inevitable, but accepting the purposeful as God plans it, in the grace that God promises to supply. Much pastoral sick-visiting will be planned to help fellow Christians find that fourfold path to victory.

Especially will this be so with those we must think of as chronic invalids, and with the physically handicapped and malformed. But here some additional ministry may well be possible. It should not be necessary to remark that the blind are not deaf, and the deaf are not mentally retarded, though we often treat them so. Nor should a pastor need reminding that the independence of the handicapped is almost the most precious possession in their lives; or that each invalid or malformed individual wishes most of all to be respected for his own sake, and not pitied for his affliction. In truth, the pastoral aim with such afflicted lives is not essentially different from what it is for all: to enable each Christian to live out his life to the fullest possible usefulness and blessing, in the circumstances and with the powers conferred upon him.

To that end the pastor will often become involved in finding work, training, resources and outlets by which the handicapped can preserve their self-support. Sometimes he will initiate friendships, plan the sharing of hobbies, call in experts, explore public or private means of assistance, or bring together (when it is wise) similarly handicapped people to share in common enterprise. Always he will seek ways to keep alive, active and useful the connection of handicapped people with the ongoing life of the church, that the individual may feel himself to be not only supported by but contributing to the fellowship in positive and appreciated ways.

At deeper levels it may be necessary to kindle effort, and repeatedly to reassure those whose opportunities and capacities are limited of the worth of endeavour and faith in overcoming obstacles. An astonishing number of great names may be cited, of those whose total achievement includes the conquest of disability—Pasteur, Milton, Beethoven, Stanley (poverty), Wilberforce ('the shrimp'), Gray ('low spirits my faithful companions'), Cowper (recurrent madness), Francis Havergal, Helen Keller—the list is endless, and needless too, perhaps, for a generation that saw the most powerful nation in modern times ruled from a wheel-chair.

Yet for the Christian heart the highest motive for effort is not emulation or ambition but dedication. The same faithfulness is possible with one talent as with ten. Difficulties are no excuse for disobedience, and if the opportunities are limited by circumstances, that is no reason for not fulfilling the obligations they bring. Nor is 'resignation' a Christian attitude: one is not 'resigned' to the will of a loving Father whom one trusts implicitly. Self-pity, self-excuse, resignation, have no enduring motive-power to sustain the invalid or handicapped. An attitude more heroic, and more permanent, is needed.

Towards this the pastor may seek to lead by urging that *every* Christian is called to live out his discipleship and express his love for Christ in circumstances that are limited for him, either by the actions of others, by heritage, by talent or temperament, by inherited responsibilities, by opportunities or the lack of them, by his own past decisions, or by habits formed, openings missed, insufficient education. The simple truth is that no Christian has perfect freedom to choose the theatre of his Christian loyalty. Ill-health, mental or physical incapacity, is but one factor among many, and not really more forbidding than some others. It was to *slaves* at Corinth (among others) that Paul addressed that bracing advice, 'Let every man, wherein he is called, therein abide with God': it is the word for the invalid and the afflicted also. An unresenting acceptance of the challenge of difficult circumstances, in reliance upon the Lord who promises sufficient grace, is the key to superb character—and a powerful testimony to Christ.

When to such general avenues of ministry are added the countless special opportunities which experience, and the infinite variety of circumstance, will open up, the demands of pastoral sick-ministry upon the pastor's time, energy, sympathy and insight may seem insupportable. Yet nothing will seem too much for the man who so earns the gratitude of hearts he has saved from resentment and repining. Nor will he ever forget the Master's verdict—'I was sick, and ye visited *me* . . .'

14 PROBLEMS OF AGE

Ministry to the aged is one area of pastoral work certain to widen in scope and increase in demand. The conquest of disease, the control of birth-rate, and rising living-standards make for an ageing society: it is estimated that three times as many people survive the age of sixty today as did fifty years ago. Their number makes them a good market for political exploitation; but their problems are deeper than political or economic adjustments can cure—or, for that matter, Christmas parcels, organised picnics, trips to the seaside, or rota-visitation by well-meaning church members. The blunt truth is that age is incurable: ministry, even at its best, can only alleviate its burden. And for most young pastors the first step towards ministry to the old is to gain a true compassion, deepening into respect, and even reverence.

The sense of the burden of age has probably never been expressed with more pathos than in Ecclesiastes 12:

> Youth and the prime of life are in themselves mere vanity, unless a man remember his Creator in the days of youth, before the evil days come, and the years draw nigh in which there is no pleasure; before the sun and the light, the moon and the stars, are darkened to eyes grown dim; before life's winter sets in, the clouds oft returning even after rain. Then all the strong guardians of the body—the soul's house— grow feeble, the limbs tremble, eating loses its pleasure as the few remaining teeth cease their function. With steadily increasing deafness, all the typical sounds of an Eastern village grow faint—even the sound of grinding corn. The sudden note of a bird startles the mind grown nervous of every change; hills, and all steep places have to be avoided because of unsteady gait—the ordinary paths have terrors enough for the shuffling uncertain feet of the defenceless. The hair whitens like the bloom on the almond tree; the bony frame grows hunched, bent and awkward like the grasshopper—and all natural desire fails. Because man goes to his eternal home, and the mourners go about the streets, there is nothing left but to await the call—before the silver cord of life is snapped, or the golden bowl of life is broken, or the pitcher is smashed at the fountain and the wheel shattered at the cistern—and one's dust returns to the earth as it was, and the spirit to God who gave it.

At least that is a great deal more compassionate than Shakespeare's almost contemptuous—

Second childishness, and mere oblivion,
Sans teeth, sans eyes, sans taste, sans everything . . .

The lean and slippered pantaloon

or W. B. Yeats's

An aged man is but a paltry thing
A tattered coat upon a stick . . .

Ecclesiastes is kinder, too, than the common assumption that the old
are inevitably mentally deficient, hopelessly out of date, ignorant,
to be cossetted, tolerated, humoured, but never taken seriously.

But compassion is not pity: it is gentleness with understanding.
Dr Anthony Bashford quotes extraordinarily perceptive words of
John Lennon: 'The thing I'm afraid of is growing old. I hate that.
You get old and you've missed it somehow. The old always resent the
young, and vice versa.' That focuses the mood of many old people
today: fear of getting older; disappointment tinged with envy of
those who come later and inherit things you never had; resentment
at the freedom, prosperity, education, uninhibitedness of youth—at
being shut out, left behind, too late—and at being treated as children
by those who owe their very existence and all else to the generation
behind them. The old do resent the young: and the young resent the
old—their wisdom, authority, claim, and obligation.

Sometimes, the resentment has cause. The rebelliousness, brash-
ness, harshness of youth, their scorn of everything the old fought for
and believed in, invites a backlash of impatience and of anger that
can only alienate, poisoning the mind and mood of age into a
bitterness towards life with which the pastor may find it very
difficult to sympathise. If this sounds extreme, it is by no means rare.
Certain normal and inescapable features of old age provoke that
protest in the soul, and the stronger, richer, more active the soul has
been, the greater the protest at life's dwindling into age. Some
abnormal complications may turn protest into barely tolerable
spitefulness.

Normal Burdens of Age

Among unwelcome but inevitable factors in growing old are:
(i) *Infirmity*—the steadily increasing helplessness which is a
vexation, a humiliation, to an independent spirit, and should be. To
be impatient with that feeling is simply not to understand. The
advancing deafness that at first one tries to hide from oneself, and
then tries hard to hide from others, that cuts one off from

conversation, laughter, even the greeting of passing friends, making one look stupid because a question goes unnoticed, or a remark is incongruously answered; the dimming of sight that makes walking uncertain, friends difficult to recognise, reading a labour, and people's facial expressions no longer an index to their conversation—these are no light afflictions.

Stiffening of joints and uncertain balance mean decreased mobility, so that getting about is toilsome, every walk an adventure, unfamiliar streets, houses, steps, a risk. Ours is a cruel world in which to be old, with restricted street crossings timed for agile people, with flashing lights that command and forbid, with everywhere printed instructions which you dimly see while you are trying to find the kerbstone with your feet, escalators, lifts, public vehicles that have no time to wait for tottering people—and for some, the bewildering, obsessive preoccupation with pain at every movement, every meal, and through the nights. Often, too, there are private, intimate problems and deficiencies which they would never name to you, but which you must never forget. You cannot *begin* to minister to old people until you understand infirmity.

No old person, even on the fringe of a Christian fellowship, should be left to struggle alone with advancing age. The visitor should not enquire about deafness, just notice, and speak clearly—not loudly. Presently, gently persuade that using a deaf-aid is no disgrace, but as sensible as using glasses—and see that the instrument actually works. Remember what a trial old ladies face to wash and arrange their hair, and pay a graceful compliment. Notice when the old teapot or coffee jug is getting too heavy, and organise tactfully a gift of one easier to handle—then give them time to come round to it! Provide a large-print Bible, and hymnbook, and other reading matter (short sections are lighter to hold) and leave them without comment. Arrange transport not only to special treats but to the regular services and sectional meetings, and especially to the Lord's Supper—but see that the car is roomy enough for ill-managed limbs and figures less slim than once they were. When need arises, see that the welfare authorities are alerted for the provision of walking-aids, domestic help, nursing or other services. Observation, tact, and care add up to a ministry of comfort which the proud old will accept silently, but not without appreciation.

(ii) *Isolation* may be as heart-breaking as infirmity. Many who now are old were shy and retiring by training and long habit: age makes them more so, and unease in the presence of a 'superior' person like the pastor will make them slow of thought and speech, anxious not to offend. Facility in making new friends decreases as the need of them grows. Mentally, too, the old often feel isolated from a world of new ways, new language, new topics of conversation, and a host of questions and opinions they do not begin to understand. The loneliness of mind possible to an old person in young company is hard to imagine. The people they knew, the places they remember, the issues they felt strongly about, the causes that once possessed their zeal—nothing is of the least interest to those around them, who know only their own world.

For many, this detachment from contemporary life is intensified by bereavement—for some, by divorce: the partner who shared the old memories and thoughts is no longer there to listen—or to disagree! Added to the mental isolation is often a sense of not being wanted, of uselessness, of not contributing to any circle or purpose. Life's drives have dwindled to sitting in a corner and keeping out of the way. In defence, the old will sometimes withdraw still further into a spiritual isolation that is scornful, critical, pretending supreme indifference to everything that is going on, resentful of all approaches —yet needing friendship desperately. The pastor will find such an attitude inexcusable—and pathetic. Says one who knows: 'In the solitude of bed-sitting rooms, in nursing homes or in guest houses, in the geriatric wards of hospitals, some elderly people live out dreary days with nothing to do, with no conscious purpose in life, with no hope in the future.' Of course there are many happy old people, with loving families and many friends, and an alert interest in life: they too will appreciate ministry, but they present fewer problems. For those whose isolation is deepest, the simplest practical steps to keep them in touch with life will have value—to see that they have literature easy to read, radio or television that works, visitors with whom they can truly converse and find refreshment of spirit. But more will be needed than this.

(iii) *Retirement* is itself a problem, and often unexpectedly so. One who has taken pride in his daily work, has enjoyed responsibility, has felt himself useful to others and seen things grow under his hand, has enjoyed the daily stimulus of workmates and colleagues, must miss a great deal that probably he scarcely valued until it had ended. A woman whose work has been her life will soon find lack of work very like lifelessness. The looked-for freedom and rest turns out to be idleness and loss of purpose, want of any daily plan or weekly pattern, and of companionship. Even husband and wife find the first days of retirement taxing: there is so little to talk about now, and so much time in which to do it.

The answer lies in *partial* retirement, if possible, for the first year or so, and *planned* retirement in any case. New interests should be decided upon, and begun, in readiness; societies and groups explored and joined; odd tasks should be undertaken—voluntary, social, church work of many kinds; especially should opportunities be sought out in which the skills and experience of a lifetime may be used part-time and at reduced pressure for good causes; study courses in new fields may be chosen and embarked upon—all before retirement begins. The action, the commitment, are important: vague, undated intentions continually postponed will be of little help. The happiest of all retirements for busy people is that which seems busier than ever—though now each task is chosen and enjoyed, keeping at bay the dreaded time when there is nothing left to live for.

(iv) *Unexpected poverty* is a sad disappointment to many older people, evoking more than a little of shame, felt injustice, and fear. Many who 'made arrangements for a rainy day' find that inflation has made their careful provision ridiculously inadequate, their thrifty foresight look foolish. This is not their fault; they can neither understand why it happened nor remedy it. They resent it, feeling 'let down' when others who squandered their income, or who never earned much, are maintained from public funds, which they themselves are most reluctant to receive.

The familiar independence of old people is not stupidity or pride, but a whole life's training, not lightly to be cast aside. Where public pensions or allowances are available, the pastor will persuade that they should be utilised, but he will need tact, and strict truth, in doing so. It will help little to argue 'You paid for it, it is yours by right'. Those who all their lives have had to count the cost of things can work out for themselves how long the pension would last if it were only their weekly contributions coming back! The pastor may urge that their life work and payment of taxes has helped to create society's present wealth, which it is therefore right that they should share; he may also urge that God uses the goodwill of a society slowly learning to provide for all, to make His own provision for His people. In practical ways, too, the observant pastor will watch for the needs so bravely hidden, the inadequate heating, food, clothes, light, the early retiral to bed, although sleep is poor, to save on expenses—and will organise discreet assistance.

(v) *The loss of religious support* is a common, and costly, feature of age. Diminished mobility, the bereavement of friends, incapacity to continue Christian work once loved, the necessity to move from the old home, losing touch with the long-familiar congregation, which itself so quickly changes that former members are soon little remembered, the removal of a long-loved pastor—many such circumstances contribute to severing of ties that once sustained spiritual life. Some, accustomed to the quiet and reverence of a Christian home, are forced to end their days in homes of others who have no sympathy with religious faith or scruples, in an atmosphere entirely alien to Christian sensibility.

Equally distressing to many older minds is the confusion, the obscuring of faith, that results from changing interpretations of the scriptures, from new views about the Christian creed, from radically differing opinions on what is permitted to the Christian. Convictions and ideals learned in childhood, perhaps idealised in memory but basic to a lifetime of religious experience and loyalty, seem to be challenged, scorned and overthrown, even by those who still pass for 'religious'. Others, who never had a religious training and have no religious experiences to remember, come to the end of life with intense spiritual hunger, and in complete bewilderment about life's meaning, worth, and destiny.

A booklet on the care of the elderly lays unexpected stress on the need that those who minister to them shall offer 'a clear statement of personal belief and the grounds on which such belief is founded'. It emphasises the deep needs of the human heart in 'the area of faith about life and death', and as to hopes, fears, motives, purposes, joy and guilt—'for which the religious, compassionate, well-informed, experienced, and articulate clergy and laity have a special responsibility'. It must be recognised that a number of people in these days reach old age deeply hostile to all religion, partly through embittering experiences, through smothered guilt, or through tragic ill-treatment by unworthy professors of religion. But others are ready and eager for spiritual counsel, instruction, comfort, and restoration to Christian faith.

Much can be done by an alert sympathy to keep older members of the Christian fellowship in touch with its ongoing life and work, by seeing that a church newsletter circulates freely and regularly, filled with the refined 'gossip' of church friendship and affairs which would be exchanged on social occasions. Reports on church meetings should be informative, written expressly for those absent, giving reasons, discussions, difficulties as well as decisions. The pastor should take care to consult older members on new proposals and convey their opinions to the deciding bodies. A little thought and organisation can keep older people, longing for something to do, knitting, sewing, making gifts for children, addressing church correspondence, making decorations, sweets, cakes, and a hundred other things—some of which could no doubt be more quickly done by younger people, or could be purchased, but the doing of which will bring intense satisfaction to those so allowed still to contribute to the work they love. Meanwhile regular worship-visiting will help make some provision in place of the means of grace so sorely missed.

(vi) *Awareness of approaching death* is again an entirely normal feature of old age. When every announcement of another's death is a fresh warning; when every year off the calendar means one less ahead; when every springtime could be the last—after sixty or so the bell tolls always for thee! The evasions natural to youth are pathetic in old age: the reality looms too near to be ignored. The wise pastor will neither obtrude the subject into conversation and prayer nor avoid it, but be aware that old people may have good reason for wishing to hear him speak of it. The vagueness, and rarity, of any Christian teaching on the Christian view of death leaves many totally unprepared. Many need reassurance, an antidote to the nagging fear of dying; some need also a fresh grasp of the reality of God's personal forgiveness and peace through the death of Christ; all need the reinforcement of Christian hope and promise.

A faithful ministry to the aged will thus often anticipate the kind of help that the pastor is frequently called to offer to the dying. Far better to discuss the great Christian themes of immortality, hope, and Christ's victory over death, while strength of mind and spirit remain, storing up the undergirding truth that will—in the end—steady the soul's passing through the open gateway to the life beyond. There is nothing morbid in thus approaching the subject that ever hovers in the ageing mind, provided that the teaching be honest, forthright, founded on scripture and not imagination, and centred firmly on the dying, risen Christ, who abolished death and brought life and immortality to light through the gospel.

Remembering all these natural, inevitable features of growing old, is it strange that ageing hearts should often feel the root of anger, the 'conscious impotence of rage' which Eliot suggested marks the old? This is not entirely a modern trait, for

> Weak, sickly, full of pains, in every breath
> Railing at life and yet afraid of death

comes from the eighteenth century; but it is a mood of age which the pastor will often meet. W. B. Yeats noticed it—

> Did all old men and women, rich and poor,
> Who trod upon these rocks or passed this door,
> Whether in public or in secret rage
> As I do now against old age?

and Dylan Thomas approved of it—

> Do not go gentle into that good night.
> Rage, rage against the dying of the light.

Sometimes resentment focuses upon special grievances, sometimes upon the family, or upon younger people, sometimes upon those most anxious to help—for interfering! But the fundamental cause is the frustration and fear of age itself. At times the pastor can help the family to understand this, and be patient; rarely, he may help the old to see it too. Certainly he must understand it for himself, and keep unruffled his own sympathy and care, if he is ever to minister consolation and peace.

The Pastoral Aims

The irreversible situation sets firm limits to what the pastor can attempt, but he must not on that account undervalue his ministry; he will aim at adjustment, acceptance, reconciliation to age, but as a positive reaction, not a negative and passive resignation. Plainly he will seek to assuage the envy and the anger, the helplessness, loneliness and fears. He will try to show how natural, universal, inevitable age is—no special spitefulness of fate against an undeserving victim! Both practically and by explanation he will strive to make the burdens more tolerable, more understandable; will help the resentful to see that no one is fairly to blame for what could not be avoided; will try to persuade the neglected that no one means to be unkind—but the young have *always* been preoccupied, too immature to understand: even the old were so once.

Plainly, too, the pastor will do all he can to bridge the gap between the old and the younger members of the family, and of the neighbourhood. It needs extreme care not to appear to be interfering or tale-bearing: yet he can help, as few can, to interpret each to the other. He can gradually instil into envious hearts that all the talk of the good old days implies that *theirs* was a richer, calmer life, with less of stress, fewer pressures, temptations or problems than young parents face today; he can help the old to appreciate that their home discipline, thrifty ways, fine example, plain wholesome food and the rest were privileges that many of today's young people never inherit.

And he can help the young to appreciate the lack of education, the long hours of work, the larger families, with little social help or welfare, the stress of two world wars, the disappointments and the fears, that make the old 'difficult to understand'. But to succeed, the pastor needs real knowledge of past years, and the ability to listen, to sift, and to turn to good advantage what he hears.

Thirdly, he will strive to retain the dignity, the self-respect and independence of the old by every possible means—never by any action, word or tone appearing to condescend, or pity, or rebuke, but practising a considerable discretion in doing good, so that pride is not wounded, and confidences are strictly kept. Finally, a Christian ministry to the old strives to evoke a positive attitude towards the remaining years, as no mere futility or loss, no protracted, useless pause between life that was and life that is to be, but itself a part of God's pattern, a reaping time, a time for maturing and deepening one's knowledge of God, for recollection, and for long, long thoughts again. Certainly old age is part of the Christian plan of life. With Christ, youth is an adventure, middle life a task, old age a harvesting, an opportunity to see more clearly what are the really important things, for deliberately recalling all that was good and gracious in a long career, for walking daily a little closer with the God who has been loved and trusted through the years, until the day comes when like Enoch we walk on and on and fail to come back. Age is

> The last of life, for which the first was made:
> Our times are in His hand
> Who saith 'A whole I planned,
> Youth shows but half; trust God: see all, nor be afraid!'

The promise God made to Israel holds good for all His people:

> who have been borne by me from your birth,
>   carried from the womb;
> even to your old age I am He,
>   and to grey hairs I will carry you.
> I have made, and I will bear;
>   I will carry and will save.

It would indeed be strange if the God who gave us life, who kindles the joy of childhood, who satisfies the exciting, clamorous needs of youth, who sustains the burden and the strain of middle life, should lack the wisdom, power or love to bring His people at the last, full of grace and peace, to inherit eternal joy.

Some Abnormal Complications

Age has of course its own sicknesses to complicate the natural weakness of advancing years. The watchful, attentive pastor is often aware of developing needs and dangers, sometimes anticipating problems before they can become emergencies. His card-index will record the family doctor's name and telephone, the addresses of close members of the family; he will know what domestic help or district nursing services are available, and sometimes he will leave his own name and address with nearby neighbours with invitation to let him know if at any time he is needed.

Ordinary household dangers are of course increased by impaired senses. The pastor will notice faulty electric wiring, the smell of gas, the smoking chimney, the loose stair carpet, and take appropriate action. He will learn of uneasiness caused by local behaviour, fears arising from undue noise or other annoyance, and sifting crotchetiness from genuine grievance, attempt to find a cure. When serious medical attention becomes necessary, the pastor will sometimes find himself mediating between family or medical authorities and a reluctant or frightened patient. He can often persuade that a consultation is necessary, introduce the possibility of surgery, be first to suggest mechanical aids or the need of constant attendance: for it is easier for some old people to assent without loss of face to something the trusted pastor advises. Sometimes he will urge that it is of little use to pray, if we wilfully refuse the help that God has placed within our reach.

Aware how much depends upon the maintenance of hope and courage, the pastor will follow up medical decisions with immediate pastoral ministry. Recuperative powers are slower in age but still wonderfully resilient, and without pretending to medical prognosis a pastor is justified in reinforcing the opinion that treatment, since it is advised, must be hopeful. Pastoral support will be most needed where signs have appeared of mental illness, sometimes inducing such shock as to destroy the patient's will to recover. The family may at once assume the worst, and their fears will quickly communicate themselves to the old. Yet sometimes the 'mental trouble' is no more than delirium due to high temperature, the side-effects of powerful drugs, the after-effects of operations, or the effect of vivid dreams on a mind too weakened in concentration to reassert control of thought and emotion, and laugh off the fears of the dark hours. Disorientation, delusion, fluctuating memory or recognition, are always distressing, and the underlying causes must be sought with the usual expert medical assistance—but there is no need to assume that the old person has 'gone mad', or that a night's rest will not fully restore the faculties. Most pastors meet this numbing dread of insanity, and learn to confront it with gently cool, even amused, understanding, allaying by a quite unemotional reaction the panic others feel, while privately contacting the family doctor to report what is happening.

'The prognosis of mental disorders in old age is probably better than one would anticipate ... The psychiatrist of today knows that many old people recover, or improve, even following psychotic breakdown.' So reports Dr Martin Roth. The cure of such conditions lies obviously well beyond the competence of the average pastor, but there is no doubt that among the factors which predispose towards favourable results is the confident, unyielding frame of mind, the positive, courageous expectation of good, which the pastor's ministry can help to sustain.

Among the serious disorders that afflict old people with special intensity, Dr Bashford names five that a pastor does well to recognise sufficiently to seek qualified help in time. (i) *Depression* can vary from 'an off day', a passing mood of discontent or disappointment, to a lasting lowness of spirits deepening into despair—when the risk of serious self-neglect, self-injury, and even suicide is fairly high. Among symptoms may be a generalised and unshakeable anxiety, an immediate fear of crisis, of emergency and imminent disaster which appears to have no identifiable cause; or a general listlessness and apathy which neglects to prepare meals, attend to necessary chores, or keep the person clean and neat.

Carelessness as to appearances, of the home as well as of the person, may first betray something being 'let go'. Sleeplessness may be a lifelong habit, the result of retirement, or it may suggest a deterioration of spirit. Careful conversation (but not direct enquiry) can discover neglect of accustomed acts of piety—the daily Bible reading and prayer, attendance at religious meetings—and reveal in turn some accumulating feeling of resentment, or of guilt, which avoids the remembrance of God. Too much attention to questions of health, symptoms, medical 'neglect', may show that anxiety is increasing about bodily conditions; but so too the deliberate avoidance of all reference to health or appetite can sometimes betray a hidden over-anxiety, even a growing delusion, about dreaded diseases, the breakdown of natural functions, or insanity.

Among the many possible degrees of depression, the pastor can only exercise a common-sense judgement, and offer a faithful ministry of counsel, scripture teaching, and recall to habits of prayer and faith. Often this is all that is necessary to achieve a more reasonable and confident frame of mind. Where this fails, and the condition seems to deteriorate, other help should be sought.

(ii) At the other extreme to depression is *mania*, a condition of heightened mental activity that loses all touch with reality and the common limitations of things, giving way to the most exalted delusions of personal skill, importance, wealth, and power, framing and setting on foot impossible schemes of all kinds; dressing up in ostentatious costumes, indulging in extravagant claims to great achievements in the past, records broken, crowds of flattering admirers; and making excessive demands on others' assent, obedience, co-operation in plans and projects ridiculously wild.

Mania is an intolerable condition to live with, and the patient's removal to constant and expert oversight and treatment is as advisable for the family as for the sick person. The pastor will probably be quite unable to offer any ministry to the patient, but his assurance that sedatives, drugs, and many modern mental skills can treat such conditions successfully will help much to comfort the family, and perhaps to assuage their self-justifying resentment at what they have suffered!

(iii) *Hardening of the arteries*, inevitable with advancing years, may reach a condition ('arterio-schlerosis') in which insufficient blood reaches the brain. Symptoms will depend on the area of the brain being starved, loss of memory, lack of concentration, unstable emotional tone, fluctuating moods, a clear mind one day, a scatter-brained muddle the next. By its very nature the condition tries the patience of those who must continually adjust to it, trying to keep the person happy. The pastor can reinforce sympathy with understanding, and possibly help the patient also to realise what is happening; but only medical skill can alleviate the trouble, provided it has not gone too far.

(iv) '*Late paraphrenia*' is a further trying development, and seems to have no known cause or cure, unless there is a psychological history to explain it. An old person, otherwise healthy and normal, may develop a deep and generalised suspicion of everyone in sight— friends, visitors, neighbours, officials, the doctor and the rest are 'all up to no good', seeking some advantage, trying to get the better of the defenceless old! Handbags are hidden away, purses and wallets put in the most inaccessible places, and when the place of conceal-ment is forgotten, that is 'proof' that suspicion was well grounded. Noises in the night, passing aircraft, rumbling water-pipes, the lights of passing cars, may all feed a persecution-obsession, playing imaginatively around death rays, flying saucers, evil spirits, witch-craft, even spiritism. A sudden concern for the reform of 'un-precedented evils and abuses that threaten all Christian civilisation' may lead to a spate of letter-writing to the press and to public figures —the more exalted they are, the more responsible for the world's state, and the more necessary it is to stir them to action.

Old fears revive, especially the single woman's long buried fear of unwanted sexual approaches. Old superstitions recur at such a time, with exaggerated terror of curses, ill-luck omens, spells, charms and the like. Many painful twinges, bad dreams, tricks of memory, and uncertainties of vision can lend new support to half-believed legends of devils, ghosts, and other 'spiritual appearances'. Especially do imperfections on the cornea give rise to strange accounts of what the patient 'can see for herself'—snakes, flowing water, moving lights, crawling insects—which alarm the hearers with fears of mental disturbance when the descriptions given are strictly accurate, and the real cause is impaired sight.

In all such symptoms it is not difficult to see the decay of mental strength, concentration, perspective, and self-discipline, allowing the accumulated ideas, impulses, fears and emotions of a lifetime to run amok, without control. Here again, understanding, unfaltering sympathy, humouring friendship, constant reiteration that the answer to all our fears is to rest in the care of God our Father and our Guardian, is the pastor's best assistance. A dilemma arises when the patient, appealing to this sympathy, seeks the pastor's support for some of the stories, explanations, protests or fears that mean so much to the aged person. It is useless to argue—the position is beyond persuasion, and an obsessive idea will, curiously, beget its own endless logical justification. Yet for the pastor to give assent to the views expressed would be dangerous, for his authority is enormous in support (worthless if he opposes!). Probably the best response is— 'Well, I have never in my life met a demon, a persecutor, a sex maniac, a ghost, so I do not know—but this I do know, that God is love, God cares, and God is watching over you.'

(v) *Senility* is the final stage, the price that must be paid for a strong body that outlives the atrophying brain. It is the decay of all the avenues of intelligence, emotion, initiative and control. Memory becomes faulty, though the patient will insist it is clear and unquestionable; because retentive memory depends upon depth, clarity and emotional associations of first impressions and their subsequent repetition, the things most easily recalled in age are the memories of early years, while the shallow impressions made by recent events, in which the old had little interest, pass immediately beyond recall. The over-active imagination produces restlessness and destroys sleep. Together with the loss of all sense of time, this can result in midnight activity, meals, walks, visits, that are inconvenient, and dangerous, but perfectly understandable. Failure of concentration makes conversation difficult: the thread is lost, and new ideas do not come, while trying to pursue them brings deeper confusion and distress. The same failure of concentration can bring a loss of mental control; ideas that once would be automatically suppressed by the inner censor of morals and manners, now float in the mind unhindered and may overflow in conversation, not because 'he is getting a dirty old man' or she 'loves salacious gossip', but merely because the inner discipline has failed. So childhood's uninhibitedness returns, sometimes with the same childish demands for attention, and sulkiness if attention is not forthcoming.

No ministry can cure, or even greatly help this condition. The more frequently that familiar and loved ideas of faith and piety can be recalled and shared, the sweeter will be the mind content and the mood. Reassurance, support, constant reminder of the simplest, most central things in Christian life in affirmations, memories, loved scriptures, hymns, prayers—but never argument, or the pressure of new ideas—will help to carry the failing soul in quiet confidence to the brink of that river beyond which life rises again to its floodtide.

'To know how to grow old', says Amiel, 'is the master work of wisdom and one of the most difficult chapters in the great art of living.' Its problems can be alleviated and redeemed, but not overcome. Yet what the pastor can do is no small contribution to its comfort, its dignity, and its enjoyment. As respectful, courteous, attentive friend, he can mediate between the generations, and between old memories and new conditions, watching for practical needs as they arise. As pastor, he can help to make the last years fruitful of mature and gracious experience, mellowing and deepening character, and stimulate the spiritual health that (especially in the last years) is no small part of total welfare. In his more priestly role, he can help prepare for age, for death, and for the life to come. And as man of God he can bring God very near in the last days when the soul's own energies of faith and prayer are too exhausted to seek God's presence for itself. Then the pastor in his own person becomes for the clinging heart the very embodiment of all God's promises, and the assurance that in the end nothing has separated from the love of God in Christ.

15 CONFRONTING DEATH

In a report on 'Health in the Individual and the Community' comment is made on the failure of so many of our hospitals to give proper attention to the psychological needs of the dying: 'the idea of the "good death" has hardly found a place in modern medical thinking.' In contrast, the work of Dr Cicely Saunders at St Christopher's Hospice, London is described. It has two closely related aims, firstly that death should be faced and accepted by her patients so that they can adopt that positive attitude toward it which enables us to turn the most hopeless situation into an opportunity for achievement; secondly, that by extremely skilled nursing and an expert balance in the use of pain-killing drugs, her patients may be kept alert and responsive to life until the very end of their own, enabling them to meet the challenge of death as fully conscious human beings. Death, says Dr Saunders, is not in itself hard; it is preparing to die which may be difficult.

Admirable as these two aims are, the Christian pastor may wonder how they are to be achieved by medical and psychological means alone, though what further aim he would himself seek is not very easy to define. So very much depends upon circumstances. The person dying may be a Christian friend, colleague, member of the congregation, and the pastor becomes involved for every personal and pastoral reason. Or the individual may be a total stranger, to whose bedside he is called by a relative or neighbour, or at a doctor's suggestion—in which case the first need is to establish a welcome. The end may have been long foreseen, or it may be due to sudden seizure or accident—in which case his immediate task will be to deal with shock, or panic. Plainly, almost everything will depend upon whether the patient is a Christian, to whom the pastor brings mainly comfort and reassurance; or a non-Christian, to whom he brings the evangel; and that again will depend upon his own theology of conversion and of death.

How much the pastor may attempt to do may be limited not only by the condition of the patient, but by whether he knows that the end is near. We may perhaps describe a Christian death as one approached with steadying confidence in the eternal love of God and the promise of eternal life; a death sensibly prepared for, faced with courage, and with forgiveness and love towards all, accepted without resentment as the Father's loving will, and consummated at last by a quiet committing of one's spirit into the Father's hands. The aim of all Christian ministry to the dying must then be to bring each individual as nearly as circumstances, condition, past life and present willingness allow, to a Christian passing—to enable each, in short, to die well.

Practical Considerations

Common-sense awareness of sickroom necessities is the more necessary where the patient is helpless and needs constant attention; the visitor will be ready to disappear and return without comment at the slightest hint. As a general rule, it would be folly to ignore a doctor's counsel that a particular patient should not be told that the end is approaching. Some doctors are temperamentally secretive, but most often there are good reasons for withholding *this* information, as the doctor considers the patient's physical, psychological and family circumstances. At the very least, a pastor should strive to consult the doctor before divulging what he thinks he knows. If the patient asks, such a question from the dying demands a truthful answer: but usually the truthful answer is, 'I am not a doctor, and I cannot tell; but if there is anything you ought to do, or want to say, it is well to be *always* prepared; none of us knows when life will close for us.' To say more, without medical authorisation, would be to incur heavy responsibility. Certainly a pastor has no right, in Christian love, to blurt out what he merely guesses.

If the suggestion of definite preparation is accepted, the pastor should act at once. A son or daughter may need to be called with urgency; and the pastor may have to resist the family in order to discharge his duty to the patient—he may be the only person the patient will trust. A letter of confession, or of forgiveness and reconciliation, may need to be written, and should be done at once—at least a written note of its contents drafted in the patient's presence—that the heart of the dying may find ease. Any last message entrusted to the pastor would be treated in the same way. If time and conditions allow, the preparation of a will is best left to a lawyer, the pastor making immediate arrangements, whatever the time of day. Where that is impossible, a note of final wishes, written in the patient's presence, and read over in the presence of a witness who also signs the record, will establish some *moral* (though not legal) authority when the wishes are reported to the family: it will also

G

afford some measure of content to the dying at having at least done his best.

Throughout a visit, the pastor will be aware how talk distracts the weakened mind, especially talk about new ideas, or any form of argument. Sentences will be clear, and short; one's manner not morbid or mournful but straightforward, confident, though sad. There need be no embarrassment at silence; there is no haste at death, and time for recollection, for unspoken companionship, is more valuable than chatter. Awareness of what is said must not be measured by articulate response; a look, a moving of the lips, may be all the patient is capable of emotionally, as well as physically, and the visitor will not withdraw the help he offers because there appears to be no answer, unless he realises that further talk is burdensome.

Similarly, it is exceedingly hurtful, as well as impolite, to whisper in the presence of the seriously ill. It is sometimes said that hearing is the last sense to be lost, and it is impossible to know with what pain or helpless embarrassment the patient may overhear his condition, his prospects, and perhaps himself, being surreptitiously discussed. Even if he cannot hear the words, to know that talk is going on, and to suspect that it is about himself, may be as distressing to the sick soul, lying

> like one in a trance,
> That hears his burial talked of by his friends
> And cannot speak, or move, nor make one sign
> But lies and dreads his doom.

Before he leaves, the pastor will consider whether any others in the household may be in need of reassurance, guidance or comfort: his presence, of itself, may often strengthen and restrain an otherwise frightened or hysterical wife or mother. How long the pastor stays will depend, of course, upon his intimacy with the household, the imminence of death, his other duties, and how many are being allowed to visit the sickroom. If he is the only one, he is probably expected to stay longer. When he does leave, the pastor will avoid an air of finality—'The Lord be with you, till I see you again'—and if he promises to return he must do so, even if news comes that he is too late. He will be waited for, and sorely missed if he fails to keep that promise.

It is always difficult to assess at such a time how far active help or guidance will be welcomed in arranging for the funeral and in making the other adjustments which the new situation will demand. A pastor must be willing, but not intrusive. He will probably learn to be ready with suggestions as to what must be done up to and just after the funeral: but to counsel a deliberate pause, perhaps of three weeks or three months if circumstances allow, before any far-reaching decisions are made. Intense grief is no aid to wisdom and a balanced mind, and with patience and prayer, the future that at first frightens and bewilders will be made plain.

For his real ministry in the presence of death the pastor needs more than common sense, sympathy and foresight; he needs a clear and simple pastoral theology concerning death, not indeed for discussion when the end is near, but to arm his own mind, inform his counsel, and inspire his prayers.

Theology of Death

It has often been remarked that death has replaced sex as the unmentionable subject, and non-Christians of considerable intellectual pretensions will often fall back upon the most naive and superstitious notions when the shadow falls too near. Lacking any confidence in life to come, modern man finds the fact of natural death and dissolution too horrible to contemplate, and turns away. Few adults have seen death; it is an occurrence for hospitals, among professionals. Its approach is not discussed, its onset is not described, the fact is referred to, when it cannot be avoided, only obliquely in euphemisms and circumlocutions—'passing on', 'if anything happens', 'had his', 'it proved terminal'. Funerals, too, become brief, professional, anonymous, although the after-care of tombs and memorials may be sentimentally extravagant. Fear of age and dread of death explain in part the twentieth century's pathetic worship of youth. Sartre's 'Death is absurd, we ought not to think about it' is indefensible; Heidegger's 'Death is an essential strand in the fabric of life; to think about death is part of living' has at least the ring of Christian realism.

For Christians, perforce, think about death a great deal, not only with the returning season of Passiontide, and the great Calvary themes that lie at the heart of the evangel and within many of our hymns, but on every celebration of Christian baptism and the Lord's Supper. Life through death is the heart of Christian experience; life through His death is the heart of the gospel. In place of the pagan symbols for death—the broken column, the snapped sword, the fallen tree, the pitcher broken, the spilled winecup, the broken lute-string— all expressing the sense of something ended, something lost, the Christian has learned the very different symbols of the empty cross, the riven tomb, the Easter lillies, the crown of life, rest in green pastures, the Father's house, the everlasting kingdom, harps and thrones, the Paradise garden and the city with the gates of pearl and streets of gold, all speaking of gain and hope, of victory and glory.

Behind the transformation of the symbols lies the transformation of the very thought of death, by Christ 'the death of death', who tasted death for every man and rose again. Death, for the Christian, has lost its sting, and the grave its victory—in this life! 'The soul's invincible surmise' that death just cannot be the end of the human pilgrimage, struggle and sacrifice, the eclipse of all faith in human dignity and destiny, the final blank contradiction of all life's meaning and value, received in Christ's resurrection God's unanswerable confirmation. What is at stake is not merely human comfort, but the significance of all man's moral endeavour, the assurance of eternal justice, the reality of divine compassion towards mankind. If death did end all, life itself would be devalued, and man but deluded dust. Hope is no opiate, but a spur; to believe that man has forever immeasurably increases his responsibility in decision, stiffens his courage to endure, prolongs the whole perspective of his effort, and endears all his relationships.

Yet such considerations, vital though they are for man's understanding of himself, are not the biblical basis of faith in immortality. The Bible's argument is that God loves man, accepts man into gracious fellowship, and in His faithfulness will never let man go. Said the psalmist—

> Whither shall I go from thy Spirit?
> Or whither shall I flee from thy presence?
> If I ascend to heaven, thou art there!
> If I make my bed in Sheol, thou art there!

And said Jesus, He is the God of Abraham, of Isaac, and of Jacob— in successive generations—yet never the God of the dead, but of the living, for all live unto Him. Add to this the promises of Jesus to His own, to give to them eternal life, to raise them at the last day; that no one should be able to pluck them from His hands; the promise of the Father's house, and the resurrection and the life. 'Because I live,' Jesus declared unforgettably, 'you will live also . . . I will come again, and receive you unto myself; that where I am, there you may be also.'

To the many questions that inevitably spring to mind, the wise pastor will pretend no final, infallible answers. He can be clear on certain great truths: the survival of personality; the final assessment of true achievement; the inheritance of life's gain, as earth's experience is carried forward to be the accumulated spiritual capital for another life; the permanence of faith and hope and love in life that is endless because divine; the preservation of values, the vindication of faith, and the victory of Life. And he can treasure certain great promises—faith to be lost in sight; rest from earth's labours; 'His servants shall serve Him'; 'we shall be like Him—we shall be satisfied, when we awake, with His likeness'.

> Therefore are they before the throne of God,
>   and serve him day and night within his temple;
>   and he who sits upon the throne will shelter them with his presence.
> They shall hunger no more, neither thirst any more;
>   the sun shall not strike them, nor any scorching heat.
> For the Lamb in the midst of the throne will be their shepherd,
>   and he will guide them to springs of living water,
>   and God will wipe away every tear from their eyes.

For the rest, the New Testament's emphasis is not upon the indefinite prolongation of *this* life, but upon change:

> Our commonwealth is in heaven, and from it we await a Saviour, the Lord Jesus Christ, who will change our lowly body to be like his glorious body, by the power which enables him even to subject all things to himself.

> We must be changed. Flesh and blood cannot inherit the kingdom of God.

As one identical life persists through all the changes in the seed, the plant, the fruit, so (says Paul) life persists unbroken through death— 'as we have borne the image of the man of dust, we shall also bear the image of the man of heaven'.

> For this perishable nature must put on the imperishable, and this mortal nature must put on immortality ... What is sown is perishable, what is raised is imperishable. It is sown in dishonour, it is raised in glory. It is sown in weakness, it is raised in power. It is sown a physical body, it is raised a spiritual body ... We shall all be changed.

Death *is* but a transformation, a birth into a new world, as fantastic, as unimaginable, as unforeseeable, as our birth into this.

That is the answer to the chief difficulty that most people experience concerning the Christian hope of immortality—the difficulty of imagination. *I have*, in sober fact, already lived in another, entirely different world; in total darkness, without eyes, in silence, aware only very dimly (if at all) of warmth and movement, a mother's pulse beat—yet alive, growing, preparing. Looking back, I can remember little (though my nervous system may); I can imagine absolutely nothing of that life, yet I certainly passed through it. Then came a vast change, a passing into this life, into a world of light and colour, of sound and beauty, of relationships and action and a manifold experience utterly unimaginable to me when I lay within the womb. But inability to imagine it did not make this world awaiting me an illusion, mere 'wishful thinking'. Moreover, in some inexplicable but real way, identity persisted through that life and into this. My body changed entirely—in size, weight, strength, power of adjustment and adaptation. Yet somehow it carried forward into this life the habit of curling up to find comfort, the heartbeat love of rhythm, a whole system of genes that determine the colour of my eyes, my hair, my temperament and gifts. All is changed, yet bears with it as inheritance a capital from a previous existence, inconceivable, well-nigh incredible, certainly unimaginable—yet certainly, scientifically, actually and literally *true*.

And it will happen just so, again, in death.

Armed with such reflections, scriptures, illustrations, the Christian pastor need not feel inadequate, confused or helpless in the face of death. He has much to say that no mocking cynicism, no proud agnosticism, can rival when the end draws near. Though in the shadow of death he will neither argue, nor preach, nor oppose, yet he will be ready with an answer for the hope that is within him, and bear in his own quiet assurance of manner a clear testimony to Christ's gift of everlasting life.

The Final Ministries

Just how this Christian gospel for the dying may best be expressed in home or hospital in the last hours of life will require considerable thought and delicate discrimination. To those who have not known the saving grace and sustaining fellowship of the risen Christ, the pastor will bring the simple, direct appeal to be saved by trusting wholly in Christ. Some will object that it is already too late to change a heart and mould a life in Christian ways. Others will strive above all for the profession of some time-honoured form of words that may or may not be understood, but probably cannot convey what the patient means to say, because they are not his own. Deathbed repentance, and even more deathbed evangelism, may have the ring of 'cheap grace' and a suspicion of insincerity. Yet the story of Calvary has an illuminating footnote in Christ's assurance to the dying thief, and since then none dares set limit to the infinite compassion of God.

Plainly, the visiting pastor cannot at this point try to lead a soul through all steps of Christian experience, or define the meaning of great Bible terms, or seek promises of amendment of life. A simple confession of the need of God's mercy and forgiveness, a sincere acceptance that Christ died for our sins and offers pardon to all who believe—these justify the pastor in giving assurance of salvation, and of life everlasting, in Christ's name. In the end, only God knows the heart of any man (including the pastor's), and the pastor will refrain from pronouncements to others on any soul's ultimate destiny. But though he does not know God's judgements, he does know the gospel. That Christ came into the world to save sinners, and that those who come to Him He will in no wise cast out—this he knows, and will seek to share, with all consideration, gentleness and courtesy, while time and breath and opportunity last.

For Christian and non-Christian alike, help may be needed in facing the experience of dying, and not only the fact of death. To speak of birth, release, and rest, may help; but the great scriptural pictures of Christ coming to receive us unto Himself; standing to welcome Stephen, in the moment of his death, into glory; loving His own right to the end; giving to His beloved in sleep; and the glorious promise that neither life nor death shall separate us from the love of God, will do more than persuasion to reassure the fearful soul. A quiet repetition of familiar and powerful words—

Whatever my lot, Thou hast taught me to know
It is well with my soul!

All the trumpets sounded for him on the other side!

In life, in death, O Lord,
Abide with me.

I am now ready to be offered, and the time of my departure is at hand. I have fought a good fight, I have finished my course, I have kept the faith: henceforth there is laid up for me a crown of righteousness . . .

Let not your heart be troubled; ye believe in God, believe also in me. In my Father's house are many mansions . . . Let not your heart be troubled, neither let it be afraid.

I will not fail you, nor forsake you.

Father, into thy hands I commit my spirit.

Such words, laden with the faith of generations, bring more steadfastness and comfort at the last than all our exhortation or our thought.

Of course, while consciousness and concentration last a brief, clear ministry of word and prayer is possible. Here, too, the familiar has most power, provided it be not merely hackneyed and unconsidered. Even Psalm 23 and John 14 can lose their significance in habitual recitation. The resurrection stories, Romans 8, John 6, John 10, Paul's great passages in Thessalonians and Corinthians, the beloved Psalms, the positive affirmations of Peter's rich epistle, 1 Corinthians 13 and Revelation 7, all yield strong comfort, and should be drawn upon as age and circumstances suggest.

The Lord's prayer, spoken very slowly, the Christian benediction, and other known prayers from scripture or elsewhere, will help the patient share in moments of praying, which should be brief and simple, and such as the patient can make his own.

> O Lord, support us all the day long of this troublous life
> Until the shadows lengthen and the evening comes,
> And the busy world is hushed,
> The fever of life is over,
> And our work is done.
> Then, Lord, in Thy mercy, grant us safe lodging, a holy rest, and peace at the last, through Jesus Christ our Lord.

Always include, too, words of confession, and the acceptance of forgiveness. It is very important, in such need, to pray not only for the patient but with him, uttering the patient's prayer. Imagine what he would say, if he could find strength and voice—and say it for him.

Verses of beloved hymns are useful for such prayer, and also for focusing faith and testimony, rekindling feeling, recalling past comforts and days of great blessing. Remembered briefly in this way, they can linger in the mind when the visit is over, bringing peace and renewed grace in the long hours of watching.

But let it be repeated that silence too can be gracious. Dying is a lonely experience: perhaps the deepest need is for a trusted friend, who stands for everything loved and believed and for a wider circle of fellow believers, simply to be there, sharing the moments, representing the Faith, embodying the hope. And one who, when the end has come, will be counsel and support to dear ones left behind.

In such ministry the pastor realises again his own dependence upon the help of God and the direction of the Comforter. But these are given. By them, a soul that has lived in faith can be assisted to 'die in the Lord—to depart and be with Christ, which is far better'.

16 SOME SPIRITUAL MALADIES

Among the larger domestic and social problems with which the Christian pastor tries to help, are some less dramatic and much nearer home, the inadequacies, difficulties and failures within Christian life itself. The aim here is authoritatively defined: 'the maturing of the saints, the work of ministry, the upbuilding of the body of Christ, till we all come in the unity of the faith and of the knowledge of the Son of God, to a mature man, to the measure of the stature of the fullness of Christ.' A full, useful, happy Christian life, steadfast under pressure, Christlike in character, contributing richly to the lives of others, is the obvious goal, but something less will often confront the pastor in his local Christian fellowship. In general, sympathy, insight born of personal and vicarious spiritual experience, and the aid of the Spirit, must help him diagnose what is wrong; the scriptures illumined by the Spirit, and *not* merely his own experience, must show him how it can be righted. It is important that the spiritual health of others should not stand in the wisdom or example of men, but in the word and the power of God.

The variety of spiritual need is endless, but some frequent spiritual maladies may provide examples of pastoral care of the unhappy Christian.

(i) *Immaturity*

Evangelical emphasis upon the wonder of conversion sometimes diverts attention from the need of continued growth and progress in Christian experience and character. Scripture rebukes the *uselessness* of the immature who, considering the time they have been Christians, should be teaching others, but still need to be taught the first principles of the gospel, being babes in need of milk, and not solid food, unskilled in the word of righteousness. Elsewhere, the *emotional vulnerability* of the immature occasions concern—'Be no more children, tossed to and fro, and carried about with every wind of doctrine, by the cunning of men . . .', while the jealous, self-assertive *divisiveness* of the church at Corinth is traced to the members being still 'babes in Christ'—a nursery of childish converts.

The steps of spiritual advance are wonderfully described in 2 Peter 1 : 5–7 : to faith's vision of the ideal must be added resolution to follow it, and growing knowledge of oneself and of the world as potential obstacles. In face of temptation from within, the Christian will need self-discipline; in face of opposition from without he will need steadfastness. Such conflicts teach the value of those regular habits of prayer and worship which the New Testament calls godliness, and teach also a better appreciation of the struggles of other Christians, producing brotherly love. Out of that growing insight and sympathy, the crown of Christian character comes within reach—Love itself. At any rung of this ladder of Christian progress the young convert may halt. The pastoral task is to discover where, and why, and this passage is a useful check list—was it lack of vision, of resolution, of self-understanding . . .? To persuade young Christians of the need to grow in Christ, 'in understanding' to 'be men', and to follow on to know the Lord in deeper ways as the years pass, is the first duty of the pastor to the convert, requiring delicacy, firmness, and sometimes courage.

The need is greatest in two related areas of Christian experience, living by faith, and expecting answers to prayer. Early experiences of the miracles of faith provide such confirmation of God's nearness and power that the young convert tends to expect marvels every day, and to see in prayer an infallible means for getting what he wants and when he wants it. He soon learns otherwise—the painful way. A sickness is not healed, a coveted examination result is not achieved, a friend is not converted: prayer has failed, and faith 'is shaken'.

The pastor of course will not question the astonishing answers to prayer, the miracles of providence—or coincidence—which mean so much to the young Christian. He knows that God ever deals with children in childlike ways. But he knows too that God's children must grow up. He strives therefore to prepare for the disappointments and delays, the harder lessons and the divine refusals, that must be faced and inwoven into faith, with growing understanding of God's ways.

The elementary lesson is that God uses means, as well as miracles, to do His will. Jesus does not create water at Samaria, or loaves and fishes in the wilderness, or a boat, a donkey, a coin: He adopts, borrows, sends for, what lies to hand. Paul advises wine for stomach upsets, organises a collection for relief of famine, welcomes human provision for his needs, enjoys the attentions of Luke to his medical welfare, with no thought that such secondary instruments infringe

upon faith in God's provision. Those for whom the whole earth is full
of God's glory see no contradiction between material and human
instruments and the divine sovereignty and love which made all for
man's use. The immature Christian must be weaned from dependence
upon 'inexplicable divine coincidences' to a more rational and
enduring confidence that God fulfils Himself in many ways, and
'Omnipotence has servants everywhere'.

Faith certainly is justified in expecting great things from God, in
counting upon His intervention in everyday affairs. Once a man is
sincerely convinced that any plan *is* the will of God, he may go
ahead, confidently leaving God to open up the way and provide the
means. The second lesson, however, is to let God have His way, to
give or to withhold, and not to fret when cherished plans go wrong.
The Bible's most magnificent chapter on faith—Hebrews 11—is not
concerned at all with the faith that trusts in God and gets what it
wants, but with the maturer faith that trusts in God and goes
without. The great heroes 'all died in faith, *not* having received the
promises'; 'faith is the evidence of things *not* seen'. It is not easy to
persuade the young Christian that the faith which 'sees the hand of
God' and has endless thrilling testimonies to God's answers to prayer,
is more 'sight' than 'faith'; that he must learn to believe that God is
at hand when the signs are withheld, that God's faithfulness is
unaltered when comforts are withdrawn.

Mature faith still prays when prayer fails of its expected result.
To those familiar with the New Testament, unanswered prayer
remains a disappointment but should never be a problem. The
proposed prayer for revengeful fire upon a Samaritan village, the
Pharisee's prayer of self-righteous pride, the ostentatious prayer that
seeks human admiration, the prayer of the unforgiving heart—all
such are unanswered and unanswerable. Paul's prayer for relief from
affliction, like Christ's prayer in Gethsemane, warn us that prayer
establishes no claim upon God, coercing Him to grant what otherwise
He would not give, or to interfere in other lives against their will, or
to change His loving purposes for us or for the world. Prayer rests
entirely upon 'Thy will be done'—the glad acknowledgement that
God knows best. Immature prayer addresses God across a gulf,
asking for what it wants; maturer prayer stands beside the God we
have come to trust implicitly, pleading only that what He wants
shall be done. The pastor who can nurture infant faith to that
measure of maturity will have laid the foundation for life rooted
unshakably in the faithfulness of God, and confident always that His
will is good.

(ii) *Depression*

The sharp fluctuations of feeling which distress young Christians are likewise symptoms of immaturity. The relief of forgiveness, the joy of knowing oneself loved, saved, set free, the excitements of new friendships and new patterns of life, often accompanied by considerable 'fussing over' and publicity, all tend to confirm that God's 'blessing' is a highly emotional experience, and the Christian life an endless thrill. The pastor will understand, and share, this great happiness: but he will foresee the need to become independent of it. He will warn clearly that, if for nervous and psychological reasons alone, a reaction is inevitable; no normal soul can live at a pitch of excitement. He will explain, too, beforehand, that while faith is greatly helped by feelings, it is not itself a feeling, nor dependent upon feeling, but often strongest when all joy and excitement are withdrawn, and the soul coldly, deliberately, without emotional help, walks obediently with God through some desert experience.

Of one of the most powerful and fruitful periods of his whole evangelistic career, Paul wrote 'we were so utterly, unbearably crushed that we despaired of life itself'. God remained faithful—but at times it did not feel like it—'We are afflicted in every way, but not crushed; perplexed, but not driven to despair; persecuted, but not forsaken; struck down, but not destroyed.' It is a sign of maturity to be able to see both sides of experience—and to admit to both. The truth is that at any given moment our emotions depend upon many factors that have little to do with spiritual realities, upon health, tiredness, digestion, temperament, physical comfort, anticipated duties or afflictions. The mature Christian, when joy and high spirits are given him, thanks God for them; and when they are withdrawn, trusts God without them. The pastor will often recommend the emotionally unstable to *memorise* Psalms 42 and 43:

> My soul thirsts for God . . . I pour out my soul . . . My soul is cast down within me . . . I say to God, my rock: 'Why hast thou forgotten me?' . . . Why go I mourning . . .

> Why are you cast down, O my soul,
>   and why are you disquieted within me?
> Hope in God; for I shall again praise Him,
>   my help and my God

—and to learn to laugh at himself.

(iii) *Doubt*

Doubt may arise from the false identification of faith with feeling, or from disobedience resulting in loss of assurance—'by rejecting conscience, certain persons have made shipwreck of their *faith*'. It may be little more than a sceptical frame of mind, repelled by the extravagant claims and superficial credulity that pass for faith; or it may be a serious intellectual difficulty in reconciling Christian teaching with strongly held convictions about the world. In appraising the nature of the doubt, in acknowledging the value of doubt in purifying religious belief from superstition and unexamined assumptions, and in leading unsettled minds to firmer conviction, the pastor will need all his skill in exposition, his wisdom with souls, and his intellectual integrity.

He will first seek to comfort and encourage. Doubt is no sin, unless it be wilfully persisted in, against all inward illumination, as excuse for disobedience. The honest mind, wrestling with problems of belief, may be sure that light will come if truly desired. It may assume that the Christian gospel has endured too long, accomplished too much, explains too many otherwise unanswerable dilemmas about human existence, rests on too great authority in the person and character of Jesus, not to be able to withstand fair investigation. And it should rejoice that at the very centre of the Gospels stand two figures whose experience should undergird every doubting soul: the man at the foot of the Mount of Transfiguration crying 'Lord, I believe, help Thou mine unbelief'; and the disciple Thomas, in the upper room, protesting his inability—or unwillingness—to believe unless convinced, and ending by protesting in the presence of the living Christ, 'My Lord, and my God'. Sometimes the honest questioner may learn much, too, from Matthew's ninefold gentle rebuke to those 'of little faith', not cast out for their unbelief, but encouraged from small faith to great faith by the words of Christ.

For the rest, the pastoral antidote to doubt is *persistent sincerity*, and *discrimination*. A man who has known the joy and strength of prayer may in all honesty go on praying, whatever his questioning, assuming no more than that prayer has been a help to himself and to others. A man who has seen the vision of true goodness in Christ Jesus may in all honesty go on following the steps of the Master, assuming no more than that history holds no better example of life well lived. To abandon either prayer, or moral loyalty to the best he knows, would be to abandon the search for truth; to hold to both is to be sure in the end to come out of darkness into His most marvellous light.

But that may not mean that everything he once believed will be as clear and certain again. Essential to mature belief is discrimination between truths that are known and tested in spiritual experience, and mere opinions that are formed, revised, adjusted or abandoned as Christian education supplies better information and guides a keener judgement. About many religious questions, affecting the origin of the scriptures and their meaning, prophecies and their fulfilment, theological and ecclesiastical issues and much more, a man may hold such opinions—and doubts—as study and experience have conferred, always aware that on some subjects humility demands an open mind, and on others a personal decision, which yet must not be imposed upon other minds. In this realm of religious opinion, freedom of enquiry and freedom to revise judgement are essential to Christian integrity.

But on the things that can be tested by faith, conscience, and obedience, a man can be sure, with a conviction unshakable by circumstances and unchallengeable by others. Thus Paul declares himself persuaded that nothing shall separate us from the love of God in Christ. He affirms that all things work together for good to them that love God. He triumphantly proclaims 'I know whom I have believed, and am persuaded that he is able to keep that which I have committed unto him against that day'. Such are the clear certainties that emerge from Paul's spiritual experience; and no man can consent to doubt his own experience—'that way madness lies'. On these, Paul builds a fourth, not yet experienced but assured by the logic of faith: 'We know that we have a house not made with hands, eternal in the heavens.' A love that will not let us go; a providence that shapes experience towards making us Christlike; a Christ wholly to be trusted to the end of time; and a firm hope—in consequence—of personal immortality: that is no mean creed. John would add the sure word of God that came to men in Christ, the life and the light of men; and the certainty of prayer: 'this is the confidence that we have in him, that if we ask anything according to his will, he heareth us.' 'By these things men live, and wholly in them is the life of the spirit': they are learned by walking with God, and not by discussion of Him.

The pastor will find very often that painful doubt is created by the failure so to discriminate spiritual convictions from religious views. A Christian may become deeply distressed to find his former opinions about the authorship of some biblical book, or some 'evangelical' doctrine, changing under pressure of new knowledge or scientific training. He *feels* that all the foundations of his faith are shaken, *nothing* is certain any more! Simply to draw the distinction between the things he knows, because so God has shown him, and the things he believes, because so he was first taught, is an immense relief to his soul. It is also the beginning of a firm conviction of the things that save, held alongside a tolerant teachableness about things that require endless investigation.

(iv) *Moral Backsliding*

When Christians withdraw life again from commitment to Christ, withholding obedience, deserting the means of grace and forms of service they had undertaken, numerous first-line 'explanations' will be offered which are not the true reasons. No soul abandons the living fellowship of Christ, the joy of Christian friendship and work, simply because of a quarrel, 'finding worship boring', or disappointment in some leading Christian. Some deeper disloyalty lies behind such a pose, prayerlessness, a seductive friendship, an enticement into more serious evil than is being confessed. Probing the true reason, and reminding of what loyalty to Christ has always demanded, may be all that is required. There is a bracing quality about Christ's own words, concerning those who put their hands to the plough and looking back prove themselves *unworthy* to be disciples, and others who start to build, or to fight, without first counting the cost, and prove themselves *unable* to finish, which powerfully stirs the slumbering conscience.

Where the cause of backsliding is spiritual malaise, a feeling that nothing has gone right, expected blessing has not been experienced, and unexpected opposition has disheartened, the pastor will turn to the epistle to the Hebrews. Addressing precisely that mood, the writer urges his readers (a) *not to forsake the assembling of themselves together*—the temptation to withdraw from fellowship appears to be a desire to avoid hypocrisy, but in fact it is to avoid the self-rebuke which others' zeal and joy would bring, and leaves us weakened by loneliness; (b) *to hold fast the profession of our faith*—for there are times when the soul needs to gather its resolution and lay hold of eternal life, vigorously affirming what it *does* know and *has* experienced through Christ; (c) *to draw near to God*—for the troubled soul so often runs away from God, hoping to return when all is well again: yet how can the heart be well without God, whose only purpose is our welfare and salvation? That passage, and indeed the whole epistle, is a marvellous cordial for drooping spirits.

Circumstances could arise in which the restoration of the wayward may require adjustment of lesser loyalties. Where—for example—a marriage engagement has been broken, or some public wrong has been committed, a violent quarrel has ended lasting friendship, or some similar obstacle remains to hinder full fellowship and remind of past failure, a pastor may advise transfer to another Christian group for a fresh beginning. No quarrel should be left unresolved, no wrong unconfessed, no clear duty run away from: but it may be better that the penitent, saddened soul find refuge and a spiritual home elsewhere, than be lost to the Christian fellowship altogether.

Following a dramatic conversion, backsliding can grievously distress a young Christian, who may find it very difficult to recapture assurance and joy. It requires some care to explain that backsliding is not fatal to Christian confidence, without suggesting it is not for all that serious to oneself and costly in witness to others. Many a soul has thanked God for Peter's story, for the Saviour's firm yet gentle re-establishing of the disgraced apostle after a threefold denial, and His acceptance of Peter's thrice-renewed declaration of love. The pastor will assure the shaken heart that God is ever more concerned with the future than with the past; that He who did not begin to love us because of what we were will go on loving us in spite of what we are; that the gospel of forgiveness is as true for the backslider as for other sinners. If we confess our sins, God is faithful to forgive; though we are faithless, yet He abideth faithful—He cannot deny Himself.

Very occasionally, obduracy and pride will prevent penitence, and the pastor may have to venture—on scriptural grounds—to warn that 'it is a fearful thing to fall into the hands of the living God'. The same faithfulness which holds on to us when we are well-meaning but weak, still holds on to us when we are rebellious and impenitent. God will not let us go: if love will not win our hearts again then judgement may. Hebrews 6 is a strange passage, but its solemn note, echoed in chapter 10, is part of God's word:

It is impossible to restore again to repentance those who have once been enlightened, who have tasted the heavenly gift, and have become partakers of the Holy Spirit, and have tasted the goodness of the word of God and the powers of the age to come, if they then commit apostasy, since they crucify the Son of God on their own account and hold him up to contempt . . . Though we speak thus, yet in your case, beloved, we feel sure of better things that belong to salvation. 'My righteous one shall live by faith, and if he shrinks back, my soul has no pleasure in him.' But we are not of those who shrink back and are destroyed, but of those who have faith and keep their souls.

God is not mocked, and a healthy fear of His judgements is a necessary element in Christian faith.

(v) *The Unforgivable Sin*

Occasionally, too, the pastor will be confronted with a fixed state of distress caused by 'a conviction of having committed the unforgivable sin'. Only rarely is that phrase from the Gospels the true source of the trouble: usually it merely provides a form of expression for a primitive terror of God, or of hell, and a refusal to believe in the redeeming love of God. It is even possible that the root cause is a strange, inverted evangelical exhibitionism. Where careful exposition offers any help, the pastor will point out that whoever is guilty of that sin will not be worrying about it! He will take the troubled soul through the passage: to call Christ Beelzebul, His works the works of Satan, evil good and good evil, is obviously to place oneself beyond the point where truth and grace can touch and change one; if we are determined to hold that truth is a lie and a lie truth, then truth itself is powerless to save us. So long as we take that stance, we are beyond conviction, beyond penitence, so beyond forgiveness. But we need not maintain that stance—even if we ever adopted it: and true penitence is *sure* to be forgiven. It may help if the pastor challenges the unhappy one to say if that is what he now says of Jesus—that Jesus is Satan, and His works are evil; if not, then he certainly is not within the solemn terms of that passage, and ought not to 'wrest the scripture to his own damnation'.

But the root cause of such fears most probably lies elsewhere, in infantile, pagan or sub-Christian conceptions of God, or possibly in deeper psychological conditions, and the real cure must begin much further back.

(vi) *Life-long Regret*

Another possible consequence of backsliding is lasting regret at missed opportunities and the disobedience that thwarted God's purpose for life. It is best to face frankly, once and for all, that this may have happened, and is now unalterable, rather than to obscure or minimise what the honest Christian heart can see for itself. What is more important is how the resulting position is to be faced and handled. On that the pastor can say two significant things. First, that God's love, likewise, is unalterable; He will not withdraw His grace or withhold His blessing because of mistakes now repented; His forgiveness is complete, and without reproach.

The second relevant truth is that many famous servants of God have found their life-work, not in the path which at first seemed their appointed way, their first choice, but later, in some revised plan. Elisabeth Fry, John Wesley, John Newton, William Booth, Dr Barnardo spring at once to mind, out of many. Not all, it is true, missed the first way by disobedience, but each discovered what seemed *to them* a second-best avenue of service. The story of John Mark's eager setting out, falling by the way, being rejected by Paul but encouraged by Barnabas, and setting forth again on a fine career of evangelism, pastoral service and Gospel-writing, is recorded for the encouragement of all who have to start again. Who, with Mark in mind, can despair of finding useful work to do for God, whatever mistakes have been made?

(vii) *Perplexities about Guidance*

The more eager a young Christian is to obey his Lord, the more anxious he may grow as to how Christ's will may be discerned. He may be impatient with the pastor's talk of 'circumstances'—yet it seems unlikely that God means me to be a concert soloist if He gave me no voice, or that He should want me to abandon an ailing wife or parents to follow some distant gleam that blinds me to duties nearer home. The young Christian will talk much of signs and impulses—though Gideon's fleece and the apostolic lot are not, by their scripture setting, recommended for mature Christians, whatever place they may have for spiritual childhood. The pastor will advise that such 'spiritual promptings' should be prayed over long and humbly; if they persist, they should be examined thoroughly in all their implications, and discussed with other trusted Christians. Then any action taken will not be based upon emotional impulse alone but *also* on the sifting of prayer and impartial counsel: such a decision will stand when the emotion deserts us and the way becomes rough. If the young Christian rejects such advice, the pastor may well warn that such an attitude suggests he intends to go ahead, whatever God wills.

The anxiety is often unnecessary. Sometimes a soul pleads repeatedly for guidance about something so plainly right that no further 'indications' could make it clearer. We do not need a revelation from the skies to tell us to do a kindness, to make a sacrifice, to give time and energy to some worthy cause, to witness to the faith. Others 'wrestle with God' for leading until their intense anxiety, and fear of doing wrong, unfit them to hear any divine voice saying 'This is the way, walk ye in it'. Such hearts need to be counselled in the *kindly* ways of God, who if we want to know His plan will surely reveal it in His good time. If we truly desire that His will shall be done, He will accomplish it in the end—despite our foolishness: there is no need to run a spiritual temperature worrying whether almighty God knows how to get His own way! Our true anxiety should be about our own willingness to obey: so often when we think we 'wrestle with God' we are in truth wrestling with ourselves.

Two scripture passages may illumine pastoral counsel. The psalmist hears God promising

> I will instruct you and teach you the way you should go,
> I will counsel you with my eye upon you.
> Be not like a horse or mule, without understanding, which must be
>   curbed with bit and bridle, else it will not keep with you

—thoughts which seem to find echo in Paul's 'Do not be foolish, but understand what the will of the Lord is', and even in Jesus' words: 'No longer do I call you servants, for the servant does not know what his master is doing; but I have called you friends . . .' Plainly, the ideal is an *understanding* of God's will, a discernment of what God purposes, and an insight into how one's own gifts, circumstances and experience may serve that purpose, together with so close a daily fellowship with Him that God 'guides us with His eye'. As an old saint expressed it, 'The heart that lives in God's company knows, by the change in God's countenance, from smile to frown, when it does wrong!' God seeks not brute beasts of burden, nor mindless slaves, but willing, co-operative servants, their minds transformed to know the good acceptable and perfect will of God.

The other instructive passage is Acts 21, where Paul is urged by trusted friends not to go to Jerusalem, and those who speak by the Spirit warn him plainly of what will befall him there. Yet he goes forward, and the counsellors retire saying 'The will of the Lord be done!' Careful analysis reveals the elements of divine guidance as Paul understood them. His journey rested on a long-settled conviction that his work in the east was done and that he must visit Jerusalem before turning westward; on a long-planned endeavour to unite gentile with Jewish Christians by an act of timely charity: neither of these purposes was lightly undertaken, nor lightly to be set aside. A man professing to follow God's leading must hold to his course consistently. Secondly, Paul listened to, and weighed, the counsel of his friends, but he knew that the decision must be his own. Thirdly, he had heard the voice of the Spirit within his own heart, and had testified to it earlier on the journey. Fourthly, the only 'contrary indications' which even the friends could argue were warnings of trouble ahead—and that did not seem to Paul any reason at all for not going forward: 'What are you doing, weeping and breaking my heart? For I am ready not only to be imprisoned but even to die at Jerusalem for the name of the Lord Jesus.' If the way forward leads to opposition and a cross, that is no proof that it is not God's will; only *self*-will ever demands that things shall always turn out well.

An understanding of divine guidance is plainly the key not only to personal obedience but to the fulfilment of God's whole plan for each Christian career. The pastor who can successfully instruct his people in this area of their discipleship, will have contributed in far-reaching ways both to their happiness and to the cause of God.

(viii) *Over-scrupulousness and Freedom*

Variations among Christians on minor matters of conduct will create numerous problems for the diligent pastor. His responsibility is many-sided; to protect at all costs the conscience of the immature and weak, to defend the freedom of others to do what they consider right, and to preserve at the same time the unity of the fellowship. He will ponder often the thorough discussion of such questions in Romans 14 and 15, and in 1 Corinthians 8 and 10.

On several details of behaviour much disputed between Jewish and gentile Christians (the observance of the Sabbath, the use of wine, the eating of meat whose slaughtering involved sacrifice to idols, or whose preparation did not fulfil Jewish ritual regulations, and attendance at public or family feasts in idol-temples, the only halls available) Paul distinguishes two main attitudes. The 'strong' conscience is robust, broadminded, decisive, clear-sighted, arguing for freedom and first principles—'the idol is nothing'; 'food will not commend us to God'; 'nothing is unclean in itself'. So it exercises boldly its liberty in Christ, enjoys whatever is laid before it, fearless of scruples, 'raising no question for conscience' sake'. The 'weak' or tender conscience is timorous, cautious, scrupulous, fearful of sinning, often unhappy and anxious about the interpretation others will place upon Christian attendance at idol-shrines, or that fellow-Jews will place upon breaches of ritual or Sabbath law. So it tends to be negative, distrusting all argument as sophistry, keeping a safe distance from 'doubtful' things. These two attitudes, the broad or lax and the narrow or strict—the tough-minded and the tender—have continued through Christian history, and divide Christians no less sharply today.

Paul's pastoral counsel embraces four clear principles. (a) Personal responsibility is paramount: 'Let every man be fully persuaded in his own mind . . . To his own master he standeth or falleth . . . Whatever is not of faith' (that is, not done out of conviction that it is right, but negligently, careless whether it is right or not, to conform to others) 'is sin.' This respect for individual conscience and conviction is imperative. Background, experience, upbringing, personal weakness, vary so widely among Christians that the intensity of temptation, the allowable degree of freedom, the sensitiveness to particular moral issues, are highly individual concerns. On some questions of conduct, the true answer must be 'others may, you may not'. When Peter asked Christ's will for another disciple he received a reply which is of wider application: 'What is that to thee? Follow thou me!' Each soul must ask for itself, 'Lord, what wilt thou have me to do?'

(b) But the freedom one claims must be granted to others: there must be no mutual recrimination, whether by the strong, despising the scruples of the weak, or by the weak accusing the laxity of the strong. 'Let not him who eats despise him who abstains, and let not him who abstains pass judgement on him who eats . . . Who are you to pass judgement on another's servant?' Each of us shall give account of himself to God, and not to one another. A mature Christian group will include many differences of conscience on matters less important, and much of the pastor's work in the community will lie in fostering the loyalty within difference, the mutual acceptance of each other's sincerity, which prevents the group splitting into mutually accusing factions. (c) Nevertheless the strong have an added responsibility, to consider the weak, to bear their infirmity, to do nothing which would make them stumble in the Christian way. It may be necessary, for love's sake, for the strong to deny themselves freedoms they could conscientiously defend, lest by their example the scrupulous be led astray into what *for them* would be danger and sin. The strong cannot always please themselves—as Christ did not please Himself—but must curb their freedom with responsibility towards all for whom Christ died. If the brother is being injured by what the strong allow themselves, then the strong are no longer walking in love.

(d) For all that, the weaker may not impose their scruples upon the stronger, so as to get all their own way. They too must move towards maturity, towards Christian freedom, and a better sense of proportion. Paul does not hesitate to rank himself among the strong, and since he expends four chapters upon instruction and explanation, and insists that indeed the idol is nothing, and the kingdom of God is not meat and drink, he evidently expects the weaker brethren to grow up and come to moral understanding. This is the pastor's tightrope. He must respect and safeguard the tender conscience of the fearful young Christian, while rebuking the censorious spirit which often accompanies it; he must gently lead towards a more robust and balanced view of what loyalty to Christ requires, and a truer discernment of what is vital, what merely trivial; and he must defend the freedom of the strong to do what their conscience allows, while rebuking the scorn and impatience which often accompany strength, and demanding consideration and understanding towards his more vulnerable brethren.

In the chaotic dissensions of today's moral uncertainties, successful pastoral leadership in this sphere is no mean achievement.

(ix) *Insularity*

Emphasis upon freedom of conscience, individual responsibility, and personal faith, sometimes multiplies difficulties for the extremely shy and reticent, tending to confirm their loneliness and self-absorption. It can also intensify, by seeming to justify, the anti-social egotism of the self-opinionated Christian. Insularity may be a temperamental trait, or the result of unsuccessful adolescent experiments in social adjustment. It can arise from unconscious inferiority inhibiting normal relationships; equally it can arise from a sense of spiritual superiority, an exclusive self-righteousness. Individualist withdrawal and egoist aggressiveness are alike failures in co-operation, and either can produce the introspective, inarticulate, lone-wolf personality. Sometimes the soul may long for friendship, but remain incapable of the necessary initiative, and of responding to others' approaches. Weaker personalities retreat into lonely, negative, isolation; stronger ones over-compensate in a schismatic antagonism to all leadership, critical, abrasive, self-righteous, taking revenge for felt unpopularity by rejecting and despising all others.

The first step in ministering to either type will be to assess the cause of such insularity. Is it a natural introversion of temperament? Is it a reaction to unhappy experiences? or a distortion of pride? The next step will be to persuade that the anti-social, isolationist spirit is wholly unchristian. Very much of the New Testament lies to hand for argument—the message of a *kingdom*, entrusted to a disciple *band*, centring in *love* and *mutual service*, a gospel of *reconciliation*, the creation of a *Church*, with the gospel ordinances of baptism, the Supper, *shared* worship, prayer and work; the one people, one body, one family, one messianic community, one temple for the Spirit, one Vine—of Christians made alive together, raised together, made to sit together in heavenly places in Christ—with all the exhortations to unity, forgivingness, mutual edification—the emphasis is constant, ubiquitous, and endless. The insular Christian is simply a contradiction in terms.

The pastor's third step will be to introduce the isolated Christian to those circles and tasks where he will be brought into relationship and held there by shared purposes. To initiate friendships would probably fail, as too artificial and self-conscious: to link the unattached to work, studies, hobbies, interests, which others share provides a basis of regular contact out of which friendship can arise more naturally. It may be useful to show the reticent and withdrawn that self-absorption is selfish when others need sympathy, help, and friendship; and to show the aggressive and antagonistic that he is making no contribution of any value, nor will he until he learns that others also know the Lord and serve Him with sincerity, and less pride. Such a personality should not be given leadership in any group, for his own sake and for theirs, but encouraged to work in a team under a personality stronger and more mature than his own.

There are of course various other spiritual maladies, and the pastor will accumulate his own list of the odd and troublesome spiritual predicaments to which Christians are liable. The approach to most will follow the general pattern outlined: first to assess the true proportions of the trouble, a transient aberration or some more serious inadequacy or wrong. What is presented as a desperate spiritual crisis often turns out to be a tiff with the boy-friend, or a wish for more pastoral attention! Secondly, to probe the real causes, in gospel light. Thirdly, to apply the insights and convictions of scripture to whatever is causing distress; and fourthly, to take whatever active steps may be called for to rearrange the life-pattern and avoid recurrence of the spiritual ailment. Complete honesty of mind, and truth spoken in love, are the pre-requisites, and always the goal is clear: a full-grown Christian soul, conformed to the image of God's Son.

17 SEXUAL DIFFICULTIES

As religion has been defined as what man does with his solitariness, so character, for later adolescents, consists very largely in what a man does with his sexuality. Failure to achieve balanced and happy self-understanding and self-discipline involves failure in maturity, and the end to any genuine religious experience and loyalty. The close relation of sexual and religious development is seen not only in their emergence at the same period of life but in the use of common language—love, devotion, worship, union; while those who find in sensual temptation their most intense moral problem frequently discover in religious devotion the most effective diversion of their unused drives. Sexuality may be said to become addictive in the sense that it can exercise an obsessive, compulsive power over personality. The pastor may occasionally be consulted by conscience-tortured sensualists, but much more often by those who find in sexual tensions the greatest hindrance to discipleship, and those for whom, perhaps because of previous modes of life, Christian conversion has provoked intense struggle at precisely this point.

General studies in psychology and in Christian ethics provide the fundamental insights necessary to wisdom in this area of pastoral ministry, but it is possible that Christian upbringing, training and zeal may create a special repugnance towards all sexual aberrations whatsoever. Sex is one field of human behaviour where condemnation habitually outruns understanding—or the will to understand. The pastor may need to remind himself that if he has experienced no special difficulties in this matter, then he owes an enormous debt to a good home behind him, and probably a good wife beside him. If he finds himself particularly repelled, or censorious, when sexual problems are presented to him, he must remind himself that more often than not such recoil springs from inner insecurity—from a repressed but active awareness of vulnerability, or remorse, which ought to make him sympathise, but which in fact makes him quick to condemn. Candid self-awareness is essential to sincere counselling, here as everywhere.

Imaginary Problems

Faced with an anxious, ashamed soul wrestling with his own (rarely, her own) sensuality, the first question for the pastor must be, Is this a real problem, or only an imaginary one? The irrational tabus that surround sex, the conspiracy of silence about it in which many young people still grow up, so far as 'respectable' conversation is concerned, and the popular misconstruction of religious teaching on original sin as another name for sex, all breed in earnest young hearts an appalling tension between spirit and flesh, between idealism and natural appetite. To this is added the necessity to hide even one's temptations, so that the soul becomes furtive, feels hypocritical, and in the end carries a weight of irrational emotional guilt, not for sins committed but for the amount of evil one has resisted!

The pastor's general teaching and preaching should help to dispel much of this muddle of earnestness and falsehood. By his plain Christian common sense he will bring enormous relief and daylight, by merely accepting the sexual nature of the healthy man and woman; by insisting on the normalcy of sexual appetite as nature's— and God's—provision for the continuance of life; by emphasising that sexual desire is *not* sinful, that the excited stirrings that beauty or manliness evoke in young minds and hearts are among the loveliest experiences of life. The pastor will not deny that there is *any* problem. But he will declare that the problem is one of circumstance, age, readiness for responsibility, and for really mature love that unites two lives totally, and does not play at doing so. He will explain that it is the urgency of the sexual drive, conflicting with natural reticence and the immaturity of other sides of our growing nature, which creates the need for discipline. That is no reason for denying that we have sexual urges, for repressing them unacknowledged into the sub-conscious mind where they will surely take revenge; or for feeling guilty about them when they are an essential part of our humanity; or for giving them free rein before we or our life-pattern are ready for the responsibilities they involve.

For the rest, the pastor's counsel will be obvious Christian wisdom: to recognise the danger of letting any strong feelings dominate the whole mind and heart, so getting beyond rational control; to guard against this danger by avoiding sexually stimulating books, films, friendships, that only increase desire without providing for its healthy outlet or control. Above all, the pastor will urge that heart and life be centred upon the perfect Man, Master, Friend and Saviour, whose we are and whom—with all our powers—we love and serve.

Sexual Aberrations

But there may exist a problem beyond mere misunderstanding and imagined guilt. Sex may already have become obsessive through physical or mental self-indulgence of which the adolescent is ashamed but against which he or she is increasingly helpless. The self-induced orgasm or relief is in reality less evil than it seems to the young mind, and it is inexcusable to play upon fabricated guilt-feelings for religious ends. Essentially, masturbation is childish sexuality, the infant still exploring its own body, and the adolescent who practices it is failing to grow up. Probably this is the best, because the true, approach: first, that the habit tends to hinder full maturity, to distort real manhood and womanhood into self-obsessed and superficial habits of feeling which will one day spoil the adult experience of love. Secondly, that masturbation, like all sexual activity, the more it is indulged, the more demanding it becomes, tending by this habit-forming power to *increase* the sexual problems of growing up, by concentrating so much on thoughts of sex as to make self-discipline still harder to achieve. Not so much in itself, but in the lack of self-control which it reveals, and confirms, it is dangerous for the future, when still fiercer temptation will arise.

The mental indiscipline which turns for sexual excitement to pornography is likewise a weakening of character, undermining resistance to evil suggestion and impulse. Ethically, the evil in pornography lies in the market it creates for those who would exploit models and authors willing to degrade themselves for money; in the contribution it makes to the coarsened, sex-imbued climate in which young people have to grow up; and especially in the attitude to women and to sex which it inculcates—the separation of sexual experience from all tenderness, consideration, love and loyalty; the false standards of beauty and vanity with which sex is surrounded; the notion of uncontrolled licentiousness without consequences which it instils. Such reasons make it forbidden fare for Christian minds, a market no follower of Jesus could support.

Psychologically, the evil of pornography lies in the constant stimulation of appetites already difficult to control; in the feeding of imagination and arousal of feeling by means of fantasy and falsehood. 'Mental masturbation' strengthens the obsessive demand of sex upon attention, intensifying the problem of achieving balanced, mature, wholly adult character. Lasciviousness, the sensually poisoned imagination, can exercise an astounding compulsion over otherwise clever and discerning minds. As a man thinketh in his heart, so *is* he, and so if he have courage and opportunity he will one day find himself behaving. That is why Jesus laid His sharp condemnation not only on the act of adultery but on the look of lust, the committing of adultery in the secret places of the imagination and the soul.

Hence, too, Paul's realistic warning that Christians should 'make no provision for the flesh, to fulfil it in the lusts thereof'—that is, provide nothing, in reading, entertainment, conversation or in any other way, for lust to feed upon. The pastor will insist that so often we make our own temptation by the things we permit our memories to lay in store. More positively, Paul adds 'Whatever is true, honourable, just, pure, lovely, gracious, excellent, praiseworthy— think about these things, and the God of peace will be with you.' Purity of mind and heart is not just the absence of evil thought and feeling, but the presence of wholesome, gentle, positive ideals and enriching imagination. The mind preoccupied with lovely things, high thought, the habit of instant prayer at the suggestion of evil, and the sense of God's love and presence at continual command, is not so much protected from impure allurements as immune, by reason of its own spiritual health. That is the only dependable safety.

Promiscuity

A pastor is not likely to be approached by those whose sexual obsession has already led them into habitual promiscuity. It would in any case be a situation calling more for evangelistic than for pastoral counsel. But in the present confusion, both in society and on the fringes of the Church, he may well be confronted with a demand to be told why complete sexual liberty is in Christian eyes a sin; or by someone hard pressed by arguments in favour of promiscuous or trial-relationships. Especially, perhaps, will he meet the specious plea that 'Love—and do what you like!' is a Christian maxim.

The full reply belongs to the more thorough discussion of Christian ethics, but the pastor may wish to arm himself with several lines of persuasion. (a) The truly Christian maxim is most certainly, 'Love God and you will do what He likes—as exemplified for us in Jesus Christ'. (b) 'Love' in Christian eyes is not demanding, self-indulgent, clamorous possession of another regardless of consequences, but a genuine respect and goodwill towards others, that treats them always as persons, never as things, certainly never as tools, to use or abuse, for one's own pleasure. The 'consent' of a partner in no way releases a Christian from Christ's law of love. (c) The Christian is, as Paul argues, totally the possession of Christ who bought him, body, mind, and spirit, to whom he must yield himself as a living sacrifice, holy, and acceptable to God. He is also, body and soul, a temple of the Holy Spirit, to be kept holy and consecrated as a shrine of the divine Spirit, not defiled or degraded by any indulgence forbidden by the divine holiness. (d) The experience of those who have indulged in sexual licentiousness is unanimous: the minding of the flesh is death: sensuality 'petrifies the feelings and hardens all within'; peace, joy, the sense of God's presence, the vision of God, all are forfeit when, in defiance of conscience and Christian ideals, we descend to levels of behaviour unworthy of our true humanity. (e) The standard is Christ: to pretend that His pure, strong, disciplined example can be reconciled with sexual licence is to call black white and good evil.

It is true of course that those who defend promiscuous sexual relationships will brush aside such arguments as of little weight: their minds are made up before discussion begins, and on other grounds. The pastor can only insist that they set their behaviour in the light of the gospel, call things by their true names, and cease lying to themselves.

Homosexuality

The whole problem of homosexuality—sexual desire directed toward members of the same sex—is fraught with difficulties for the Christian counsellor—traditional, emotional, psychiatric, sometimes criminal, and personal. The average pastor's immediate problem is to enter sympathetically into such a condition, overcoming his initial repugnance, or disgust, sufficiently to begin to understand. Homosexuals complain bitterly of the attitude of churches and 'clergymen' who 'wish that homosexuals could be strangled at birth' and who substitute a slow social strangling, an imprisonment for life behind bars of social ostracism. It is charged that 'most church members still believe that homosexual acts are contrary to the will of God for human sexuality, and therefore sinful'. A considerable burden of irrational guilt (it is said) is made more heavy by the self-righteous disapproval of the religious community. 'It is not to be recommended that a homosexual in distress should go to a minister . . . the scars of mishandling by ill-informed and incompetent ministers remain upon many a Christian homosexual'—the scars being defined as rejection by God, by Christ, by the church, or perpetual schizoid concealment, and a deplorably low level of maturity.

When to this highly emotive protestation is added the suggestion that this devaluation of a whole class of men is a myth which the righteous foster 'to keep their own homosexual elements rigorously dissociated from their own self-awareness', we suspect that self-righteousness and self-justifying accusation are not all on one side. Others blame scriptural authority, especially in the stories of Sodom and Gomorrah, and Paul's condemnation of 'abusers of themselves with mankind', as the source of the traditional Christian reaction. F. R. Barry says 'this peculiar reprobation' has been indubitably bound up with the biblical stories; yet he also shows that modern biblical scholars think it very doubtful if the stories were ever held to refer to homosexuality until Jewish revulsion against Greek decadence sought scriptural foundation. Sherwin Bailey argues that Roman law, severe against the homosexual corruption of minors, had at least as great influence in moulding Christian thought. Rome's reason's were presumably social and military: at any rate more is behind this attitude than biblical literalism. The medieval church prescribed penances and other spiritual penalties, but rarely surrendered homosexuals to the civil magistrates.

The truth is that traditional Christian repugnance towards homosexuality arises more from ignorance, from a horror of deliberate sexual perversion of the young, from imagination (fed by graffiti) of what homosexuals actually do, from the disgust aroused by male prostitution, and from fear of its consequences in prison, in the army, and in similar single-sex environments. Behind it lies also the strong intuition that whereas heterosexual relationships are natural and purposeful, homosexual acts are unnatural, meaningless except as sensual self-indulgence, and a perversion of nature's true intent.

This may all be unsatisfactory to the protesting homosexual, but it is not merely unthinking or insensitive self-righteousness, or deliberate cruelty. Nor is sympathy entirely withheld: Barry says: 'in itself it is no more wicked or morally culpable to be an invert than it is to be blind or to lack a limb . . . Inverts must be released from the guilt complex which will drive them into yet deeper introversion.' He appeals that homosexuals shall not be cold-shouldered, or treated as a class apart. A strongly evangelical discussion rehearses the scriptural pronouncement but goes on 'It cannot be over-emphasised that there is nothing wrong with homosexual inclinations. Like other deviations from normal which date from birth or from early upbringing, they must be accepted and lived with if they cannot be corrected . . . Homosexuality . . . describes the constitution of a man or woman for which he or she cannot be held responsible' (C. G. Scorer).

It is clear that whoever would counsel in this field has some careful

thinking to do and some fine discrimination to exercise. It is
estimated that something like five per cent of the population is
predominantly homosexual, of whom perhaps one in five may be
overtly recognised as 'effeminate', queer, gay or 'pansy'. There are
of course infinite gradations of homosexual orientation, from latent
homosexuality, which is barely conscious, only revealed in crisis-
situations, and tends to accuse others in unconscious self-defence, to
the wholly homosexual, who avoids at all costs all relationships with
the other sex. Barry suggests that sex is always to some extent
ambivalent—normal heterosexuals can sometimes feel a keen
attraction towards certain members or types of their own sex also.
Kinsey's six-place scale, from wholly hetero- to wholly homo-sexual
probably over-simplifies.

The causes of homosexuality are highly debated. It is thought by
some that a homosexual stage is normal in every boy's growth—
possibly because the physical changes of puberty are first observed
in one's own body, and easier to explore in others of one's own sex
while shyness and fear still inhibit approaches to the other sex.
Masturbation belongs to this phase, and should pass with it as the
adolescent's sexual development matures into full heterosexual
normality. (a) Some adult homosexuals may thus be only retarded or
arrested in development, possibly through weakness of character, a
cowardly avoidance of the risks of personal confrontation with the
opposite sex, involving possible rejection or extended responsibility.
One who is basically inadequate, or fearful of proving so, may well
prefer at first the secrecy of self-stimulation and later seek similarly
timid partners. Many virile men hold homosexuality in contempt as
the refuge of the weakling, with a private suspicion that all men
could be homosexual if they refuse to grow up. There could be
medical reasons behind such arrested development, but it is likelier
to be psychological in origin; the pastor may be able to probe the real
causes, illumine the situation, and lead toward normal heterosexual
orientation, especially where the original fear of sexual rejection has
taken on religious rationalisations in its defence.

(b) In other instances, adult homosexuality may be due to
regression, under exceptional stress or 'breakdown', to an earlier
stage of life which was less complicated, less demanding. Regression
is a familiar psychological mechanism of self-defence, the stage of
earlier and more comfortable existence chosen varying with the
patient. Where the stress causing it is linked to problems of love,
sexual rejection, or fear (as of venereal disease), the regression may
well be to the furtive fantasies of adolescence and the acts that then

gave secret relief and pleasure without the dreaded consequences. Here pastoral counsel will probe the causes of the regression, seeking to explain the mechanism, in the expectation that once the illusion of return to adolescence is destroyed, the homosexual symptoms will disappear. It may be necessary to retrace the steps of normal growing up, seeking friendship among both sexes and gradually accepting the risk and responsibility of confrontation, out of which heterosexual love can grow.

(c) *Conditioned* homosexuality is more deeply seated and will require correspondingly greater investigation. An abnormal relationship with one's parents in an embittered home; a 'mother-fixation', the man so idolising his mother that no other woman can ever displace her; a violent sexual experience in childhood (rape, assault, seduction); any traumatic experience or psychotic condition that chooses sexual action for its symbol—may have this result as adolescence passes into manhood and womanhood. Infatuation with certain types of people, as one's teacher or athletic hero, may contribute; 'infantile terrors' associated with women guardians, nurses, teachers, may also distort natural affection. The clue may lie in some quirk or eccentricity—aversion only to fair-haired women or to bearded men, for example, or homosexuality combined with claustrophobia. Considerable skill would be required to uncover such causes of the adult orientation, and properly qualified psychiatric treatment may well be necessary. But the cause being discovered and illuminated, it is always possible that conditioned—or artificially induced—homosexuality may be cured.

(d) The *constitutionally* homosexual presents a very different problem, however, and qualified opinion is much more pessimistic about reorientation to normal sexuality. Among the possible causes discussed are genetic conditions, hormone deficiencies, some psychosomatic disability—a psychological inversion or deprivation—making the condition in either case a clinical rather than a moral disorder. The condition is then likened to blindness, deformity, left-handedness, in being congenital, beyond the subject's control or cure by act of will, and morally neutral, as tone-deafness or colour-blindness is morally neutral. It is just 'the way the person is made'.

Before this condition, pastoral counsel can only be ameliorative, giving support and understanding, advising acceptance of the handicap as others must accept blindness, epilepsy, a family entail of insanity, as one of the conditions set for discipleship. As Scorer says, 'the homosexual can serve his God and his fellow-men in his particular calling as profitably as any other: . . . he learns of his condition, understands his limitations in certain directions, and adjusts his life accordingly.' Sherwin Bailey uses the phrase 'a handicapped person' and Barry speaks of homosexuals as a class of 'deprived people' cut off from a full share in the common life, for whom society ought to feel responsible as it does for its otherwise handicapped members, meeting them with compassion rather than indignation. The homosexual 'has to learn to accept it, live with it, and make the best that he can of life in spite of it'.

The pastor's main practical difficulty is, plainly, to distinguish the more vicious *perversion* that seeks carnal gratification without responsibility, discipline or love; the arrested or regressive homosexual who suffers an artificial and perhaps temporary *deprivation*; and the *constitutional* homosexual who carries a possibly incurable handicap throughout life. And then to offer what analysis, illumination, friendship, counsel and comfort he can, always referring to medical and psychiatric experts conditions beyond his own power. He will recognise that it is of little use to call for the exercise of 'will power' when the causes are beyond the will's effective field of operation. He will realise the uselessness, and possible tragedy for two souls, in advising marriage as 'God's will in all sexual matters'— as Barry suggests, it would be as sensible to advise a colour-blind man to take up painting.

Some homosexuals, among them professing Christians, resent deeply the church's disapproval of homosexual *acts* between consenting adults—a disapproval which either drives those who seek sexual gratification with other homosexuals out of the churches into the homosexual ('gay') clubs, or private unions, or compels them to live hypocritically. 'Their spiritual pastors and masters have usually counselled a lifetime of chastity which they themselves would almost certainly never have had the strength to maintain.'

But what else *can* the Christian pastor recommend? In the parallel situations, is he to direct every widower, bachelor and spinster to the nearest brothel, or arrange for private service? The homosexual *condition* may be beyond the will's control and so beyond blame: but the temptation to give way to it in homosexual *acts* is under moral control, and a man is justly blamed when he fails to control his carnal nature by rational and moral considerations. In most people's eyes, the acts themselves are revolting; the necessary concealment is at once an acceptance of deceit into the pattern of life and a confession of something publicly shameful; the effect is to alienate from normal society and to increase the tendency to self-pity and specious self-justification; while homosexual habits and liaisons make increasingly difficult any steps towards reorientation and final cure. To talk of chastity as beyond one's strength misses the vital point in Christian reaction: in this as in all other human tensions and demands the pastor will point to the sustaining grace of God and the compassion and power of Christ as the only resource that can keep life clean, whatever the handicap or circumstances. It is by no means the homosexual alone who has to depend on that resource in a celibate self-denial—in or out of marriage.

In some countries, homosexual activities between adults are no longer criminal: but society always has acted, and most States still do act, rigorously to protect the young, the vulnerable, or those persuaded under duress to share in such behaviour. When in consultation the pastor learns of such activities, his position is intolerable. A teacher, youth leader, or guardian of an imbecile, may 'confess'—or boast—his conquests, relying upon confidentiality. To condone, even by silence, is to become an accessory and share responsibility for harm done to others. At the very least, the pastor must warn that unless such conduct is proved to have ceased, he will report it to the police authorities. Most pastors would want to make sure it ceased, by reporting it in any case.

For good and ill, for joy and great misery, sex holds enormous place in most lives. In helping men and women to handle the issues it raises, the Christian pastor is often tested to the utmost, both in wisdom and in patience. He may often wish he need not become involved, especially in the darker sides of sexual behaviour. Yet if he fails his people here he will fail them badly. Almost alone in western culture the church stands for purity, chastity, true love, married joy and strong family loyalty: and among the young and middle-aged, the key figure in that Christian campaign is the local pastor, teaching, preaching, counselling and practising the Christlike way. Those whom he leads into lifelong happiness in this field will thank God for his ministry, and remember him with lasting affection.

H

18 THE ADDICTED

An addiction is clearly a self-imposed sickness, but it is extremely difficult to keep both sides of that description in mind at once. On the one hand, to those long sheltered from coarser temptations, or redeemed from such evils by sudden conversion, the important words are 'self-imposed'. The addiction is deserved; the sufferer is a 'victim' only of his own evil habits; talk of 'sickness' is sentimental hypocrisy, for no one contracts alcoholism by infection, only by drinking. The society which talks lightly of alcoholism as a 'disease', which spends millions a year combating cancer and billions a year promoting alcoholism, is merely evading responsibility; every intelligent citizen and father knows that social conditions, the exploiters of human weakness, and the individuals who succumb, are very much to blame for the resulting addiction. The only hope for such is to break the evil habit by self-mastery, or by a *true* conversion which will end it at a stroke. The more severe our own struggles, the more critical our judgement tends to be, and the more instinctive our revulsion, even though criticism and revulsion be tempered by sorrow.

On the other hand, to those who deal with addicts, the important word is 'sickness'. They know how utterly helpless the alcoholic, the inveterate gambler, may become; how useless it is to look for 'self-mastery', or even for sufficient mental grasp to 'lay hold of the gospel' however simplified its presentation. The ill-used nervous system still craves for its narcotic, the weak mind for its spurious excitement. Not all who profess heartfelt faith in Christ, and a passionate longing to be saved, find their besetting sin immediately conquered. Some, like the prodigal son, must trudge a long and wearisome way homeward before the fatted calf is tasted; the process of salvation is for them as for Peter one of stumbling, rebuke, denial, and renewal. The evangelist may perhaps retain his illusions about instant salvation: the pastor usually knows human nature better. Moral sickness may be part of the sinner's judgement, but it is still *sickness*, and those who defend this viewpoint remind their critics of the scorching parable of the Pharisee and the publican, and the matchless words, 'Neither do I condemn thee; go, and sin no more.'

Those who believe in Jesus, Friend of sinners, and in the gospel as the power of God unto salvation, know also that nothing is to be gained for the sinner himself by denying moral responsibility. They remember too that saving faith may lack intellectual comprehension, may even lack words, may be merely the reaching of a hand to touch Christ in the crowd, a despairing 'Lord, remember me!' or just the heartbroken return from repeated falls to seek yet again the Christian friendship of some circle of redeemed people whose compassion gives meaning to the gospel. Above all, Christians may not forget that it was Jesus who first spoke of sin as sickness, and of Himself as the Physician. Granted that the analogy is only partial, that this sickness is often the fault of the patient, *the Master knew that as clearly as we do*, yet still defended His ministry in medical terms, and 'bore our sicknesses'. There is no gainsaying that supreme directive. The pastor has to school his mind to think of sinners in Christ's terms; and then, with heart the humbler for his readiness to condemn and withdraw, must walk beside the sinner in saving companionship.

Addiction to Alcohol

Alcohol is strictly a narcotic, which by depressing the higher faculties of judgement, moral sensitivity, and self-consciousness, produces anaesthetic effects in some, short-lived, specious geniality in others, and an equally abnormal belligerence in yet others. Its evil moral, social, marital, economic and criminal associations apart, its crucial danger lies in the addictive nature of the drug, from which none can presume immunity, and whose effects are cumulative. Alcoholism is the addictive stage where, despite all consequences, control over drinking has been lost, the demand is compulsive, and withdrawal of the drug produces acute physical and mental distress. Clinebell says that alcoholism is twenty times as prevalent as all other addictions combined in western Europe, Britain, and the United States; others say that its incidence is five-and-a-half times that of cancer; the World Health Organisation ranks it fourth greatest health problem in the world.

Exactly why a foolish, self-deceptive, extravagant and dangerous social habit should in so many become a 'self-perpetuating vicious cycle', obsessive, irresistible, utterly destructive of physical health, mental and moral capacity, family life, career, and sanity, is debatable. That alcohol undoubtedly diminishes control over intelligence, judgement and will has suggested that psychological causes lie at the root of the craving—as a subconscious mechanism by which tense and unstable people seek psychic relief. The parallel with addictive gambling, where no physical effects are involved, supports this; as does the testimony of hard-drinking criminals that the need ceases in jail, where drink is not available, to reappear on release. For vagrants, retarded minds, and 'drop-outs', alcohol certainly provides anaesthesia—the resource of the 'mindless'.

On the other hand, the effect of alcohol on senses, nerve centres, liver and general health is plainly physical. It has been argued that some irreversible change occurs in the alcoholic's organism; 'in this sense, alcoholism is incurable' though treatable—the alcoholic will never again drink in controlled fashion. The analogy of diabetes is cited: some biochemical condition has arisen in which sugar in the one case, alcohol in the other, proves highly dangerous, in the latter case creating so violent a craving that taking alcohol can induce the temporary insanity of *delirium tremens*, withholding it can produce equally violent symptoms of distress, loss of control, and abject helplessness. That, in some cases, 'inherited drunkenness' may be part of the cause, and certain drugs can make the body reject alcohol, also tend to confirm some physical basis for the condition—though whatever physical predisposition is present would remain inoperative if alcohol were never taken. To indulge at all in a habit so manifestly evil in its effects, to be unable to resist social pressure, and especially to persist when first signs of deterioration give solemn warning, argue some moral weakness, some sad insufficiency in the life-pattern, underlying all else; the strong and happy Christian soul is not likely to succumb to this particular snare. The pastor will be aware that ethical and religious deficiencies are part of the explanation, and ethical and religious motive forces must be part of the cure.

Where the alcoholic genuinely seeks the pastor's help, a great step is already taken towards cure. If the approach is from within the worried family, the pastor will have right to seek interview with the alcoholic on their behalf, but it will be essential to get on to terms of sympathy and confidence with the patient himself: nothing can be achieved by lecturing or hostility. It may be necessary to advise that the family cease to shield, or even to restrain, the alcoholic: only abandonment to his self-chosen life may bring the self-realisation which deliverance requires. As a tactical step, the pastor may even consider that a temporary separation of husband and wife may be the way to expose how desperate the situation is: but this will need great care, foresight of possible consequences, and confidence in the sober partner. Of course if the alcoholic has previously been within the fellowship of the church, the pastor's approach is simplified.

The physical effects of alcoholism require the immediate advice of a trusted medical authority, who may prescribe hospital treatment or the use of alcohol-repellent drugs. Willingness for such consultation is a useful test of earnestness, and of the prospect of success. At the same time, it is essential that the patient shall not imagine his problem is an affliction for which the cure lies in medicine. He must be made to realise clearly that his problem, his enemy, is alcohol, and that only he can resist its hold; he cannot be delivered without his own initiative, and co-operation at any cost. That is why the pastor will wish to bring the patient quickly to the issue of religious faith: in the last resort only the renewal of the patient's conscience and moral strength can save him. Steps toward this will include clear conviction that dependence upon alcohol is *wrong*, that indulgence in a habit so self-destructive is wilful folly amounting to *sin*. Unless this conviction is created, a religious deliverance is improbable: a man cannot confess before God, seek forgiveness for, and ask grace to overcome, something which he half-believes is not nearly as serious or sinful as others make out.

Where the patient rejects the religious conviction, confession, and surrender to the saving power of God through faith and fellowship, the pastor must rely on human and ethical forces for such help as he can give. To abandon the patient because he is unsympathetic to religion would be unchristian, though the task is made infinitely more difficult when he refuses the only adequate help. Prudential arguments about what alcohol is doing to him and to his home, and ethical arguments about his duty to himself and to others, with the firm realisation that he needs external help from somewhere, will be the minimal steps toward renewal. The alcoholic must be left in no doubt that alcohol is not for him, not in any circumstances, not at any time, not in the smallest amount; that every act of resistance is a firmer step towards cure, and every weakening can plunge him into worse horrors, made more powerful by reaction to temporary abstinence.

In all cases, the story of the patient's decline, its excuses, hidden motives, predisposing causes and futile attempts to resist, will need to be brought into the daylight of consciousness, sympathetically but very frankly, that the patient may clearly understand himself. But also that the pastor may clearly understand the circumstances which contributed to the tragedy. It is of little use to attack the result if the predisposing unhappiness, tension, anxiety or fear remains. Such probing and assistance may carry pastor and patient far beyond the original problem: new home relationships, change of employment, and of environment may be demanded—nothing can be too radical to solve such a problem. In every case, too, the whole pattern of life may be changed. The times of greatest temptation must be so organised as to be full of other interests and company; unhelpful friendships must be replaced by supportive ones; activities must be arranged which will supplant those associated with drinking, every emotional, intellectual and habitual bond with the enemy must be broken. Any understanding group might share the redemptive task, but a living church fellowship should be the ideal social environment in which the patient finds, together with friendship, example, and confirmation of the supernatural powers of the gospel, a confident expectation of change in him which in itself is a powerful incentive, and a gentle, sharing understanding of his penitence and regret. If within that fellowship he finds one who has come his way, he will be blessed indeed; or the pastor may introduce him to someone in another fellowship who can share his story. In any event, it is well not to leave responsibility for rehabilitation to everyone in the group: some selected individual or couple should be assigned to this personal task as a very deliberate and dedicated act of service for Christ.

The fellowship of 'Alcoholics Anonymous' is a non-sectarian version of the same group-therapy. Its recovery programme—the famous 'Twelve Steps'—covers admission of helplessness; fearless self-examination; confession, belief and commitment towards God 'as we understand Him', with surrender and prayer; repair of injury to others; meditation to discover and do the will of God; and sharing this message with other alcoholics. In addition 'AA' provides regular companionship, social activity, mutual support, specialised treatment, and discussion. Even for those helped by a Christian fellowship, such a programme offers additional support in the dangerous leisure time.

The pastor's concern will extend beyond the patient to his family, who may possibly have contributed to the problem and will certainly have shared the pain; his care for them will be part of his general pastoral ministry, but also a major factor in strengthening the faith and resolve of the alcoholic. To help the husband or wife to understand the total problem, to win support, and hope, for recovery, will be essential to success; much of the reorientation of life will also require their co-operation. Often the pastor can alleviate some of the immediate domestic problems alcoholism has caused, and may need to arrange protection for the family. If the attempt at recovery fails, or is prolonged, the pastor may achieve much in helping the husband or wife to remake life for themselves, not consenting to be wholly destroyed by a partner's excess.

The pastoral ministry to the alcoholic will thus extend into marital, evangelistic and pastoral counselling for all connected with the patient, each needing help in different ways. For the family as a whole, the 'countenance', sympathy and friendship of a pastor and his Christian fellowship can be vital help towards keeping a home together and preserving dignity and hope. The redemptive effort involved is extensive: the end when achieved more than rewards all the labour, prayer and patience it entails.

Addiction to Gambling

As on so many subjects, the pastor will have to make up his own mind to what degree, and for what specific reasons he considers gambling unchristian; but even those who find it possible to defend the mild excitements of an occasional 'speculation' must agree that compulsive gambling is a psychological disorder, a spiritual tragedy, and an unrelieved evil. There appears in some characters, male or female impartially, a special vulnerability to gambling intoxication that develops into mania or 'craze', a pathological condition to which gambling becomes a necessity. No physical or biochemical basis for the craving is suggested, but some doctors, prison officers and welfare workers are convinced that gambling can assume the proportions of at any rate a mental obsession. All control, and foresight, are lost: the gambler continues when he knows he has no further resources, no good fortune on his side, no hope of restoring his position. He cannot stop, but lives on dreams of scooping the pool, and to that end may borrow, steal, embezzle, rob home and family. How desperate the situation may become is illustrated in the estimate of an honorary psychiatrist to 'Gamblers Anonymous', that one in five members had made at least one attempt at suicide.

It is at the point where gambling has become compulsive that a pastor is likely to be appealed to by those who share the degradation and loss. Much that was said about ministry to the alcoholic is relevant here: the varied approach; the possibility of a religious experience that delivers from the habit at once, where the sinfulness of the habit is accepted; the need to rely on other arguments where Christian premises are rejected, though these are much weaker; and the need for supportive counsel. In the prevailing muddle on this subject, it may be difficult to reach clear conviction that gambling is inherently wrong; the pastor must not assume that every gambler is dishonest, avaricious, mentally deranged or suicide-prone. But at least it should be possible to argue that gambling is stupid, dangerous and evil for anyone in whom it becomes a compulsive 'possession'. Surrender to *any* compulsion or 'mere habit' which thus gains control of the Christian's time, resources, and interest, is a betrayal of the absolute Lordship of Christ; in so far as gambling achieves gain through others' loss, it is a failure of love, a 'stealing by consent of the robbed'—like persuading a child to give up its pocket-money for rubbish. To the extent that the motive is cupidity, gambling is self-condemned. In looking to luck, chance, good fortune or fate as the directive force in life, gambling contradicts that trust in the providence and direction of God under which the Christian should pass his days. To mislead by poor example others whose character is less mature and resistant, and to lend active financial support to those who live by exploiting them, is to fail in caring for the weak. The social-economic argument that such passage of wealth in the community without relation to productivity, merit, or social good, should appeal to all Christians with any conscience about inequality and world poverty. The association of gambling with crime, poverty and despair is an ancillary reason why Christians should avoid it altogether. All of which may be more dramatically and personally summarised in the question: Would Jesus do it?

Where such considerations fail to convince, the pastor can only appeal to the self-interest of the man being ruined, enlightened now by his experience, or by the carefully marshalled evidence of what has happened to others. Admittedly, reason can carry little weight to a mind habitually dependent upon chance; foresight of ultimate disaster will seem mere pessimism to one who daily lives upon the hope that the next wager will bring riches; indeed, the clearer the danger the greater the excitement! Unless ethical and religious arguments convince, or the dangers arising for his home and his employment prove sufficient warning, it may be that only a conspiracy to expose him unsheltered to the full extent of his losses, and to public shame, will bring the gambler to his senses.

Where, however, there is a desire to reform, the pastor should again listen attentively to the story of decline, analysing causes and motives, isolating areas of probably recurring temptation. As with alcoholism, remedial steps can include far-reaching changes in the pattern of life. The wife or husband of the gambler may be given full executive authority over the family income and possessions, not in mistrust but to remove temptation. An employer, properly approached (perhaps by the pastor) may consent to pay salary into the employee's banking account, from which only the partner can draw—by mutual agreement. Where specific causes of the habit have been brought to light, as boredom, loneliness, worry, felt inadequacy, envy of others' affluence or home or holidays, pressure of debt or hire purchase payments, and the like, it will be necessary to deal with these before the temptation will be finally removed. A change of locality, employment, or friendships may be necessary to sever old associations, and always it is necessary to devise and *set on foot* substitute activities for the times of greatest stress. The church fellowship may offer interests, occupations, new responsibilities, sponsoring friends, who will assist in rehabilitation, while in some districts, 'Gamblers Anonymous' can reinforce pastoral and church ministry in numerous ways.

The absence of physical craving, and a lower level of social tolerance, make addiction to gambling a little easier to cure than alcoholism, but the way back to thrift and responsibility is long and hard nevertheless, and may necessitate psychiatric treatment in the end. Even Christian friends are slow to trust the former gambler, and much sympathy, friendship and patience must be added to counselling skill to help such a soul find deliverance, safety, and self-confidence again.

Addiction to Drugs

The prevalence of drug addiction will be brought under the pastor's notice as distraught parents confide in him that sons or daughters are experimenting with drugs; as addicts themselves seek of him in near-despair the help and sympathy no one else will give; and as he realises that the young people of his own fellowship must not be left ignorant or confused about the danger, or about Christian reaction to it. One young man whispering boastfully about his experiences or 'kicks' can lead to others, perhaps more vulnerable, making perilous trials. Frankness and information are the only safe prophylactics.

For the present purpose a drug may be defined as any substance not normally required by the body, which is introduced to modify any of its functions, whether curatively, or for the sake of pleasurable, sedative, or stimulant effects. Addiction may be described as the compulsive taking of drugs on which the user has become dependent, either socially, to conform to the mores of his group; or psychologically, as constantly needing the feeling of well-being or of tranquillity which the drugs provide; or physically, where sudden withdrawal of the drug produces symptoms of distress and pain, often exceedingly severe. Sometimes, psychological dependence is referred to as drug *abuse*—a defensible, curative usage being un-

H2

necessarily prolonged or intensified; the word *dependence* is then used to mean actual physical dependence only, the condition requiring expert medical attention and treatment. There are a small number of 'therapeutic addicts', usually now of middle-age or older, whose addiction results from medical prescription begun before the seriously addictive properties of some substances were fully understood; their behaviour is not seriously affected under controlled doses, sometimes under special licence or at treatment centres.

The appalling mental and physical results of drug addiction are now plain to all who take the trouble to investigate, but at the same time an exceedingly profitable underground market has sprung up for the exploitation of the young in search of excitement. It operates in part upon the threat of blackmail, and in part upon the torture suffered by those made dependent upon supplies if withdrawal is threatened. In order to educate against the dangers, and to convince addicts who seek help that he knows what he is talking about, the pastor needs at least some elementary knowledge about the more familiar addictive drugs:

Amphetamines are 'pep' pills, used to increase energy, properly obtainable only on medical prescription, though many doctors deny that they have any proper medical use except for a few rare disorders. These do not usually create physical dependence, but more and more have to be taken to produce the desired results—an increasing psychological dependence. Amphetamines can produce severe disturbance of personality and behaviour, especially violent aggressiveness. Dr N. W. Imlah records that of five thousand admissions of amphetamine-addicts to mental hospitals in Japan in 1955, twenty-six per cent were still in hospital ten years later.

Barbiturates are 'sleeping pills', which can create physical or psychological dependence if the therapeutic dose is exceeded. The drowsiness induced is of course dangerous to car drivers, and in combination with alcohol their effect can be very serious. Since barbiturates cannot cure, but only hide the underlying causes of restlessness and tension, increasing doses tend to be needed, and overdose—often taken desperately to produce desired effect—can be fatal. Easy availability and familiarity also tends to make easier impulsive attempts at suicide.

Cannabis, which contains one of the oldest drug-derivatives, opium, goes by many names—hashish, grass, Indian hemp, pot, bhang, dagga, marihuana (marijuana)—and is used in many forms, as resin, flowers, leaves in cigarettes smoked as 'reefers'. Cannabis has no medical use, and it is a criminal offence in some countries even to possess it. It produces an effect like cheerful drunkenness, an excitement invariably having sexual overtones. The most widely used drug, it is believed by many to be the least destructive—some say, less harmful than alcohol.

The World Health Organisation reported that 'Cannabis has acute and chronic effects on the individual user and the community. Cannabis is a drug of dependence, producing public health and social problems, and its control must be continued. Users often take it to the exclusion of all other activity . . . Cannabis distorts perception and the sense of time . . .' Some experienced doctors hold that a large proportion of heroin addicts started on 'soft' drugs like cannabis—cannabis especially producing the kind of exhilaration in which suggestibility to other drugs is greatly increased.

Heroin (di-acetyl morphine, a derivative of morphia) is 'by far the most widely used, and the most rapidly and completely destructive of all known drugs' (Dr Imlah). McNaughtan remarks its effects upon behaviour, but its greatest peril is that it rapidly establishes physical dependence; the consequences of its use are described as 'dreadful' and of its withdrawal as still worse. Early death often results from heroin, and most morphines adversely affect the reproductive processes.

Cocaine at first produces exhilaration and cheerfulness, but addiction brings depression, mental confusion, loss of moral values, a marked motor restlessness ('the leaps'), tremors, slurring of speech, serious decline in general health, and in extreme doses, convulsive seizures. Delusions of persecution, hallucinations, and the delusion of 'bugs creeping under the skin' are common mental results.

Hallucinogens cause disturbance of perception, and loss of contact with reality. Best known 'psychedelic' drugs are 'LSD-25' (lysergic acid diethyl-amide), the 'fantasy drug', 'STP', mescaline, and psilocybin: all induce illusions and hallucinations, producing experiences similar to those of the schizophrenic. They are extremely powerful, minute doses being effective, and the reactions provoked are wholly unpredictable. Of LSD Dr Imlah says, 'Under its influence, a man has rushed at the headlamps of an approaching car in the belief that he was catching huge yellow butterflies, while others have become acutely suicidal.' Another authority suggests that LSD may cause damage to the chromosomes. Aldous Huxley's famous experiment with mescalin produced the report that intelligence was unchanged, the will was weakened, and vision much intensified (but would the intelligence making the report declare itself consciously incapacitated?).

Alcohol, Nicotine, must be included in the list in simple fairness to young defenders of 'their' drugs, since both are addictive and demonstrably harmful. Alcohol has physical, personality and social consequences no less widespread or damaging as those of other drugs; Bewley (Proceedings of the Royal Society of Medicine, London, 1968) says 'the largest problem of addiction in the United Kingdom is . . . alcoholism'. Nicotine has proved carcinogenic effects, especially (but not only) lung cancer, and psychological as well as physical withdrawal symptoms. It greatly weakens the case against other people's choice of drugs if they suspect that they are being blamed, not for the use of harmful drugs as psychological crutches, but only for a different, more original, preference.

The dangers involved in drug addiction are of many kinds and degrees. Dependence upon some regularly repeated stimulant, sedative, or intoxicant is itself a confession of inadequacy; the continual demand for increased dosage, and fear of withdrawal, or sheer inability to end the habit, abjectly confesses the lack of freedom and self-determination. It is usually held that, except in a few cases, the use of drugs does not lead to mental *disease*, but does lead to mental, moral and physical deterioration. Drug addiction and personality disintegration go hand in hand, each promoting the other, and the extent of an individual's vulnerability cannot be foreseen. Lichtenstein and Small vividly describe the decline in responsibility, the illusory fears and jealousies, the aggressiveness, the depression, the mental and moral disintegration, which drug addiction produces—the addict is usually ready for any lie, crime or violence to gain supplies. D. W. Vere, speaking of the rapid and deep disintegration of personality, uses of the incidence of drug-taking in one English district the phrase 'the epidemic of ruined lives'. With the authority of a Reader in Therapeutics in London University, he adds: 'the therapeutic prospects for dependent persons are known to be poor. Results in the United Kingdom resemble those of the United States Public Health Service Hospital at Lexington, where only sixteen per cent of patients remained off drugs such as diamorphine for seven years, and sixty-four per cent relapsed, died, or were untraced.'

Incidental dangers are no less serious. Drug addiction necessarily brings the young person into the fringes of the criminal community, where he may easily be drawn into further illegal adventures, and on to other, harder drugs than he first intended to experiment with. The influence of most drugs is such that he can be induced, or himself desire, to do entirely uncharacteristic things, violent, sexual or criminal, while 'not himself'. Further, the addict's dependence upon drug supplies makes him easy prey to criminal pressure, blackmail, and duress, by those who can provide them if he co-operates, withhold them if he does not. He may be reduced to *any* means of gaining the necessary price; the pedlar may withhold the softer, cheaper drugs in order to introduce the addict to the more profitable harder drug, completing his enslavement; most desperate of all, the young addict may be (and often is) forced by his own abject dependence upon supplies to become a pusher, only getting what he must have if he succeeds in tempting others to begin their own destruction.

No reasonable and healthy-minded group of young people

presented with the total picture of the dangers involved would willingly let themselves in for such wholesale degradation and abuse. It is often the fascination and curiosity of an unknown experience, combined with ignorance of its true nature, which makes them willing to try. The pastor will want to make sure that at any rate they cannot hold him responsible for that ignorance.

It is frequently said that we do not know what makes individuals turn to drugs; good home backgrounds and higher than average intelligence (as among student groups) will be found among addicts as often as 'bad' homes and low intelligence. Curiosity about 'exploring inner space' and 'way-out experiences'; general rebelliousness against accepted mores and restrictions; the tendency to follow slavishly any trend that the media of communication publicise as fashionable; the highly profitable exploitation of the weak and the young by manufacturers, importers and hawkers; the subtle advertising done by 'pop' lyrics and suggestion—all have place among possible causes. One of the falsehoods canvassed by defenders is that the habit is 'modern—of the twentieth century': the truth is that 'millenia ago the Amerindian had his mescalin, the Siberian tribesman his psilocybin, the middle east man his alcohol' (Vere): drugs belong to a culture that in every sense has not yet come of age!

But causes run deeper: 'it is not the drug that is the problem'. Tension predisposes to any form of indulgence that promises release; so do heavy examination programmes, unhappy love-affairs, failure to find satisfactory employment or frustration in it, felt inadequacy in sport, study, or social poise and success; the craving for excitement betrays thorough boredom with a dull, repetitive, unrewarding existence, aimless, purposeless and meaningless. Sharing few of the goals and ambitions of secularised, materialistic, acquisitive western culture, the young find no substitutes but those which offer a new experience 'in another world', whose attractiveness is naturally increased when the society which they despise condemns it!

So, as Vere eloquently argues, the basic cause is a spiritual one—a religious vacuum. 'Emptiness', emotional deprivation, the 'nothing' at the heart of youth, is the clamorous cause, to which all pastoral concern must address itself. The deepest condemnation of our civilisation is that the young should feel the need of drugs, not that they should take them. We must save young people not merely *from* the evils which others, for gain, thrust in their way, but *for* something infinitely better, more satisfying, secure—for life abundant.

The rehabilitation of those who have fallen is a long, laborious and discouraging task. *Medical* treatment is of course essential for those physically dependent. Withdrawal from the drug must probably be slow and prolonged. Hospitalisation, or commitment to recognised treatment centres, will usually be recommended, and pastors will support such suggestions, advising truthfully that under proper control treatment may be far less unpleasant than the addict may have been told. *Psychological* analysis and therapy may be needed to uncover the predisposing states of mind—heredity, inferiority, conflict, introversion, some deeply buried childhood experience of rejection, terror or despair, inadequacy in some cherished ambition, rebelliousness provoked by mishandling. Only skilled probing and interpretation can reveal and assuage the situations that made drug experimentation seem a valid means of escape. As always, to counsel psychiatric help demands great caution. The implication of insanity may not be far already from the patient's mind, and must be avoided at all costs. The doctor may best know when to make the suggestion, but in any case it should be delayed until considerable confidence has been built up between the addict and the pastor, and the suggestion can be received without suspicion, resentment, or shock.

What *religious* assistance the pastor can offer will depend much on the patient's co-operation and the help of the Christian fellowship and the home. That a pastor becomes involved at all is promising: but much more will be required that neither a cry of despair, nor an expectation of miracle in answer to prayer, can guarantee. Reasonable discussion of the dangers and weaknesses of drug-taking may persuade the more intelligent, but few people act from rational considerations only. One doctor warns that horrific pictures and uninformed emotional reactions do not help, but he does not suggest what, in dealing with the less intelligent, will offer any hope of reform. Fear is a powerful motive, and in such an emergency it has rightful place in changing motivation and behaviour in those less amenable to reason—and there is ground enough for letting the addict be factually and firmly shown the way he is going. Religious warnings—of judgement or hell—are not likely to have any weight with those who have long ceased to let conscience influence their conduct, and are much more likely to alienate all trust.

Much needs to be done *socially* and practically towards re-patterning the addict's life-style; family support needs to be re-established, and employment found—in spite of obvious difficulties. Some change of environment may be advisable, without breaking frequent contact; and new hobbies and friendships, occupations and responsibilities must eventually replace the lost, if spurious, excitements. It is here that truly religious forces are brought to bear, in the Christian love and compassion that sets about healing and renewing a soul. Other Christians, of great understanding, patience, constant openness, and ready availability, should be engaged—poverty of after-care is the main reason alleged for the many relapses into renewed addiction. The demands are high, patience is sorely tried, the ex-addict invades so much of the new friend's time and interests; yet unless the supporting friendship is available *whenever* the patient is under pressure, alone, anxious, depressed or bored, he will very easily feel rejected, and seek out his old friends and habits.

This is why the only final answer to the addict's problem is a living faith in 'the Friend who sticketh closer than a brother'—the *ever-present*, never rejecting, ever supporting God who is always 'for us'. A transforming religious experience is the one solution for the addict. He needs to be shown, as McNaughtan suggests, that 'Faith in God is a better support than drugs'. As Vere says, 'Just as an empty stomach needed to be filled with bread, so an empty life needed to be filled with Christ . . . It takes a deep influence in a life to enable it to stand against its only, distorted, source of pleasure. It must be a displacing influence, a filling influence.' And he adds the testimony that of the five drug dependent persons known to him who have been lastingly relieved of their dependence, three attained this through some form of religious experience, and another through marriage to a stronger personality.

Therein lies the pastor's resource—the power of God, and a supportive Christian fellowship. For Jesus still comes to seek and to save those who are lost.

DEEPER INSIGHTS

19 ELEMENTARY PASTORAL PSYCHOLOGY

The Christian physician, aware that all healing is divine healing does not on that account doubt that the evidence of healing will lie in measurable conditions like temperature, heartbeat, returning strength and prompt reflexes. The accepted medical functions and norms by which he affirms that the patient is well again do not contradict, but in fact prove, that God has been at work; the Christian physician will describe the process, and prescribe for convalescence. Exactly so, the Christian psychologist, analysing, defining, explaining the healing of some distressed mind and soul, and advising on healthful changes of attitude and environment, does not for a moment doubt that Christ only is the Saviour of men from every spiritual ailment, affliction and evil. He too delights to trace God's healing hand, and to demonstrate the curative power of grace, the therapy of obedient faith. When he expertly diagnoses a human need, analyses its causes, defines accurately the steps by which it may be met, he is explaining, but not explaining away, the process of cure; not denying God's intervention but describing God's method. That some psychologists are atheists, some arrogant, some amoral, and some seem obsessed with sexual explanations, is no reason to dismiss a whole area of dedicated knowledge and skill concerned with mental and spiritual health. The truth is, that every pastoral counsellor is dealing with the forces, problems and mechanisms that belong equally to the field of the psychologist; the only question is, whether he blunders along blindly in supreme ignorance of what he is handling, or has sufficient knowledge to guide what he can do, *and to prevent his attempting what he cannot.*

The dangers cannot be too strongly emphasised. As no one unqualified in medicine should ever advise a patient on medical matters, so no one unqualified in medical psychology should ever attempt to help a psychotic, a paranoic with delusions of grandeur or of persecution, a manic-depressive, alternating between elation and despair, a schizophrenic, anyone insanely violent, or any person so mentally disordered as to imagine that he is normal and all other people abnormal. Nor dare the pastor attempt to use psychotherapeutic methods beyond his own training and responsibility—methods whose potential side-effects and ultimate risks are probably beyond his understanding. The pastor will find enough opportunities for ministry to a score of mental and spiritual maladies, without pretending to a competence he does not possess: *the insane must be committed to those qualified to help them*, and any pastoral care exercised only under expert direction.

Even in problems amenable to pastoral guidance it is well for the counsellor to know what he is about as he probes a man's past, analyses his present attitudes, and proposes revision of his ways. Moffatt makes John say of Jesus, 'well did He know what was in human nature': the pastor who seeks sufficient psychological understanding to preserve him from unforgivable blundering is but aiming to share that divine insight into human hearts. It will help him not only to understand other people, but to understand himself—his own prejudices, impatience, and limitations. Above all it will quicken and deepen his pastoral sympathy, as with sharpened, better informed, more inward understanding he shares the problems of his people.

Analysis of Mental Life

Pastoral psychology, like educational psychology, industrial psychology, social psychology, chooses its own starting-point and uses its own terms in concentrating upon its own special interests— the moral, social, and religious problems that confront the pastor. Inevitably, therefore, it is one-sided, and in summary form it is in danger of caricaturing a vast subject. Keeping that caution in mind, and evading controversies, it is useful to begin with man as a *dual* creature, a body-mind, whose physical elements and limitations deeply and constantly influence the mental elements, while the mental as deeply, constantly, and mysteriously, influence the physical. So closely inter-related are the two sides of man's being that we conceive of them separately only in abstract thought, and with effort. Though the proper field of psychology is the mental life of the body-mind entity, it can never forget the physical concomitants of mental experience—the sentient and motor nervous systems, the brain cells, sense organs, the hungers, appetites, pleasure-pain reactions, sexual differences, physical limitations of strength and concentration, the morbid or distorting effects of physical affliction, deficiency, malfunction, or disease. No attempt to help the distressed soul will be effective if it forgets the body—nor will it be truly

Christian if it forgets that the body is God's, by creation, redemption, and the indwelling of God's Spirit.

It is convenient to identify in the stream of conscious mental life features that have to do respectively with knowing, feeling, and willing, recognisable aspects or phases of mentality, modes of psychological experience, distinguishable in thought though never entirely separable in fact.

The *cognitive* process receives sensations from the 'external' world (including the subject's own body), recognises their significance for its stored experience, so as to 'perceive' objects, persons, situations, and 'apperceives' the new awareness by building it into the existing stock of memories, adjusting what is already known to take account of the new information. By reflecting rationally upon the result, the mind sharpens its awareness, discovers relationships between things known, and deduces still further truth by perceiving in what *is* the underlying regularities from which prophecies can be made of what *will be*, and *must be*. By detaching from objects actually experienced the general impressions or images into which they can be analysed, the mind attains 'ideas', to which it can then attach words, names, symbols, in order to recombine them into new patterns by the power of (inventive, aesthetic or theoretic) 'imagination'. Both reason, which analyses, and imagination, which recombines, enormously extend the simple sense-experience by which the mind knows and interprets its environment. When analysis, comparison, evaluation and recombination of ideas, are deliberately directed towards some conscious purpose, so that only significant ideas are selected for attention, we are *thinking*; when they are enjoyed for their own sake, we are daydreaming (*'imagining'* in the popular sense); and if we pursue imagination to the detriment of reason, we are indulging in *fantasy*.

The *affective* (feeling) aspect of conscious mental life is the source of all response to environment, to ideas, and to experience generally—the consciousness of the way things 'affect us'. The tendency to feel, or be affected by, any object or experience is inborn (inherited) though particular emotional responses may be learned or copied from others. Feelings range from a basically physical disturbance of consciousness (like hunger) to an exalted spiritual response (like adoration); from simple, unanalysable states like fear or anger (the 'primary emotions') to complex states (like awe = wonder + fear + humility; contempt = disgust + superiority); from mild to overmastering in degree; and in tone from pleasant (with concomitant desire to prolong or intensify) to unpleasant (with concomitant repugnance and fear). Feeling is of all mental states the most subjective and relative—the same fact, rain, may bring joy to the gardener, vexation to the holiday-maker, despair to the expectant child, fear to the flood-victim, awe to the worshipper of the rain-god. Adler's distinction between emotions that are *conjunctive* (tending to unite people in good will—social cohesiveness, sympathy, appreciation) and those that are *disjunctive* (tending to antagonise and divide—anger, contempt) is important in social and religious contexts. Some would confine the 'primary emotions' to fear, anger, love, holding that all the rest are combinations of these; others include as primary joy, sorrow, disgust, repugnance, surprise, wonder, 'positive or negative self-feeling', 'tender emotion', sympathy, and even honour, surprise, approval and disapproval. All feeling impels to action—fear, to resistance or flight; anger to punishment or revenge; love to gestures or deeds of identification; the word 'emotion' focuses this 'impulse to motion'. Whether feelings *produce* physiological changes (in blood circulation, respiration, glandular secretion) preparatory to appropriate action, or *are* simply the awareness that such changes are taking place, psychologists have never decided.

The *conative* aspect of conscious mental life includes that positive and initiative response to objects and situations by which we seek to react to environment and bring about changes in whatever has affected us. Feeling is the more passive side of personal response, though it moves toward action; volition, will, the process of conation, is the more active side of that response, not only prompted by, but itself strongly reinforcing feeling. Will is so intimately concerned in most religious and pastoral issues as to demand detailed attention. But 'all consciousness is motor' in the sense that everything in mental life, every thought, impression, belief, feeling, idea or habit tends towards action, being inhibited only by the tendencies towards action of other, contradictory thoughts, impressions, beliefs, feelings, ideas or habits. *Inaction is the balance of opposing impulses*—a vital principle in understanding character weaknesses. To be conscious is to react to stimuli; to cease to react is death; the whole process by which the living organism strives to react is 'conation'.

This threefold analysis, convenient for description, must not obscure the unity of conscious mental life: there is no act of *knowing* without sufficient interest being *felt* to cause attention and prompt *reaction*; there is no *feeling* without some *known* object or idea to stimulate and focus it, and some *prompting* to pursue the resulting pleasure or avoid the resulting pain. (Where the known object or stimulus is so vague as to seem absent, we speak rather of a mood than a feeling—an 'objectless feeling' such as anger, resentment, which however immediately seeks to identify a cognitive stimulus, and an objective target). Conscious life is a continuum of impressions, interpretation, emotional experience and reactions of choice, in which pure, isolated, or abstract cognition, feeling, volition, never occur. In different religious philosophies, different forms of religion, and different religious persons, either thought, feeling or will may predominate, but a balanced and satisfying religious life will involve the whole personality: truth, tradition, memory filling the mind with belief and conviction; feelings of gratitude, trust, devotion, peace, joy kindling and sustaining the inner life in such belief; and prompting to approved conduct and service, the will being wholly responsive to the truth, emotions and ideals which religion inculcates.

Instinctive Dispositions

The stream of conscious mental life has also certain strong currents of movement, inherent patterns of its own, instinctive impulses which constitute the basic *drives* carrying life forward in the individual and the race. Instincts are channels along which the original life-force in each individual finds expression; they provide the springs of all energy, in saint, thinker and sinner; out of them is built up all mental experience and they determine the ends of all activity. The instincts are the raw material of character, and their emotional energy is the dynamic of life. Nevertheless man is no longer regarded, as once he was, as simply a bundle of thrusting instincts each seeking its own end-satisfaction: he is the vehicle of a life-force which manifests itself in clearly discernible instinctive drives which form part of the biological inheritance of all normal members of the species.

Full discussion of the nature of instincts would begin with the physiological reflexes, automatic reactions barely conscious—as blinking, mouth-watering. Like these, instincts are *connections* (between outward or inward stimuli—sense impressions, thoughts—and feelings, desires, impulses to action) *which are unlearned*, are sometimes barely conscious, but which yet serve some purpose. But even when the stimulus is absent, the *tendency* or *disposition* to react in patterned ways is present, so that an instinct is usually defined as a deep-rooted, hereditary disposition, innate and unlearned, to respond in regular ways to given situations, so as to attain a desired biological end, though often without foresight of that end. Where a *reflex* is specific and unalterable, an *instinct* is much more general, embracing attention to the stimulus (cognition) aroused emotion related to it (affect) and the impulse to respond (conation); it is also much more subject to modification by training, redirection, ideals. Instincts are shared by all normal members of a species; dispositions to particular talents and capacities are the 'gifts' of private individuals.

The older 'instinct psychology' multiplied human instincts to include most unlearned tendencies or activities—crying at pain, starting at sudden noise, jealousy, play, curiosity, sleep, constructiveness, acquisitiveness, language, appeal (the call for help), suggestibility, habit-formation, and others. It is more enlightening to see a few instinctive drives towards fundamental biological ends as creating numerous subsidiary tendencies and habits:

for example, the fundamental need of every organism, the need *to be*, to find itself and assert itself in the struggle for existence, will find expression, in different conditions, as the 'nutritional instinct', as the 'acquisitive instinct' (to ensure future existence), as self-expression, as self-preservation in danger, which will evoke 'instinctive fear'; and again, against foes produces pugnacity; against overwhelming odds, flight, and in situations not understood but potentially dangerous, curiosity. The same basic drive *to be* will prompt also the 'instinct' for security, which may require constructiveness (for the den), or in competition with others, caution, even jealousy. The basic drive towards self-reproduction may be a consequence of this same urge to assert one's own existence, or a distinct inherent disposition; it will prompt all activities and responses related to sex: self-display, rivalry, mating, and at one remove, the parental 'instinct' with all which that includes of constructiveness (for the nest), defence of the young, nurture, and sometimes self-sacrifice. The reproductive ('sex') instinct is one of those not immediately obvious but latent until physical changes or environment provide appropriate and effective stimuli. It is much debated whether gregariousness ('herd' instinct) is again self-preservation seeking protection in numbers, not a distinct disposition; derived from it are suggestibility, imitation, attraction-repulsion, group-play, 'appeal', the 'instinct' for communication (language); it is arguable that habit-formation, play, most fears (except, in the infant, the fear of loud noise and the fear of falling), language, and perhaps jealousy, are more acquired than innate. Sleep is like hunger a physiological need whose satisfaction is 'instinctive'. *Self-preservation, self-reproduction* and *gregariousness* (the preservation of the individual, the species, and the group, respectively) are probably to be regarded as the truly fundamental biological instincts, modes of the essential drive of the living organism to continue to be itself. Other deep-rooted inherent dispositions, like imitation, pugnacity, fear, will rightly be called 'instinctive', as arising from the primary instincts, rather than as themselves instincts.

Each basic instinct and derived instinctive disposition has its powerful attendant emotion—pleasure accompanies the satisfaction of each instinct, pain marks its frustration. Thus they constitute our *motives*—that is a 'motive' which appeals to an instinctive emotion as an end to be gained, or avoided—so *moving* us to action. Self-preservation can evoke aggressive feeling, anger, fear; sex evokes 'tender emotion', physical passion, parental pity, jealousy; gregariousness evokes feelings of loyalty, distress at separation—and the like. *It is in these instinctive emotions that the great driving forces of life really lie.* For good and ill, they determine what interests us; scenes, objects, impressions, people, appeal to us primarily because they stimulate our basic or derived instinctive emotions; ideas likewise move us to heroic endeavour, emulation, sacrifice, degradation or self-destruction, as they appeal to the same fundamental instinctive emotions. In civilised man, these simple, fundamental drives become overlaid and modified in a thousand ways: yet beneath all the modifications it is these same inherent demands of our nature that determine, in the last analysis, our goals, ambitions, and achievements. Each 'drive' aims at 'satisfaction', and so is felt as a 'want'; a want when defined and accepted by the self is 'desire', and such instinctive desire, enormously reinforced by the attendant emotions, is the force of life itself thrusting towards its biological ends.

That is why the thwarting of instinctive drives and emotions is so dangerous. Blocked, they become not less powerful but more so. Other methods of control or diversion must be found: mere denial that the instinctive forces exist in us, mere damming of their outlet by wholly negative, rigid self-discipline, is attempting to hold back the elemental forces of life itself, and must lead to trouble, whether by paralysis, inversion, or explosion.

Our understanding of people will not be greatly affected if instead of speaking of inherited instincts, instinctive drives and instinctive emotions, we prefer to speak of human 'needs' or 'inherent concerns', in order to avoid the biological emphasis and underline the great complexity and modification introduced by training, custom, and rationality. Man, it is said, is *now* far more than a fixed pattern of instincts. Human nature as we know it has certain primary needs— of *security* (when denied, this originates anxiety in all its forms); of *self-assertion*, the need to be a person in one's own right (when denied, this originates varied neuroses, 'split personality', frustration, resentment and the like); and of *sexuality*, including all forms of sensuous comfort and pleasure. These three original concerns determine all interests and responses, and are the raw material of character. This representation is plausible enough, but the direct link with the fundamental nature of life, with the body-mind organism and its biological ends, and so with its instinctive emotional drives, is also important: to speak of 'instincts' keeps this biological context of psychology in mind.

On either choice of terms, it is possible to name (i) the *original direction* of the drive, the end it normally tends to fulfil (as self-protection is the normal end of fear); (ii) the *perversion* of the drive, when its normal outlet is stemmed (as phobias and anxieties of all kinds are the perversion of fear—vanity is the perversion of self-display; avarice, of acquisition; lust, of sexual desire); (iii) the positive and profitable *redirection* of the drive, its '*sublimation*' (as alertness and caution are the healthy, civilised redirection of primitive fear). Civilised conditions and social custom seriously inhibit the expression of elemental need, denying free rein to man's aggressive or reproductive impulses, for example; inevitably, a great surplus of energy and of associated emotion lies waiting to be released by appropriate stimuli, sometimes creating exaggerated, uncontrollable outbursts of passion where least expected. Alternatively, the surplus emotional energy may be driven underground to cause hidden trouble deep within the soul. In every generation, man must find means of harnessing, controlling and capitalising the elemental forces within himself if the individual life is to be fulfilled, and civilisation advance. But however refined, ordered, altruistic man's behaviour becomes, the energies that still carry life forward are nevertheless those that derive from the original biological thrust of life working in instinctive ways towards biological ends. It is true that man as we know him has been both born of nature, with a powerful biological heredity, and nurtured by history, tradition, and environment: but nature is as determinative as nurture—'man is more born than made'.

Achievement of Selfhood

Every organism, says Hadfield, is compelled to move towards its own completeness. There is no motive in life so compelling as this hunger for fulfilment; 'the mind is a becoming' (Jung) and the urge is towards *integration*, the rational, purposeful unity of many forces harnessed in one personality. As the fulfilment of any one drive brings pleasure, so the fulfilment of the total harmony of fundamental drives brings happiness, the felt welfare of the whole self. But, as all experience shows, such harmony is not innate. Just as, in intellectual life, a chaotic stream of sensations, ideas, memories has to be sifted by interest and attention, interpreted and ordered by reason, and so organised into consistent knowledge, to produce the sane mind—just so, in the affective and conative life, a chaotic stream of instinctive drives, emotions, desires, motives, has to be harmonised, reconciled, organised, to produce a sound, consistent character.

There is nothing *given* in the elemental drives of the living organism to ensure their harmony, or to preordain their integration into a unified personality. The urge towards self-preservation, for example, will conflict, if the young be endangered, with the parental 'instinct' to the point of self-sacrifice. The ('herd') impulse to seek and hold the approval of the social group will often conflict with sexual or aggressive impulses whose satisfaction would outrage and alienate the group. The conflict of instinctive drives can tear personality to pieces, drain all psychic strength, destroy decision of mind and peace of heart. Internal conflict can also produce alarming symptoms of neurasthenia or psychosis—breakdown, phobias, distressing anxieties, sleeplessness. When to the lack of harmony among the basic drives of the organism are added contradictions and conflicts between these and the inherited culture, the custom, the precept and example of one's group, and one's own conscientious standards of morality, the area of distress grows wider. Then indeed another law in the members wars against the law of the mind and brings the soul into subjection. Romans 7 is the classic exposition of this theme of intro-personal conflict.

The moral task of the growing personality is therefore one of integrating the inherited and acquired elements of psychic life, so attaining the strength, peace and happiness of an ordered, consistent personality. Psychologists speak much, therefore, of 'systems' or 'constellations' of related drives, motives, desires, emotions, ends, with their implied ideas, beliefs, and insights; of the organisation of mental life around chosen themes, often themes accepted from the cultural traditions of the group. Such systems of organised instinctive emotions, desires, ends, variously called 'sentiments', 'interests', may be numerous: the same individual may have a sentiment of emotions, desires, beliefs, centred in citizenship, another centred in his home, another centred in religion, another in his career, and yet another in some hobby or sport. In each system, certain of his ideas, thoughts, memories, emotions, desires, instinctive drives, beliefs and responses have become integrated, and so his reactions in each field are consistent, strengthened, and predictable. A strong sentiment organised around patriotism will inhibit the possibility of treachery; a strong sentiment of honesty and truth, will make it 'impossible' for such a man to steal.

When one or two such systems absorb a man's inner life, his will be a strong, 'single-minded' enthusiastic character; when several systems cohere, they may reinforce each other, and the same man be a good citizen, father, workman, churchman and golfer. Where the systems do not cohere, a man may well be torn between public duties, family loyalties, his work and his love of sport. Where two systems conflict—for example, one earnestly religious, the other sensual and self-indulgent—the man will be now one thing, and now another, and neither with his whole heart. The whole secret of personal power, inward harmony, and happy self-realisation, lies in the successful organisation of the biological forces within the soul together with the social, cultural, moral and religious patterns by which they have been overlaid.

The factors involved in such a process of self-organisation are varied: (i) Simple *habit* creates a pattern which subsequent stimulation of the instinctive dispositions tends to follow with less attention and effort. This is one of nature's economies; we do innumerable things without concentration, because a habit once acquired tends of itself to repetition. Thus the adult is less at the mercy of momentary impulsive response than is the child. Nevertheless, this creates a problem when the habit is one of which we come to disapprove. Original instinctive emotion reinforced by repetition without attention becomes very difficult to change; to the 'force' which created the need is added now 'the force of habit', tending to unify attitude and behaviour for good and evil. (ii) *Environment* tends to encourage or inhibit the instinctive drives with a view to comfortable and secure adaptation to circumstances. The nutritional and acquisitive aspects of self-preservation which made primitive man a hunter are modified almost unrecognisably in modern city life into far-reaching ambition, and even (some psychologists suggest) into refined forms of hunting—collecting rare and priceless objects, or hunting criminals! Especially do social example and sanction, expressed in custom, tradition, parental training, and education, extensively modify the elemental nature of the growing personality. The sexual drive, by nature promiscuous and casual, becomes transformed by economic necessity, the need for social cohesiveness, and the parental 'tender emotion', into a strong family bond. The aggressive and pugnacious impulses that derive from self-preservation facing danger are modified into tough foreign policies and scientific research. This modification of instinctive life by a 'psycho-social environment' in which the organism adapts to tradition, custom and social pressure, is one of the traits peculiar to man.

(iii) Another uniquely human trait severely modifying instinctive behaviour is intelligent *reflection, anticipation, and thought*. Reflection includes remembrance of past responses and their consequences, self-criticism, self-approval, and remorse. Anticipation includes foresight of possible consequences and conflict with other desirable results. Thus man profitably accumulates his own and others' experience and foresees his way, again being delivered from momentary, impulsive reaction to immediate stimuli. Thought has been defined as postponed response, intelligence pausing to control the instinctive process in the light of consistent and unified ends. In this way, the blind, all-or-nothing reaction to instinctive emotion characteristic of the child (and the animal), evident in outbursts of fury or unreasoning fear, is exchanged for the considered, measured and deliberate (i.e. organised) response of the mature adult. Creative imagination may divert the original instinctive drive towards wholly new channels by conceiving outlets for the residual energy far distant from its original biological ends: the sexual drive has produced as much poetry, literature, drama, music, painting, foster-care, social reform for children, scientific research and religious mysticism, as has any other single force. This is achieved by the intellectual conception of abstract ideas, relations, and symbols, and the transference to them of the fundamental interest and energy. That is the function of thought and imagination in the civilising of instinctive life.

(iv) However, '*purposive action* is the most fundamental category of psychology' (McDougall) and the most powerful factor in unifying the instinctive responses of man to his environment. As thought postpones response, opportunity arises for rational purpose to intervene in the choice of *which* response, for which foreseen and approved end, shall be made. Thus the systems of organised responses to instinctive impulses are built up, and each comes to act as a whole. Any stimulus within the family sentiment, for example, or the patriotic sentiment, appeals not only to the elemental instinctive emotion of sex, or of gregariousness, but to a now complex, highly organised and unified system of ideas, feelings, beliefs, purposes, all of which contribute to the pattern and the force of the response made. As one, two, or three 'master sentiments', controlled by one, two or three dominating purposes, emerge in the developing character, so behaviour becomes increasingly unified and consistent. Ultimately, the individual's acts of volition will focus into *choices* the impulses already organised into these ruling sentiments: the self, in willing, is in fact the self as identified with such a master-sentiment, in so far as an individual may be said, loosely, to have several 'selves', or co-existent spheres of reference—family, work, religion, recreation—within which he lives. In any conflict, the strongest sentiment will probably decide which response is made: even a comparatively weak desire arising within the religious sentiment will overcome a quite strong desire arising in a sentiment— say sport—to which the individual attaches only slight importance compared with his religion. By the time this degree of organisation of the instinctive life is reached, personality is becoming fairly well developed and character is approaching stability.

(v) But what determines such ruling purposes? The capacity for reflection, self-criticism, and creative imagination, enables man to hold before himself abstract concepts of goals or states of being which he would choose to attain, and then to strive toward them. Psychologically, such imagined ends of behaviour are *ideals*, even though morally they may be reprehensible—the false ideals of the libertine, the drunkard, the ruthless killer. In the capacity to form and follow such ideals lies all humanity's power of progress—or degradation:

ideals morally or scientifically approved as beneficial to the race are the 'block and tackle' by which man hauls himself forward. The power of the ideal, whether good or bad, consists in its stimulation of one or more systems of disposition, by offering the means of satisfaction, attracting to itself, and so focusing, the instinctive emotions and promising harmony and self-realisation. If the promise prove illusory, the choice will be seen to have been in error, the ideal a false one; but 'the ideal alone is able to stimulate the will and so to organise all the instincts into one harmonious whole'. It is not too much to say that consistent and stable character owes as much to the ideals a man holds as to his physical, social and cultural environment, as the powerful influences integrating his inherited, instinctive dispositions into strong, unified personality.

(vi) Ideals, however, are not spun out of the air, mere fictional or fantasy goals unrelated to the real world. To move the reluctant will, overcome conflict within the soul, and persist through years of discouragement and frustration, the chosen ideals around which the soul is to organise its behaviour must be rooted in convictions about reality and the nature of life and the universe. The final organising factor, therefore, is a *philosophy of life*, which may be no more than a vague outlook absorbed from the family and education; may be a deliberate rejection of all idealism, a cynical, materialist, fatalist, or sensualist egotism; or may be a self-conscious commitment to some religious, philosophic or political creed. The integration of personality around any ideology is the fruit of social training, experience, and personal decision, establishing a special set of psychological ideals, which gain immense force from tradition and group support but operate essentially as a powerful internal drive. In the case of a religious philosophy of life, this is further intensified by the conviction that invasive spiritual powers are available to faith and prayer, by which inherent moral energies can be reinforced.

Karl R. Stolz declares that 'the majority of persons suffering from curable mental disorders stand in need of an adequate philosophy of life, of life-giving convictions which will sustain them in their hour of perplexity . . . We require a sense of the worthwhileness of life, a constant conviction that we are in league with cosmic energy, that we are engaged in an adventure in friendliness with God. Religious ideals lift us above the gross and transient elements, the ebb and flow of our personal fortunes . . . supply the background of encouragement and hope which makes life not merely tolerable, but dignified, fruitful, and serene. (Religion) is the rallying centre of the forces of personality.'

It is not surprising that religious life and language often bear marks left by incorporation and integration of the instinctive forces of personality. There is much, for example, in religious hymnody, in the doctrines of love and the Fatherhood of God, and in the pre-occupation of the religious with questions of chastity and the hallowing of marriage, to remind us that sexual emotions are being re-directed and refined in religious faith. The gregarious disposition finds higher resolution in the strength of religious loyalty, the value placed upon fellowship, and on the continuity of group tradition, and in the conviction of continuous companionship with God. The self-preserving impulse adds its own weight to religious ideas like salvation, refuge in God, and personal immortality. This is only to say that religious faith is essentially and relevantly *human*, addressed to man and adapted to man in his creaturely need, offering a positive and fruitful outlet for drives otherwise dangerously self-destructive.

Unfortunately religion can also, from the psychologist's point of view, create dangers of its own. Over-emphasis on religious obedience, neglecting personal freedom, can produce lame and deficient person-alities incapable of full moral responsibility and initiative. Reliance on doctrines associated with eternal damnation can invent spurious fears which harass already tortured souls. Unbalanced (and un-biblical) attitudes towards sex can produce rather than heal intense spiritual conflicts. Even the exaggeration of family loyalty can result in fixations upon father, mother, or home which prevent full develop-ment in sons and daughters. Insistence upon one rigid pattern of experience can engender a spurious conviction of personal guilt as the necessary pre-requisite of the relief of divine forgiveness. The tenor of some popular hymns is a longing to return to infantile security and to reap a reward of safety and comfort for ever—a dream which may encourage in weaker personalities a regress to infantile dependence that actually undermines character. Superficial, errone-ous notions about prayer can sometimes weaken initiative and transfer responsibility. Psychologically as well as socially, there is probably nothing quite so bad as bad religion. Yet that is an inverted testimony to religion's power, and leaves no reason to doubt that, at its best, as one authority on clinical psychology expressed it, religion is the only complete cure for neurosis—the life based on fear—because it substitutes a life deliberately built upon love, trust, and confidence in the final and unshakable basis of security, the love of God.

Man achieves maturity, stability, and safety only when he

integrates all the elements of his nature—instinctive, environmental, and ideational—in organised selfhood: if such integration fail, what remains is a tension of conflicting impulses that either tear the soul apart or remain in uneasy balance, threatening outburst at any time. The process of self-organisation is gradual, scarcely reaching recognisable fruition until the storms of adolescence are subsiding; the process can also be costly, in struggle, self-denial, and unhappiness. Success or failure is usually ascribed, by religious people (including pastors) to strength or weakness of 'the will'. The nature and function of *will*, therefore, needs careful consideration. But before that can be attempted, it is necessary to describe the other side of psychological experience, even more important to pastoral understanding of people and their problems, the mysterious and powerful realm of the 'unconscious' that lies behind and beneath the stream of conscious mental life.

20 THE LEVELS OF LIFE

Pastoral teaching and counselling would be a great deal easier if all that went on within personality and between persons did so on the 'surface' level of conscious awareness of the world, ourselves, other people, situations, and our own clearly understood reactions to them. But life is never that simple. Mental life in fact proceeds, and behaviour is affected, on five levels at once: beside simple consciousness are group-consciousness, self-consciousness, subconsciousness and unconsciousness, to complicate the cure of souls.

> With *group-consciousness*, the pastor is not greatly concerned. It is most evident in so-called 'crowd psychology', characterised by contagious emotion (for good and ill, for enjoyment or fear); by transient impressions, easily fading as the crowd disperses; by multiplied suggestion, so that the crowd readily join in what few are bold enough to initiate; by decreased intelligence, and by diminished responsibility. A deeper group-consciousness is possible where the group is more permanent than a mere crowd, and where the uniting interest is not superficial and accidental but deep and important, as in a Christian fellowship. Then the dynamics of group discussion, shared decision, teamwork, mutual stimulation and support, become important to the pastor as spiritual leader.

On the *self-conscious* level we are aware of ourselves being aware of the world, other people, objects and situations, aware of ourselves thinking, feeling, acting, by habit or by decision. Self-conscious life is reflective, self-analytical, self-approving and self-critical. Some, it is true, are only dimly aware of their own mental processes, finding introspection and self-analysis uncongenial and difficult. To others, the inner world is the most real, and the most readily understood: especially to those unhappy in personal relationships or defeated by external circumstances. Many Christians even identify introspection, a preoccupation with one's inner states of mind, with spirituality, and the mood appropriate to religion. Much 'evangelical distress' is thus self-induced by endless self-questioning and self-accusation.

Excessive self-consciousness is the root of much pride, preventing endeavour by the fear of failure, or of appearing foolish. It occasions a Hamlet-like indecisiveness which can see no problem or situation directly, but only its own reactions, fears, and motives. It is necessary sometimes to insist that absorption in one's own spiritual states is selfish, and that the only true index of character, good or bad, is behaviour. Another danger attached to excessive concern with one's inner states is self-deception. Self-analysis may threaten a sore point of memory, of personal relationship, or of realised prejudice, and the self-communing mind shies away to invent entirely different explanations of one's opinions or conduct, rationalising both in ways more acceptable to ourselves. Jesus' sharp indictment of long public prayers offered, not in genuine piety but 'to be seen of men', sets a standard of self-understanding and honesty that applies in many directions—to the preaching that is mere self-display; to the intellectual scepticism that hides moral rebellion; to the excuses behind which we hide our failures; to the bias arising from having begun life in some circumstances of which we are now ashamed—or brazenly defensive; to the things we do, or defend, 'on principle' but which turn out to be merely reflections of our upbringing or our personal advantage.

Much of this is not hypocrisy, the deliberate and deceitful pretence to others of motives and opinions which we do not in truth possess: on this level it is the half-aware self-deception of one who on examining himself cannot easily accept his own verdict, and substitutes another, fully persuading himself of its accuracy. The deception may of course be deeper, in the subconscious, or even the unconscious, mind—though it is not then precisely a *self*-deception: the man will then simply not know the springs of his own attitudes and actions. Few religious beliefs or opinions are in fact held on rational or intellectual grounds: most are grounded in upbringing, group loyalty, the power of tradition, or in some real or fancied advantage in being identified with some particular point of view. Thouless describes eloquently the protestations of an atheist about the incredibility of the Genesis story—which in truth arose from the elopement of his fiancée with a Sunday-school teacher!

This rationalising process often illumines the attempts of people in distress to offer most unconvincing reasons for what they say or do, and their resistance to all reason or persuasion when the counsellor seeks to correct their attitude. One must never argue with the offered explanation, but pierce to the true motive, and deal with that. Another device by which an uneasy self-awareness is often evaded, is the projection of one's own attitudes, motives, tendencies, weaknesses, on to other people. Very argumentative people blame others for being dogmatic and unreasonable; the inwardly proud see pride in everyone; the untruthful suspect every speaker of lying; a lady may violently dislike another for the sentimentalism, or untidiness, that reflects her own character. 'We personalise our unrecognised failings, and hate in others the faults to which we are secretly addicted' (Hadfield). Inversely, we may tolerate wrongs in others because we tolerate them privately in ourselves—or because we understand the struggle too well and dare not condemn.

'Know thyself' is ancient wisdom: the pastor's insight into the tricks his own mind plays upon himself will often help him read beneath the surface of explanations and 'confessions' which his people bring to him, and discover the real problems behind the ones they talk about.

The Subconscious Level

The subconscious level of mental life comprises all that realm or store of impressions, memories thoughts, ideas, feelings, beliefs, motives, ideals, all that awareness of scenes, people, events, names, ourselves, skills, and the rest, which are not at any given moment present to consciousness but *which are within recall*, or nearly so. Freud preferred the name 'pre-conscious', because at any time this wealth of mental furniture can be brought into consciousness by our own act of will, or by any remark, picture, scene, that 'reminds' us. Things temporarily forgotten are 'brought again to mind' from beneath the mind's threshold of consciousness, immediately attention requires them.

A vast hinterland of conscious life lies on this subliminal level. It is part of nature's economy of attention and effort. If at every moment we actually heard and felt everything available to conscious-ness—the ticking of the clock, the feeling of our clothes, our breath-ing, pulses, heartbeat, the room temperature, the moving wind, the sound of traffic and children, the objects just at the fringe of vision—we would be too distracted to concentrate upon or remember *anything*. Yet all these impressions are being received: if the clock stops, or a car back-fires, a child screams, the temperature falls, we are at once alerted. We act subconsciously, also: we adjust our stride for a hill, our steps for a stair, without thought or attention; we put out the lights, lock up for the night—and have to go back to see if we did so.

The 'subconscious mind' stores things dimly impressed, irrelevant to immediate needs, overlaid by other things, and things to which we prefer not to attend (as a person we dislike, passing on the street), yet keeps them within reach, to be recalled sometimes with surprise— 'Oh, yes, now you mention it, I do remember seeing her in the main street yesterday!' Very strangely, the subconscious mind sometimes works at a problem without our attending to it, and comes up with a sudden insight or explanation in whose formation we seem to have no part— 'I never thought of it at the time, but while I was dressing it came to me: she was supposed to be in Paris yesterday, not London, so I knew the holiday was cancelled!' Problems that seem intractable at night, or in a period of pressure, may be suddenly resolved in the morning, solutions we never worked out step by step presenting themselves complete and obvious. Waterhouse speaks of the subconscious 'incubating' impressions until they become memories, permanent notions; and advises that this facility be used in sermon preparation by letting subjects 'simmer' before attempting to write.

Most people can perceive for themselves the influence of subconscious impressions or emotions upon their own actions and attitudes, though occasionally the pastor will meet with surprise, and even anger, if he brings into consciousness links that the person being counselled prefers not to acknowledge. The less thoroughly trained a professional man is, the more he is likely to exaggerate the outward symbols of his status, in dress, office furniture, brass plates and framed certificates. The wider the clerical collar, the narrower the confidence beneath it! Many advertisements impose upon subconscious associations: the white coats, balances, flasks, test-tubes, laboratory desks and scientific jargon which surrounds the statement that A's pain-killers are 'scientifically proved more pure and powerful' than any other, lend to a wholly unsupported assertion an entirely spurious authority. A whole doctrine, such as predestination, may be rejected as 'illogical, dangerous nonsense', not because the speaker has understood its meaning and assessed the arguments on which it is based, but because he dislikes Paul, with whose writings it is popularly associated. In the mouth of a revered preacher, the same ideas might become at once reasonable and profitable, though no more understood than before. A hymn may be disliked because it was the favourite of a girl-friend who proved fickle.

All new information, of every kind, is assessed and absorbed by every investigator, either with the concurrence of, or against the resistance of, the existing stock of knowledge and opinion, not all of it present to the conscious mind, but available, and subconsciously influential in the assimilation or rejection of new facts. All prejudices are opinions subconsciously conditioned, amenable to no rational analysis or refutation simply because the real reasons why they are held are not logical but associative, emotional, or intuitive. Reverie is the indulgence of the subconscious, letting the mind throw up its own associations and images without directive concentration—though the links and underlying relationships can be traced afterwards if desired.

Such 'subliminal' influences upon human thought and behaviour are often described as 'unconscious', and the issue is one of degree. The term 'subconscious' is better confined to those determinants of thought and attitude which, though hidden at the time, can with reasonable self-knowledge and candour, be brought to conscious attention and their influence recognised—perhaps with some assistance from a forthright friend. To help Christian people towards such self-understanding, so clearing the way for more honest, free, and vigorous self-criticism, is the task of every teacher; for the pastor it may involve deeper emotional and moral self-assessment, but often it is all that is necessary to restore a more fair and sincere frame of mind in those who have been resentful, suspicious, prejudiced, or unforgiving.

The Unconscious Level

The unconscious level of mental life comprises all that still vaster store of impressions, thoughts, ideas, feelings, beliefs—all, in fact, that has ever passed through consciousness—*which lies below the reach of voluntary recall*, being made available for recapture only by other, indirect means. The existence and importance of the unconscious level of life are beyond doubt: some forms of hysteria, phobias, manias, acts performed under hypnosis for which the doer can offer no motive or explanation, links certainly discoverable between present attitudes or anxieties and distant, totally 'forgotten' events in childhood, meaningful dreams, and significant or repeated mistakes, and many other common experiences bear witness to this 'underworld' of personality. From it arise the hidden springs of much of our conduct, mood, and attitudes, of some of our rationalisations, and many of our antagonisms. Between the conscious and the unconscious levels of life is a constant interaction, though the unconscious is known only by its effects, becoming understood as the dynamics of unconscious influence are laid bare.

The content of any individual's unconscious mind extends beyond all that ever entered his consciousness; *all* his past is there, including experiences—infantile and ante-natal experiences are examples—of which he was never conscious. Some tendencies and dispositions which arise from brain-structure and nervous system; habits associated with physiological processes such as breathing, digestion, blood circulation: elements of our physical make-up—our height, colouring, slowness of speech or changeable temperament—which we owe to distant ancestors and racial origins, all this may never have entered consciousness as motives, influences or aims, yet goes to make us what we are. All that we have ever experienced, sensed, thought, felt, willed, desired, imagined, remains 'somewhere' to be thrown up in shock, fever, hypnotic trance, or the long regressions of old age, into conscious memory. All unsatisfied desires, consciously or even unconsciously suppressed and denied, recede into the unconscious level of mind, to agitate from time to time, and sometimes to explode. All undeveloped potentialities, the 'glimmerings' of artistic, or inventive, or intellectual talent that never had a chance to shine, remain in the hinterland of conscious life as an unrealised source of discontent. Of especial importance to the influence of the unconscious mind on conscious life, however, are (a) unconscious influences derived from childhood experiences, and (b) unconscious influences arising from repression.

(a) Freud spoke much of infantile sexuality, meaning the influence in later life of those biological components of the infant's nature which in due time become the mature sexual instinct in all its aspects; he ascribed most mental troubles to the growing child's failure to adjust to this developing sexuality. The ruthless selfishness and extravagant passions of infancy, too, become suppressed as incompatible with the demands of others, upon whom comfort and security depend, and sometimes the suppressed emotions remain to distort later relationships. Neglect, cruelty, loneliness, fear, rejection in childhood all remain 'buried' in the unconscious mind to threaten later life. To have been the eldest child may leave dispositions towards masterfulness, jealousy, or compassion; to have been the youngest child may leave dispositions towards anxiety, fear of bullying, or a demand to be pampered; to have been the middle child may leave dispositions towards insecurity, indecision, uncertainty of selfhood and of status. A healthy young woman, terrified of travelling through tunnels or removing a dress over her head, *may* have been unconsciously experiencing again the very prolonged and difficult labour of her birth; a strong and 'difficult' lad who deeply disliked his younger sister to the point of complete indifference to her, did not know, even when he had been told, that his attitude was governed by the accident that a continental holiday, long looked forward to, had been cancelled to pay the costs of his sister's birth. 'Buried', 'forgotten', 'lost' childhood experiences remain throughout life to contribute powerfully, though unconsciously, for good and ill, to our conscious selves.

(b) Repression is the process whereby the instinctive impulses and their attendant emotions are *barred out of consciousness* because circumstances, conscience, social disapproval, or conflict with preferred ends, make them painful, contradictory, and unacceptable. Repression, it must be remembered, always works unconsciously: it is not the conscious and deliberate control of an instinctive impulse, but the denying of its existence, the disgusted refusal to accept that it could be there in us, at all, the insistence upon burying it out of our own sight. The conscious suppression of many desires is essential to civilised life and disciplined self-control, the inevitable means of adjustment to society and the development of personality. To express all impulses and desires would be contradictory, self-destructive, savage; self-integration implies the denial of some that others may be satisfied: for example, the denial of the promiscuous sexual impulse that the parental instinct might be satisfied. Unconscious repression, on the other hand, which merely ignores such impulses, rejects the possibility that they exist, refuses to resolve the tensions created, or to find positive outlets for the emotions generated, is dangerous, the source of much 'unconscious conflict', mental distress, neurosis, exaggerated reaction and irrational fear, of hysteria and even of insanity. Horrible scenes, memories, emotions (as from war-time) may likewise be repressed, the conscious mind simply refusing to remember them, driving them underground, where nevertheless they can cause serious neuroses, and force their way into consciousness as nightmares. Repressed emotions, memories, desires are not destroyed; they provoke civil war between the conscious, approved self and the repressed, unconscious self: 'the unconscious is unconscious because there is an active force keeping it out of reach of the conscious mind' (Lee). This force is repression, and its strength is evident in the resistance it opposes to any attempt at unveiling and resolving it— resistance expressed in fear, anger, anxiety, even suicide. Such unconscious influences can lie dormant for years, to be triggered-off in later life by emotional stress, shock, illness, or mental breakdown, and reappear with astonishing tenacity and power.

The pastor needs at least to be aware of the so-called 'mechanisms' of unconscious life that illustrate further its many-sided influence and suggest means of controlling, or manipulating, its innate energies:

(i) Freud made much of 'parapraxes' or *faulty acts*—slips of the tongue, mishearings of something said, misreadings, forgetting duties or promises—which are not purely accidental but betray unconscious attitudes, revealing motivations too deep for conscious recall. Of course, fatigue, illness, excitement, fear, may weaken concentration and control; but at other times unconscious motives may be at work: we fail to post a letter because we dislike the person addressed; we leave things behind in homes we are happy to revisit—not in others; a wrong medical prescription was traced to long buried malice towards the patient; a mistaken name easily slips into conversation because one part of the mind is 'deeply' anxious about that person; when we say 'selfish' for 'unselfish', or 'I did' for 'I did not' we sometimes speak more truthfully than we intend. It is well to remember that most mistakes are innocent, and unconscious motivation needs to be clearly proved, not cleverly imagined.

(ii) The psycho-analyst's process of *free association* attempts to get beneath the rational and censored expression of the mind's contents, by allowing relaxed, spontaneous, free utterance of whatever ideas 'float' to the mind's surface in an undirected, alogical chain or flow of words. The assumption is that the links between ideas are not in truth free, but the result of past associations established by long-forgotten experiences. From a random starter-word such free utterance may reveal a tendency to return upon certain key-ideas (as fear of the dark, nudity, hatred of cats) which are thereby seen to be significant; or, when certain links between ideas seem inevitable, one idea may be avoided (repeated mention of a woman, never her husband, for example) the hesitation and change of direction revealing a significant inhibition; or when some places in the mind are approached in a long session, the patient may stir, stammer, wring his hands, and the like, unconsciously revealing inner tensions in that mental area. When the contents of the unconscious are thus induced to rise to conscious memory, the explanation and the cure of mental symptoms often follow.

(iii) Much the same self-revelation of the unconscious has often been achieved under *hypnosis*, which induces a trance-like sleep in which the barrier of self-consciousness and self-censorship is passed, the range of memory increased, and the relaxation required for free association more easily attained. The possibility of implanting healing and constructive suggestions in the troubled mind during periods of hypnosis demonstrates that manipulation of the unconscious, as well as its uncovering, is possible by this method, though earlier exaggerated claims are no longer made for it.

(iv) Another form of free, undirected and uncensored mental revelation is the *dream*—'the royal road to the interpretation of man's mind' (Freud). The meaning may be straightforwardly clear, as the hungry dream of eating; or the dream may be a kind of self-analysis which it requires considerable skill to interpret. The patient's reactions when relating the dream may reveal where its emotional significance lies; while the frequently recurring dream is sure to be significant of the state of the unconscious mind. Some hold that the dream is a safety valve, relieving hidden tensions and pointing towards solutions. Certainly many dreams reveal deep-buried conflicts, fears, desires, attitudes; a recurrent dream of falling may betray an inner insecurity about one's status, finances, or marriage. On the other hand, many dreams are due simply to internal or external stimuli—indigestion, excitement, pain, memories, lights, sounds, temperature, discomfort; habit, temperament, and other idiosyncratic factors also affect dream-experiences. In those that are significant of unconscious states, some symbolism is usually apparent.

(v) *Symbolism* is of course the language of the unconscious mind, since if the true state of mind were plainly expressed, the underlying cause would be a conscious one. Most primitive, and childhood, thinking is in images rather than in words and abstract concepts, and to these the mind returns in relaxed, undirected thinking, in reveries and dreams; images express what is felt rather than what is understood. When the image has similar meaning for various people, as with flags, or the cross, the image becomes a public symbol; but when the image expresses an individual's unconscious state, it is a private symbol whose meaning is not at first clear. Anxiety about one's preaching ministry may well find expression in dreams about unsteady pulpits; an over-anxious car driver may dream of terrible *train* accidents; dreams of lost coins or gems may symbolise anxiety about distant children out of touch. Much ingenuity is expended on the endless number of symbols in which (or *into* which) sexual fantasies may be read: some of these are doubtless valid, for dreams of sexual search or satisfaction are as natural as the dream of athletic prowess to the man who has lost a leg, and most objects that occur in dreams can be likened to *something* related to sex experience. Emotions or inhibitions revealed in the telling, and the frequency of the supposed symbolism, would be relevant clues to the symbol's significance.

The tendency to symbolise by inversion is probably a reaction against something that causes trouble. The dispositions we are unconsciously repressing provoke the symbol of their opposites, not only in dreams but in conscious life also. The abnormal attitude or behaviour may turn out to be the reversed symbol of some repressed normal activity: the fiercely repressed sexual nature of the intense evangelical may find its symbol in extreme Puritanism, in fierce opposition to all mention of sex, family-planning, abortion, or even of women. Excessive sexual desire may produce erotic dreams or dreams of martyrdom for purity's sake. In waking life, a student may fret himself into near-despair about an examination, not because he is anxious to pass, but because he is anxious lest passing will bring promotion, separating him from his girl-friend—yet he is bound in conscience to do his best. The over-anxiety that unmans him is in fact symbol of the repressed conflict of desires. Cynicism may be the inverted symbol of a repressed guilty conscience: as Fosdick said, Conscience is so often the voice of the repressed *good*.

Unconscious symbolism lies also behind identification with one's friends and colleagues, with the heroes or villains or victims of film, novel or play, so as to enjoy or suffer by empathy what in conscious life we would be ashamed, or afraid, to experience. The old doctrine of *catharsis* rests on this: the great artist in painting, drama, poetry, music, providing the symbolic expression of things buried deep in the unconscious life, so that by giving them name, form and expression, we are 'cleansed' by aroused fear, or pity, anger, or humour or admiration. That great drama, especially, operates upon two levels, that of conscious interest and involvement in the story and the characters, and that of the release of unconscious motivations and tensions, may hardly be doubted. Another form of unconscious identification is projection, which seizes upon (or imagines) in others the attitudes, desires, and motives being rigorously repressed in oneself—and does so without even subconscious awareness that it is one's own inner conflict that lends violence to the accusation.

(vi) *Suggestion* operates unconsciously as well as subconsciously— its effect being sometimes too deep to be voluntarily recalled to consciousness. The presence of an idea is a suggestion that it be adopted, unless inhibited by contrary ideas. Any idea clearly realised has already aroused sufficient emotion to stir interest and attention, and it tends to move towards action: therein lies the power of suggestion. So the child acts, speaks, feels, as its mother does, 'naturally' we say, meaning unconsciously. 'Suggestion is unwitting imitation': it gives to environment its power to mould personality. 'Suggestibility', the liability to accept suggestions from social atmosphere, status-example, the expectation of others, varies with individuals, but is always a more powerful factor in education than either memory or reasoning. The influence upon corporate behaviour of the school uniform, badge, and tradition, and the strong effect of crediting children with intelligence, responsibility, and good intentions, before they are evident, illustrates the power of suggestion in moral spheres. Response to suggestion is generally unconscious and spontaneous up to about six years of age; more deliberate, though still largely unconscious, up to eleven; more critical and self-conscious in adolescence, though the influence of the herd and of the other sex is often unconscious—and hotly denied! In later life, still, beliefs and attitudes are transmitted more by suggestion, atmosphere, dramatic presentation, confident and repeated assertion, embodiment in status-symbols (the professor's gown, the bishop's gaiters), and traditional statements, than by reasoned argument. Suggestion is a prime factor in psychotherapy, too; to replace deleterious suggestions with healing, advantageous ones is to remove the cause of trouble at its source.

Of course, the response to suggestion may not be precisely what is expected, or intended: *response* is negative as well as positive. There is a 'sha'n't' period in most children's lives; a chaotic, awkward period in most adolescence. Because children, especially, can be contra-suggestible, a clever but disliked teacher may be less successful than a less competent but more sympathetic one. Older people, too, can become contra-suggestible, by habit, in self-defence, or for the sake of drawing attention to themselves. But suggestion-to-the-contrary is still suggestion, and its influence is powerful. In order to harness the power of the unconscious by advantageous suggestion it is necessary to arouse the appropriate antecedent mental state, while *not* arousing (if necessary, suppressing) any competing and conflicting mental state —this is the meaning of persuasion, when done on the conscious level, and of 'subliminal suggestion' when done by hypnotic or similar subtle approach to unconscious motivations. The antecedent state moves of itself into action when thus not inhibited. The positiveness of a suggestion adds to its power: every mother knows that 'Be brave' is more effective than 'Don't cry'; 'it is manly to own up' is stronger than 'it is mean to lie'. Thus, a measure of control is established over behaviour, and over character development, by selecting and controlling the suggestions which shall be allowed to pass into conduct, by countering one undesirable suggestion with another, desirable, one, and by storing the unconscious with abundant positive and approved suggestions—as by regular devotional exercises.

(vii) *Displacement* is a mechanism for resolving conflict by the substitution of a symbol for the real object of tension, and then transferring psychic energy to the symbol for safer outlet. George Eliot's Maggie Tulliver wrought out her generalised ill-temper against the grown-up world, and against her brother in particular, by battering her doll. So others channel thwarted protective and parental emotional dispositions towards household pets or horses. Such displacement of repressed emotional energy may be a useful safety-valve; it may explain otherwise irrational obsessions, or resentments, or fears—the real object of these being hidden by the new, unconscious and inexplicable substitute; and it explains 'transference', the focusing upon the counsellor of the thwarted affection or dependence which is causing tension. Where the displacement is towards an outlet morally admirable and socially useful, it is usually called 'sublimation'; it has then an important place in mental and moral therapy.

(viii) *Compromise* is perhaps less an unconscious mechanism than a failure to find any effective solution to unconscious tensions. On the subconscious level, the distraught, self-divided mind reveals the attempt to go two ways at once, to obey two contradictory impulses at the same time or with swift alternation; and a similar situation may obtain in the unconscious mind, only revealed by thorough probing— or by an illuminating experience like conversion. So Paul later brings to consciousness a conflict that once drove him madly to persecute: 'I do not understand my own actions. For I do not do what I want, but I do the very thing I hate . . . I can will what is right, but I cannot do it . . .' Hamlet's uncertainty of aim and changing mental moods provide an intellectual parallel, with the root-cause, the conflicting loves for father and for mother, hidden this time from the sufferer. Compromise at an unconscious level may produce entirely inconsistent behaviour—frequent sexual unfaithfulness alternating with abject and heartbroken penitence and generosity towards the wife; it may sadly enervate the soul, as strength is expended in internal, though not conscious, conflict; and it can develop disabling neurotic symptoms, and ultimately a split personality.

(ix) *Regression* is essentially a flight from tension, refusal to handle decisions, responsibilities, or guilt, by declining to grow up (arrested maturity) or by mentally reverting to infancy again. All adults have their childhood within them, with memories of being sheltered, defended, comforted, shielded from deserved consequences. Normally, these are deliberately left behind; maturity, freedom and responsibility are welcomed. In weak personalities, childhood memory is cherished wishfully, nostalgically, and adult responsibility is feared. But the desire to remain a child is repressed by parental, social, even physical pressures, with inevitable tension, which may drive the personality backwards into childishness and a pathetic dependence upon parental or pastoral approval, affection, direction, and support. Sometimes such adult regression manifests all the petulance, tearfulness, exhibitionism, wilfulness (and even bed-wetting) with which the child demands attention—though the patient will be wholly unaware of the real nature of the symptoms, and will rationalise them in a most grown-up way. Here, too, the 'transference' to the pastor or psychotherapist of the dependence which it is no longer possible to focus upon the parents, may offer the clue to what is happening, and the task of disengagement, always necessary with transference, will be correspondingly more delicate.

The most discussed, most powerful, and often the most misunderstood, manifestation of the influence of the unconscious mind upon conscious life is the famous 'complex'. The terminology varies with the teachers: it is clearest to keep the word for *unconscious* associations of repressed instincts, memories, desires, emotions, fears, ideas. As on the conscious level of life all the contents of the healthy mind move towards integration by organising sentiments, and either consciously suppressing or unconsciously repressing all ideas, emotions, desires that are inconsistent with them, so, within the unconscious mind, the tendency to integration remains active. The repressed ideas, memories, wishes, emotions, desires, themselves tend to coalesce into unconscious sentiments around dominant themes, gathering strength from organising other elements, and reinterpreting other repressions, in the light of the main unconscious interests. It is these dynamic, though unconscious, 'constellations' of ideas, wishes and the rest, with their attendant instinctive emotions, which are complexes, and which exercise at least as powerful an influence in the total life as do the conscious sentiments. Where such an associated system of ideas, feelings and wishes can be brought into consciousness (as when Barry says the golfer tends to see bunkers in running brooks, and golf in everything) it is simpler to speak of obsessions. Where the source of the trouble is clearly felt and understood—as with a *sense* of inferiority—there is no complex, since there is nothing unconscious; the situation then is much easier to deal with by conscious self-understanding and self-discipline. An inferiority *complex*, or a sexual *complex*, is wholly unconscious, and much more difficult to cure.

Emotional complexes form when strong instinctive impulses conflict—for example, when self-assertion and self-preservation pull different ways, or dependence and independence, or romantic love and self-love in the adolescent. Whatever is repressed gathers to itself ideas, fantasies, memories, associated impulses, desires, emotions; any stimulus which appeals to one element in the system— a memory, or scene, or temptation—may trigger-off the whole complex with all its dynamic, constituent emotions. The patient, and all who know him, are astonished at the totally uncharacteristic and uncontrolled, unheeding, outburst, which may wreck career, character and reputation in one insane rebellion: none having guessed the pent-up forces gathering through the years in a soul not healthily integrated, or even balanced, but clamped down rigidly by un- conscious repressions—until the clamps broke. The morally self- indulgent, who repress conscience and their 'better selves', and the morally ascetic, who repress their lower nature, may alike become morbid, even neurotic. The 'uncivilised' elements of personality, unacknowledged and repressed into the unconscious mind, form 'mental abscesses' which poison and menace conscious life.

The more serious effects of morbid complexes are beyond pastoral competence to handle. Extreme physical symptoms like paralysis, or blindness, are possible as the patient seeks escape from intense unconscious conflicts by flight into helplessness. Such hysteria is not cowardice, or malingering, but illness. Some psychotherapists trace every neurosis to a complex: the paralysis of fear, neurasthenia due to exhaustion of mental energy in internal conflict, anxiety- neurosis, perversions of various kinds, have all been so explained. But other manifestations of complexes may yield to pastoral ministry. Dreams may reveal the strength of unconscious mental systems, especially in nightmares, and simple explanation may bring relief. A fear-complex will not yield to argument and persuasion (any more than any other complex will) since the causes are un- conscious; nor will it be helped by running away from the situation, since the causes are within the soul. Suggestion may help, as with the child terrified of cats given a toy dog to go to bed, to keep the cats away—though the cats were but symbols for bullying school- mates. Or other depth-therapy may be required.

An inferiority complex may arise from childhood subjection to bullying or contempt within the family; from—say—a weakly child having a lisp, or a handicapped child placed in an athletic school. It can arise from social promotion into circles where a poor education or an uncultured background begin to be significant; or from failure in some ambition or test which leaves a permanent psychological scar. The symptoms may be very varied. A hidden inferiority may be revealed by professed inability to join in normal social relation- ships, perhaps to the point of producing physical alibi—pain, sciatica, paralysis; the unconscious wish is to prevent comparison with others, to evade having to sustain a social front. A tendency to boast inordinately about little successes, or to invent imagined triumphs in which the ego satisfies itself as to its immense superiority; even a turning to wrongdoing to demonstrate courage and daring in dramatic ways, may betray the unconscious sense of inadequacy. Conceit, by which the subject seeks to convince himself as much as others; excessive criticism of others, a common defence mechanism against unconscious inferiority; the bold-front 'I do not care what people think!'; the habit of name-dropping and recalling, unnecessarily, brief encounters with distinguished people—all such poses show the inferiority complex influencing conscious behaviour, though the subject could not say why. Even excessive deference and humility, though apparently (and sometimes actually) a confession of conscious inferiority, may also be a defensive device by which hidden inferiority seeks to avoid being snubbed.

All such symptoms, where they arise from unconscious mental systems, will yield nothing to reason, threats, punishment, or ridicule, being below the level of conscious attention. Sympathy, analysis, to help the sufferer understand the true nature of his conflicts and realise the deep springs of his fears and discontents— such are the indirect methods to which unconscious strains may yield. A timid, 'lazy', shy, rebellious child, to whom school and all its demands are simple torture, will find no help, only bitterness, in being shamed, punished, threatened, or rejected; a wise teacher, finding some one thing which the child does well, and organising for that one thing to be shown off to an appreciative class, may be astonished at the swift transformation wrought in the whole personality, just by finding itself approved, and superior, in one direction. As the unconscious mind ever exerts its influence by devious ways, so the circuitous method is ever the right way of manipulating its power.

Even so elementary an introduction to depth psychology should convince the pastor that more than one level of living, of explanation, and of help, must always be in his caring. It suggests too that the patient is often the least qualified to diagnose the real nature of his trouble; a cautious and kindly step-by-step guidance towards self-understanding is often his sorest need. A better appreciation of the sub-liminal forces that affect conscious living adds a new dimension to the value to be set upon worship, daily prayer and Bible reading, the Christian insistence upon love, peace, and daily trust, as storing the hinterland of life with positive and healing associations and suggestions. Penitence too, confession, forgiveness, are seen in new light, as 'clearing the drains' of unconscious life, setting the deepest parts of personality in the clear light and peace of a gracious relationship with God. This is by no means to reduce Christian faith and devotion to humanist levels of auto-suggestion: it is merely to say that the divine provision matches the human need, that the spiritual experience of the saints has within it the oldest and deepest wisdom in the world.

21 MORAL PSYCHOLOGY

It is with *moral* psychology that the Christian pastor is chiefly concerned, with the development, the distortions, and the dangers that affect the quality of conduct, attitude, and personal relationships among his people. When normal character-development fails, it is necessary to examine the processes behind moral decision in order to understand what is wrong and how it may be remedied. The common explanation of all wrongdoing, that either the individual 'cannot help his character—it is all due to his background', or 'he is just weak-willed, he could be better if he tried' may sound charitable, but is it true? and if it is, what may be done about it? Some examination is plainly necessary of the influence of individual background upon moral development, and of the meaning of 'weakness of will'; more positively, the psychological methods by which character may be changed or strengthened, and the inner resources of moral power available to Christian hearts, equally need to be understood, if the pastor is to deal sympathetically and effectively with moral problems.

Background Influences

(i) The moral influence of *heredity* is real, but limited, and it is important to recognise that limitation if heredity is not to be made an excuse for inertia and despair. Much that is attributed to heredity is in fact the result of early childhood training and example. There are no genetic mechanisms by which bad temper, pride, meanness, alcoholism, sexual perversion, can be transmitted. We do inherit certain predisposing factors, as for example a physiological nervousness, excitability, or sensitivity, which may make us susceptible to provocation and swift to react: whether that basic psychological equipment makes us neurotic, is transmuted into talent, or disciplined into normal moral sensibility, is *not* predetermined—it is within our own choice.

We inherit of course the instinctive predispositions already described, with their attendant emotions, as the pattern of the life-force within us all; their integration into admirable or despicable sentiments is the result of our own self-discipline. We also inherit intelligence, the fundamental capacity to learn, to adjust to new situations, and to apply experience to new circumstances. With the emergence in human development of intelligence, the process of integration becomes self-conscious and self-directing. Ethical development is undoubtedly related to intelligence, as that makes us more critical of ourselves, of the examples set before us, of tradition, and of dogma, but the contribution of intelligence to character is rather one of degree than of quality: moderate intelligence can co-exist with admirable moral qualities and selfless devotion to others' good.

Inherited, too, is the basic physical groundwork of personality in the bodily conditions that influence all mental life, the thyroid, adrenal, pituitary and other endocrine secretory systems which affect the individual's mood, moral sensitivity, reactions and determination. But here again to 'influence' psychological development is not to govern or predetermine the *direction* which character shall take; the same physiological equipment may be well-used or ill-used, according to the purposes adopted and the values pursued.

A right explanation of the limited place of heredity in character formation will offer comfort to the distressed without undermining responsibility. It provides assurance that nothing innate and unalterable stands in the way of change and success, while acknowledging that some men's problems are, by nature, harder than most.

(ii) *Environment* has a similar potent, yet limited, influence upon character. In one sense, environmental influence is immeasurable— it covers the effects of climate, race, geography, language, history, home life, culture, education, the technological level of society (tools, training, industrial processes and opportunities available), moral and social habits, standards, religion, and all else that forms the matrix of the developing individual. Powerful effects can follow either from single events that leave permanent impressions, as shock, fright, illness, bereavement; being an only child, pampering or neglect or loneliness; or from the general atmosphere of life, as pessimism, cynicism, uncertainty, violence, fear, antagonism. Character obviously takes its shape to some extent from the mould in which personality is constantly being formed.

Yet 'it is not being in a slum but copying the slum's ways that creates the slum type'. A similar external environment can produce very different character in different individuals; as an Irishman said, 'You can bring up a litter of pups in a cowshed, but ne'er a bit of a moo will they give.' It is the individual always who determines (a) whether the environment in which his life is set shall be allowed to govern his aims, horizons and endeavour, or not; (b) whether it will evoke from him a positive or a negative reaction, whether he will conform, by surrendering to its pressures, or rebel by reacting against and rising above its influence; (c) what elements in the total environment will be allowed to provoke a positive, and what elements a negative, reaction. A city boy growing up between a canal, a railway, a park and a brewery will doubtless be influenced by them all, but not equally or in the same direction. The truth is that one's psychological environment consists in those factors in one's total surroundings which one *consents* to take into life as either pressures to yield to or perils to resist. Paul writes to certain who are 'in Corinth' and 'in Christ': living in two worlds, they are influenced by both, but they choose their mental environment and so make for themselves their own moral world.

This insight, too, retains responsibility and hope of change, while freely admitting that life and circumstance set for some souls enormous problems of self-discipline and resistance, as they offer to others enormous advantages of example and inspiration.

(iii) The most potent element in environment is however *parental training* and family example. Though no one inherits pride, in some from the earliest years parental attitudes can instil a sense of one's superiority to all other children that becomes insufferable, and almost ineradicable. Much that seems to be inherited, because it appears so early, is so deep-rooted, and so exactly reproduces the character of the parents, is in fact the infection of suggestion, of imitation in the circumstances most favourable to deep and lasting impressions. Infantile responses to mother-love and mother-care (perhaps especially breast-feeding) and to parental discipline, set up patterns of reaction and relationship which continue to influence the individual on into his own marriage and parenthood; the relationship of his parents to each other, and the image of each on his own half-aware yet observing mind, sets standards to attain or examples to avoid for the rest of his life, though there is no reason of course why, with growing insight and wider experience, his reaction to family norms should not change.

Imitation has far greater place in childhood's patterns of conduct than either persuasion, entreaty, or command. A concrete example of any action not only reinforces the power of suggestion but demonstrates that the act is possible and desirable—or undesirable. For, given the immense psychological power of suggestion, reinforced by affection and discipline, the choice remains with the individual whether to react positively, or negatively, to be attracted or repelled.

A pastor may, if he have sufficient courage and tact, make occasion to comment on the commoner mistakes of early moral training, as part of his ministry to the Christian home. Few children, for example, hear adults discussing *good* ideas, good actions, good people, with half the animation and interest with which *bad* ideas, actions, people are examined and condemned: the impression that evil is more important and exciting is inevitable. So, without thinking, we normally pet and fuss over a naughty child and ignore a good one—with the same effect. When we *tell* children what to do, or not to do, instead of leading them to examine, analyse and criticise a situation, and so reach their own understanding of right and wrong, fair and unfair, we are *teaching* them to rely on others, on prevailing group-custom, for their moral decisions—a habit we shall condemn them for, later on. If we discuss all questions on a level of expediency, consequences, welfare, career-ambitions, we cannot pretend surprise if they show little reverence for purely moral judgements, for the imperative ought, and the costly duty. If we rely mainly on punishment to inhibit undesirable behaviour, we are actively teaching that such behaviour is all right if the consequences can be avoided—it is being found out that makes it wrong! If we suggest that something is good and fine in proportion to its effort, cost, and pain we are deliberately imparting the doctrine that goodness is unpleasant, and every pleasure evil. From all we know of character formation and the importance of the dominant sentiments, it is clear that indoctrination with particular Christian beliefs is far less important to the ultimate pattern of life than the development of a strong religious sentiment—a whole system of ideas, feelings, interests, habits, goals, happy memories, hero-worship, associated with God, Christ, church, Sunday, Christian friends and homes, Christian music and festivals—all making the basic Christian beliefs 'come alive' in a 'constellation' of dispositions and attendant emotions which will *comprise* a Christian character.

Seeking to understand, and to explain, the behaviour problems of others the pastor will allow full weight to these background influences of heredity, environment, and childhood experiences; yet never let his patient forget that no 'influence' is determinative: we choose our response, making the 'background' serve us—for good or ill. Whether we achieve what we have chosen will depend in large measure on our 'strength of will'—whatever that may mean.

Strength of Will

Inability to break a habit, control a passion, or sustain a good intention, is commonly attributed to 'a weak will'. Where this approximates to the true cause, it is often the predictable result of the appalling doctrine that the strong will of the growing child must be 'broken' if he is ever to be disciplined. It is of little use to complain of weak character if we set out to destroy that on which strong character depends.

The will is central in the teaching of Jesus: His message of the kingdom is essentially an invitation to find fullness of life and joy in the identification of our will with the will of the Kingly Father. Of Himself, Jesus could say, 'My sustenance and refreshment is to do the will of my Father', and at the great crisis of His life His own reaction is simply, 'Not my will, but Thine be done'. For Jesus, the act of will is decisive, and revelatory: it is not enough to say 'Lord, Lord' unless we do the will of the Father in heaven; nor, on the other hand, is it fatal to say 'I will not' if afterwards we repent, and obey. It is the act of will which clarifies belief: 'he who willeth to do God's will shall know of the doctrine.' For Jesus, the will, the deed, expresses true character: the impulsive intention, the unconsidered promise, the conventional profession of godliness, signify nothing without the resolution to do, to be, and to obey.

But what is this 'will', and why is it so significant? Organisation of the instinctive dispositions and emotions into coherent sentiments —patriotic, domestic, religious or whatever—is never totally success- ful: some contrary impulses remain, either consciously suppressed or unconsciously repressed for the sake of self-integration. *Will* is the identification of one (or more) of the dominant sentiments of personality with some proposed course of action; if not the total self (because of the residual conflicting elements) yet almost the total self moves towards the purposes and satisfactions focusing one of the dominant sentiments, resolves to attain them, and organises thought, feeling and action to achieve the approved end.

The resolve to enlist and fight because danger threatens one's country means that the stimulus of danger and the presented appeal for enlistment have evoked from the total sentiment of patriotism a complex response of desire to assert oneself, an impulse of pugnacity, a wish to do one's duty, a desire to recapture the comradeship and excitement of former military experience, to reassert old skills or authority—and so on. The self, moving to identify itself with this total sentiment of patriotism, inhibits contrary impulses arising from other sentiments (ambition for promotion in present career, desire to remain in one's family) and assents to the course of action which will give the patriotic sentiment fullest satisfaction. In another personality, the family-sentiment, or the career-sentiment, being stronger and more inclusive of many impulses, desires, interests and goals, and being more closely integrated so that all its forces operate together, may inhibit the patriotic sentiment, faint and ill-organised, and the man resolves to stay at home.

Many of the individual's actions are of course mere reflexes of the nervous system (blinking, sneezing), or habits made effortless by repetition (walking, shaking hands, eating); it has been estimated that some ninety per cent of adult behaviour is involuntary. Only where new responses, involving choice between alternative impulses, are required is the act of will, identifying the self with some one course through its appeal to some dominant sentiment, a fully conscious, deliberative, and effortful experience.

Closer analysis of the process of *will* reveals: *want*, as a blind tendency towards particular ends ('to be rich—no idea how!'); *appetite*, as the rise of a blind want into consciousness with awareness of pleasure, pain, unrest, a sense of not being satisfied; in *desire*, that feeling of unrest is directed towards an end explicitly recognised as a good, a goal worth reaching; and desires are organised into *'universes of desire'* (Mackenzie)—all related, compatible, and mutually supporting desires tending to be aroused by the same stimuli; the 'universe of desire' plus other mental elements such as associated beliefs, ideas, fears, memories and the rest, would form what others call the sentiment. The strength of any particular desire will depend on the strength of the 'universe of desire' in which it belongs, the sentiment in which it is organised: an occasional, isolated desire would usually be weak and easily inhibited by stronger systems of desire. If a single element in a total situation is desired (say better wages) but not the total situation with all its consequences (great responsibility, longer hours, moving to a new district), then the desire is negatived, and remains a *wish*. If however the whole situation, the element desired, its cost, and its consequences, is assented to, then the self moves to identify with the course of action required, in an act of *will*.

From another angle, *reflex actions* are the basis of all our response to stimuli; where alternate responses demand comparison and selection, *attention* is required; and when attention is self-consciously directed toward a desired object and its offered satisfactions, so that the self consents to the necessary course of action, and organises mental life towards its accomplishment, we recognise an act of *will*. It will be seen therefore,

(a) that *will* is regulative, not creative. It selects among the presented impulses, responses, desires and emotive suggestions those which, in organisation with other desires and goals, will achieve the greatest overall satisfaction;

(b) that the motor-continuum of involuntary impulses to action arises not from the will but from the instinctive drives and attendant emotions. Will organises, rather than originates; it intervenes in the conflict of impulses. The strength which moves towards achievement is *not strength of will* but the strength of the emotive ideas, suggestions and desires which will manipulates;

(c) that will involves intellectual elements—a *pause* inhibits impulsive tendencies to immediate response, holding action in suspense; in *deliberation*, attention oscillates between alternatives, comparing possibilities, estimating consequences, aligning the proposed courses of action with the main purposes of life. *Decision* is then the approval and acceptance of one course, surrender to its impulse and identification of the whole self with it;

(d) that thus sustaining an idea before the mind, imagining the act and its consequences, remembering, judging (especially the judgement that we *can* do what is in view), and above all the act of selective attention which manipulates activity by manipulating the ideas which the mind entertains—all *intellectual* elements—all this is of the essence of volition.

Such an analysis of the volitional process throws much light on the problems of the weak will, and on the processes by which character can be improved. 'Character is the completely fashioned will'—an integrated personality in which the several organised sentiments which comprise the mental life have been so unified that fully developed desires, directed towards fully understood and accepted goals, issue in fully efficient actions with the least possible conflict with contrary sentiments or desires. Since life's energies are not derived from the will at all, but from the instinctive emotions, it is useless to call upon the will to 'make a supreme effort', 'to screw its strength to the sticking point'. The only strength which will possesses lies in the original impulses which it observes and judges, among which it selects, and which it organises into action.

Similarly, the analysis shows that will controls behaviour by attending to, and selecting, the antecedent psychological states. By inhibiting—drawing away attention from—the mental state which would otherwise issue in action, and substituting—turning attention to—another mental state tending to issue in another action, we decide what action shall occur. The process is parallel to that of purposive thought, or reasoning, where the goal—the solution of some problem, the construction of some argument—is attained by attending to, selecting, and pursuing, those ideas which are relevant to the purpose on hand, and not attending to those ideas which are irrelevant. In volition, we attend to, select, and pursue, those emotive impulses, or desires, which lead to the chosen result. The decision of will stabilises the idea selected, as a strong suggestion held with assent before the mind, and its own emotive force urges the suggestion into action.

Man's freedom of will lies, thus, in his choice of what he will mentally attend to, and cherish, in his inner thought and imagination. The 'effort' of will lies in concentrating upon ideas, desires, goals, that may demand some cost of comfort, the suppression of conflicting desires, goals, and sentiments, the sacrifice of immediate for long-term satisfactions. Since we cannot follow all goals at once, nor satisfy all 'selves' at once, will is the expression of the 'accepted' self, the organised 'self' in which a common and accepted purpose or standard of values has assigned to each impulse, feeling, idea, desire and goal its allotted place in the life of the whole personality. The more integrated the personality, the stronger the will—for more, and better unified, impulses are focused in its chosen courses of action, and fewer and weaker impulses oppose them.

The same analysis exposes the essential truth about the weak will. 'As soon as the self ceases to function as one integrated whole, it ceases to be one self,' personality disintegrates into rival selves. The chaos of contradictory impulses, ideas, feelings, goals, that results is usually described as 'weak', inconsistent character; its explanation lies in the inability of the self to identify itself in any organised, harmonious way with any one sentiment or purpose; or, in some cases, rival sentiments are so balanced—religious loyalty and family loyalty, for example—that any proposed action appealing to one also appeals to the other, and the will hesitates, vacillating between the two. The forces that should be organised into a unity of purpose that would give to will its firmness and determination, are deployed instead in conflict with each other, cancelling each other out—the result is obviously 'a weak will'. The self cannot function as will, because there is no single harmonious self, only competing, mutually destructive 'selves'. Any newly presented situation requiring choice— a fresh temptation, a new opportunity, or challenge—cannot appeal to one strong and organised sentiment, because none has been formed: the reaction of the individual to the new situation is then unpredictable, inconsistent, impulsive. He has not the inner integrity of purpose to choose consistently, and a choice made one day will be revoked the next, when social pressures, change of mood, or new ideas, refashion his reactions.

Weakness of will thus arises from disorganisation, which prevents any one or two interests from predominating. The resulting confusion and weakness is sometimes made worse by attempted rationalisation: we invent persuasive reasons for what are in fact contradictory attitudes, until 'we do not know what we think'. Sometimes we attempt to keep different sentiments and desires in separate compartments of the mind—a sentiment of religion, in which our behaviour, speech, and deportment are all that can be approved by religious people, and an entirely separate sentiment (say) of sport, in which our behaviour, speech and deportment are such as would outrage the pious. Any issue which infringes upon *both* areas of life will leave the will in utter confusion.

Stolz usefully distinguishes the *integrated* personality, the *unintegrated* personality, and the *disintegrated* personality. Of the integrated personality he observes one danger—narrow, entrenched interests of small intrinsic value. The will expressing these will be strong, even violently so, yet ultimately ineffective because too narrowly based and in conflict with reality. An exclusively religious man may be determined to keep his family from contact with 'the wicked world'; he will fail because the maturing family will inevitably react, and because they must come to terms with the world in order to feed, obtain employment, and the rest. A break-up of the too-narrow sentiment may be required, introducing wider goals, before healthy re-integration is possible.

The unintegrated personality may have good thoughts, impulses, desires, among others, but has no co-ordinating master-interest—good or bad—to make the components of personality a working whole. The cause may be indolence, infantilism, even possibly physiological, or the effect of dominance by an over-bearing personality in childhood. Complete inability to integrate is subnormal: and in all such, will must be weak, unpredictable, and easily persuadable.

The disintegrated personality has receded from a unity once achieved—'gone to pieces'. Deep disappointment, failure, sorrow, may so affect life's closely organised drives as to disrupt personality itself, leaving the shattered self a mere chaos of impulses, emotions and desires. The chosen guiding principle of life may prove unworkable, unsafe, or simply untrue, and all life's plans collapse. Will, henceforth, must be vacillating, indecisive; for the self is divided, without integrity. In this lies the supreme importance of ensuring that the basic principles upon which one builds life and character have reality and truth; religious fantasy, pious makebelieve, a 'blind faith' which experience is bound to destroy, are not just nonsense, but dangerous, for they can ultimately destroy, psychologically and morally, those who build upon them.

Weakness of will, then, arises from failure to marshall the instinctive forces of life behind consistent and lasting purposes. Superimposed upon this fundamental psychological situation may be secondary factors that further weaken the will—strong emotion, the power of habit, accidental counter-suggestion, discouragement, and the like. Each requires attention if the will is to gain ascendancy and strength. Such strengthening of will is one of the chief steps to be taken to improve, protect and mature an unsatisfactory character; another, is to explore what sources of moral strength beyond man's own are available to Christian faith.

22 MORAL THERAPEUTICS

Since the fundamental cause of moral weakness is the divided self, we strengthen the will not by 'moral effort', nor by penitence, nor even by prayer, but by unifying once for all the self which the will expresses. Decide what you *really* want, and the necessary will-power is at hand, whatever else may be lacking. How this unity is to be attained will vary with different individuals: for some, understanding of the cause effects a cure. Conflict, however, is only possible among smaller, narrower sentiments; once a dominant, widely inclusive sentiment emerges within personality, inner conflict is greatly diminished. Hence the need for a dominant, broad-based, and dependable ideal, so obviously right, so widely satisfying, that all rival purposes are either taken up into it or left behind. 'What the will requires for its strength and development is not training but inspiration' (Hadfield).

The purpose of the ideal is to provide for the self a stimulus, a goal so challenging, so satisfying, that personality may be organised around it safely, absorbingly, and permanently. It must therefore appeal to basic instinctive drives of human nature, offering the maximum of fulfilment; it must recognise the social situation in which the individual life is set, so gaining co-operation and support; and it must be so well grounded that no experience, however tragic, can disprove its validity and leave the soul to disillusion and despair.

Here the Christian pastor has immense advantage over every other psychotherapist. For the Christian ideal is by definition (a) *all-inclusive*, involving the total dedication of life to God in Christ—family, work, friendships, career, leisure, body, mind, spirit—in response to total redemption. (b) It offers positive and lasting *satisfaction* of the deepest longings of the self, in life renewed at its source, self-realising in larger dimensions than all previous experience could promise, abundant in its range, its values and its joy, and eternal. (c) It is *socially conditioned* by an enriching fellowship, and socially orientated by the demand for outgoing love, in feelings of compassion and deeds of service. (d) It is *objective*, in that it centres the soul upon the will and purpose of God in society and the world about us, not upon our own inward experiences, hopes, and fears; God's kingdom and righteousness absorb the personal forces that else would preoccupy the soul with its own inner strife and struggle. (e) The Christian ideal is *positive*, involving only such self-discipline and self-sacrifice as may be justified—in Jesus' words—'for My sake and the gospel's', and in promoting the larger good of the community. (f) It is *sustained* by a total world-view, a philosophy of life and interpretation of the universe, in which its vision of the perfect life and the perfect world are rooted in the loving purposes of the kingly Father, who is at once the Origin, the Sovereign, and the Goal of all that is.

Moreover, this sufficient ideal has three features that operate powerfully towards the unification of the inner life: (g) is is *personalised* in the Figure of one who at once commands respect, admiration, and worship. Childhood's potent disposition towards imitation, and the equally powerful moral impetus of emulation, are both capitalised in Christianity's presentation of the Hero-Christ, an ideal infinitely more effective as a focus about which the energies of life may be organised, than any abstract ethical doctrine, however lofty. (h) But the Hero-Christ is also the Saviour-Christ, who by identifying Himself with us in our need, and standing in for us in peril, has evoked the two most powerful moral forces of the human soul—gratitude, and love. Through its gratitude, the soul may attain every virtue and yet remain unself-righteously *humble*; through love for Christ all the emotive forces of personal attachment, confidence, delight, desire to please, and to be worthy of approval, are harnessed at once around the ideal Figure. This is the 'expulsive power of a new affection' by which countless lives have been converted and constrained to goodness, heroism, and compassion. (i) The ideal is nevertheless also an *internal* standard, an inspiration and a censor within the soul. The Christian ideal exercises its selective judgement at the place where the will controls suggestion, and either assents to or inhibits the emotive energies evoked by presented ideas. This inward 'fellowship with Christ' is the most powerful influence in Christian character. The loss of Christ's presence, and of inner peace, is itself the test, the strongest inhibitor of evil at the inward centre where alone the will can exercise its function of selectivity. The self, fully identified with Christ, recoils at the suggestion of evil, and inhibits the forces that move towards its execution; it supplants the evil suggestion with that of retaining the approval of Christ, the Lord of life, and substitutes for its emotive force, love and gratitude toward Christ on whom rests all life's hope, security, and purpose.

Such centring of life around the Ideal, who is at once the highest vision of the intellect, the focus of emotional energies, and the unanswerable censor within the soul, frees the will from enervating conflicts and liberates the forces of personality for unified expression: in this light the insistence of Jesus upon single-mindedness gains new significance. 'No man can serve two masters . . . Seek first the kingdom of God and his righteousness . . . No man who puts his hand to the plough and looks back is suited to the Kingdom . . . Unless a man leave father and mother . . . sell all that he has . . . sit down and count the cost . . . cut off hand or foot, and pluck out his eye . . . take up his cross . . .' Paul, too, held himself as bondslave of Christ, bought with a price, constrained by His love even to madness; for Paul, to live at all was Christ—whose he was and whom he served. This is the source of that immense strength of will—in Jesus and in Paul—which no threat of suffering, no toil or disappointment, could exhaust. Divided interest saps power; 'surely, half-heartedness, wavering, faltering in love or faith or purpose, the hopeless toil of living two lives—this is one chief source at least of much of the unhappiness and unrest, the weariness and overstrain, the breaking-down, in modern life' (Paget). The pastor will find, almost without exception, that gloomy, timid, morose, and defeated Christians are simply those not yet fully committed to the Christian way of living, divided within themselves, consuming their own strength in internal discords—and wondering why the Christ they only half-love does not give them 'victory'.

Specific Weaknesses

A character generally strong may, of course, reveal weakness in particular directions or in particular circumstances: (i) *Habit*, for example, made almost involuntary by repetition, exposes weakness by resisting change. A strong emotional impulse, sorrow, shock, or horror at the consequences of the habit, or the moral revulsion which accompanies conversion, may break the established connection between stimulus and response. Psychologists tend to favour sudden rather than slow breaks with undesirable habits; the immediate decision 'brings out the fight in us'; it establishes the encouraging fact that the habit can be broken; and when the first break is violent and dramatic, sufficient emotional force usually remains in memory to rekindle revulsion and resolution when temptation recurs Establishing a new habit to supplant the old (sweets for cigarettes, a regular engagement on the evening usually spent over alcohol) will succeed better than merely concentrating on breaking the old; especially, the new habit of instant prayer, by which the mind in the moment of danger immediately turns to Christ and His approval, may be all that is needed—provided that the thought of Christ has for the individual sufficient emotive force. The assistance of others may provide invaluable support in the struggle if wisely arranged. The resolution to break a habit may be communicated *privately* to some trusted friend whose good opinion it is desired to retain; resolution is then reinforced by the fear of 'letting down' the friend, without the risk of public humiliation if a widely publicised reform proves only gradually successful.

(ii) Any single strong *emotion* can weaken and frustrate the will, causing uncharacteristic conduct or reactions, as when fear, under some immediate threat to personal safety, may overwhelm all sentiments of duty, loyalty or even religion; or when strong sexual desire may suddenly erupt in an otherwise self-controlled individual, and the will stands irresolute and ashamed. A candid, self-understanding watchfulness, and a careful organising of time and habit to avoid the situations which bring temptation and opportunity, is an obvious strategy of defence; but the best safeguard against emotional weakness is a strong counter-emotion. A deep dread of moral defeat, a strong *feeling* of shame, a true and pure passion for a worthy partner, are more powerful weapons than some cultivated— or pretended—pose of unemotionalism. Some words of Jesus, of Peter, and of the epistle to the Hebrews, all suggest that the most reliable antidote to fear of men, and fear for one's own safety, is a healthy, reverent 'fear' of God—and the principle of meeting emotion with counter-emotion has the widest application.

(iii) An unexpected weakness and indecision are sometimes provoked by *counter-suggestion*, which confuses the mind and hampers the will. A specific proposal, excellent in itself, wholly in line with an established sentiment, happens to be put forward by a person we dislike or distrust—and we hesitate, prevaricate, 'wisely take time to think it over'. The pastor himself may be reluctant to recognise how often his want of enthusiasm for some suggested change in the Church programme—or for some theory affecting biblical interpretation—is influenced more by the person or school from which it emanates than by its intrinsic merit. So often, 'judicious hesitation' is only counter-suggestion weakening decision! More familiar, and more serious, is the counter-suggestion that arises from the presence and opinion of others, family, workmates, friends, whose persuasion, whether spoken or silent, is to depart from the normal pattern of character and do what others expect and approve. The impulse of group-consciousness, prompting the wish to be supported and admired, tells strongly against personal conviction and desire to be loyal to one's standards, and an unsuspected weakness is revealed. It should be sufficient for the pastor to point out what is happening, and help the individual to see in truer perspective the larger issue which he is sacrificing for the smaller personal prejudice, or for immediate personal comfort. To be strong, a man must learn to distinguish principle from prejudice, and must frankly accept that occasionally loyalty to principle may involve social discomfort. The Christian, at any rate, cannot surrender the direction of his conduct to the pressure of any group alien to his primary loyalty to Christ as Lord.

(iv) A larger problem may underlie this particular source of weakness. Through no fault of their own, many modern people live upon *hedonist assumptions*, derived from the atmosphere of an age which tests all things by their utility, and measures utility by personal happiness and welfare. In its grosser form, this means living for indulgence and enjoyment, but in more refined forms it may imply that the worthwhileness of any endeavour will depend upon 'how it turns out'—that is, on results satisfactory to the person concerned. We even judge what is the will of God by whether a course of action is likely to be 'crowned with spiritual *success*'. When the moral significance of high principles, unswerving truth, and loyalty, irrespective of results, have not been learned in childhood, the adolescent and the adult are placed at serious disadvantage in a world where truth may be costly, where integrity involves many sacrifices of opportunity, where honesty may be a costly policy, Christian character call for determination, and Christlikeness be rewarded with a cross. Much that is blamed as weakness, especially in young Christians, is really the inbuilt disillusion of a superficial evangelism, false to the realist gospel of Jesus and the heroic element in true discipleship. A truer exposition of New Testament Christianity, especially of the open-eyed realism of Jesus, is the only prophylactic, or cure. Most young people, at any rate, are willing enough, and strong enough, for spiritual warfare, if they are not wilfully misled by older Christians eager for cheap 'decisions'.

(v) Nevertheless, *discouragement* can be a serious specific cause of moral weakness. The disheartened defeat themselves. For example, 'a man is a slave to bad habits only so long as he thinks he is'. A man must firmly believe that a habit can be broken, so that the effort to break it does not call up automatically the counter-suggestion 'I am bound to fail'. Similarly, a man must believe that the downdrag of a poor background is limited in effect and can be overcome.

We never resolve upon actions we believe impossible, nor upon any reform so long as we blame our parents, forbears, circumstances, for the mess our lives are in; the one fatal obstacle to rebuilding character, says H. H. Farmer, 'is for the patient to become possessed by the thought that he is merely the passive victim of forces over which he has, and can be expected to have, no control.' Psychological determinists can never allow their patients to share their view! The Christian pastor will appeal, of course, in face of all discouragement and despair, to the redemptive purpose of God, the healing power of divine love, the invasive energies of the divine Spirit, the long testimony of the Christian Church to the transforming power of Christ. 'Modern psychotherapy confirms the old religious belief that to give power to the will, confidence and faith in the possibility of victory are essential' (Hadfield). The pastor will also understand the value of examples, multiplied within the Christian fellowship, of that divine victory at work: he will see that the weak are fortified repeatedly by the friendship and support of those whose personal histories bear witness to the difference Christ makes.

Conversion

But not all in need of moral help are responsive to Christian therapy and religious counsel. For those who are not, there is little the pastor can do, apart from offering continuing sympathy and friendship, and maintaining unfailing openness to any change in attitude. He cannot be expected to show people how to make a success of unchristian living! Instead, he must often point to Christian conversion as the only prescription for moral health and salvation. He needs therefore to understand clearly what conversion means and implies—and no less in pastoral work among new converts than in evangelistic effort. A psychological description of conversion is not an ultimate explanation of it, and in no way controverts the religious account of its source in divine love and power. For those who have experienced it, Christian conversion has unmistakable transcendental reference—grace, love, power have entered life from 'outside' the self, and life henceforth is not to be lived from a self-chosen centre for self-chosen ends on self-engendered resources, but for Him who has given the soul new life and new goals to live for.

For all that, conversion may have a purely secular, even pagan, form: the longing for rebirth is older, and wider, than Christianity. A personality dominated by a particular sentiment may under emotional stress, change of circumstances, illness or the like, become totally

changed, the dominant interest replaced by something very different—
even by its opposite: a careless, irresponsible, superficial person may
become serious, dedicated, concerned; a man long noted for family
loyalty may break out in wholly unpredicted sexual license. Often it is
possible afterwards to look back to 'symptoms' of the coming change,
in signs of discontent or inward struggle, and then to the resolution of
that discontent or struggle by the sudden irruption into conscious life
of the energies hitherto repressed. Former emotional drives have been
transferred to new foci, organised into new sentiments, and released
along new channels of expression, while new emotional energies have
been evoked or released by new concepts, experiences, ideals: through
a child's death, perhaps, a man turns from obsession with sport to new
care for his family; a growing boy transfers something of his
admiration, affection and protectiveness from his mother to his girl-
friend, with new, hitherto latent, emotions adding their force to the
new sentiment. All such reorientations of personality are psychologically intelligible: a repressed system of energies, desires, concepts,
memories, goals, gains unexpected force through some climactic
experience and 'takes over' conscious life, the will moves to identify
the self with the new dominant sentiment, and life is changed. The
former dominant sentiment is now repressed, and long pent-up
energies are released in the exhilaration of spirit, perhaps also in
exaggerated reactions.

When the experience provoking such a re-centring of personality
is a religious event—hearing a sermon, meeting a Christian whose
life and testimony kindle conviction, an illness given religious
significance, some shock of fear or shame; when the new centre of
life is God or Christ, and the effect is submissive acceptance of an
ideal which addresses the self with divine authority and promise,
demand and succour; and when the release or redirection of suppressed energies results in dedication to Christian purposes and the
flooding of the soul with spiritual peace, exhilaration and joy, we
speak of *Christian* conversion. Often the term is reserved for sudden
and dramatic change from irreligious to religious character, from
sinfulness to Christian discipleship, but it is important for the pastor
to remember that there are other forms, no less valid or Christian.

The 'once-born' Christian may have known no emotional upheaval,
no dateable transition from unchristian to Christian, because from the
beginning of conscious moral responsibility his inner life has been
organised into a strongly Christian sentiment, his beliefs, emotions,
goals and norms integrated around Christian ideals as gradually, and
with as complete permeation of his life, as the rest of his education.
Even in such a life-history, however, there will have arrived eventually
a moment when for the first time, consciously and independently, a
decision is taken, an act performed, a duty fulfilled, in which the
hitherto subconscious assent to all things Christian becomes excep-
tionally personal, deliberate, voluntary and final. At the same time,

the pressure of Christian teaching, example, and habit becomes no longer simply an outward discipline but an inward constraint and delight. The moment may arise without conflict or resistance, may appear to be wholly in line with all previous development, but it will nevertheless fix and register the life's own allegiance to Christ in a new *personal* depth of commitment.

A form of conversion no less significant is experienced by those whose religious zeal is itself transferred to new channels and new loyalties by some revision of religious concepts, some wider religious ideal: one need only mention the 'conversions' of deeply religious men like Paul, Luther, Wesley. Something similar marks the experience of some of the great mystics. It is possible, further, to speak of varying emphases in conversion. That of Zaccheus was mainly a moral change; that of Peter an emotional one ('Thou knowest that I love Thee'); that of Nicodemus intellectual—the perception of new truth; that of Cornelius, the fulfilment of a religious pilgrimage; that of Paul a surrender to revised religious convictions and pressures long accumulating. On missionary fields conversion often has a social emphasis (as it had for Joseph of Arimathea and the converts at Pentecost) as a public identification with the Christian community, with all its risks and implications. This is only to say that the incoming of divine light, love and power is never stereotyped, but adapted to individual personality-structure and to personal need.

In evangelical circles, however, the word 'conversion' is usually reserved for the dramatic change of life-style from sinful to Christian, more or less suddenly, and accompanied by conviction of sin, repentance, a new insight and trust (faith), and a new self-understanding, issuing in a reorientated personality wholly dedicated to Christian ideals. Normally the experience is expected to involve a moral crisis, in which former goals, attitudes and emotions are repudiated, and new generally opposite ones embraced; together with a new, confident awareness of divine aid, in forgiveness for the past and help for the future. Personality is re-centred around Christ, accepted as Saviour from all evils and Lord of life, replacing 'self' as the centre of reference and the spring of decisions. Re-orientation accomplished, 'the peace which passes all understanding disperses the demons of gloom and depression and floods the personality with joy, hope, and the assurance of oneness with God' (Stolz). The familiar underlying psychological mechanism is here at work: a formerly suppressed or repressed sentiment of 'better' moral feeling and idealism, gathering strength from some external or internal stimulus, erupts into conscious life to find expression in new directions of volition and reintegrate the personality around a new pattern. Paul's later references to his own conversion leave no doubt that the Damascus experience was the final outbreaking of a new self after a period of 'subconscious incubation' (William James) that began at least as early as the death of Stephen, and probably before that—an internal struggle, against conviction and submission, of which his violent persecution of Christians was but the inverted expression. But though the experience may be thus *described*, such a total change of the self cannot in practice (or in logic) be 'self'-generated: the operating force is the power of the Spirit working through the life-giving word of God.

Adolescence, the natural time for personal explorations and adjustments, for the formation of psychological sentiments and the integration of the inner life, for great decisions of many kinds, is also a 'normal' time for conversion. That such religious experiences are not simply manifestations of immaturity is shown by the way they vary with individual disposition, and by their permanent effect on the subsequent character and career. The conversion experience is moulded, too, by the social conventions of the religious group in which it occurs. Sudden, dramatic conversions are not in fact the 'norm' in Christianity, since over very large sections of the church they do not occur—or only rarely. This group-expectation has as much to do with evoking 'adolescent conversions' as adolescence itself, and certainly as much as sexual disturbances.

Many religious conversions occur between the ages of twelve and twenty-five. It is as meaningless to dub these 'merely adolescent' as it would be to nickname those which occur in old age 'merely geriatric', those due to the testimony of a boy-friend, 'merely Romeo-initiation', those inspired by a fiancée, 'mere Julietism', 'valetudinary' those brought about by serious illness, and those occasioned by the fear of death 'thanatological'. The game is easy, but what insight or explanation do derogatory semantics convey? As well speak of marriage, ambition, social idealism, university education, military service, as 'merely adolescent' because they also first come into view at that period of life!

Nevertheless, *some* of the force, the joy, and the relief of Christian conversion in youth undoubtedly derives from the release of energies generated by the awakening and growing sexuality, and its diversion into 'love for Christ' is psychologically, as well as religiously, a very significant event. So much tension, so many new experiences, opportunities, responsibilities, fears and dangers crowd the adolescent years, that the finding of anchorage, social acceptance, and support, a Person to love, a Hero to worship, relief from guilt-feelings, and the answer to insistent intellectual questions, all at once, is bound to be an overwhelming experience. The all-or-nothing response, the exaggerated accounts of pre-conversion sin and post-

K

conversion virtue, the exuberance and barely-directed energy slipping over into impatience—what *could* be more natural? The perceptive pastor will understand the ebullience, the alternations of emotion, the hunger for repeated experiences of similar intensity, the reaction that must set in. He will be ready for it all. But he will, for all that, value beyond all other fruits of his pastoral work these climactic occasions when the young—or the old—are brought to the life-changing decisions in which all Christian truth is *realised* and all Christian grace floods the soul.

But just because he values such events, and longs to see them often among his people, he will be on guard against pressing young people for premature decisions. Even a superficial understanding of the profound nature of conversion should warn against blundering intervention into the delicate mechanisms of mental life—not to add, trying to force God's hand. When emotional disturbance, or guilt-feelings, are artificially induced in the hope of producing the required religious response, or when social pressures and religious warnings are used to evoke decisions, professions of faith, or the acceptance of obligations for which the personality is not yet prepared, the pastor could well be faced with reactions opposite to those he wanted, and with consequences he cannot handle. In any case, the simulated conversion, though produced for the best reasons, leaves such psychological and spiritual scars, such a confusion of emotions and of ideals, such deep disappointment and self-distrust, that religious disillusion and ultimately scepticism are almost inevitable. Unwise evangelism has probably produced in the long run as many hardened, unreachable sinners as it has produced matured Christians—the 'failure-rate' of converts of the more sudden type appears fairly high, judging by church membership figures. And each 'failure' is an individual far less likely than ever to be attracted to Christianity, or patient with its claims.

Such caution over *unwise* evangelism merely underlines, however, the reality and moral power of the valid conversion-experience by which many of the distortions and deficiencies of human character can be cured, and life reorientated 'at a stroke'. Because it is so far-reaching, it cannot be hastened; because it is so potent, it may not be induced; because it has to do with God and the human soul, it must not be engineered; because it vitally concerns human life and destiny, it must never be counterfeited. In the possibility of and the gracious invitation to, radical regeneration in Christ, lies all the Christian gospel to a world otherwise without resources, without redemption, and without hope.

Corrective Strategy

Christian conversion does not solve all problems at once, and the pastor will need often to counsel further steps of practical moral wisdom in handling the spiritual difficulties which younger and older Christians face. In general, such wisdom lies in using *positively* the insights offered by moral psychology. (i) One constant source of trouble is temptation, whether as enticement to evil confronting us from without, or the inclination towards evil which prompts us from within. The distinction is in part misleading: to allure us at all, any temptation must appeal to something within us; we are always our own worst tempters.

Of course the pastor will emphasise that temptation is not sin. It is one of the most remarkable traits in the portrait of Jesus that He 'was in all points tempted like as we are', and the words have been a comfort to generations of hard-pressed converts, together with the inference drawn, 'He is able to succour them that are tempted'. We dare not imagine that His temptations were in any way unreal, or pretended, or on some ethereal plane far above ordinary experience, for then the scriptural inference would not hold, and the picture given in the Gospels would be misleading. The plain truth is that without temptation none should find maturity, or strength or character: that is why Jesus said to Peter, 'Satan hath desired to have you, that he may sift you as wheat: but I have prayed for thee, *that thy faith fail not . . .*'—and not 'that you may be excused temptation.'

But if temptation is not sin, it easily leads to sin, unless well handled. One necessity is unblinking self-knowledge, that recognises with utmost candour one's own moral danger, that refuses to rationalise or justify the evil suggestion, or merely to repress it by denying its reality even to ourselves; but frankly acknowledges that some things are dangerous for us if not for others; that some company always finds us at our weakest; that 'a serious clinical interest in the social aspects of certain behaviour patterns' is sometimes the deceitful name we give to playing with temptation. A young Christian must learn to expect sin to be deceitful—that it never brings the pleasure it promises, and always brings the retribution that it hides; that he always chooses evil at the expense of some good, and is inevitably poorer in consequence; and that the issue of temptation is immeasurably serious, demanding some ruthlessness in cutting off occasions of evil—as Jesus said, 'It is better to limp into Life with one foot than to jump with both feet into hell.'

The intellectual aspect of will's function, as selecting between presented suggestions, underlines the truth soon learned in experience: that the result of any spiritual conflict is usually settled in the first moments of conscious danger. Passions toyed with, thought about, by their very nature monopolise attention, and draw to themselves the strength and concentration of the whole self, which is then naturally powerless to prevent the suggestion moving into action. The key to victory always lies in the thoughts we attend to. In the mind sensitive to Christ's disapproval, and already filled with whatsoever things are true, lovely, pure and excellent, no idle wandering fancies offer opportunity to evil. Choosing what to think about, you choose your character—the old saw is approximately true: Sow a thought and you reap an act; sow an act and you reap a habit; sow a habit and you reap a character; sow a character and you reap a destiny. So Paul acutely affirms, as the central strategy of spiritual warfare, the Christian's purpose 'to take every thought captive to obey Christ'. For if Christ is Lord and Censor of that inner realm of thought, imagination and desire, He is Lord of all, and temptation has no power.

(ii) For all that, temptation is not always conquered, and one vital element in moral therapy must always be a clear and healthful technique for dealing with failure, and its resultant guilt and distress. The emotional reactions of remorse, self-accusation, and shame must not be deprecated, since in them lies much of the moral energy for renewal: they must be diverted. The disturbing memory, with its attendant feeling of revulsion and shame, must become the focus of strong new associations of forgiveness, relief, gratitude for favour shown in pardon. A mental catharsis of confession is necessary, in which all self-justification and self-deceit are finally removed, and all shelter from personal responsibility is abandoned. The conscience needs not appeasement but cleansing, and the heart needs not excuse but the assurance of a loving forgiveness. The depth and power of such an experience will depend upon a truly redemptive religious faith, and upon an adequate conception of what forgiveness costs. Cheap pardon cures nothing and cleanses no one. But the pastor has a story to tell, and an authority to declare divine forgiveness through the cross, which can effect purging and renewal of the stricken personality. He will insist that the forgiveness of God must be *accepted*, rested upon, rejoiced in, as accomplished and settled. Continually to seek pardon for the same offence is want of faith. 'If we confess our sins, he is faithful and just to forgive us our sins, and to cleanse us': true penitence freely admits the need of that, and true faith simply takes it for the truth, and relies upon it.

How far penitence should be made public is a question for pastoral discretion. It is very doubtful if, in practice, public confessions do any great good to compensate for their obvious dangers. Where the offence has been public, attendance at worship and especially at the Lord's Table, with the obvious approval and welcome of the pastor, is sufficient notice to those who know the story that all is well again. Where the offence has affected other individuals, confession to them, with restitution wherever possible, is a necessary part of penitence, and provides great support against repetition. Who else needs to be told, a wife or family for example, will depend upon circumstances, but in general confidences are better kept, and reticence respected. It is often well that the pastor himself does not know details, lest his own position between various parties become intolerable. Provided that no wrong is merely hidden, no person injured by silence, the pastor will be content that penitence be sincere, reform genuine, and a better foundation be laid for future Christian obedience.

(iii) The power of suggestion, so potent for evil, may also be employed positively for good. When the premises of a betting shop prove an irresistible temptation to a former gambling addict who yet must pass them in the course of his work, it may help greatly to go with him, and standing before the door tell forcefully the story of a recent suicide, in wretched circumstances, of one driven to despair by gambling, and then take him straight to meet the family. So a new set of associations has been created, charged with counter-suggestions which will recur at that spot. An individual wallowing in self-pity is best lifted out of it by awakening pride— 'You are surely not the kind of person to let that sort of treatment spoil you—I have always thought you could take that in your stride!'

A mother who was becoming over-enthusiastic about her small boy's 'second sight' and ability to see visions even of dead relatives, was turned from this socially rewarding 'boast' by the pastoral remark 'I should not worry—he shows no other signs of mental deficiency; he is alert, and sharp and intelligent enough to outgrow it.' On the whole, the positive suggestion is always more powerful than the negative one: the wise mother distracts a naughty child; the cool father obtains the dangerous blade by offering an apple; the young vandal who destroys the garden's beauty is best given a garden of his own, and helped to plan it. Concentrate hard upon getting to sleep and you will lie awake all night: attempt some mental task, like composing a letter, and you may not finish it. The hermit fleeing to the desert to avoid temptation found he had taken it with him. So one does not best meet evil with punishment, or command, but with attractive alternatives. That is indeed the basic moral strategy of Christianity—'overcome evil *with good*'.

One application of this positive power of suggestion, the daily Bible reading and prayer, has already been mentioned: but one caution is necessary. An idea held before the mind, even in prayer, is still exercising its power of gathering to itself emotive force. To pray, long and earnestly, against a temptation is but a pious way of dwelling upon the alluring idea; pray against drink, and you will find it fills the mind! Instead, prayer should be *for* other things, and away from the immediate danger; it should be a specially powerful way of 'changing the subject' before one's attention; of switching the mind from the evil that entices, *not* to seek strength against it, but to worship and adore the purity of Christ and the glory of God. For another basic technique of Christian moral wisdom is, never to meet problems head-on, but always indirectly. In some realms, the harder we try the less we succeed; and the surest antidote to anything wrong is to substitute a positive good.

(iv) The most potent example of such moral substitution of good for evil is called sublimation. Essentially, it implies the conversion of the instinctive forces within the self from their normal outlet—which may for social or moral reasons be disapproved—to one deliberately chosen and of positive value. As we have seen, the fundamental emotive energies cannot be eradicated, and it is dangerous to repress them by refusing to acknowledge their existence: the healthy and productive solution is to find constructive and socially approved forms of expression, to capitalise the inherited instinctive forces for chosen spiritual ends. Just as, in the process of civilisation, primitive hunting becomes dauntless exploration, naive curiosity becomes scientific research, anger sublimates into moral indignation and fear into wise precaution, so sexuality, baulked of natural expression, may drive downwards into perversion, but may also reach upwards into socially useful, enriching and valuable expression, in social care, vicarious motherhood, school-teaching, medical skill, poetry, music, painting, sculpture, the creation of all lovely things.

The pastor has ample opportunities to guide individuals under stress, seeking to control or to deny their passionate nature, to find healthful and satisfying outlets in new careers, or hobbies, or public service. Hadfield wisely protests against the idea that sublimation is the solution to every emotional problem: he insists that one cannot sublimate an instinctive drive that has never been awakened, nor one that has been rigorously repressed by shutting the mind and memory against it. Hadfield is condemning the 'perverted idealism' which denies man's animal nature altogether. But that is another problem. Where the emotional stresses of a passionate nature—aggressively violent, pugnacious, self-assertive, sexual, maternal, gregarious—are causing trouble, the right solution must be to find approved outlets, socially useful and personally satisfying. It may require investigation and ingenuity; aggression, pugnacity, may be found very useful in pursuing unpopular social causes; self-assertiveness has useful outlet in political life; caring for others' children, or defending the handicapped child, will absorb all the maternal affection most women can spare. There is certainly work enough waiting to be done in the world to provide opportunity and outlet for unused energy—if the pastor can only persuade that moral health and satisfaction are to be valued above the affluence of rubies.

Moral therapy rightly seeks a cure for what has gone wrong in individual character: but the Christian ideal is not exhausted in that negative, 'nothing the matter' well-being. Stagnation turns sour, even in the basically good character. There is an innate creativity, a forward-moving dynamic, inherent in the truly sound Christian character which provides its own safeguard against danger. The goal is one never yet reached, except by Christ; the Christian presses toward that mark for the prize of the upward calling of God, never counting himself to have attained, but leaving the things that are behind as he reaches towards maturity, the measure of the stature of the fullness of Christ. The pastor will ever cultivate that upward-stretching spiritual ambition which never rests upon its laurels or counts its victories, but presses on. For he knows the most basic of all principles of Christian moral wisdom—that no man falls from his steadfastness if he grows in grace, and in the knowledge of our Lord and Saviour Jesus Christ.

23 MENTAL THERAPEUTICS

The positive application of psychological insights is as relevant to mental as to moral problems, remembering how tenuous is the distinction between them, and provided always that the pastor keeps in mind the limits of his competence in handling mental trouble, and is firmly resolved that *'the insane must be committed to those qualified to help them'*. So long as these reiterated caveats be taken seriously, the pastor may often observe, and seek to alleviate—or seek help for—a number of minor mental ailments not uncommon in our stressful society.

Mental Ailments

(i) *Infantilism*, the nostalgic regression to childhood security, dependency, exhibitionism, and petulance, which was noted as one of the mechanisms of the unconscious mind, may of course become a seriously incapacitating condition; it may also be manifest in milder forms, and then can be actually aggravated by some religious attitudes. In general, the adult emotions of courage in danger, fortitude before difficulties, confidence in the face of anxieties and responsibilities, have never been allowed to develop, the personality suffering 'fixation' in childhood's attitudes, relationships, and care-free satisfactions. A vague sentimental symbolism is preferred to clear thinking, and an equally vague habitual infirmity of purpose replaces mature decision. The individual is often vain, and still more often extremely sensitive and easy to offend, magnifying trifles, and resenting any want of attention or appreciation.

Kimball Young estimated that of three thousand Protestant hymns studied, the predominant motif of more than half was the longing to return to infantile security and to reap a heavenly reward. A hymn like

> Safe in the arms of Jesus,
> Safe on His gentle breast,
> There by His love o'ershaded
> Sweetly my soul shall rest . . .

illustrates infantilist religion, at once unhealthy, unscriptural, and a distortion of the manly faith which Christianity inculcates—a faith which faces all kinds of adversity, adventure, risk and conflict in the confidence that when we have fought a good fight and finished our course, *then* we shall find underneath us the everlasting arms. The pastor who is aware of the danger will avoid the sentimental comfort that undermines realism and retards maturity, and eschew all maternal, nursery, and childhood analogies. He will be alert, too, to the dangers of a 'feminist' presentation of religious truth, the softer, romantic, emotional appeal, and the feminine Christ of art and of many devotional manuals. Such an emphasis repels masculine personalities, and panders to the child in all of us, to the reluctance to grow up and face the real world. The mature Christian must be psychologically weaned to live in the adult world, exercise his own judgement, accept his own responsibilities, enter into spiritual freedom, no longer leaning upon others' directions nor upon codified regulations—Paul would say, even of the divine law—but answering to his own Master and following his own vision with courage and realism.

One more serious form of infantilism is the so-called 'oedipus' complex, which Freud once thought all children possessed: an intense jealousy of the father's position and privileges with the beloved mother, even to the point of wishing (like the Greek youth) to destroy the father and claim the mother for itself alone. Intense antagonism between the boy and the father, the girl and the mother, can arise from or be complicated by this subconscious (or even unconscious) jealousy, and growing sexual awareness can add its emotional overtones to the personal conflict. Where developing adulthood, and a growing interest in members of the other sex of one's own age, do not cure this mother- or father- fixation, some deep-rooted cause may be suspected, calling for expert analysis and patient, detailed recall.

(ii) Similar to infantilism in motive and effect is *invalidism*, a mental regression to some earlier experience of illness in which the individual was sheltered, pampered, excused all responsibility, forgiven all tantrums, and allowed his own way. Faced long afterwards with real adversity or conflict, the mind 'remembers' this happy state, and reverts to it, even to the extent, sometimes, of reproducing the symptoms of the illness. The cause may be a desperate craving for sympathy, an underlying anxiety-state, or retreat from some painful circumstance that defies solution; the cure will be to remove the cause if possible, and in any case to lead the patient to see the explanation of his reaction. Somewhat different are the professional neurotics who retail their operations, symptoms and distresses merely

for self-parade, to demand attention, to inflate their own importance
—or because they have no other conversation. The cause here is more
a character-defect than a mental maladjustment: the cure may
lie in some new compelling interest, or opportunity, in face of
which all 'nerves', 'heart trouble', and 'poor health' will suddenly
take wings.

(iii) Infantilism and invalidism are both instances of a broader
tendency of troubled minds to escape from reality into *fantasy*, where
problems disappear and conflicts never arise. In the child, such
fantasy is natural; the invisible playmate, the magic world of 'let's
pretend', enlarge the child's experience and exercise the precious
gift of imagination; in the adult, the fantasies of luck, of some sudden
and fantastic turn of fortune, of an Aladdin's lamp conferring omnipotence, a Cinderella romance awaiting the neglected, a 'sleeping
beauty' hope of eventual awaking to everything the heart could
wish, are pathological. The weak personality lives upon what might
have been, to escape from the person he is; he 'cherishes high ideals'
behind which to hide from himself his real failure; he resents all
criticism, because he carries deep within himself the fantasy of his
own perfection—if others could only value him aright! He is over-
scrupulous about his own conduct and censorious about others,
because he cherishes the idea that he is morally without reproach.
Where the child knows that he is pretending, the adult indulging
morbid fantasies identifies with his fantasy: he can live for years
really believing that beneath his weak timidity is a born fighter, if
need should call for it; beneath his most unfortunate lack of training
is a wonderful talent; beneath his want of opportunity a truly great
brain; beneath a plain exterior a *true* beauty that despises artificial
aids; all failure and ineffectiveness are merely unfortunate setbacks,
obscuring the real gifts, capacities and good intentions which time
will surely reveal!

Religion often nourishes such fantasy-making. Prayer is sometimes represented, without conditions or limit, as a means of persuading Omnipotence to interfere with the natural sequence of
events. Faith is sometimes offered as an opiate, sheltering from all
adversity, an agency by which the universe may be made 'to waive
its laws on our behalf'. Plain truth-speaking is considered in some
Christian circles to be ungentle, and so unchristian—lies become
'misunderstandings', violent quarrels become 'a clash of personalities', plain swindles are said to be 'an unspiritual way of doing
things'. Heaven, for some, appears as the recovery of the lost womb,
the mother's arms, where all is effortlessly safe and comfortable! It is

God's work to remove all obstacles, resolve all problems, answer all questions, and make us happy.

When the fantasy threatens to fail, the weak take refuge in 'breakdown'. A fantasy of power, of being able to accomplish anything if it is really desired to do so, may suddenly give up trying, and show mental and physical symptoms of serious incapacity, rather than admit that some problem has defeated ingenuity and determination. A fantasy of moral perfection, faced with disillusion, will break down into total moral helplessness to avoid a crisis of exposure. The student living upon his fancied academic prowess will *actually* collapse into helplessness before an examination which would expose his illusions. Physical pain and muscular paralysis may accompany the loss of all mental control, to evade the loss of the treasured fantasy of competence.

'The beginning of personality reconstruction is the exposure of cherished fallacies' says Stolz. The fantasy-escapist has to be led to recognise, realise, and acknowledge, the nature of his imaginings; to accept the objective world; to take into his thought the hard facts of life's injustice and risk, and into his courage the harder facts of suffering, disappointment, and tragedy. Counselling such a person must demand time and almost infinite patience: but in the end he must see life, himself, and other people in a truer perspective, and accept his own situation with a candid, unpretending faith.

(iv) At the opposite extreme stands the personality that nurses its anxieties in a more or less permanent mood of *worry*, which—if its immediate occasion be removed—will soon find or invent other things to dread. Conscious fears define their object and prompt protective measures; the perpetual anxiety-state is diffused over many real or imaginary objects and inhibits effective action. It is usually due either to some threatening impulse within ourselves— we fear 'breaking out' in cruelty, spitefulness, lust, madness; or to arrested emotional development depriving us of normal courage and fortitude of adulthood. Sometimes the unrecognised object of fear gains a symbolic expression. We 'cannot stand heights', because an inner insecurity about ourselves, our abilities, our status, has made falling from a height our symbolic anxiety—the recurrent dream of falling, in a dozen forms, will often provide the clue to 'acrophobia'. A suppressed fear of exposure (sexual or moral) could explain the fear of open spaces (agrophobia); a memory, or an imagination, of something that has happened in dark, confined places, can explain claustrophobia; many undefined anxieties are unconscious memories of fearful experiences of childhood.

Some phobias are merely mental idiosyncrasies which a man can live with, finding some amusement in his harmless oddity; others, that are the index to generalised anxiety, may need to be probed. A subconscious desire for what is feared may explain anxiety: a man wishes to be promoted, fears he may not be, and fears the new responsibility which promotion threatens. Anxiety can even be desired for its own sake: the individual feels disappointed, even cheated, if the worst does not happen. Some anxiety-states, again, are due to suppressed memories of wrong done and never confessed, of conscience stifled, leaving a generalised feeling of guilt and a lack of assurance of God's favour: these may be especially difficult to relieve, because the connection with the past wrong is usually rejected. In other instances, to uncover the cause, and if possible to remove it, to impart relevant counter-suggestions of confidence, and to initiate some alternative and worthwhile concern (some person or cause worth worrying about) to side-step the anxiety, will probably help.

Apart from breakdowns due to disillusion, fantasy, anxiety, or arrested development, other similar maladjustments, or neuroses, occur simply because normal people are under excessive tension or strain. A *situation-neurosis* may be due to no more than the tension inseparable from a given situation—bereavement, unemployment, a broken engagement, and the right handling of the situation is the cure of the neurosis. A *character-neurosis* may result from some character-trait, or general character-structure, indulged by parents but in adult life proving unsatisfactory and ruining desired relationships, or career. A reorientation of personality around new ideals will clear the neurosis symptoms also. Deeply-buried memories of neglected or over-disciplined childhood may leave disproportionate timidity and a compulsion to placate others; or may leave a hyper-tense dramatising of the self, acting as though always before an admiring audience, demanding continual praise and approval, or else breaking down into petulance and dependence. Retracing causes into childhood reminiscence will probably uncover, and cure. *Conversion-neurosis* manifests a definite symptom as substitute for the true cause of tension—physical vomiting representing 'being sick of one's remembered cowardice'; a hand-washing or hand-wringing habit may symbolise fear of moral or social stain. A fixed idea, a perversion, or an obsession like kleptomania, may be the conversion-substitute for a hidden anxiety, which must be brought to the surface of consciousness, that the symptom may disappear.

(v) Excessive *emotionalism* creates both mental and moral weakness. Deficiency of emotion paralyses response, initiative, and action, for emotion makes ideas vivid and urgent, and provides energy for reaction. But in psychic development emotion always has a head-start on both intellect and volition, and requires to be restrained lest it continue to dominate personality long after infancy. Maturity brings poise, stability, and is moved deeply rather than impulsively and passionately. Immaturity indulges in emotion; maturity uses it. For emotion should issue in action: when feeling is often stirred without appropriate expression in action following, a cold, unemotional paralysis is likely to develop, an inability to feel deeply enough to respond to any situation. Moreover, an emotional experience may come to be cultivated for its own sake, as a shield against reality, a refuge from duty, so that people can be 'deeply moved' to pity, or by horror, or by religious truth—but moved to do nothing. The feeling of sympathy, of moral indignation, of compassion, is mistaken for charity and assistance: one may contemplate the photograph of a starving child, or an actual homeless family, or some outrageous social evil, or a 'moving' film or theatre performance, all with the same ready emotion: for pseudo-compassion demands no effort, decision or sacrifice.

Here again religion must bear some blame for sometimes encouraging emotional escapism, in dramatic and aesthetic forms of worship not even intended to affect conduct; in excitable, unrestrained ejaculations, exaggerated language, noise and movement assumed to be evidence of sincerity; in confusing fervour with truth. It has sometimes encouraged abnormal introspectiveness, producing Christians absorbed in their own emotional states and craving continual 'uplift' and spiritual excitement. The pastor should learn to recognise the emotional child in the unhappy, intense, unreliable, and sulking Christian. He will need to explain gently, to expound the shallowness and uncertainty of living by feeling instead of truth and principle. Most of all, he will teach his people to value the emotions that unite—sympathy, joy, delight in each other; and to beware the emotions that divide—anger, disgust, fear, envy, resentment. To introduce such a distinction is already to reflect, to evaluate, and to restrain, which is the first step towards emotional maturity.

(vi) Hadfield speaks of a 'submissive instinct' related to the need to obey the tribe, the 'herd', and sees it as perverted in *masochism*, the pleasure that some find in being over-mastered, and others in self-inflicted pain. In Christianity, this inverted delight in suffering is doubtless complicated by the story of Christ's passion, and by the challenge to take up the cross. To suffer for the cause of Christ becomes a proof of Christian excellence: then, to suffer at all becomes for some an excellence in itself. Pain, adversity, unhappiness, self-torture, are sometimes said to be 'transfigured' by Christ's example even though they be needless, profitless, morbid and cruel. The ancient church's exaltation of martyrdom, the Roman Catholic devotion to the crucifix—the tortured Body growing with the centuries ever more hideous with pain—and the Puritan valuation of self-discipline as an end in itself, all display a masochist tendency which is wholly foreign to the message and story of Jesus. The pastor must oppose it at all points, as unhealthy, dangerous, and untrue to the love of God and the joy of Christ.

Masochist misapplication of Christian moral heroism may partly explain also the persecution mania which affects some religious people. For most modern Christians, martyrdom is at a safe distance and only theoretically a Christian ideal. Persecution-mania is of humbler origin—mere self-pity more often than not; resentment at others' rejection of what *we* think religious faithfulness, but what *they* see as hypocritical, soured, and self-righteous pride. Occasionally, the root cause may be displaced projection—our own severe criticism of others being represented as their unjustifiable attitude towards our own loyalty to principle. Under no circumstances can taking pleasure in *any* kind of suffering be reconciled with Christian compassion, or the kindness of God, or the promise of the gospel.

Curative Procedures

Nearly all the twenty-five or so main varieties of mental therapy, by which such ailments may be treated, assume that no absolute line can be drawn between what is physical and what is psychical in the human 'body-mind'. The pastor will never treat the soul in the abstract, but only the total personality, remembering that in any individual in trouble, physical health may need as urgent consideration as spiritual well-being.

(i) The general method of therapy is to *help the patient understand* his own story, to unlearn habitual responses to recurring situations and learn new ones, and (often) to see the world no longer with childhood's eyes. The troubled soul must be made aware of its *real* problem: thereon, the individual must very largely cure himself. Responsibility for decision, and for the exercise of faith, cannot be evaded, or passed to the counsellor; the patient must at least put himself in the way of the healing forces available—it cannot be done for him.

Some firmness is required in making the patient face reality. Power to overcome difficulties lies in facing them, never in evading, whether through palliatives, distractions, drugs, or flight. It may be necessary to provoke a crisis of clarity, decision, and deliverance, and the skilled therapist will often expose insincerities, penetrate pretence, confront souls with the truth, lead patients to wholly unwelcome self-understanding, and drag into daylight the evasions, self-deceit, inconsistencies that underlie mental ill-health. The neurotic is usually living in a private world, judging all things from a very private standpoint and interest: he has to be made to see (not simply told) that the world, and himself, are set in the wider perspective of others' judgment and interests, also. The process of self-exposure is neither easy, nor pleasant: but it contains healing.

(ii) The methods of *substitution*, by which troublesome emotive suggestions implanted in the mind are replaced by profitable ones, and (iii) of *sublimation*, by which the instinctive emotional energies are acknowledged, accepted, and diverted to socially useful and satisfying purposes, apply to mental problems exactly as to moral ones. (iv) The value of *analysis* in psychological healing follows from its place in dealing with the unconscious mind. By the relaxed, free association of ideas, by skilful questioning, by objective interpretation of attitudes, emotions, fears, significant mistakes, prejudices, and (with great reserve) reveries and dreams, the hidden sources of distress or neurosis can be uncovered. Because so many disorders originate in the unconscious 'stores' of memories, associations and emotions of childhood and youth, 'reductive analysis' seeks to trace present mental conditions backwards to their causes: adolescent laziness, for example, may be due to a childhood insulated from all effort, to parentally indulged conceit which leaves all effort to others, or to parental severity which has left so deep a dread of disapproval that the youth thinks it better to do nothing than to risk doing wrong. For analysis to succeed, it is essential for the patient to *realise* the true origin of his trouble, and not merely to conceptualise it, to accept it on the counsellor's authority, nor simply to 'admit' the connection with some early guilt just because 'confession' is expected of one who consults a pastor. 'None are perfect, we are all sinners' means nothing for psychological healing—nor for spiritual grace—unless a true and submissive conviction of responsibility lies within it. But if the source of the present difficulty be realised, and its relation to the present problem be understood, as elements of the earlier experience (fears, resentments, passions) are being reproduced in present attitudes, then the unconscious obstacle to the flow of the mind's own healing energies is removed.

Just how mental analysis effects cure is debated. Certainly, the elements of personality which were excluded from the process of integration into sentiments, and repressed into the unconscious mind, are by analysis brought again into harmony with the self, no longer repressed but acknowledged, and consciously redirected or disciplined. Either way, their potency for trouble is greatly diminished. The attendant emotional drives for which no useful outlet had been found are now harnessed by the will's control to the chosen ends of life, their latent energies used for constructive and no longer for destructive purposes. Moreover, some part of the power of unconscious pressures lies in their mystery: the troubled mind fears the internal forces it cannot understand, and dreads obsession, insanity, 'possession', or simple helplessness. Explanation banishes the mystery, dispels the fear; the buried causes being brought into consciousness, the symptoms frequently disappear.

Thus illumination of itself can cure. But analysis needs completion in re-association. The unconscious memories, the repressed fears, desires and aims, must be reintegrated around fresh purposes and interests; detached from the original attendant emotions of terror, resentment, lust, they become attached to new emotions of confidence, co-operation, shame, purity. In this way, the energies that have been disturbing gain positive direction and value, and the haunting memories now evoke happier and healthier responses that serve the chosen ends of life.

(v) Because the mentally distressed need, at some point, a general reassurance of the value of effort, of the significance of their personal lives, and encouragement to persevere, the same value is set in mental as in moral therapy upon a positive and well-grounded *philosophy of life*. For the pastor this means, of course, a recourse to faith and the Christian gospel, but even some non-Christian psychiatrists have sought to rebuild a lost faith, or to guide towards discovery of a new one, to undergird the sick soul. Some, too, have prescribed participation in Christian worship, for the sake of its healing power. The positive suggestions condensed into a well-planned and well-conducted worship-service are all good: they offer solace, challenge, intellectual nourishment, and reassurance, by means of objectively presented, and shared, hymns, prayers, scripture and fellowship. In such an atmosphere self-assessment can be balanced and profitable; anxiety and resentment—even discontent—can be resolved; self-indulgence, self-pity, irrational fears, impatience, are all seen in new light; and a strength not one's own is expected, experienced, and absorbed.

(vi) With religious assurance and spiritual healing should go also active enlistment in outgoing social *service*, within church or neighbourhood, in which the troubled personality can find relief from its introspective moods, its loneliness and self-absorption, its fears and sense of uselessness. Many in psychological trouble need not a vacation but a vocation—they are not overstrained but under-motivated: and often the best cure, or the final part of it, is to become involved with others more handicapped, whose courage and peace will shame self-pity; and with causes beyond personal well-being, whose demands will evoke the unity of purpose and the strength of will which the weaker soul needs.

Sources of Power

Whether we deal with mainly moral, or mainly mental problems, of all remedial ministries that of reinforcing the individual's moral strength will probably be called for most frequently. The 'pathetic moral impotence' of modern society has often been described—the high ideals, and far-reaching social programmes, that fail for lack of moral initiative and determination, leading to impatience, cynicism, violence, or despair. Amid the ever-increasing pressures of modern life, frequent 'nervous breakdowns' and the almost endemic neuras-thenia expose the lack of reserves, the perpetual strain and inward fatigue, with which many live. Nor is the modern church remarkable for any greater effectiveness or power. Where apostolic Christianity was vibrant, dynamic, transforming, its most characteristic experi-ence of the Spirit, one of joyful moral triumph and invincible endurance, modern Christianity is dogged, tenacious, earnest—and wistful.

It is of little use to urge the weak to 'Be strong'. The psycho-logical conditions of power follow clearly from the nature of mental life. All human energy lies in the instinctive emotions: though the reserves vary to some extent with health, temperament, and training, the unexpected resources manifested in emergencies by apparently ordinary people show that the notion of some 'inner reservoir of strength', limited in capacity, is false. The energy *available* is immeasurable, given health and the natural rhythm of effort and rest. Most fatigue is mental in origin. One cause of the exhaustion of strength is *mental inhibition*—by boredom, loss of concentration, the acceptance of negative suggestions—as that we shall fail, or that the effort is not worth while, or that we have not the requisite ability. Want of zeal, conviction, and hope, drains energy immediately.

Another cause of exhaustion is the *conflict* of incompatible ends, the loss of that integration in which strength of will lies, the indecision which wastes energy in striving to settle what shall be attempted, and then approaches it with depleted resources. This is why, in the older religious language, 'recollection', the regathering of the soul's internal powers in periods of cultivated tranquillity and self-concentration, is so often prescribed for 'exhausted' lives. A third cause of exhaustion of strength is *dissipation*, when interest and energies are scattered over multitudinous trivial purposes. We cannot give ourselves wholly to more than few things: each venture we endeavour is at the price of something else. Superficial, trivialised lives are not so much weak as wasteful. And *aimlessness* is equally enervating—when we have no purpose at all to kindle enthusiasm and evoke energy, no enterprise to sustain by its challenge and inspire by its very greatness. We are never so exhausted as when we are doing nothing in particular; to be evident at all, energy must flow, and the condition of renewal is expenditure. The pastor will often insist that God never confers power, so that we may then look around for ways in which to use it: God gives the *task*—the power is manifested in the doing of it.

But the psychological conditions of power are not the whole secret. In the biblical view, man is essentially a vehicle for forces beyond his own: a clay image of his Maker inbreathed with divine life; a 'candle of the Lord' divinely illuminated; the shrine of a spirit destined to return to God who gave it. The New Testament is focused upon the inbreaking of God in Christ, and in the Spirit, to redeem and to transform. 'The rule of the Spirit of life in Christ Jesus' is Paul's explanation of his deliverance from the power of enslaving sin. Whether man is the vehicle of divine or demonic forces, of good or of evil, is for man to choose; but his hope lies not within his own energies, but in the power that flows *through* the soul in which Christ's Spirit dwells.

Where Christians speak of divine grace, or the Spirit, others may speak of man as the channel of the Life Force, the *élan vital*, the evolutionary thrust of which man is the temporary bearer and highest expression, or the divine immanent in the universal process. Christian faith finds such notions vague and unsupported beside its own certainty of the intervention of healing and redemptive forces in history in Christ, and the experience of inward renewal possible to all who pray. The many-sidedness of that invasive energy has already been illustrated—faith, assurance, confidence in the conservation of values, and the friendly nature of the Power behind the universe;

a world view that centres in Christ Jesus, Image of the invisible God, sufficient clue to man's past, present and future; the power of Hero-worship motivated by admiration, gratitude and love; the illuminative and recuperative powers of prayer; the redemptive energies released by a conviction of divine pardon, the compassionate fellowship of Christ, and the enabling of the Spirit; the steadying influences of Christian friendship and private devotion; the enrichment and healing of shared worship; the outward-turning, stimulating challenge of active service for God and men—all these contribute to the spiritual healing that Christ offers to the troubled mind and soul.

And all this the pastor has at hand as he attempts to minister to the distressed. Teaching, the impartation of ideas, the kindling of insights, is but part of that ministry: to persuade men to respond and to commit themselves to Christ, to stir them to faith and action, is the greater part. In the last resort, therefore, the crucial question to the mentally and morally sick is still 'Do you *want* to be healed?' And as of old He who asks possesses the compassion and power to make the question meaningful, and the answer all-important.

24   ALL SORTS OF PEOPLE

People differ. The pastor who gets that trite maxim firmly into his mind and method will save himself much perplexity and wasted effort. Professor Lloyd Morgan's five pups made their point. Reaching a barred gate, all failed to get through at the bottom; three discovered that the higher bars were wider apart, and got through; the fourth continued to struggle below; the fifth lay down and whined. The experiment being repeated for twenty minutes, they did the same each time. Personality differences are innate: which means that they are natural, inexplicable, and unchangeable—even by religion. The notion that all individuals are able to enjoy the same religious experience, by which their differences will be ironed out, has no support in scripture, in experience, or in common sense. Jew and Greek, barbarian, Scythian, bond and free, male and female, all are one in Christ Jesus: but they are not all equal, nor all alike.

In outlook, temperament, character, Peter was not John, nor Andrew Thomas; nor was Mary Martha, or Mary of Bethlehem very like Mary Magdalene. Nor did Jesus do or say anything to lessen their natural differences, or seek conformity to one type of personality. Indeed, when Jesus expounds His redemptive work, in Luke 15, He draws attention to the variety of people He comes to save—some like sheep straying, needing care; some, like coins, accidentally lost, needing to be discovered; some, like the prodigal, wilfully lost, needing to learn their lesson; some, like the elder brother, lost in uncharitable self-righteousness, needing to be humbled. The Master would never say, 'They are all sinners' and leave it at that. Above all others, Jesus would *discriminate*: the Christian pastor must learn to do so too, constantly, habitually, and perceptively.

The continual temptation, of course, is to pigeon-hole the infinite variety of the human soul—which is stupid. All one can truthfully do is to indicate some of the bases upon which humanity plays its incalculable permutations. (i) The ancient Greeks observed a correlation between physical and psychical characteristics in naming the four chief 'humours' of personality after the supposed four chief fluids of the body—blood, phlegm, bile, 'black bile'. Men, they said, are sanguine, phlegmatic, choleric (irritable) or sad. The relation of 'temperament' to glandular secretions is more complicated than that, but a measure of truth lies here, although what is often called 'temperament' may more accurately mean the tone and mood of personality, determined by life's general experience, making one habitually optimistic, or pessimistic, trustful or suspicious, confident or cynical. A sunny, hopeful, resilient temperament is a gift of God. The slow, steadfast and unemotional are often most reliable, loyal, consistent. The 'irritable' are also the excitable, enjoyable people, impulsive, generous, swift in reaction, in sympathy, and in understanding. The melancholic tend to feel deeply, in true friendship, sharing joy and pain; to see danger, and to carry others' responsibilities—they are often artistic, sensitive, profound, supremely honest. In inexplicable ways, they just *are* such people: in any crisis, one turns immediately to find optimistic possibilities, another to stolid reflection, the third to swift reaction, the fourth to 'face the worst'. They do not choose so to do; they are probably unaware of doing so; life, or teaching, may modify their nature, but nothing will change it.

(ii) All conscious life has cognitive, affective and conative aspects, but individuals vary considerably as to which aspect predominates, and in what proportion. Those in whom cognition is strongest are the 'intellectuals', much occupied with information, reflection, the patterns of objects, the abstract connections of things, and of ideas. As Christians they are given to arguing 'principles', to discussing theology, analysing situations and people, to study of the Bible, and to theorising about everything. Often they are satisfied with theorising—somewhat contemptuous of emotion, and frightened by their zealously active fellow Christians. They cannot help these tendencies, and are not to be blamed for them. But they do need to be taught that 'no heart is pure that is not passionate; nor safe, that is not enthusiastic': nor is faith of any use without works.

Those in whom emotion is strongest are often impulsive, changeful, easily persuaded, easily discouraged; they are warm-hearted, zealous, infectious in their enthusiasms, and often deeply loyal. They tend to despise 'head religion' and 'works'; but to bring a passionate sincerity to Christian devotion, worship, and fellowship. They too cannot help their nature; though they need to be warned that without intellectual direction and forethought, emotion may become undisciplined, misleading, and dangerous; without expression in Christian action and conduct, it is valueless, deceitful, and will die.

Those in whom the will seems strongest are often impatient of theorists and emotionalists alike—they judge only by deeds, by things accomplished, battles fought, results achieved; they give no credit for good intentions or for proper feeling. They tend to act alone, mainly because intellectual explanations and plans, and emotional persuasions, needed to enlist others, seem so much wasted time. 'To see it and do it' is everything, and if others do not see and do at once, they are not worth waiting for. Such activists are often valuable; they need, of course, to be reminded how wrong-headed, hurtful, and costly, unconsidered and unplanned action can be; how much needless opposition is stimulated by failure to communicate intentions and explain reasons; how much real damage to one's own cause can result from impatience with others' feelings, loyalties, and fears. Sometimes, too, the activists need to be reminded that sustained, humble and gracious work springs oftenest from hearts that know how to wait upon the Lord.

The pastor will often be surprised at unsuspected resources of emotion in 'intellectual' people, who patiently amass facts and figures with which to fight for some social cause about which they feel deeply, though silently. He will find that some emotional people can rouse themselves, and others, to passion—without ever losing sight of their goal. There are hard-driving activists who know well how to appeal to reason, to imagination, or to emotion, as each may serve. There are no 'pure types'. Nevertheless the pastor will find that much of his public instruction and private counsel will be aimed at fostering a balanced, and tolerant, religious life, in which each factor has its due, but only its due, place.

(iii) The psychological differences between male and female ought to be too obvious to need description, although every statement made is debatable, and every generalisation finds many exceptions. It is usual to trace all feminine psychological characteristics to women's biological function as mothers, the fulfilment of which requires, for example, steadfast personal relationship to ensure protection and provision while caring for the child—and a special relationship to the child also. Thus, to obtain and to hold a mate, fending off rival claimants, is more important to the female than to the more promiscuous male, for whom *biologically* the personal relationship means less. Whether this be the explanation or not, it is generally true that most women are more concerned with persons, with personal relationship, with personal character, than with anything else at all. Where men can be interested in things, like machines, in abstract ideas, theories, principles, beliefs, or justice, women will usually see these as the possessions, the ideas, principles, attitudes of individuals—likeable or disliked, trusted or suspected.

The personal relationship being important, women will be pleased by flattery, though well aware that it is flattery; men are said to be pleased by it, too, but do not recognise it! From the bearing of children arises woman's far greater capacity for enduring pain, and their superior courage, though men will suffer more for abstract causes and ideals than most women see as necessary. From the care of children arise woman's tender patience with the sick, ailing, and helpless, and their immense compassion; yet man's patience in catching fish, or tinkering with machinery, will exasperate women. From the training of children is said to arise the tendency of women to want to manage others, seeing what is best for them more clearly than they can see it for themselves. This is mistaken for wilfulness, or 'bossiness' when it is in truth well-meant (though excessive) 'mothering'. From the facts of child-bearing, too, arises the woman's greater sense of the child's 'belonging' to her, indissolubly, whatever happens later in life; the child is literally and physically of her flesh and blood in a way that men do not usually feel—or understand. Possibly that is why, however faithless and antagonistic the child becomes, the woman rarely breaks with him, as the man is willing to do—thinking her 'soft'.

From the mother's protectiveness towards the child issues, it may be thought, the greater 'deadliness' of the female, her ruthless and (to herself) unsparing dedication to keeping and defending her own. She is, too, quicker at scenting danger to her interests and those of her circle: much more tenacious of those customs, rules, moral qualities, and social codes, in which experience has shown safety to lie—and so far less ready than men to experiment with new modes of behaviour, which could destroy what the woman feels it essential to conserve.

Persons, values, and attitudes are less matters of analysis and logic than of swift judgement and feeling-response: woman's concern for them, therefore, makes her more intuitive and less deliberatively rational, than man—and more imaginative. Feminine 'fickleness' is really woman's swift, intuitive, and emotional response to changes in relationship, where men value more their loyalty to abstract ideas and 'unchanging logic'. Feminine 'deviousness', cleverness (or 'cunning')—the gift for indirectness in approaching any goal—is due to their superior understanding of persons, plus imagination. Because language, and writing, are means of inter-personal communication, women are usually more articulate than men, and better linguists. In later life, a woman's home, her opinions, her work, her 'rights', become her 'children'—and she defends them with the old tenacity. It is probable that, for physiological reasons, woman is more constantly and more regularly reminded of sexual matters, and also of the passing of the years: it is said that women are far more time-conscious, far oftener in a hurry through life, than are most men, who face no such drastic limitation upon the functional lifespan.

Many of these 'feminine' traits—innate conservatism, nearness in thought and feeling to the sources of life, intensity of personal relationship, high valuation of moral and personal qualities, in-tuitive and down-to-earth judgements, and concern for the young—tend naturally to make women appreciate religious insights, disci-pline, and support. Traditionally, too, woman has been the more vulnerable, emotionally and socially, and religion has been her consolation, while most informed and thinking women are aware that Christianity has done more for women, for children, and for home, than has any other civilising factor in society. For all these reasons, women are often the pastor's best allies, the church's best supporters and workers, and most loyal defenders. If they tend sometimes to resist change, 'irrationally'; if they cannot be bothered with constitutions, rules, and standing orders, only with 'how nice the President is'; if they consent to support educational reform in the Sunday School *only* if they can keep the class they have taught for years—these are but the defects of fine qualities the men never had! Just as the men's argumentativeness, resistance to persuasion, tendency to remain on the fringe and avoid getting involved, impatience of emotional pietism, and often unimaginative 'logic', are also defects—from a pastor's point of view—of that hard-headed quality which women rarely possess but which, when it is on your side, is invaluable.

Feminine psychological characteristics do not depend, of course, upon a woman's being actually married, and a mother—only upon her being naturally constituted for that function. Single life will to some extent modify and transfer most of the natural traits. Men like to suppose that unmarried women inevitably become crabbed, soured, misanthropist; when that does happen, the cause lies more often in the educational and vocational deprivation which has un-fitted them for independence, than in mere lack of the enriching companionship of men! Unmarried men, also, can become emotion-ally, and socially, thwarted, misfits, misogynist. Bachelors are, as often as not, made so either by health (as epilepsy), or by circum-stances (as having dependent parents)—in which case they may become as embittered as women in similar case. Or they are homo-sexual; or they have been so absorbed by a mother-fixated ideal that they have never found a woman able to be both sweetheart and mother; or they are bachelors by disappointment, having lost the woman they wanted, and are now resentful, or fearful of a second humiliation. Some men delayed decision, through weakness of character, or circumstances, until they became too fixed in ways to risk the disturbance of a shared life. And all these reasons—with some others—may explain why individual women remain unmarried. No pastor in his senses will embark upon matchmaking, whatever his feeling that two lonely people could be so much happier together. But he will be aware of the particular problems of single life; will remember that the causes may be very unhappy ones; and will be ready sometimes to offer careful counsel concerning any psychological or spiritual obstacles that have distorted attitudes to marriage.

(iv) A much more technical classification of 'types' is assayed by some psychologists. Jung's distinction of introvert and extrovert has become popular jargon, because it answers to a difference most people can recognise, though the terms merely indicate extremes between which the majority are ranged. Basically, the extrovert is the outward-turning personality, friendly, easily adjusting to new acquaintances, gregarious. He is often emotional in a shallow way, given to external interests, as sport and shared hobbies. Absorbed in what goes on around him, he shows little self-consciousness, is rarely embarrassed or anxious, rarely takes offence, always ready to help and to be helped. The extrovert is often dominated by sense experience rather than thought, and sometimes given to sensual pleasures; his is the 'enjoying nature', and he makes always a good companion. If he refers at all to his inner feelings and thoughts, he will tend to assume that these are the same as everyone has— 'everyone knows . . .' Some extroverts tend to make swift, intuitive, dogmatic judgements, often on superficial evidence. They tend also to look after themselves and expect others to do the same. The more thoughtful extroverts are given to analysing and classifying endless objective facts, ignoring inward experience and their own psychological reactions.

Basically, the introvert is the inward-turning personality, retiring, shy, finding it difficult to make new friends, reticent about expressing his feelings, though they run deep, usually absorbed in his own thoughts, inward investigations, mental states and reactions, and very self-conscious. The introvert is therefore usually a solitary, easily offended, or embarrassed, sometimes suspicious of others' approaches, self-reliant, anxious about many things but chiefly to be left alone, and reluctant to receive help. Some introverts rely on their sensations, but mainly those of inward-looking, intensely-feeling type; they are frequently unhappy, over-sensitive, under-communicative; others, the prophets and poets among them, see and feel truth with great inward certainty, needing no external authority and no evidence other than their own perception. One danger is that such inward inspiration may lose touch altogether with the external world, and become inarticulate to others—as in some painting, poetry, and music. Introvert thinkers are sometimes arbitrary, obstinate, relying entirely on their own insights and conclusions, disdaining argument and even consultation. Nevertheless, when left to himself, the introvert will often feel unfairly neglected, or perhaps inferior.

Whether men are on the whole more extrovert and women more introvert is doubtful, though often assumed. The entire extrovert would of course be a chaotic, characterless automaton responding helplessly to external stimuli, lacking all thought, conviction, and personality. The entire introvert would be beyond social contact, withdrawn, eccentric, sometimes alienated to the point of insanity. The mainly-introvert regards the mainly-extrovert as superficial, finding it hard to appreciate such easy adaptation to environment as other than hypocrisy; the mainly-extrovert thinks the mainly-introvert to be odd, unfriendly, self-righteous, 'a misery', and of little practical use. On the other hand, given some common ground of work, games, political or religious ideas, opposites can discover a mutual attraction, and a rich friendship develop, each complementing the other.

E. S. Waterhouse suggests, significantly, that the introvert tends toward religion and the life of the church, and the church tends to attract only introverts. The 'inwardness', intellectualism, and 'spiritual emotion' which characterise the church's life, prayer, inward piety, self-examination, 'the soul's experience of God'—all are plain, and welcome, to the introvert, baffling and pointless to the extrovert. Yet Peter, Thomas, Matthew, among the Twelve, do not strike one as introverts; and Christian history testifies abundantly to an extrovert quality of discipleship, clearly demonstrated in the activity, energy, and courage, of explorers, reformers, missionaries, statesmen, soldiers, leaders of great social causes, and many others. There is warning here for every pastor, and church. The possibility of limiting ministry, and fellowship, to one type of temperament only, is very real; and the danger of valuing only one type of response to the gospel—that of the 'deeper' introvert. Christ came to seek and to save extroverts also—and their active, practical devotion to Christ's cause and standards of conduct, is at least as genuine an expression of faith as the introvert's deep thoughts and spiritual moods. Pastor and church must devise both attraction, and modes of work, for the Christian extrovert—and teach some of the introverts to like him!

(v) Another technical attempt to relate psychological temperament to physical organisation may be noticed for the insight offered into common personality-traits. There are individuals, it is said (as by Kretschmer), in whom the *digestive* system predominates— 'comfortable', deliberate, easy-going people, such as Pickwick, the fat and jolly monk, the fat woman. Such are 'nature's friendly reconcilers'—nothing is worth quarrelling about for long. They are also said to be naturally conservative in outlook, and eager to conform, for the sake of peace. There are individuals in whom the *muscular* system predominates, hard, physically strong people, glorying in laborious work and exercise, sportsmen, soldiers, manual workers. Such are usually energetic, combative, aggressive, restless; they tend to use other people, to mount crusades, to defend existing and familiar principles—though sometimes these individuals are against authority, iconoclastic, if that gives better outlet to their energies. They share some qualities with Jung's extroverts, and are not often troubled by over-scrupulousness. And (the theory continues) there are individuals in whom the *nervous* system predominates, highly strung, sensitive, cautious, often sceptical and self-restrained people; poets, thinkers, the ascetic, scientists, philosophers. Often they are tense, rarely fully relaxed, and reserved—approximating again to Jung's introverts. They tend also to be conscience-ridden, with a strong sense of sin, and little helped by either ritual or authoritarian theology.

Since the basis of this differentiation is physical, we might expect physical conditions to emphasise it. It is asserted that alcohol tends to make the first group sociable, the second belligerent, and the third confused; that the muscular group like noise and plenty of space, but the nervous group hate noise and choose snug corners and sheltered places. Faced with trouble, the 'comfortable' group will seek, and offer, friendly sympathy; the muscular group will work off adversity in vigorous action; the nervous group will withdraw and brood. Some would add that the way an individual sits will reveal his type—lounging, alert, or tightly twisted; and that even in sleep-positions the same differences are discoverable.

(vi) A number of minor, or less systematic, psychological differences may be mentioned together. Two fundamental *types of will* have been described, without explanation: the explosive will tends to reach a decisive resolve impulsively, with bewildering suddenness, and eagerly; it may also change its resolve equally suddenly. The obstructed will is inhibited, tends to postpone resolve, to reach decisions only under pressure, and then to be stubborn, obstinate and 'mulish'. In the former type, thought clearly grasped tends to lead to action; in the latter thought tends to lead to more thought.

Attempts have been made to differentiate personalities which react to *abstract ideas* from those which respond only to *concrete situations* and demands. Some are moved to great effort and sustained action by imaginative ideals, such as 'truth', 'political principles', 'justice', 'social ownership and control', 'musical integrity'. They will recognise and be loyal to such ideas wherever they are met. Others are unmoved by abstracts, but will identify energetically and loyally with personal leaders, organisations, causes, churches— remaining only dimly aware of any finer points of teaching or principle involved. The 'abstract' people will often be denominationalists on theological grounds; the 'concrete' people will be loyal to the church where they find greatest kindness, friendship, and spiritual help.

Another significant difference marks the *imaginative* from the *unimaginative*. Some see truth in words, logical steps, arguments from facts; others see truth in pictures, and persons, and stories. By imagination we enter another's situation to sympathise and share; we explore new possibilities, solutions to present problems, or ideals never yet attempted, or responsibilities we never thought to carry. Imagination is the great liberator of thought; without it we are imprisoned within past and immediate experience. But imagination varies greatly: some have little, or it has never been awakened; even those who possess it differ. Some, probably the great majority, imagine visually; scenes, people, whole pages of books or of music, easily 'come to mind'. Some imagine audially, recalling conversations, remarks, even tones of voice, and able to invent conversations with ease, which others find impossible. The pastor will sometimes feel quite helpless in the presence of people who appear entirely callous, unmoved to pity or to action by another's tragedy, or by distant distress; unable to see or feel beyond 'what sinners deserve'; dominated by their own prejudices and narrow experience. He must learn that such are not always as wicked as they seem, but just deficient, bereft of God's greatest gift to the human mind—imagination.

William James' distinction of the *tough-minded* and the *tender-minded* may turn largely upon this presence or absence of imaginative power. The 'tough' act on ideas, doctrines, principles, on 'hard experience of the real world', riding rough-shod over considerations of gentleness, sympathy, and others' hurt. To the 'tender' such considerations are paramount, and no idea, doctrine or principle is worth anything if it is careless of human suffering. But beside imaginative identification with others, the quality of emotion affects this distinction. The harsher, driving passions tend to be ruthless even when directed toward good ends; the tender, sensitive emotions restrain strength and inhibit ruthlessness. The tough may sometimes do more good in the world, and the tender do less damage.

Finally, among these less systematic distinctions, we may notice a difference in the capacity to think of one or more things at a time. There are *one-track*, *two-track*, or *multiple-track minds*: it is not always a question of deliberate selfishness, or of self-will, but of mental inability to hold more than one suggestion, or argument, or point of view before their attention. One-track minds just do not *listen* to alternative proposals: they seize upon one, decide for or against it, and commit themselves at once. They do not truly discuss: they form and hold an opinion, and while others are speaking are merely re-arranging their own thoughts and arguments in defence of that opinion, never listening or weighing what is said; when they next speak they do not reply, but continue their own argument. Two-track minds tend to see all things in black and white, and to make a positive or negative response, never consenting to compromise, to seek a middle path, or find a third and better way. Multiple-track minds can usually see, and argue well for, all sides of a question; excellent in thorough investigation and free discussion, their temptation is to hold judgement in suspense too long, and never reach clear and settled conclusions.

In the light of these and other distinctions between people, the endless variety of humanity produced by birth, background and experience, the pastor can scarcely avoid 'placing' himself in each suggested classification, coming to terms with his own temperament, limitations, psychological tendencies, and mere habits of thought and attitude. He should come to know the individual features of his own mental and spiritual make-up with the same objective, impartial and unregretting coolness with which he remembers the colour of his own eyes and the shape of his head. And he should know when to merely recognise his own temperament 'doing its stuff', when to be amused at himself, and when to take more deliberate steps to compensate for his own preferences and prejudices.

He must seek the same objective and impartial understanding of all the varying people to whom he is called to minister, with a mind as flexible, as open, and as appreciative, as he can cultivate. Other people, no less than himself, are what God, background, and life have made them: in the limited areas of voluntary moral endeavour he may persuade and hope to change them: but in the cast of their minds they are no more changeable—and no more responsible— than in the cast of their features.

One result of this, usually hard to accept, is that people must vary also in their capacity for certain kinds of religious experience. We usually assume that all in our congregations, and indeed all whom we seek to evangelise, are equally free, and able, to grasp and apply the truths we teach; seen from a pulpit, human nature is regarded as pure and unconditioned 'spirit', fully capable of making unhindered response to the gospel—*if the heart is willing*. We would not assume anything like this with regard to equal ability in art, music, scientific or philosophic discussion. All that has been said of innate temperamental and other psychological differences among individuals shows that we may not assume it in religious understanding and experience either. Much will depend on how the truth is presented—abstractly, imaginatively, argumentatively, or in warm simplicity and sentimental stories—whether certain types of people will be as ready, and as *able*, to respond as others might be. The Master said that even the 'good soil', which received the word, brought forth some thirtyfold, some sixtyfold and some an hundredfold, in fruitful results. There is no common level of religious appreciation and understanding. Even among the Eleven in the upper room Jesus had many things to impart which the disciples were *not ready* to hear.

Some dear and godly souls will never grasp clearly the doctrine of the cross, or the implications of the trinitarian formulation of theology: they know little, but they love much. Some eager and earnest students of all things Christian, profound and honest minds devoted to divine truth, will never bring themselves to shout 'Hallelujah!'—even at the last trump. There are five-talent disciples as well as ten-talent ones, and they receive the Master's 'Well done!' And there are one-talent people who could earn the same commendation. The pastor who sets out to make all people around him into *his* kind of Christian will meet early and deep disappointment; and if he tries to minister to extroverts in his own introvert way, he will get nowhere. The question is always, how will that man, that woman, *being that sort of person*, best follow Christ's way out of their problem, and through their own appointed path of discipleship. Christian experience and Christian fellowship will in time modify some mental traits and habits, and lend a new colour to temperament; something nearer to balance and wholeness will come with the years; but the basic pattern of personality, its psychological framework, is set, and will change very little to the end.

It is thus a mistake to seek to change one's psychological 'nature' other than by correcting obvious weaknesses with counter-balancing strength. The secret of happiness lies partly in organising life and work in line with temperament, and not athwart it. Nor should contrasts within the family, or within the Christian fellowship, be deplored. They must be expected: they should be appreciated for the richness they contribute, and the variety of service and ministry they make possible. Such openness to all sorts of people requires large-heartedness in the leader, and some elaboration in the church's regular programme. But the ultimate question about every element of personality is not what is its explanation, but how it can be used for the glory of Him who, in our nature, redeemed mankind for God.

25 THE PASTOR'S CARE OF HIMSELF

The immense range and depth of any earnest and effective pastoral ministry makes utter nonsense of the complaint sometimes canvassed, that modern pastors lack a clearly defined role in society. The most elementary acquaintance with the tensions and frustrations, the broken relationships and moral tragedies, the mental distress and spiritual desolation, that abound in contemporary society makes ludicrous any suggestion that a conscientious pastor today has too little to do. Nor is the pastor's so-called 'search for an identity' any more understandable if its real source lies in 'the ache of unused capacities'. Frustration is sometimes a pretentious name for feeling too good for our job: but even an introduction to the scope, demands, and skills of pastoral care should dispel such over-conceit of ourselves. Surveying the field of pastoral need, the best-trained pastor can only exclaim—as even an apostle was constrained to do—'Who is sufficient for these things?'

It is rewarding to examine carefully what Paul means. His poignant self-questioning was occasioned, not by depression but by the immensity of the task to which he felt called: to be commissioned by God to speak such truths as would bring to some, who believe, the very fragrance of life; and to others, who reject the truth, the horrible odour of death. How, he asks, can any one mind or heart be *sufficient* for work like that? The word he employs was used by the Baptist of his not being *worthy* to loose the sandals of the Messiah, and by the centurion of his not being *worthy* that Christ should enter his home. In the Pastoral Epistles the word is used of one *competent*, sufficiently gifted, for teaching and for leadership. To the Corinthians, the word is used of the *resources* by which one man can hope to carry the responsibilities, impart the strength, attain the wisdom, sustain the patience, which Christian ministry demands. A man will not long attempt the pastoral tasks we have outlined without asking himself if he is personally worthy to be doing such work; if he can ever be competent; if his own mind and heart and faith will ever be big enough to succeed. On all three counts, the answer is the same: it is God who makes us fit, competent, and resourceful—'Our sufficiency is of God.'

Even so, such assurance must prove ineffective if common-sense

310

precautions are ignored, or if the deepest motives that first make a man undertake pastoral work do not continue to operate.

Precautions

Though Paul was sure that God could make him sufficient, he yet knew that any man, despite preaching to others, could in the end be 'disqualified'. Pastoral responsibility is an exposed position, and the pastor a man like other men. (i) It is only common sense to bear in mind the special *personal dangers* inherent in pastoral work, the precautions needed against temptation and scandal, and the mis-understanding of the pastor's role which may lead a man to carry more than his due responsibility. He is a wise man who never seeks to make decisions for others, or to direct events beyond his personal competence. (ii) The warning bears repeating against the temptation to *rely upon one's own experience*, enlarged by memories of previous case-histories, as equipment for facing each new pastoral situation. This must bring disappointment, for no two persons or problems are ever the same. It can bring, too, an undermining sense of having little to give; our experience 'runs out' and we begin to question if anything we have known can fit some new need. The cure is *always* to turn back to the gospel, to the New Testament's many-sided exposition of the manifold grace of God, taking the problem afresh each time to the fountainhead of all Christian counsel and support— which is not experience but the inexhaustible evangel. To do this demands care, discrimination, imagination, a full knowledge of divine truth, but it provides a never-failing resource of ideas, insights and power.

(iii) *Depression* waylays the pastor more insidiously than the preacher. The inspiration of the public occasion, and the hope that at least someone in the crowd may have been blessed, are both denied to private and individual ministry. Moreover the pastor hears many sorry, and even sordid, stories: the very sensitiveness to misery and evil which makes him a pastor also makes him vulnerable to moods of discouragement, and to occasional despair of human nature. The emotional weight of some secrets and the insoluble tangles of some lives can cloud a man's whole week, unfitting him for other tasks— and for other company. A man must *realise* this danger, and watch his own reactions. Nor must he feel guilty when, having shown a stricken and still tearful visitor to the door, he returns to plunge into play with the children, or a family celebration. His prolonged indulgence in emotional sympathy will do nothing at all to resolve the problem or to help the now absent soul. Nor will an accumulated sadness and despondency equip the pastor (any more than emotional distress equips the nurse) to be confident and cheerful when the next need arises. This implies no insincerity: it is a realist assessment of what actually helps people in trouble, and of one's own emotional vulnerability.

(iv) When conspicuous *failure* with some problem plunges an earnest pastor into near-despair, it is probably because he has over-looked the strict limitation that circumscribes his work. Always, in every situation, he is dependent upon others' co-operation. In worship, in teaching, in sick ministry, at weddings and funerals, in marriage and parental counselling, and in the private interview, he can only offer the truth, point a way, suggest a course of action, sustain with sympathy and prayer. Decision, acceptance, response, are not his, and he must not burden himself with responsibilities that he cannot, in the nature of things, discharge. To give all he has, to do 'as much as in him lies', is the limit of his charge: he will last longer in this ministry if he learns to limit his hope—though not his aim.

(v) To set bounds to one's emotional involvement, and limits to one's expectation, is to approach the strictly professional attitude. Yet *professionalism* is itself a serious temptation in pastoral ministry. The elaborate 'office', fixed hours of consultation, obtrusive card-index, formality of bearing, and high-flown technical jargon, are all evidence that the pastor is moving from the role of the Christian friend, God's servant for God's people, towards something more distant, authoritative, and self-important. By such means, a man is not merely taking necessary precautions, but beginning to insulate himself against all spiritual involvement, even if he is not also beginning to exploit the pastoral situation for his own status and pride. He may indeed continue to do much good, especially for people impressed by such show of efficiency. But he will alienate those who find it hard enough to bring themselves even 'to have a word with the pastor', much less 'to arrange a consultation'. In the end a pastor may well find that he has fallen between the couch of the fully professional psychological consultant on the one hand, and the footstool of the wise and trusted Christian friend, on the other.

(vi) The greatest danger in professionalism is that of growing *cynical*. To the fully professionalised mind, the scientific, professional, and organisational aspects of the work become paramount; each 'case' ceases to be significant except as an example of a theory, an item in a day's case-load; non-relevant factors, like family opinion, employment, emotional disappointment or fear, religious affiliation, being outside the scope of professional enquiry tend to be ignored. It is an easy step to become condescending or glib in speaking of God, sin, or human sorrow and death; to suspect every client of stupidity or malingering, to disbelieve every story, discount every description of distress, assume the worst motives, and find some moral turpitude beneath every tragedy. Few who move so far from Christian charity will long remain pastors: but the temptation to lose faith in people and in all idealism, must be foreseen.

(vii) It is strange how insensitive a pastor may become to the spiritual need, and even distress, of *his family*. Domestic prayers, and shared church worship, which should provide the atmosphere for frank discussion, shared doubts and fears, may fail to do so, and the very closeness of the family can impose its own reticences. The pastor as father will need to watch his own young people with the same care that he devotes to others, and not scruple sometimes to seek the counsel of youth leaders or fellow deacons about their spiritual welfare. He will acknowledge that his sons and daughters face the same difficulties as other young people, and that love itself may blind him to their failures, and their dangers. Without shirking his responsibilities, he may sometimes request a colleague to speak privately to his son or daughter, lest familiarity should rob Christian counsel of its weight, and make warning appear as threatening. A specially difficult duty in the family context is that of marriage counselling: a pastor may well feel that whatever other share he takes in the marriages of his own children, the preparatory interviews, and perhaps the administration of the vows, should be in other hands, if full weight is to be given to what is said and done.

When illness or trouble falls, most Christian families pray together, yet it is easy for the pastor to omit to pray with his own sick child or wife, perhaps because he fears to seem officious. When wife or child is removed to hospital, the family visit to the bedside will usually lack the frankness and solemnity of a pastoral call: there is a keeping up of appearances, and of courage, which is meant to be kind but which prevents the outspoken question, or complaint, or fear. 'Wanted—a pastor!' wrote a minister's wife to a religious paper after a serious illness. She had received love, sympathy, desperate concern—but not ministry. A private word to hospital chaplain or personal colleague is all that is needed. Involvement in other's homes, cares, and children, can be no excuse for neglecting one's own home or wife or children, for ignoring family occasions, for failing to share your children's maturing. 'Let him first rule his own home well' is an apostolic requirement from pastors, and for 'rule' it is permissible also to read 'Let him first love, and care for, and watch over, and support, his own household well'.

(viii) The common-sense *need to know oneself well* faces the pastor in various aspects of his ministry, but merits a final emphasis. A thorough and candid self-understanding is achieved, not in some penitent fit of pious self-examination and 'reconsecration'—which may be a good beginning but of itself achieves little—but by living with oneself observantly, self-analytically, impartially comparing oneself with others, not to praise or blame oneself or them, but simply to note differences and enquire *why*. Any mature man, but especially one caring for others' souls also, should be fully aware of his own susceptibility to flattery, to sex-appeal, to criticism, and to discouragement. He should be acutely aware, too, of what in other people particularly annoys, irritates, or antagonises him, clouding his mood and betraying his fairness of judgement—and why. It is stupid to pretend this never happens: the only open questions are, on what occasions, and why, and how best to compensate for his own weaknesses. A mature mind will ruthlessly dissect its own rationalisations, its changing moods, its specious arguments and insincere excuses; it will sometimes catch itself out in special pleading, illogicalities, and the prejudiced presentation of evidence. A mature soul should form a just estimate of its own gifts, capacities and strength. On the one hand he should be aware when this knowledge makes him jealous of others more gifted, and when it hinders his willingness to attempt what others think him capable of doing. On the other hand, he is a wise man who understands his own limitations, and who will not be cajoled, flattered, or bribed into accepting positions or undertaking obligations that he knows God has not equipped him to fulfil.

The self-aware man knows the chips on his own shoulder, his deficiencies in education, in family background and cultural opportunity. He should have taken the exact measure, too, of the lasting consequences in him of any past sins, and while rejoicing in forgiveness know how to reckon with the fact that neither the nerves, the memory, nor the unconscious mind ever entirely pardon. So, when he catches himself avoiding reference to certain subjects, or certain people, avoiding particular themes in preaching, or the mention of specific Christian duties, he will understand why; and he will know whether attention should be paid to it, without over-compensating.

A self-understanding pastor can hardly be ignorant of his own aptness or inaptness for personal relationships. Shyness, withdrawal, a fear of criticism, or resentment at disapproval, an inability for small-talk, contempt for the niceties of social intercourse, a tendency to chatter nervously lest serious subjects be started, an opposite tendency to preach, or to offer spiritual counsel at every opportunity, a greater ease among older people—or among younger ones, a fear of involvement, or of self-disclosure, a tendency to become facetious when nervous, and morose when left alone, an unwillingness ever to say anything meaningful or stimulating lest it give offence—a score of such habits and reactions shape relationship to others, and each has its personal and private explanation. A man cannot, without strain or hypocrisy, be other than himself; but he should know himself, and what makes him so; and whether in this detail or that he should correct a fault, or cultivate a gift, to enable others to get on with him more smoothly.

Such precautions against pastoral failure seem elementary and obvious, yet experience suggests that neither the temptations of pastoral work nor the need for self-understanding can be taken for granted—or fewer breakdowns would occur.

Motives

Negative precautions will not sustain a pastoral ministry: a man needs positive and enduring motive-resources to renew his zeal and rekindle his hopes continually. In all his involvement with other people's problems, distresses, sins, frustrations, needs, joys, unhappiness, illness, bereavement and death, the pastor undergoes a drain upon his own spiritual strength, and a constant challenge to the depth of his own faith. True, he will also discover, often to his grateful amazement, that such work can bring its own mysterious reward of grace and inspiration. The promise, 'whosoever loses his life for my sake and the gospel's will save it' will come alive just when he feels his strength is at an end, and he will realise after some period of especial strain how wonderfully he has been upheld. But apart from such occasional grace, two deep and enduring motives will nourish the zeal and patience of the pastor who sees his work in scriptural light.

(i) The description of Christian ministry in Ephesians 4 has pastoral emphasis: 'the equipment of the saints, the work of ministry, the edifying of the body of Christ, until we all come to . . . the measure of the stature of the fullness of Christ' may not be accomplished without preaching, but it certainly will not be done without pastoral care. And the total ministry so described is set in the astonishing context of the steps God has taken to bring alienated hearts into the sevenfold unity of the Spirit—the descent of Christ in incarnation and His glorious ascension in victory. It was customary in Rome for a general who returned in triumph from some great campaign to distribute gifts and rewards in celebration, captured booty to the soldiers, slaves and promotion in rank to the officers of his army. So, says Paul, Christ at His triumphant ascension appointed some to be apostles, some prophets, some evangelists, pastors, teachers, for the work of ministry. To be made ministers at all was His celebration-gift to His men. Indeed, the ministry is His ascension-gift to His church. Even more, their ministry is the continuation of His work on earth. And more yet—their ministry is the prolongation of His ministry as the risen, victorious Christ, no longer humiliated and rejected, but exalted. In the pastor's office, no less than in his spiritual experience, he is raised up to sit with Christ in heavenly places.

Shorn of theological metaphors, this means that the pastor goes among needy souls and into the dark places of human experience (a) not alone, or on his own initiative, nor to do simply what he thinks best, but as representative of the risen Lord, and to convey the grace of the triumphant Christ. (b) He goes, too, not upon his own resources but as the vehicle of a love that has been proved at Calvary sufficient to redeem, as the channel of a power that has been shown sufficient at Easter to break the spell of evil and impart ever-lasting life. (c) In consequence, he goes with the under-girding confidence that in this universe goodness is stronger than evil, truth more enduring than lies, love wiser than hatred, and life mightier then death. To meet men in their need, sin, and despair, with this strong conviction makes immense difference to his attitude, his hopefulness, his expectation of success, as he confronts each new situation.

The truth may be more concretely expressed. Among the resurrection stories we find repeated reference to Christ the risen shepherd—the risen pastor. Immediately before His death, Jesus recalled the prophecy that the shepherd would be smitten and the sheep scattered, adding the promise, 'but after I am risen, I will go before you'—the shepherd's usual position, leading his flock and calling his own sheep by name. At the Easter tomb, the angels echo that promise, 'He goeth before you, into Galilee'; and John's story of the risen Christ beside the lake preserves the words, 'Feed my sheep . . . my lambs'. The writer of the epistle to the Hebrews, looking back upon the great event, speaks of 'the God of peace, who brought again

from the dead our Lord Jesus, that great shepherd of the sheep . . .'
And in the one glimpse of the after-life which the Apocalypse
allows, we see Him who sits upon the throne 'sheltering' the saints—

> They shall hunger no more, neither thirst any more;
>   the sun shall not strike them, nor any scorching heat.
> For the Lamb in the midst of the throne will be their shepherd,
>   and he will guide them to springs of living water

—Pastor to the end.

Watch the risen Christ moving among His friends, and the full
meaning of that title, 'risen Pastor', becomes clear. He ministers with
infinite compassion to heart-broken, bewildered Mary, blinded with
tears, haunting in passionate grief the last places where she had seen
her Lord. He leads the erring Peter, step by step, to the retraction of
his threefold denial by a threefold confession of love, forging meanwhile a new loyalty, a restored confidence, a deeper gratitude and
dependence. He meets Thomas in his doubts with understanding,
invitation, and blessing. So too the risen Pastor drew near to two
disappointed, mourning disciples, probed their sorrow, and opened
to them the scriptural purposes of God until their hearts glowed
with understanding. Then at Emmaus He broke bread with them
and made Himself known. Finally, still as Pastor, He gathered His
men about Him above Bethany, and sent them out to His world-
task with the promise of His companionship and His power.

Such is the timeless pastoral purpose of Christ towards His own,
that continues in every pastoral ministry, making every pastoral
heart a channel of His caring. Who could want greater incentive
than that? Yet there is a motive that strikes even deeper, still closer
to Christian experience, compelling pastoral endurance.

(ii) 'Who is weak and I am not weak, who is disgraced and I burn
not?' Paul asks the Corinthians; 'I want you to know how greatly I
strive for you . . . though absent in body, yet I am with you in
spirit' he writes to the Colossians. Such imaginative and emotional
identification with others is both the very heart, and the high price,
of pastoral care. Until the pastor can leave professional self-insulation,
moral condemnation, and personal distaste, out of his relationship
with the distressed and needy, he cannot begin to appreciate either
the problems of those who come to him, or the emotional and
spiritual despair with which they face them. In Ezekiel's oft-quoted
figure, he must 'sit where they sit', even (in more modern transla-
tion) 'sit overwhelmed among them', before he can be appointed
watchman for men's souls.

But this very principle of identification, which is the heart and the price of pastoral success, is the distinctive characteristic of the greatest Figure in scripture, 'the Servant of the Lord'. This is the splendid prophetic portrait of Him who would come, anointed by the Spirit, to bring good tidings to the afflicted, to bind up the broken-hearted, to proclaim liberty to the captives and the opening of the prison to them that are bound; to comfort all who mourn, to give them for ashes a garland, and the oil of gladness instead of mourning, the mantle of praise instead of a faint spirit—every single one a *pastor's* task! A bruised reed He will not break, and a smoking, flickering wick He will not quench, but He shall bear our griefs and carry our sorrows, being wounded for our transgressions and bruised for our iniquities. The Servant serves God by serving men, and giving His life a ransom for many.

And when the rationale, the central determining principle, of this service of God and men is sought, it is found in the familiar yet penetrating statement, 'He was numbered with the transgressors'. 'The Lord has laid on him the iniquity of us all . . . He bore the sin of many' because *He* first became identified with sinners, and 'sat where they sat'. This is the characteristic of the Servant that impressed Luke, as he quotes Christ's utterance of the fateful words in the Upper Room, 'He was reckoned among the transgressors'. It is the mark of the Servant which stirred Paul's amazement, as he contemplated Him who was 'made to be sin, who knew no sin, so that in him we might become the righteousness of God'. It is the truth that becomes luminous in the epistle to the Hebrews as the central meaning of Christ's redemptive work—'He who sanctifies and they who are sanctified have all one origin. That is why he is not ashamed to call them brethren . . . Since therefore the children share in flesh and blood, he himself likewise partook of the same nature . . . He had to be made like his brethren in every respect, so that he might become a merciful and faithful high priest in the service of God . . .'

Thus the principle that sustains a pastor in the sadness and strain of ministry to the desperately needful, is nothing less than the out-working of that same 'Servant-principle' *by which he himself was saved*. He learns in his pastoral caring, probably to a degree to which few other Christians ever learn it, the real meaning of being 'numbered with the transgressors'. So he comes closer to the heart of the Saviour than any other can who has never taken on his own heart something of the sin and sorrow of humanity, and felt

> Desperate tides of the whole great world's anguish
> Forced through the channels of a single heart.

A man cannot refuse, or withdraw, or count the cost too high, with-out by implication challenging that same identification with sinners in which lies all his own hope of redemption.

The continual rediscovery of the grace available to those who truly lose themselves in the service of others for Christ; the realisa-tion that to them it is given to perpetuate the pastoral ministry of Jesus in His risen companionship and power; and the understanding that the deepest principle of pastoral care is at the same time the closest fellowship with the Servant of the Lord, surely supply incentives that can carry a man far and long in the pastoral cure of souls. But is anything more needed, in the final reckoning, than the gracious compliment, 'Inasmuch as ye did it unto one of the least of these my brethren, ye did it unto me'?

SOURCES, BIBLIOGRAPHY AND ACKNOWLEDGEMENTS

Books, booklets, articles used and recommended:

BAILEY, D. SHERWIN, art. *Homosexuality and Homosexualism* in J. Macquarrie (edit.) *Dictionary of Christian Ethics* (SCM Press, London 1967)

BARRY, F. R., *Christianity and Psychology* (SCM Press, 'Torch Library' London 1933)

BASHFORD, ANTHONY (Clinical Theological Centre, Nottingham, England) art. *Care of the Aged* in Mitton C. L. op. cit.

CLINEBELL, H. J. art. *Clergyman's Role in the Alcoholic Emergency*, in Mitton, C. L. op. cit.

GUNTRIP, H. in private lectures; also, *Psychology for Ministers and Social Workers* (Independent Press, London 2nd enlarged edition 1964)

HADFIELD, J. A., *Psychology and Morals* (Methuen, London 15th edition, 1949)
   The Psychology of Power, in Streeter, B. H. (edit.) *The Spirit* (Macmillan, London 1922)

HAMILTON, J. D., *Ministry of Pastoral Counselling* (Baker, Grand Rapids, US 1972)

HUGHES, T. HYWEL, *Psychology of Preaching and Pastoral Work* (Allen and Unwin, London 1933)

IMLAH, Dr N. W., art. *Drug Addiction* in Mitton, C. L. op. cit.

'JOINT PASTORAL CARE of Inter-Church Marriages'—Recommendations of joint working group established by British Council of Churches and Roman Catholic Church in United Kingdom, 1970

LAKE, F., (Clinical Theological Centre, Nottingham, England) art. *The Homosexual Man* in Mitton, C. L. op. cit.

LICHTENSTEIN, P. M., and SMALL, S. M., *Handbook of Psychiatry* (Kegan Paul, Trench, Trubner, London 1944)

LEE, R. S., *Principles of Pastoral Counselling* (SPCK, London 1968)

MACKENZIE, J. S., *Manual of Ethics* (Book 1: Psychological) (Tutorial Press, London 5th edition 1920)

MCNAUGHTAN, A., art. *Drugs* in J. Macquarrie (edit.) *Dictionary of Christian Ethics* (SCM Press, London 1967)

MENZIES, R., *Preaching and Pastoral Evangelism* (St Andrews Press, Edinburgh n.d.)

MITTON, C. L. (Editor), *First Aid in Counselling* (T. and T. Clark, Edinburgh 1968)

PYM, T. W., *Psychology and the Christian Life* (SCM Press, London 1921)

SCORER, C. G., *Bible and Sex Ethics Today* (Tyndale Press, London 1966)

STOLZ, K. R., *Psychology of Religious Living* (Cokesbury Press, Nashville, US 1937)

THORNDIKE, E. L., *Elements of Psychology* (A. G. Secker, London 1905)

THOULESS, R. H., *Introduction to the Psychology of Religion* (Cambridge Press 1936)

VERE, D. W., *Drug Dependence—A New Poverty* (Christian Medical Fellowship Publications, 56 Kingsway, London, England 1971)

WATERHOUSE, E. S., *ABC of Psychology* (Epworth, London 4th edition 1933)

    Psychology and Pastoral Work (University of London Press—Hodder and Stoughton, London 1939)

Sources, and further reading:

PREFACE Terence, Heauton Timorumenos l. 221

CHAPTER 1 Further reading: P. Johnson *Pastoral Ministration* (Nisbet, Welwyn, Herts., UK); W. E. Oates *The Christian Pastor* (Westminster Press, Philadelphia, US 1964); A. W. Blackwood *Pastoral Work* (Baker, Grand Rapids, US); *Pastoral Care and the Training of Ministers*—British Council of Churches' Report of working party consultation with Institute of Religion and Medicine (Eaton Gate, London, UK)

CHAPTER 4 Further reading: Godfrey Robinson and Stephen Winward *The Church Workers' Handbook* (Judson Press); Oswald Chambers *Spiritual Leadership* (Marshall, Morgan and Scott, London)

CHAPTER 6 Wisdom of Sirach 37: 7–15 (RSV); J. D. Hamilton op. cit. p. 77; Wisdom of Sirach 37: 19

    Further reading: H. J. Clinebell *Basic Types of Pastoral Counselling* (Abingdon Press, New York); F. Lake *Clinical Theology* (Darton, Longman and Todd, London); W. E. Oates *Introduction to Pastoral Counselling* (Broadman, Nashville, US); C. Wise *Pastoral Counselling* (Harper, New York)

CHAPTER 7 Further reading: W. Robinson *Christian Marriage* (James Clarke, London); see 'Joint Pastoral Care . . .' (above); *Marriage, Divorce and the Church*—Archbishop of Canterbury's Commission on Christian Doctrine of Marriage (SPCK, London)

CHAPTER 8 R. Menzies op. cit. p. 77

    Further reading: W. L. Carrington art. *The Bereaved* in Mitton op. cit.; N. Autton *Death and Bereavement* (SPCK, London); C. S. Lewis *A Grief Observed* (Faber, London); Margaret Towie *Begin Again* (J. M. Dent, London)

CHAPTER 9 R. Menzies op. cit. p. 93

    Further reading: D. P. Thomson *Aspects of Evangelism* (Church of Scotland Research Unit, Crieff, Scotland); F. Brown *Secular Evangelism* (Salvation Army Youth Work: SCM Press, London); R. Menzies op. cit. (especially)

CHAPTER 10 J. D. Hamilton op. cit. p. 107

CHAPTER 11 George Eliot *Mill on the Floss* Bk v chapter ix

    Further reading: H. G. Dickinson art. *The Sixth Form Agnostic* in Mitton op. cit.

CHAPTER 12 Further reading: Paul Tournier *Marriage Difficulties* (SCM Press, London); W. L. Carrington *The Healing of Marriage* (Epworth Press, London)

CHAPTER 13 Further reading: V. Edmunds and C. G. Scorer *Some Thoughts on Faith Healing* (Tyndale Press, London, for Christian Medical Fellowship); L. D. Weatherhead *Psychology, Religion and Healing* (Hodder and Stoughton, London); *Bulletins* of the Churches' Council of Healing (No. 3, July 1968 was on Faith and Healing) (from 16 Lincoln's Inn Fields, London); W. L. Carrington *Spiritual Healing and Christian Counselling* (T. and T. Clark, Edinburgh, for Guild of Health—leaflet); A. Graham Ikin *Background of Spiritual Healing* (Allen and Unwin, London); *Help for Handicapped People* (information issued by Government Department of Health and Social Security, London, at regular intervals); *Health: Medical—Theological Perspectives*, preliminary report of Consultation at Tubingen 1967 sponsored by World Council of Churches and Lutheran World Federation

CHAPTER 14 owes much to A. Bashford op. cit. including quotations from W. B. Yeats and M. Roth, and medical information; Shakespeare *As You Like It* Act II Sc. 7 l. 163f.; W. B. Yeats *Selected Poetry* (Macmillan, London) p. 104; A. Bashford op. cit. p. 86; two quotations from *The Role of the Churches in the Care of the Elderly*, a booklet issued by the National Council for Old People's Welfare (26 Bedford Square, London, England); Charles Churchill *Gotham* Bk 1; W. B. Yeats *Selected Poetry* (Macmillan, London) p. 105; Dylan Thomas *Miscellany* (J. M. Dent, London) p. 31; R. Browning *Rabbi ben Ezra* stanza i; Mayer-Gross, Slater and Roth *Clinical Psychiatry* (Cassell, London) p. 477; Amiel *Journal* September 21 1874
Further reading: Simone de Beauvoir *Old Age* (Deutsch Weidenfeldt, London); Paul Tournier *Learning to Grow Old* (SCM Press, London)

CHAPTER 15 Report of Chichester (UK) Conference (1968) on *Health in the Individual and the Community*; Tennyson *The Princess* l. 330
Further reading: M. Luke *Death and the Christian* in 'Health: Medical-Theological Perspectives' (see under chapter 13); N. Autton *The Pastoral Care of the Dying* (SPCK, London); J. Hinton *Dying* (Penguin, Harmondsworth, UK)

CHAPTER 16 Further reading: M. Lloyd-Jones *Spiritual Depression, its Causes and Cure* (Pickering and Inglis, London)

CHAPTER 17 F. R. Barry *Christian Ethics and Secular Society* (Hodder and Stoughton, London) p. 181; S. Bailey op. cit. p. 153; F. R. Barry *Christian Ethics* . . . p. 179; C. G. Scorer op. cit. pp. 118, 120; F. R. Barry *Christian Ethics* . . . p. 178; Kinsey in C. L. Mitton (edit.) op. cit. p. 183; C. G. Scorer op. cit. pp. 120f.; F. R. Barry *Christian Ethics* . . . p. 179
Further reading: F. Lake op. cit.; H. Kimball-Jones *Toward a Christian Understanding of the Homosexual* (SCM Press, London); N. Pittenger *Time for Consent* (SCM Press, London); R. F. R. Gardner (Gynaecologist and Minister) *Abortion: The Personal Dilemma* (Paternoster Press, Exeter, UK)

CHAPTER 18 H. J. Clinebell op. cit. p. 161; N. W. Imlah op. cit. p. 176; A. McNaughtan op. cit. p. 93; N. W. Imlah op. cit. p. 177; P. M. Lichtenstein and S. M. Small op. cit. pp. 101–110; D. W. Vere op. cit.

p. 6; p. 3; p. 8; A. McNaughtan op. cit. p. 94; D. W. Vere op. cit. pp. 9, 10

Further reading: A. J. Wood *Drug Dependence*; K. Bell *The Needle, the Pill and the Saviour*; K. Leech *Pastoral Care and the Drug Scene* (SPCK, London)

CHAPTER 19 J. A. Hadfield op. cit. (*Psychology and Morals*) p. 72; W. McDougall in F. R. Barry *Christianity and Psychology* (SCM Press, London) p. 25; K. R. Stolz op. cit. p. 335

Further reading: W. McDougall *Outlines of Psychology*; *Introduction to Social Psychology* (Methuen, London); A. F. Shand *The Foundations of Character*; W. B. Selbie *Psychology of Religion* (Clarendon Press, Oxford); T. Hywel Hughes *New Psychology and Religious Experience* (Allen and Unwin, London); W. L. Carrington *Psychology, Religion and Human Need* (Epworth Press, London)

CHAPTER 20 R. H. Thouless op. cit. p. 82; J. A. Hadfield op. cit. (*Psychology and Morals*) p. 41; E. S. Waterhouse op. cit. (*Psychology and Pastoral Work*) p. 187; R. S. Lee op. cit. p. 17; F. R. Barry *Christianity and Psychology* (SCM Press, London) p. 50

CHAPTER 21 J. S. MacKenzie op. cit. p. 47; K. R. Stolz op. cit. pp. 185f.

CHAPTER 22 J. A. Hadfield op. cit. (*Psychology and Morals*) p. 99; Bp. Paget quoted in T. W. Pym op. cit. p. 101; H. H. Farmer *Towards Belief in God* (SCM Press, London) p. 230; J. A. Hadfield op. cit. (*The Psychology of Power*) pp. 88f.; K. R. Stolz op. cit. p. 214; W. James in R. H. Thouless op. cit. p. 203; J. A. Hadfield op. cit. (*Psychology and Morals*) pp. 193f.

Further reading: K. Jaspers *General Psychopathology* (University Press, Manchester, UK); H. Guntrip *Mental Pain and the Cure of Souls* (Independent Press, London)

CHAPTER 23 Kimball Young—see K. R. Stolz op. cit. p. 346; ibid. p. 333; J. A. Hadfield op. cit. (*Psychology and Morals*) pp. 187f.

Further reading: J. A. Hadfield *Psychology and Mental Health* (Allen and Unwin, London); Wayne Oates *Religious Factors in Mental Illness* (Allen and Unwin, London); M. Gregory *Psychotherapy, Scientific and Religious* (Macmillan, London)

CHAPTER 24 Prof. Lloyd Morgan in E. S. Waterhouse op. cit. (*ABC of Psychology*) p. 106; E. S. Waterhouse op. cit. (*Psychology and Pastoral Work*) pp. 81f.; Kretscher as summarised by H. Guntrip in private lectures, and referred to by K. R. Stolz op. cit. p. 178 (also Sheldon *Varieties of the Human Temperament*). The three types are given the unbeautiful names, Viscerotonic, Somatotonic, and Cerebrotonic

CHAPTER 25 F. W. H. Myers *St Paul*

Acknowledgements

For kind permission to make the quotations detailed above, thanks are due to Abingdon Press, Nashville, USA (for quotations from K. R. Stolz); to Professor Duncan Vere and the Christian Medical Fellowship, London; to the Tyndale Press, London (for quotations from C. G. Scorer); to Hodder and Stoughton Ltd, London (for quotations from F. R. Barry); to Associated Book Publishers Ltd, London and Methuen and Co. Ltd,